# EASTERN
# UPLAND
# SHOOTING

*With Special Reference to Bird Dogs
and Their Handling*

by
## DR. CHARLES C. NORRIS

Foreword by George Bird Evans

**COUNTRYSPORT PRESS**
Traverse City, Michigan

A small offering to the memory of
my shooting dogs, especially
Saddie Sportstone
Maryland Dan
and
Chester Valley Fleetwood

# ACKNOWLEDGMENTS

I wish to thank Mr. G. Dawson Coleman, owner of the Lebanon Kennels, for reading the chapters on "The Shooting Dog" and "Handling and Major Faults," for valuable suggestions regarding the material therein and also for permission to reproduce the photograph of the fine pointer, Lebanon Tim. I also wish to express my appreciation to Dr. William F. Lentz, professor of Veterinary Anatomy, chief of clinic and director of the Small Animal Hospital at the School of Veterinary Medicine, University of Pennsylvania; and to Dr. Mark Allam, associate professor of Surgery at the same institution, for assistance in preparing the chapter on "The Care of the Dog"; and to Mr. Seth Gordon, the able executive director of the Pennsylvania Game Commission, for supplying data regarding shooting accidents. I wish also to express gratitude to Mr. C. M. B. Cadwalader, Mr. Richard C. Bishop and Mr. Bob Nichols for help in securing photographs. I am indebted to Mr. Charles Schwartz for a number of photographs, including the silhouette endpaper, as well as to Mr. Leo A. Luttringer, Jr., chief of the Division of Public Information, Pennsylvania Game Commission, and to Mr. Percy T. Jones for many fine pictures.

Thanks are due to the following publishers and authors for permission to use quotations from the books and articles listed:

*American Field,* Chicago, for excerpts as indicated in the text.

The American Kennel Club, New York, *Complete Dog Book* by R. W. Tauskey and others.

The Boston Society of Natural History, Boston, *The American Woodcock,* Memoirs of the Boston Society of Natural History, Vol. IX (1936), No. 2 by O. S. Pettingill, Jr.

The Charleston Museum, Charleston, *The Auk,* and *Birds of South Carolina,* 1910, by Arthur T. Wayne.

Geoffrey Blès, London, *How to Shoot,* by Robert Churchill.

Doubleday and Company, Inc., New York and Mrs. G. Bambridge, London: "Dinah in Heaven" from *Limits and Renewals* and *Rudyard Kipling's Verse:* Inclusive Edition 1885-1932, copyright 1891, 1934; "Mc-Andrew's Hymn" from *The Seven Seas,* by Rudyard Kipling, copyright

# Acknowledgments

1893; "The Power of the Dog" from *Actions and Reactions,* by Rudyard Kipling, copyright 1899.

Doubleday and Company, Inc., New York, *American Game Preserve Shooting,* by Lawrence B. Smith.

*Field and Stream,* New York, for photographs and excerpts as indicated in the text.

Houghton Mifflin Company, Boston, *A Natural History of the Birds of Central and Eastern North America* by Edward Howe Forbush.

G. P. Putnam's Sons, New York, *Mark Right* by Nash Buckingham.

Remington-Putnam Book Company, Baltimore, *Green Days and Blue Days* by Patrick Chalmers.

*Scientific Monthly,* American Association for the Advancement of Science, May 27, 1927, article on Woodcock by J. Grinnel.

Charles Scribner's Sons, New York: *The Little Minister* by James M. Barrie; *The Isle of Long Ago* by Edwin C. Kent; *Shotgun Psychology* by Lawrence B. Smith, Seeley, Service and Company, Ltd., London, *Shooting* by Leslie Sprak (Lonsdale Library).

# TABLE OF CONTENTS

| | | |
|---|---|---|
| I | THE SHOOTING DOG | 13 |
| II | HANDLING AND MAJOR FAULTS | 58 |
| III | THE CARE OF THE DOG | 69 |
| IV | THE GUN AND AMMUNITION | 106 |
| V | SHOOTING HINTS | 139 |
| VI | THOUGHTS ON METHODS AFIELD | 167 |
| VII | THE RING-NECKED PHEASANT | 180 |
| VIII | THE RUFFED GROUSE | 216 |
| IX | THE AMERICAN WOODCOCK | 252 |
| X | THE BOBWHITE QUAIL | 292 |
| XI | RAIL | 319 |
| XII | SCENT, WOUNDED BIRDS, AND TOWERING | 347 |
| XIII | EQUIPMENT | 365 |
| XIV | GAME FOR THE TABLE | 384 |
| | BIBLIOGRAPHY | 397 |
| | INDEX | 405 |

# A Man of Principle

Writing about Dr. Charles Norris is writing about the past, both because an era ended with him, and because he was so much of that period when in England and America the concept of taking game with style emerged from the Victorian and bloomed into the glory of the Edwardians.

The game gun, as we know London bests today, had taken form soon after Charles Camblos Norris was born in 1876. Laverack had given the sporting world his bloodline of gun dogs together with his book, *The Setter*; Llewellin was exporting his Wind'em setter strain to America; game birds were still abundant on this continent, and Eastern gunners with the means to do so were pursuing the sport of shooting over dogs with a fervor equal to their dedication to their professions or industry.

Living in the rarefied atmosphere known as the Main Line, Biddles and Cadwaladers and Norrises knew the best of both Northern and Southern shooting, in addition to their own rich Pennsylvania and New Jersey game lands. While still students in the University of Pennsylvania Medical School, Charles Norris and his classmate Williams Biddle Cadwalader, together with their close friend Lynford Biddle who was in the Law School, shot grouse and woodcock in Pennsylvania and New York State and around Ellsworth, Maine. When in practice later, Dr. Norris gunned bobwhites on the estate of his cousin, Dr. Henry Norris, at Rutherfordton, North Carolina, and elsewhere in the South.

A few years ago a book dealer brought to my attention an 8" x 14" leather-bound journal of Joseph Kreider, the gun dealer in Philadelphia containing daily records of sales from July 1893 through December 1894. There are the following entries of sales to Charles C. Norris:

> *8/7/1894  50 16 ga. Club Nitro 2-3/4 dr. E.C. 1 oz. (illegible) $1.50*
> *8/25/1894 50 12 ga. smokeless E.C. 1-1/8 8c $1.50*
> *L.C. Smith Gun, 12 ga. 30" 7-1/4 lbs. $57.10*

Charles Norris was eighteen at that time. He shot three L.C. Smith guns over a period of years until he had his Purdey built in 1929.

My early impression of Dr. Charles Norris was formed from his first letters to me written in a bewildering prescription hand on what became the familiar gray-threaded stationery from Fairhill – there were to be ninety of them during our rich nine years. I pictured him tall, lean, mid-sixties, a successful professional man living a storybook shooting life.

When Kay and I and our setters were invited to Fairhill in 1954 we were welcomed by a warm, courtly, somewhat short and rather plump man with balding white hair and pleasant blue eyes behind steel-rimmed glasses, older than I had expected. Seeing him at last, I somehow grasped how far in the past his medical career had been. He was flanked by a classic pointer-and-setter brace, both very fat and a little condescending.

I came to know that he addressed both the white-and-liver Nellie and the orange belton Charm as "Sweetie Girl," to which each responded.

Fairhill, aloof on its high wooded ridge, centered around a lone man with two dogs, three house servants, and a chauffeur. He kept two cars, "in case one of them broke down"; his chauffeur had a car of his own, but it would have been inconceivable to rely upon a servant's car; his most recent Packard, dark blue, was never quite satisfactory because it wasn't black; with two Purdeys and a Churchill, one Purdey was used mostly on rainy days.

Joining Dr. Norris at the drawing room fire before dinner after our first shoot at Amwell, he greeted me with: "You'll find cleaning implements upstairs in the gun room."

Kay laughed, "George brought his own. He's already cleaned his gun."

After retiring as head of Obstetrics and Gynecology at the University of Pennsylvania Medical School in the early forties, Dr. Norris wrote *Eastern Upland Shooting*, published in 1946. It is a splendid book, reflecting the judgment and experience in coverts of a mature sportsman with class.

Reading the first five chapters you will see why Dr. Norris and I were such close friends. It is characteristic that he should open his book with "The Shooting Dog" and continue discussing dogs for the next two chapters. During our visits at Fairhill conversation seldom strayed far from dogs. Dr. Norris was partial to bitches, and Nellie and Charm were constantly with him – at his feet or lying in a chair next to him in the drawing room, waddling in front of him around the grounds on Fairhill, or one at each side of his chair at dinner. Each had her chaise lounge in his bedroom. Following the blue Packard on our gunning trips up to Amwell I could see them sitting upright in the rear seat, with Dr. Norris relegated to the front seat beside the chauffeur. They maintained their weight by frequent excursions to the kitchen where they were slipped morsels by the cook and maid, against Dr. Norris's orders, orders that had no bearing upon his reaching down at the table to share some choice dish. During later visits, our Dixie was a favorite of his – "that nice little thing."

In *Eastern Upland Shooting*, the chapters "The Gun and Ammunition" and "Shooting Hints" are sound observations on game guns and how to shoot them. I find his comments on the 28-bore interesting at a time before the small gauge had become popular.

I don't think anyone has written more thoroughly about gun care than Dr. Norris. The Thomlinson cleaner he mentions on page 129 was regularly used at the time he wrote. It was an effective alternative to a brass brush, and I have a couple of them in my gun cabinet and still use them. Looking back, I recall reading Dr. Norris with unquestioning acceptance. Now that I have more mileage on me together with more experience, I still find very little to differ with in his opinions on guns.

The friend he mentions on page 115 as having been fitted by three London fitters was, I am certain, Lynford Biddle, whose "little Purdey" went to Dr. Norris and later came to me – a gun in top condition, capable of serving another generation or two of fortunate gunners.

One mystery that has persisted through the years since *Eastern Upland Shooting* was published is the term "rim" that occurs repeatedly in "Shooting Hints." Several readers have assumed that it was a typo for "rib" that was allowed to slip through. I am not so sure. Knowing Dr. Norris's concern for accuracy, I can't imagine his having let this happen. He had a fondness for British sporting terminology, and it is possible that "rim" was an esoteric reference in his time to the gun rib or top of muzzle. His professional secretary, who typed the manuscript for this book as well as his medical books, was trained for accuracy, and while not conversant with shooting beyond this project, would not likely have misspelled "rib" repeatedly.

"Game for the Table" is fittingly the final chapter of *Eastern Upland Shooting*, just as game on the table is the ultimate experience with it. Here, as much as anyplace in the book, Dr. Norris has indulged his tastes. His use of "good butter" and "good cream" makes a cholesterol-conscious man shudder, but that was the way with food at Fairhill and much *fin de siècle* cuisine.

I am only now beginning to appreciate the scope of the Bibliography in *Eastern Upland Shooting,* a list that could serve as a guide to early shooting books. Many of them were in the sporting library in the upstairs study at Fairhill adjacent to the gun room with its bouquet of Hoppe's No. 9.

When the estate was settled, the sporting books were purchased intact by a dealer who came to Fairhill to appraise them. A cousin, the next-in-line Norris to come into a life tenancy at Fairhill, remarked to Kay with a tone of surprise: "Charlie's fishing and hunting books brought a high price." Considering the items that were among them, the dealer no doubt made out handsomely.

Dr. Norris gave me my copy of *Eastern Upland Shooting*, inscribed, before our first visit to Fairhill; it is now underlined throughout, where certain passages speak personally to me. He was considering a second edition but the publisher didn't go through with it.

After its publication, *Eastern Upland Shooting* remained comparatively unknown, partially due to a sluggish market for sporting books. Titles that are eagerly sought-after and now bring high prices were lying dead on bookstore shelves or were returned to the publisher and allowed to go out of print. In the 1950s and '60s, copies of *Eastern Upland Shooting* could be had for $15 and the name Charles Norris, like that of Nash Buckingham, was almost unknown to a new generation of shooting men. Having written about them, it has been gratifying to see the interest in both men grow. It is particularly pleasing and important to have Countrysport Press bring out this edition of *Eastern Upland Shooting*.

The fate of the guns of well-known sportsmen holds a fascination for gun fanciers. I have written of Dr. Norris's "little Purdey" that came to me as my choice of his three London bests. The location of his Churchill 12-bore with its two pairs of barrels is unknown to me at present. The second Purdey 12-bore #25383 with one pair of 27-inch barrels already has its odyssey, which I have traced through the hands of at least seven persons – dealers, collectors, private owners.

Dr. Norris told me he had it built in 1929 as a woodcock gun – "It's really too open for pheasants." (It is choked .000" right barrel, .010" left.) At his death in 1961 it went through a family connection to a gunsmith/dealer in the Philadelphia area. It was then sold to a New Jersey collector who kept it in his collection until the early '70s, when he traded it, with a second gun, to another collector. It then went to a gun dealer who traded it to another dealer, who subsequently sold it to a Pennsylvania M.D. Somewhere during its twenty-eight years wandering, the barrels were reblued, the chambers lengthened from 2-1/2" to 2-3/4", and the stock replaced bearing an escutcheon with three initials no one seems able to identify, suggesting that at least one more individual was involved in the chain. Finally, a single trigger has been installed. Other than mention of Dr. Norris's name being on the trunk case, I have detected no warm appreciation that this was Charles Norris's gun, and I would wager that at no time during the past almost three decades has this gun been carried in coverts and fired over pointing dogs.

It is painful to contemplate that such a set of circumstances could ever involve a gun of mine. I can't conjecture what concerns Dr. Norris may have had about those other two guns; I can say, knowing how he knew me, that he was certain his little Purdey would be with me for my own forever.

As I write this, the December day is going down with a sunset glowering through leaded lines of hemlock branches, and I wonder what it looks like at Fairhill. I lay my hands on the little Purdey and feel a warmth that is twenty-eight years gone, bringing back much of what Dr. Norris and I knew. But there is more. What a man writes is that part of him he leaves behind, and as I turn the pages of *Eastern Upland Shooting* I find *the ache of memory there*.

GEORGE BIRD EVANS
*Old Hemlock*
*6 January 1989*

*Nature and Books belong to the eyes that see them.*
—Ralph Waldo Emerson, "Experience."

*The one absolutely unselfish friend that man can have in this selfish world, the one that never deserts him, the one that never proves ungrateful or treacherous, is his dog. A man's dog stands by him in prosperity and poverty, in health and in sickness.*
—George Graham Vest, "Eulogy on a Dog," in Johnson County Circuit Court, Warrensburg, Missouri.


YOU can walk into a shop and, in ten minutes, buy a gun; and, if you are a good shot, probably can perform fairly well with it. If anything happened to the gun you can buy another just like it—or a dozen if you have the money. Such is not the case with a dog. Of the two, the dog is the more important, and not only the more important, but much the harder to obtain. A really good shooting dog which can adequately handle all "four varieties" is a rarity, and not merely a matter of money.

In the days of our grandfathers, almost any dog could find game. Today, game may or may not be wilder and harder for a dog to handle successfully, but it is certainly scarcer. The scarcer game is, the more necessary it becomes to have the services of a first-class dog. Without a dog, upland shooting is a poor, drab, lonesome, and generally unsatisfactory, business. Much of the joy of shooting is dependent upon the companionship of a favorite dog. Fatigue and loss of interest soon develop for the solitary hunter who has been accustomed to watching a fine dog do his work. Even if birds are few and the bag light, the presence of a dog, quite apart from companionship, adds a never-failing and constant interest. Although a dog cannot be rated by price, a man will generally have better sport and kill more birds with a $500 dog and a $50 gun than if the prices were reversed.

For some unexplained reason, the pleasure of shooting over your own dog further enhances the enjoyment. No one likes to see the work of a handsome, well-trained, competent dog more than I do, but shooting over someone else's dog, no matter how good he may be, is not quite the same thing as shooting over your own—best of all, if you have bred and trained him yourself. The first awkward point of the youngster, and the time he makes his first retrieve, with a look which says plainly, "Is this what you want me to do," are red-letter days on the calendar of the owner-trainer.

Some men look on a dog merely as a means to an end—often they are fine sportsmen and good shots. It may be that they are too busy with other affairs; they may and often do admire and like a dog, but realize that a trainer does the work better than they could. A different situation exists for the man with a shooting in the South, where a string of dogs is often required and a trainer is almost a necessity; but for shooting in the northern and eastern states a large number of dogs is not required.

The sportsman who is shooting over a good dog will find ten times as many birds and have nearly ten times as many opportunities as the one without a dog. This is particularly true where pheasants are plentiful, as these birds will often run out of the path of an advancing gun, and, without a dog, consequently be passed by. Two experienced men may kill a good many grouse without a dog, as, even with that really scarce article—a good grouse dog—many birds will not lie and will be flushed out of range. However, without the added interest given by the presence of a dog, I, personally, would not bother to hunt this splendid bird.

With a large, strong bird, such as a pheasant, it is inevitable that, no matter how careful the gun may be to try to center his bird and not to take too long shots, there will be a certain number of cripples. While a pheasant has any strength left he will run, and a wing-tipped bird may travel a quarter of a mile or more. Without a dog nearly all these birds are lost. The fact that there will be a certain number of cripples is, perhaps, the one black mark against shooting, and should make every decent man exert every effort to secure such birds and save them from the wretched fate which otherwise awaits them.

It is a matter of satisfaction that the Pennsylvania Game Commission has recently urged the use of a dog. H. L. Betten believes that pheasant hunters should be compelled to use dogs. Almost any dog is better than none—for all can be taught to hunt. Various breeds have been taught to point, including collies and mongrels. There is even record of pigs which were taught to hunt and point. One of these, a sow, was taught by Richard Toomer, a keeper in the New Forest, to seek game, back, and stand. An illustration from Daniel's *Rural Sports* (1802), depicts "Slut, The Pointing Pig." It is said she was staunch. She pointed black game, pheasant, snipe, partridges, and rabbits. Under tutelage she improved rapidly, and in a few weeks would retrieve birds—even cripples which had attempted to escape. Her scenting ability was excellent; her pace was generally a trot. She obeyed well, and evinced pleasure at the sight of a gun. She dropped like a setter. Slut was black, with three white feet, and weighed seven hundred pounds. When five years old she was bought at auction by Sir Henry Mildmay.

According to Mr. James Day, James Hirst of Rawcliffe, about 1820, taught a large black sow to point grouse, which she is said to have done as accurately as any dog. Mr. Hirst was in the habit of shooting from the back of a bull. This strange entourage resulted from the gentleman's strenuous objection to paying taxes on horses or dogs. According to the record, therefore, at least two pigs have been taught to point game. That the pig's sense of smell is acute is well known. They have long been employed to assist in locating truffles in the Black Forest.

There are only three breeds of dogs commonly used in upland shooting: namely, setters, pointers, and spaniels. Which of the three is to be selected may well be influenced by the type of terrain to be shot over, the variety of birds chiefly found, and the choice of the individual sportsman. All are fine breeds and each has its advantages and adherents. The pointing dogs are faster, cover more ground, and hence generally find more birds. The spaniels are closer workers, splendid dogs for really thick cover, and, therefore, rarely pass by a bird. True, the birds may sometimes be flushed a bit farther away, but if care is taken not to shoot out of range this merely pushes the sport up a notch or two.

Often, in the case of pheasants, shots over points, especially in the open, are not particularly sporting. I have missed many such birds and have occasionally seen much better shots than myself do likewise. There is no excuse for it, however, and I believe this statement to be correct. Furthermore, for securing crippled birds, especially pheasants, a good spaniel is generally better than either a good setter or pointer. The spaniel follows foot scent whereas the pointing dogs are apt to depend largely on body scent and hence are not, as a rule, expert trailers. For grouse, woodcock, and quail, pointing dogs are generally preferable.

With the advent of the pheasant, which, during the last quarter of a century, has become so plentiful, the popularity of the spaniel —due to the proclivity of this bird to run and seek dense cover— has greatly increased. The pheasant is a large bird, is easy to breed in captivity, does well in farming districts, and seems destined to continue and to increase in popularity and abundance. This, coupled with the fact that it does not lie particularly well to a pointing dog, makes it likely that, as time goes on, the spaniel's popularity as a field dog will increase. In England, spaniels are used extensively, and pointers and setters are rarely employed for pheasant shooting. Spaniels are fine, handsome, merry little dogs, possess delightful dispositions, are good retrievers, and give very attractive shooting. In this country, however, there are still more pointing dogs used than spaniels. Individual excellence in any of these breeds may well be the reason for its selection.

*Pointing Dogs.* Whether a setter or a pointer is selected is purely a matter of choice of the individual sportsman—he may get a superior dog of either breed. Pointers usually develop earlier than setters, and, as a dog's life is unfortunately short, an extra year of experience is decidedly an asset. Pointers are believed by some to retain their training better than setters, to be more easily staunched, to require less pre-season work, and generally to be more biddable. Perhaps the education of the pointer can be forced a little more while the setter may require a little more judgment and experience in his training. Probably there is no great difference in this respect so far as breed is concerned, although individual dogs, naturally, vary widely.

To me, the pointer generally appears more intense and stylish on point. Pointers probably stand hot weather better, and perhaps require less water, although both breeds need plenty of it. Pointers do not collect burrs to the extent that setters do, and so the gunner is saved the time-consuming deburring that is generally required at the end of the day, or even during the shooting. Pointers do not collect snow balls on their feet as do setters, when used on damp snow nor do their coats ice up in cold weather. For actual shooting the pointer does about as well in cold weather as the setter. Pointers are easier to keep clean, and generally speaking, are more popular with field-trial men. Hence there are probably more celebrated pointers than setters before the public.

Mr. Coleman says: "In my opinion, there are several reasons why the pointers have done better than the setters in the major field trials of recent years:

1. In the professional trials, all stakes go to the trainers, and they can break a pointer derby quicker and more satisfactorily than they can break a setter. When they attempt to break a setter as a derby, they often take something out of the dog which can never be returned.

2. For some reason, during the past twenty-five years, there have been more men of means interested in campaigning pointers as field-trial dogs than there have been men interested in campaigning setters. Thirty or forty years ago, the situation was just the opposite.

However, the average southern field-trial dog is hardly the type required for a shooting dog. In the North and in the New England trials many fine setters are seen.

On the opposite side of the ledger, the setter withstands cold better than the pointer, although, if wet, the latter dries off much more quickly. Setters are apt to have sweeter dispositions and for this reason are perhaps more popular with the man who makes a companion of his dog, or who owns only one or two. Both, however, usually possess excellent dispositions: disposition is chiefly a matter of how a dog has been handled. Setters do not get cut so much with briars and, because of their more protective coats, are thought to make better covert dogs. However, this also is largely a matter of the individual. When worked hard on rough grass or stubble, the tops of a pointer's toes may get sore and raw. This is not so likely to occur to the setter. Setters are generally better retrievers from water. Both are handsome dogs, but I think the setter the more beautiful of the two. As may be seen from the foregoing, superiority of one or the other is more a matter of the individual than of the breed. Both are good.

*Field and Bench Dogs.* It is unfortunate that there is a wide rift between the field and the bench dogs' standards. Although both types were originally bred and developed for field work, years of subsequent breeding for the bench alone, without much regard to field qualities, robbed many of the show dogs of their original usefulness.

A year or two ago, at the Madison Square Garden Show, I was admiring a beautiful orange and white setter bitch. She looked as if she had everything. I asked the owner if he had ever tried her on birds. He said that, when she was two years old, he had put her down one afternoon and she had picked up so many burrs that it had taken nearly a year to get her coat back in condition. This is not the attitude of all bench-show men, but it is the attitude which has resulted in ruining many setters for field work.

Judging dogs only on their field qualities has resulted in somewhat different conformation than that usually seen on the bench. The latter are apt to be a little larger and heavier, with longer heads and better coats. Field dogs may be found in various sizes. They are generally more streamlined and often have snippy muzzles, rather high-set ears, and a tendency in the tail to curl upward. Mr. Coleman says:

I entirely agree with you that we should endeavor to get better-looking types of dogs to be used for shooting and also for the field trials.

While it may not be possible to breed field-trial dogs that win regularly on the bench, I still maintain that we can breed much better type dogs than we are now doing.

Mary Montrose won the National Championship at Grand Junction three times, and, after her last win, won Best of Bitches in Madison Square Garden. This would indicate that we can breed good-looking field-trial dogs, rather than the snippy type of individual which so often runs.

I am not familiar with bench show standards of points but believe that they should call for a dog that is physically built to run smoothly and with pleasing action.

I have seen several bench show pointers that performed creditably in the field. . . .

My uncle, Edward R. Coleman, told me that, in the early 90's, he had some very excellent Irish setters for shooting dogs. . . .

I feel that breeding to the bench show type has had a decidedly bad effect on the Irish setter.

During the past year, I have been campaigning a dog called Lebanon Tim. In the last eight months, he has won the National Amateur Quail Championship, the All American Championship on Prairie Chickens, and the National Amateur Pheasant Championship.

While I know he is not a dog that could win much on the bench, nevertheless he is very well proportioned, and many field-trial men have told me he is the best-looking field-trial dog they have seen in some time. . . .

Mr. Coleman is entirely too modest. Lebanon Tim, quite apart from his splendid field qualities, is a dog which even the most exacting sportsman would be proud to own.

It is to be regretted that some agreement between the authorities governing bench shows and field trials cannot be reached. The dog shows sponsored by the English Setter Club at Medford, New Jersey, and held in conjunction with their field trials, are steps in the right direction. If it were necessary for every dog to have a field-trial win before becoming a bench champion, and for every field-trial champion to have a bench win, the ultimate result would be an improvement in both setter and pointer.

Setters and pointers are essentially shooting dogs, and it would seem that some recognition of their field qualities should be incorporated in the bench standard. As a matter of fact, the bench standard, i.e., conformation, should idealize the most efficient type of dog for field work. There exist, however, many difficulties in such a plan, not the least of which is that, in the show ring, it is impossible to judge scenting ability, desire to hunt, and many other desirable field qualities.

As things are at present, the man selecting a shooting dog has a better chance of obtaining those qualities which he desires from field-trial or shooting-dog stock, than from show blood. It is true that some dogs have won championships both on the bench and in the field, but these are rather exceptional individuals, for generations of breeding chiefly for conformation have not helped the field abilities of the average show dog. This applies to both setters and pointers.

*Setters.* Only three breeds of setter are employed to any extent in the field today: namely, the English, Irish, and Gordon.

One often hears the term Llewellin setter. The Llewellin is a strain of English setter—not a breed. About 1790, the Reverend A. Harrison, who lived near Carlisle, Cumberland, England, started breeding setters, and kept his strain pure for thirty-five years or more. In 1825, Edward Laverack, a resident of Whitechurch, Shropshire, secured a pair of Harrison setters. These were the celebrated Ponto and Old Moll. Mr. Laverack bred his strain for nearly half a century. R. Purcell Llewellin, of Pembrokeshire, obtained setters from the Laverack kennel, and these probably formed the foundation of the strain now often spoken of as Llewellins. Exactly what additions to the Laverack blood were made by Llewellin has been the subject of considerable controversy. At all events, some Laveracks and a number of dogs from the Llewellin kennel were imported to this country in the early seventies and later. The latter were sometimes termed the Field Trial breed. The first field trial in this country was run near Memphis, Tennessee, on October 8, 1874.

These importations have done much to improve the breed of English setters in America. Prior to this the early setters (or natives, as they are sometimes designated) were, more or less, a mixture of setter breeds descended from importations that had come to this country during Colonial days; from them were developed certain strains, such as the Gildersleeves, the Campbells, and others. An authoritative history of the setters and pointers in America can be found in A. F. Hochwalt's volume, *The Pointer and Setter in America.*

As early as 1485, setting spaniels were employed to point game for the net ("Stonehenge"). These were probably the progenitors of the setter. Of all the setters, the English is usually the choice of the shooting man. Although Irish and Gordons are occasionally

seen in field trials, the dominant setter is the English, and there
are undoubtedly more good shooting dogs among this breed than
any other. However, ask half a dozen old-time gunners what was
the best dog he ever shot over, and the chances are that about
half will answer, "an Irishman." This most handsome of all setters
perhaps owes his downfall as a field dog to his "fatal" beauty,
since of late years he has been bred chiefly as a show dog.
Furthermore, his deep mahogany coat, attractive as it undoubtedly
is, makes him difficult to see against autumn tints. The early Irish
setters were red and white dogs, but the white has now largely
been bred out. The modern Irish setter is apt to be less birdy,
and does not usually exhibit so much keenness and class—in either
hunting or pointing—as does the English.

A number of breeders have attempted to bring back the Irish
setter into popularity as a field dog. Notable among these is the
late Dr. G. G. Davis, whose article in *The Dog Book,* by James
Watson, describes how splendidly Irish setters can be developed
into field dogs. The Irish setters of the bench are a little more
slender and leggy than the English.

Irish setters have the reputation of maturing late and being hard
to train. It is notable, however, that the celebrated English
authority, R. L. Russell, in his admirable book emphatically denies
the latter allegation, and believes they are as easy to train and
handle as any other breed. Horace Lytle is of a similar opinion.
There are relatively few red dogs seen in the field trials today.
Years ago I owned an Irish setter bitch, and only wish I could
now get as good a dog of any breed.

Gordons are often a little heavier than other setters, and have
the reputation of being somewhat slow, careful dogs, and, as age
increases, of sometimes showing not quite so sweet a disposition.
Usually they have excellent noses, and are reputed to use foot
scent more than some of the other breeds. They are said to be a
one-man dog. The official publication of the American Kennel Club
states:

It is easy to see why the field-trial handler does not take kindly to the
Black and Tan. He wants a dog that develops early, has natural speed and
independence, and can easily be trained to handle kindly for anyone

capable of working a dog in public competition. Not only that, he also prefers a dog which will be perfectly satisfied to spend his leisure hours in a kennel, and does not require close companionship of his handler and trainer.

Were it not for their dark color, which is fairly hard to distinguish in the field, they would be popular, inasmuch as they make good covert dogs, especially for woodcock. As a matter of fact, black, while not so conspicuous as white, shows up fairly well. The Gordon is far easier to see in cover than the Irish setter. I am not at all sure that the importance of a dog showing a predominance of white has not been overstressed by some sportsmen. A good deal depends upon custom, and what the gun gets in the habit of looking for. White is more important in cover than in the open. However, there is no getting around the fact that, except on snow, a white or chiefly white dog can be discerned more easily in all settings. Today, relatively few of the fine old breed of Black and Tans are seen in the field.

One of the first field trials run in this country was a match between a native Irish setter, Joe, Jr., and the now famous English setter, Gladstone (imp. in utero), which was won by the former. The race was decided upon the number of points made. On Monday night the score stood: Joe, Jr., 34 points, Gladstone, 30 points. At the conclusion of the match, Tuesday evening, Joe, Jr. had a total of 61 points and Gladstone 52. The race was unsatisfactory for many reasons. Since then, however, English setters have been predominant in the setter world, and their widely advertised superiority combined with their splendid field qualities have placed them in the forefront among shooting dogs.

*Pointers.* These dogs have improved greatly during the last twenty-five years, and as a result of their excellent field quality are now the most popular of all pointing dogs with many sportsmen. It is important to utilize either field-trial or shooting-dog stock, rather than strains which have been employed for generations only for show purposes.

The Papes or black pointers are rarely seen at present. The German shorthairs are popular dogs in certain sections of the country. Wirehaired pointing griffons are said to be excellent dogs, and especially adapted to grouse and woodcock shooting.

*Droppers and Crossbred Setters.* The best that can be said for these dogs is that they may be good individuals, but are likely not to be so good as a purebred. The reason they are apt to be inferior is that owners of really good dogs would not be likely to permit the use of their dogs for crossbreeding. Despite this, an exceptionally good crossbred shooting dog is encountered occasionally, but such individuals become rarer as years go on and owners become educated. Such an experienced shot as Bogardus advocated the dropper as the best of all field dogs. The great disadvantage of crossbred dogs is that they do not breed true, and are liable to deteriorate in the second generation.

Crossbreds and droppers require just as much training as straight-bred dogs. The original outlay for the thoroughbred pup is relatively small. Thoroughbreds are handsomer and more valuable than crossbreds or droppers. Dropper is the term applied to the progeny of a setter and a pointer. Crossbreds imply a cross between two different setter breeds. The English and Irish cross often results in black progeny. Droppers in the first generation may resemble either ancestor. In subsequent generations throwbacks often occur. At an earlier period both droppers and crossbred setters were more common than they are today.

*Spaniels.* The two most frequently employed breeds for field work are the cocker and the springer. There are two standards for cockers recognized by the American Kennel Club: the American and the English. They are fine, handsome, companionable little sportsmen. The American type cocker is often a black or red dog, which makes him fairly hard to see in cover. However, because of his restricted range, this is less important than in the wider ranging setters or pointers. He is also a little small for hard work in heavy cover and, since many have been bred for generations for a show dog or pet, his field qualities have probably not been helped. The English type is the more workmanlike, and generally preferable for field work.

The most popular spaniel for field work is the springer, a larger and often parti-colored dog, weighing about 45 pounds and in size about 18½ inches at the shoulder.

As previously stated, spaniels are fine dogs, especially for heavy cover, and make good retrievers. They are particularly suitable for pheasant shooting, and it seems likely that, because of their beauty, good hunting qualities, and fine dispositions, they will become more popular in the future.

Spaniels can be taught to hunt both fur and feathers, or to shun the former. As is well known, the well-trained spaniel works fast and merrily at a range not exceeding thirty to forty yards, and flushes his birds without pointing. Upon flushing his game he should stop, or, preferably, drop to a sitting position, and should retrieve only when the command is given. Some spaniels give a warning bark or whine when they are on scent.

Both the cocker and springer have an excellent nose and use foot scent more than either of the pointing breeds. It is necessary for them to be well trained, or otherwise they will range too far and put up many birds out of gunshot. A badly trained spaniel in this respect is a most irritating beast. He should stop at command.

Owing to their small size and willingness to face heavy cover, their eyes are particularly susceptible to injury, not only from briars, but also from foreign bodies, such as weed seeds, and this despite every prophylactic care. As a consequence, chronic eye soreness is common among working spaniels. They are also great burr catchers, and deburring is often a long, tedious procedure.

Field spaniels and some other breeds are employed in the field. Retrievers can be taught to work well, and are fine, intelligent, strong dogs.

According to Dr. D. B. Ruskin, the first recorded importations of Brittany spaniels to America were made by the late Louis A. Thebaud, in 1912. The Brittany spaniel is said to be easily trained, and is a good retriever.

A few Brittanies have done well in shooting-dog and other stakes. They are the only spaniel that points and have been described as an ideal old man's shooting dog. This perhaps is a somewhat left-handed compliment, and hardly does justice to a fine breed. I have never owned one, but believe a good individual should make a very satisfactory shooting dog. They have somewhat the appearance of a small setter, except for the absence of tail. The ears are set a little lower and the muzzle is not so square. Usually they do not possess quite the speed and range of a fast setter or pointer. They are said to possess a keen hunting instinct, to develop early and readily become staunch. They are easily handled, have good dispositions, and are handsome. They excel on grouse and woodcock, and also do well on pheasants. I believe that there will be more of this fine breed seen in this country in the future. There are plans to include field work for the bench champion, as is done in England. This is a step in the right direction and should do much to maintain the field qualities of the breed.

After all is said and done, the selection of a dog is an individual problem, and what will be ideal for one sportsman may not suit another. As stated, the predominance and the variety of game sought, the terrain, and other factors should enter into the choice.

*Dog or Puppy.* Whether to purchase a pup or a broken dog is also a matter to be decided. Nothing is pleasanter to shoot over than a dog you have trained yourself, unless it be one you have also bred. In this case the gun is acquainted with all the dog's proclivities—his good and bad qualities—as is the dog with his master's. Also the dog can be taught to obey low spoken orders and other special details of training that the owner desires. Dogs generally work better for their original trainers than for anyone else. The pup is more of a gamble, as he may not turn out well or may die of some infantile ailment.

Training a young dog is, for many persons, very interesting and enjoyable work. It is not a job for the total novice. It definitely requires patience, absolute self-control, time, and a training ground containing birds. It is impossible to train without the latter. Without these, the amateur had better send his charge to a professional. Contact with game birds is essential. Even broken dogs tend to lose their keenness and to become careless when birds are scarce. In passing, it may be said that it is almost impossible to train and shoot at the same time—one or the other is sure to suffer. With the amateur, both generally suffer—especially the former.

Training is not an especially hard job, and there are many excellent books on the subject. I found much valuable information in *The Whole Art of Setter Training* by R. L. Russell, *How to Train*

*Your Bird Dog* by H. Lytle, *Spaniels and Their Training* by F. Lloyd, *Training and Handling of the Dog* by B. Waters, *How to Train Hunting Dogs* by W. F. Brown, and *Elias Vail Trains Gun Dogs* by E. B. Moffitt and Elias Vail. These are fine expositions of the subject, and Russell's little volume is particularly pleasing because of his evident love of dogs and his conservatism. A few good books on dog training are an excellent investment. They are of inestimable value, not only to the man who intends to train his own young dogs, but also to everyone who proposes to handle broken dogs. Some men have an especial aptitude for training. The experienced handler will accomplish more by a stern, quiet word, or even by pointing his finger at a disobedient dog, than will others by wild shouting or more vigorous methods.

When the young dog is about six to nine months old it is advisable occasionally to bring him into the house; let him ride in a motor car, and be taken around with the owner, in order that he may become accustomed to the presence of strangers and surroundings other than the kennel—in other words, may acquire manners and learn how to behave himself under the conditions he will face in later life.

*Desirable Qualities.* Select a young dog of registered stock and one whose ancestors possess the qualities desired in the pup. Bold, aggressive, active, energetic, sturdy, high-headed young dogs, which are good feeders, are best usually. However, sometimes the ugly duckling turns out to be the finest dog. The medium-sized are preferable. Of the two, I prefer a large rather than a small dog, especially in a setter since it can be seen more easily. Many people, however, like the small dogs as they eat less, take up less room, and are easier to lift over a fence. There should be nothing weedy about the pup, which should possess good bone. A good coat is a sure indication of health, and health is vital.

Except against snow, white is the easiest color to see in the field. This is especially noticeable on dark days and toward evening. For this reason it is desirable, when selecting an English setter or a pointer, to secure one in which this is the predominating color. A dark head and a dark spot on each side help against snow. Even marking is desirable, but not important. Puppies become darker as they mature. Ticking is inconspicuous or absent in the young pup. Even a five- or six-months-old pup may be almost white, but by two years of age may have developed heavy ticking. Heavy ticking may detract considerably from the conspicuousness of the mature dog.

Attempts to test the scenting of a young pup by hiding food, and the like, are practically worthless and may well be disregarded. Many puppies will point chickens or sparrows. Precocious pointing is no particular indication of individual merit, and, like the child prodigy, often does not fulfill its early promise. When a pup points a sparrow or chicken it is generally sight pointing. Precocious pointing may lead to an overdevelopment of the pointing instinct, and to false pointing. Some strains of both pointers and setters point more readily and earlier than others. Those which develop the characteristic late come out all right generally, but are disheartening to train. Of the two faults, it is preferable for the shooting dog to possess a little overdevelopment of the pointing instinct rather than an underdevelopment. The latter are often hard to staunch. Even after they have been staunched, these dogs have a tendency to get too close to their birds, and as a result flush many of them. They may slow up and even road, but do not point readily enough. Any dog may make a mistake and bump or occasionally get too near the bird, but the type under discussion does so too frequently. There may be no tendency to chase and the dog may stop in its tracks at the flush. The dog may have had plenty of experience and possess an extra good nose, and scenting conditions may be favorable. The dog may be very biddable. The fault is that he does not point easily. If punished too severely, the dog may become birdshy.

With a pup under six or eight months of age little can be foretold regarding its future hunting qualities. In the field, flash pointing is a good sign. At this age, rather more than an inkling of later conformation can be guessed. Close-coupled dogs generally stand hard work better than those of extremely rangy build. The latter are often "hard keepers." However, there is no absolute rule, since much depends upon the individual. Other things being equal, it is best to depend upon the breed standards and the quality of the parents. It is advisable to take an older puppy in the field; then to look for an attractive manner and action of a positive type, and to observe the dog's gait and his general behavior. The pup should be tested for worms, and if found, these should be eradicated without delay. At about three to four months the pup should be immunized against distemper. A number of technics are employed. I prefer the Laidlaw and Dunkin procedure. It is best not to buy a pup under ten weeks of age, and not that young if a long train trip is necessary for its delivery.

*Selection of a Trainer.* If the owner himself is not going to train his dog, it must be sent to a trainer. The dog's whole future may depend upon the selection of the right one. Other things being equal, there are advantages in selecting a trainer who specializes in developing shooting dogs, and one who is not away "making" trials for long periods during the training season, and whose chief interest is in field-trial dogs and winning stakes. If the trainer's quarters are fairly accessible to the owner it is an advantage, as in this case the latter can occasionally visit his dog and observe its condition, and determine how the training is progressing.

Conditioning a dog is an art. Much depends upon what the dog is being prepared for, as well as his temperament and other factors. If the dog is naturally fast, and great speed is desired, perhaps an hour, or an hour and a half, every other day will be sufficient. Certainly prolonged or too frequent work will affect his speed. Most shooting dogs, however, are required to go for at least half a day and be able to repeat the following day. For such conditions the dog should be worked up to what will be required. Unless for field trials, public trainers do not often err on the side of too much regular exercise.

It is well personally to look over the trainer's outfit, interview the man, see how he feeds and takes care of his dogs, how many he has, and in what condition they are. Often trainers take too many dogs, and the temptation to continue taking one or two more is difficult to resist. A man can handle just so many dogs; beyond this number his charges will suffer from lack of work. There is no reason why the average shooting dog that is to be used afoot in a not very open country, and in which stamina rather than great speed and range is desirable, should not be worked four or five times a week for at least two hours; and, after the dog has rounded into condition, for an even longer time. The average shooting dog in the North is often required to perform for five or six hours a day, and perhaps repeat for two or three days. If this is the case, he, naturally, must be worked up to it gradually. Shorter hours and less frequent work are sometimes advisable if speed is required.

In many training establishments a dog does not get this amount of work. It is as necessary for a dog to have an adequate amount of work as for a flier who is required to have a stated number of hours in the air before being granted a license. It is the hours in the field and experience with birds that count.

This is what Mr. Coleman says about training and conditioning. He and his senior trainer, Jake Bishop, are certainly entitled to speak authoritatively:

I agree that many trainers often take too many dogs to work.

We used to take about 10 or 12 to the prairies each year and found that this was all that two men could reasonably train and condition. . . .

In Alabama, we work our broken shooting dogs three to three and a half hours at a time, but find that, if we work them more than four or at the most five times a week, they get stale.

In breaking a young field-trial dog in Canada, we never run him more than an hour at a time and about four or five times a week. At the end of the season, in the South these dogs are worked from one and a half to two hours at a time and from four to five times a week, depending upon the individual dog.

I quite agree with you that we should pay professional public trainers more for breaking each dog and thus encourage them not to try and work so many dogs at a time.

The general public have very little idea of the value of real broken shooting dogs. Many are advertised for $25 to $50, but I have rarely seen a high-class broken shooting dog which did not stand its owner at least $200 or $300, provided he sent it to a professional trainer.

Many field-trial trainers delegate the training of shooting dogs to an assistant. When possible, it is preferable to select a trainer who, personally, can give the dog experience with the varieties of birds which the owner expects to hunt. Training grouse dogs, for instance, is a specialty. Foster properly stresses this point.

If trainers could be persuaded to give their charges more time in the field, and value their services accordingly, the training period could often be materially lessened. This would mean taking fewer dogs to train, but this could be compensated for financially. It must be remembered that the cost of properly feeding dogs, especially hard-working dogs, must be taken into consideration by the trainer. Few owners would grudge a few extra dollars for better food and hygiene for their dogs. Trainers are generally honest, hard-working, ill-paid men. As a result of the latter condition, they have to watch their cost account closely—a fact which does not always help the dog's health or training.

By giving the dog nearly daily work, I have trained a young one so that he could be shot over quite satisfactorily in a little over one month's time. This dog, however, was already yard broken and was a rather exceptional individual. Furthermore, dogs require daily exercise to make them physically fit and to maintain their health. Another factor to be considered when sending a dog to a public trainer is the danger of infestation by parasites. These are all too common everywhere, and are especially prevalent in the South. Whenever a group of dogs are gathered together, with new dogs coming in, more or less constantly, this danger greatly increases and is a real risk. Besides intestinal parasites (tapeworms are usually transmitted through fleas; hookworm is acquired chiefly from infected soil), there is the filaria or heartworm, which is transmitted by mosquitoes. In training quarters the latter are particularly difficult to guard against.

Some training establishments require all dogs that come for training to be protected against (immunized or having had) distemper. Dogs may readily be shipped to a trainer during the incubation period of distemper, and hence constitute a real danger to all unprotected dogs unless a rigid quarantine is routinely practiced. It is only courting trouble to send to a public trainer a dog which is not immune to distemper.

Some public trainers keep their dogs on wire, in an effort to prevent hookworm infestation. Others require a health certificate with all dogs coming for training. The latter is an excellent precaution. It should embody the results of a recent examination of the dog and the findings regarding fecal and blood examinations. If a certificate of health were routinely required, it would go a long way to eliminate the dangers of distemper and parasite infestation sometimes present in training quarters.

The other alternative would be for the trainer to keep all dogs in quarantine until his own veterinary had examined the dog.

At the completion of the dog's training, the owner should visit the training quarters in order to acquaint himself with the trainer's methods of handling the dog, the words of command, the use of the whistle and signals, what faults he must watch for. This is only fair to the trainer and to the dog. Any conscientious trainer will welcome the opportunity to demonstrate the methods of handling, as such knowledge greatly enhances the subsequent satisfaction of the owner.

When the dog arrives home, and before he is placed in the kennel with the owner's other dogs, and in an uninfected kennel, there should be a fecal and blood examination by a competent veterinarian to make certain that the dog is not a carrier of parasites which have been picked up while away. A microscopic examination is the only certain way to exclude intestinal parasites and heartworms. These examinations should be made at once, and regardless of the dog's apparent health. A careful owner may well insist upon a second examination two weeks later. Prevention is far easier than cure, and once parasites become established in a kennel their eradication is extremely difficult, not only from the dogs but also from the kennel and yards. The returned dog should be examined for fleas, and dipped if necessary. The same quarantine and precautions should be exercised upon the purchase of a new dog, and visiting dogs should not be permitted the opportunity to infect either kennel or dogs.

Instead of securing a pup, the purchase of a trained dog may be decided upon. This has many advantages. For one thing, the prospective owner can have a trial or demonstration and see exactly how the dog works. It is obviously necessary to know what is desired. If the prospective owner's knowledge is limited, he may get an experienced friend to help him in the selection, or if he knows a really reliable trainer he may entrust the choice entirely to him. However, a trial and actual shooting over the dog for a couple of days are preferable, for a dog can make or spoil a day's shooting. The dog on trial should have good food and a rest of at least twenty-four hours. It should also be remembered that with a strange handler and surroundings the dog will definitely be handicapped and cannot be expected to exhibit his top form, but it is better to adopt the policy of rejecting all dogs immediately which do not come up to the standard required. This may mean some trouble and the trying out of a number of dogs, but is worth while in the end. A really good dog nearly always has good blood, has had experience, and must have good health. The trial should be a thorough one, and should embody work in the open and in the thickest cover available. The former should demonstrate speed and range. The latter will show whether the dog will come in and work properly in covert. The path-runner will never be a good covert dog. A dog that will modify its range according to the requirements is essential, and to do this, as it should be done, is by no means a common attribute.

Before finally concluding the purchase, it is advisable to have a competent veterinarian make a fecal examination for intestinal parasites, and a blood examination for heartworms. In this connection it is worth remembering that a recent worming, while it may not eliminate all intestinal parasites, will result in a great reduction in their number, so during the period immediately following the administration of the vermifuge the microscopic examination of the feces is less reliable, and may be temporarily negative. It is well also to find out if the dog has had distemper or has been immunized, and if the latter, what method has been employed.

Gunshyness is something which will not show up without an actual test. Deafness can often be more or less concealed by an unscrupulous seller. Do not put off the purchase of the dog until the last minute.

EVALUATION OF SHOOTING DOG. Some of the points to be considered in the evaluation of a pointer or setter are:

*Breed:* This is entirely a matter for the prospective owner to decide upon.

*Sex:* There is not much difference in the hunting qualities of the two sexes. The dog is generally a little larger and perhaps a little bolder. The chief disadvantage of a bitch is that twice a year, generally spring and fall, she will come in season. Most healthy adult bitches come in season about every six months; others have intervals of five or ten months. Variations in periodicity are common. The duration of the estrual period averages about twenty to twenty-one days. Ill health, acute and chronic infections, anemia, and hence hookworms and many other conditions may cause irregularities, which usually manifest themselves by delay in the onset of the estrual period. Even though it is possible to shoot over a close-ranging, obedient bitch, while in season, care, lest a *mésalliance* occur, must constantly be exercised. It is not safe to keep bitches in an open yard while in season. I have seen a police dog climb a seven-foot wire fence like a monkey. At this time, bitches are also somewhat of a nuisance around a kennel, as they will attract every stray dog in the neighborhood, if kept in the open, and tend to promote fights among all males. The bitch will not usually accept the dog until the eighth or tenth day. It is at this time that the swelling of the external genitalia becomes most pronounced and the discharge changes from bloody to mucus.

Some men think that the bitch is a little more clever, that she develops a little earlier, and that she is easier and quieter to handle than a dog. Bitches are not so apt to roam away from home. One definite advantage of the bitch is that, if desirable, she can be used as a matron. Incidentally, it is not wise to breed an old virgin. Spayed bitches are not generally desirable, and the surgical operation itself carries a definite mortality. X-ray sterilization, while easily accomplished in the human, is uncertain and difficult in the case of the bitch.

There is a general belief that spaying (removal of the ovaries) causes bitches to become sluggish and fat. This belief is questionable and possibly results from the fact that women who have been submitted to a similar operation frequently put on weight. In women, the increase in weight is due, not to the removal of the ovaries per se, but to the fact that the ovaries have been diseased and the disease has impaired the woman's health, keeping her below her normal weight. When the diseased ovaries are removed, her general health improves and she has a chance to regain her normal weight. The chief things that the woman suffers from, as a result of the operation, are a nervous imbalance and vasomotor disturbance. The bitch, being less highly organized, rarely suffers from such conditions; certainly not to the same extent. The chief disadvantage of spaying, apart from the risk of the operation, is that the bitch can never be bred. If she turns out well, this may be a great disappointment to the owner. I am not in favor of the operation.

Another point to consider is that if the owner's set up is such that he cannot isolate the bitch during her estrum, she will probably have to be sent to a boarding kennel. Apart from the expense, the exercise yards of many such establishments are often far from hygienic and the likelihood of picking up parasites is considerable. All bitches that have been exposed in this way should be tested for intestinal parasites on their return. The possibility of acquiring filaria, distemper, and other infections should also be borne in mind.

In their later life, bitches are not infrequently attacked by mammary cancer, which generally proves fatal, although a certain proportion can be saved by an early radical operation. Anyone who has kept a bitch, especially if she has been made a companion and has lived in the owner's house, will recognize the truth of Kipling's lines:

> Something a wanton—more a thief;
> But—most of all—mine own.
>> —Rudyard Kipling, "Dinah in Heaven," *Limits and Renewals* and *Rudyard Kipling's Verse*: Inclusive Edition.

*Age:* A shooting dog's best working age is from about three to eight years. After that, he generally slows up, but can often be hunted until nine or ten, or even in some cases a little older. Old dogs often make up in experience for what they have lost in speed and range.

An old dog is apt to be gray around the muzzle; his teeth, especially the front ones, are worn sometimes to the gums; but the condition of the teeth is not a certain criterion of age, as it is in a horse. Worn teeth, however, suggest age and are rarely present in a young dog. Usually the dog under three years of age has whiter, cleaner teeth than when he is older. The eyes of an old dog often show a bluish tinge, and the lower lids may droop, exposing the haws. The bluish tinge is often due to cataract, which in dogs is frequently slow growing. He is less active and as a result, may put on weight. For the same reason, the nails are likely to be long. In old age he often assumes an attitude with the hind legs slanted well under the body, hocks bent more than normal (or somewhat cow-hocked) and he appears as if he were preparing to sit down. Deafness is common.

*Registration:* Every dog should be registered. It is an assurance of the purity of the blood and date of birth. It adds unquestionably to his value individually and as a sire or dam. There are two associations which register dogs in this country, namely, The American Kennel Club, 221 Fourth Avenue, New York 3, New York, and the American Field Dog Stud Book, 222 West Adams Street, Chicago 6, Illinois. It is a good thing to register in both.

*Blood Lines:* A knowledge of the pedigree is important. First-hand knowledge of the field characteristics of both parents is of even greater value, and, if information regarding the grandparents is available, so much the better. "Like begets like" may not always follow, but good dogs nearly always carry good blood. It is a mistake to buy a dog on pedigree alone, but it is rare to find a class dog that does not carry good blood. So-called fashionable blood lines, while they enhance the value of the dog, may not always carry the qualities desired by the shooting man. It is for this reason that first-hand knowledge of the parents is desirable.

The quality of the dam is quite as important as that of the sire. If she has been bred before, knowledge of the quality of her previous progeny is always valuable. There are many good shooting dogs that are not fashionably bred, or even registered. Registered dogs, carrying good blood, command higher prices, and there is also a distinct satisfaction in owning a well-bred dog. Furthermore, for breeding purposes, the well-bred dog is decidedly preferable. For the average shooting man, however, individual merit is far more important than pedigree.

Blood lines are perhaps the most important thing to go upon in the selection of a puppy. They are also especially important when choosing a bitch, if breeding is contemplated, for in this case fashionable blood will add greatly to the value of her progeny. There are a number of well-known setter and pointer sires whose progeny are likely to be fine, level-headed shooting dogs. Others are not so noted in this respect. The number of field-trial wins alone is not always a reliable criterion.

*Intelligence and Disposition:* Dogs, like men, vary markedly; naturally the more intelligent the animal the more desirable he is. No two are alike. Some are cunning and sly—this is generally the result of bad training, but is, nevertheless, a trait strictly to be avoided. All really superior dogs are above the average intelligence.

A timid dog is to be avoided. A bold, headstrong dog, while harder to train, accepts punishment and retains training better. A dog may be made timid by severe punishment, but a naturally timid animal is not fit for field work and will be a constant source of annoyance. For the man who proposes to make a companion of his dog, the animal's disposition is especially worth considering. Again, much depends upon the way in which the dog has been treated. Most dogs have fine dispositions, and a man of wide experience can readily understand Lord Byron's famous epitaph:

Near this spot are deposited the remains of one who possessed Beauty without Vanity, Strength without Insolence, Courage without Ferocity, and all the Virtues of Man without his Vices. This Praise, which would be Flattery if inscribed over human ashes, is but a just Tribute to the Memory of Boatswain, a dog.—George Noel Gordon, Lord Byron, Inscription on the Monument of a Newfoundland dog.

Setters, particularly, seem to be blessed in respect to good disposition. Most of the really great dogs—those possessing unusual style and class—are high-strung but amenable to training, though requiring more judgment and experience to educate, and, later, to handle. There are some dogs which seem to be almost devoid of brains or intelligence. Level-headedness is of the utmost importance and should not imply lack of class.

*Health:* To do good work in the field, a dog must possess good health. No dog with a handicap of a heavy infestation of parasites can stand up under hard work, although with a light infestation he may show up fairly well for a time. Some dogs seem to have thinner skins or to be clumsier than others; at all events, they easily get cut on barbed wire and brambles.

Fear of thunder or lightning is a difficult thing to detect except during a storm. Dogs having such a fear are not necessarily timid in other respects. Their fear may be a result of lightning striking near them at some time, or they may be like some people who are naturally afraid of such disturbances. This neuroticism is often a nuisance, and there is not much that can be done to effect a cure. It has no relation to gunshyness or blinking. The chief thing is to prevent the dog from injuring himself or running away when a storm occurs. If the complete confidence of dogs has been gained, they may sometimes be satisfied if they can be with their masters during thunderstorms. Others wish to get into some hole or under a bed. For the hole-seekers, if an entryway is affixed to their kennel, with a winter carpet covering the entrance, they have opportunity to cower in this dark retreat during the storm. One thing is sure—punishment of any kind makes the condition worse. Even with the best of treatment, fear of thunder and lightning often tends to get worse as the dog becomes older.

*Character of the Seller:* Selling of worthless, gunshy, deaf, or otherwise undesirable dogs to the uninitiated offers great opportunities to the gyp. It is worth while to pay more money to a dealer who has a reputation to maintain than less to a fly-by-night whose only object is to get the purchaser's money.

Reasonably often a good dog can be secured from a gunner or guide. While the breeding from such sources may not average quite so high as that of dogs bought from professionals, and the finer points of training may not have been instilled so thoroughly, such dogs often make up for these lacks by their wider hunting experience and by having had more birds shot over them. Professional trainers naturally do not like to kill too many birds. Such dogs are, perhaps, less likely to be infected by parasites, especially those from the North. While this is not a hard-and-fast rule, rarely does one find a good dog in the hands of a poor shot.

*Training:* While it is natural for a dog to hunt, he is useless for shooting purposes without adequate training. The prospective owner not only should know who trained the dog, but, if possible, how many birds have been killed over him. I do not wish to labor the point, but it is necessary to stress the fact that to be a well-trained dog the animal must have had plenty of experience—the more the better. It is also well to know whether the dog has been hunted alone or in company with other dogs, and the varieties of game he is accustomed to handling.

*Biddableness:* Under this heading comes obedience in general, willingness to carry out orders, and whether the dog is accustomed to working to voice, whistle, or signals. It is a great disadvantage to have to shout loudly; hardly anything disturbs game as much and makes it so wild as the human voice. As long as the dog is within hearing, nothing is gained by loud orders. A whistle, especially a low one, is less disturbing. Signals, however, are ideal. As a matter of fact, the intelligent, experienced, well-trained dog needs few orders, and may go all day with scarcely a word spoken to him.

*Desire to Hunt:* This is largely an inherent instinct, but one more pronounced in some strains and individuals than in others. It can be encouraged only, not instilled by training. It is what makes a dog quick, busy, and industrious. Add to these gameness and, of course, condition, and you have the ideal combination to keep a dog going at the end of a long day and to bring him out the next morning, stiff but anxious to hunt. Without this attribute no dog is worth training.

*Range:* How much range a dog should have is a moot point. Field-trial men properly stress its importance, for, obviously, the more ground covered the greater is the likelihood of finding birds. The dog which, in his hunt, cover thirty miles will, other things being equal, find twice as much game as the dog which covers fifteen miles. With the old-time abundance of birds, range was not so important as it is today. The type of terrain on which the dog is to be hunted is a matter sometimes not sufficiently considered by the field-trial enthusiast. In a flat, open country, where a dog can be seen for perhaps a mile, the range can hardly be too great—always providing that the dog will handle, is steady on point, and will work to the gun. But this is not the kind of terrain generally found in the Northeast.

The trouble with the skyline dog is that it often does not work to the gun, and much good, near-by cover is passed without being investigated. There is a limit at which range becomes desirable. There is no question that the dog possessing extreme speed and range will find birds, but there is doubt as to what share of shooting his handler will get. Too much "Go on" and not enough "Whoa" is a just criticism of many field-trial dogs.

The ideal dog is one which will both go out in the open, and come in and work close to the gun, when required. To an extent, a dog can be taught to do this, but it is often extremely difficult. It is a mark of intelligence. The methods of dragging heavy chains, sacks, or long ropes; leather straps suspended so that they trip the dog, and other halting devices, are sometimes employed to shorten a dog, but often, when these impediments are removed, the dog resumes his natural range. Constant hacking will also shorten the range, but at best it is a difficult and tiresome procedure. Unless this sort of dog is constantly hacked, the tendency generally is for the range to increase until such time as it is decreased by advancing years. Some professional trainers believe it an easy thing to shorten range, but this has not been my experience.

The best thing to do with a dog which has too wide a range is to dispose of him to someone who wants a bigger-going dog. Just how much range is most useful depends upon the terrain, the method of hunting, and the owner. In this connection it may be well to bear in mind that the average gun wants a dog which will give him shooting, and if the dog is stylish, handsome, and will produce a thrill when on point, so much the better. No one wants a mutt, but it is most unfair to dub all short-range dogs "meat dogs."

About one hundred yards in the open is a fair average range for the man afoot, but there are times when the gun may desire to send him double this distance. I confess to the liking for a dog which is a little mechanical as far as quartering is concerned, and one which works out ahead of the gun and quarters his ground in *s*'s or flattened circles. It matters little which he does, although it is preferable to have him turn outward, for it is obvious that if he turns backward toward the gun he will be covering some ground which he has already been over. I do not mean to imply that the intelligence and initiative of the dog are to be totally submerged in attaining his objectives. How close the range should be in cover is a different matter. In much of the woodcock cover in Nova Scotia a dog is lost if his range exceeds 25 or 30 yards: On the other hand, I know good grouse covers in Pennsylvania where a dog can go out double, or even triple, this distance.

A good working rule for range is that the dog shall be in sight most of the time and never get out of touch with the gun. The gun wishes to hunt birds and not the dog. Nothing is more exasperating than to have to spend most of a shooting day trying to find a dog which is forever getting lost. If I have heard it once, I am sure I have heard a hundred times: "He must be on point. The last time I saw him he was going out to the left"—or in whatever direction he was last seen. Sometimes he has been found on point, but many more times the dog has been off on a hunt by himself.

A man likes to see his dog work birds and make his points; indeed, this is perhaps the best part of a day's shooting, but this is often impossible if a dog has extreme range. It matters not how steady the dog may be, the longer he is on point the greater likelihood there is of the bird running out, or flushing prematurely. Furthermore, the dog that is far away from his trainers, and kept on point for an unduly long time, may readily develop the habit of flushing and even chasing. There is no logic in having a dog make a point 250 yards in the path of the advancing gun. A closer-ranging dog would come to the bird just as certainly, but a little later, and when the gun has approached nearer. Furthermore, a big-going dog has probably overlooked good near-by cover. Such a dog, which will not accommodate his range to the requirements, is a nuisance, and birds will be passed because half of the ground is not hunted.

Dogs should keep in advance of the gun and should not cut back or run in straight lines. Almost the entire question of range is dependent upon terrain. What may be big going in one country may be short in another. The intelligent, well-trained shooting dog is constantly working to the gun and not hunting for himself. Occasionally, dogs are taught not to cross a fence or leave a field until so ordered. This point is more common abroad than here. It is useful when shooting on a restricted area or if approaching a highway. When a brace of dogs is used they should have about the same speed and range, and should hunt independently. Each of the dogs in a brace should supplement the other's weaknesses. If one is a poor retriever, the other should make up for his deficiencies. Except for grouse or woodcock, two dogs, provided they are really well broken, is a nice number to hunt if the country is not too tight. In a close country the dog's range should be restricted and when shooting alone one dog can cover all the ground that is necessary. If a brace of dogs is used it is desirable to have them about the same size, but easily distinguishable. Occasionally a combination of a pointing dog and a spaniel is employed. Under such circumstances the spaniel is usually kept at heel and used only for retrieving, and occasionally sent to work some especially heavy bit of cover. A retriever is also sometimes used in a similar capacity. This latter is a frequent practice abroad. Two dogs in a yard get more exercise during the off-season than one, and a single dog is often lonesome. Also, with a spare you have one to hunt in case anything happens to incapacitate the other. A dog and bitch make a good combination, and there is no danger of a kennel fight.

*Speed:* This is closely associated with range. Certainly the more speed the better, provided the dog does not go too fast for his nose. A few flushes are inevitable, and are generally overstressed by the novice. A dog, going very fast, often cannot stop himself in time when he gets bird scent, and may be on top of game before he is aware of it. The question of speed is therefore closely associated with nose and scenting conditions, as well as with terrain. A running fool is useless. To be of value, the dog must be hunting, i.e., searching for game. Great speed may be merely the result of the driving system of training; this is infrequently observed among shooting dogs but is seen fairly often among field-trial performers. Even an especially conditioned dog will tire after approximately two or three hours of very fast work, so that, while it is desirable that the dog be fast, industrious, and keen, exceptional speed may be a detriment. On the other hand, the slow, pottering grass prowler is even worse. The well-gaited dog runs without much up-and-down motion and appears to be smoothly and effortlessly pouring over the ground. He is really running much faster than he appears. This becomes especially noticeable if one compares him with a less well-gaited individual. Some dogs, like men, seem to be able to get through thick cover much more easily than others.

*Hunting and Searching:* The shooting man wants his dog to find birds. Unless the dog hunts the likely cover, utilizes the wind, and takes every advantage of existing conditions, he will never be an extra good bird finder. Bird-finding is of chief importance. Speed and range, although pleasant to watch, are merely means to an end. If the dog is to be useful, it must hunt as well as run. No matter how fast the dog is, if it does not search for birds it will never be a great bird finder. It is the desire to find birds, plus experience and nose, which make some dogs much better bird finders than others which may have equal or even greater range and speed. It is the quality to search, and to do this as rapidly as conditions permit, that should be looked for.

*Nose:* It is common to hear of a dog, with a "choke bore" or "long-range nose," or other terms, all of which denote exceptional scenting ability. Whereas dogs do vary in this respect, there are many other factors which enter into the question. A clever handler may do much to make it appear that his dog has an exceptional scenting ability. The man who says that last week he saw his dog wind birds at 50 or 60 yards may be telling the truth, but the probabilities are that some special conditions were present. So little is actually known regarding scent that it is sometimes difficult to arrive at a clear definition. As a matter of fact, most well-bred, healthy bird dogs possess good scenting powers, and what most of them need is to learn to use this ability properly. Of course dogs vary in their scenting ability, and, obviously, the better his nose the more useful he is to the sportsman.

Dogs should not flush birds too often, but they have to learn by experience how close they can approach safely. Different varieties of game differ in this respect, and the type of cover and scenting conditions also play a part. Thus, the woodcock holds well and permits a close approach, while the grouse must often be pointed from a distance. Well-trained dogs seldom flush wilfully. This is in part what is meant by learning to use scenting ability properly. It may be well to remind the novice that scenting conditions are poor in the spring. Some men believe that incubating birds have the power of withholding scent. The rank vegetation at this season also makes for poor scent. This subject is discussed elsewhere under the heading of Scent.

*Steadiness:* Flash pointing—the pause before the jump-in—is an inherent quality greatly developed by generations of training and breeding. Steadiness—the holding of the point—is almost entirely the result of training, and can be taught any dog. A dog which will regularly or even frequently break point and flush before the gun arrives is useless and a constant source of annoyance. However, steadiness does not imply holding a point regardless of the action of the bird. The dog would detract much from his value and be little more than an imbecile if he solidly held his point when a bird had run out from him and might be a hundred yards away, with the scent irrevocably lost by the time the gun could come up. On the other hand, it is absolutely necessary that a dog hold his point as long as the bird remains "pinned."

It should not be necessary to repeat that intensity and style are desirable. Field-trial men prefer their dogs to stand high up; however, many careful, eager dogs may crouch more or less; and, to my mind, this does not detract from their appearance, provided the crouch is not one apparently induced by fear of punishment. A high head generally denotes body scent, which is admirable, or sometimes indicates an effort to see the bird. It is often an inherited quality.

For preference, dogs should go boldly and high-headedly to their birds. However, some excellent ones are catlike in their method. That noted setter, Mohawk II, was an exponent of the feline approach. Many of his progeny also drew and crouched until the scent was established. Accurate location is of importance. Failure to do so often results in a difficult shot.

One sometimes hears an owner boast of a setter or pointer which never puts his nose to the ground. This is nonsense. All dogs do so occasionally—so-called foot scent may be all that is present. Dogs handle foot scent differently. Some follow the foot scent until the body scent is encountered. The pointing dog should not trail with nose to the ground, like a hound, but otherwise this is a satisfactory method. Many fine dogs, on first noticing scent, raise their heads and draw to the bird. Still others leave the trail, quarter their ground, endeavor to utilize the wind, and thus locate the quarry. Much probably depends upon local conditions, as well as the individual characteristics of the dog. The dog should not potter, but locate quickly. Although a high tail is now fashionable, its only real advantage is that in certain kinds of cover, such as tall grass, the pointing dog is more easily located. English sportsmen formerly used to require that the tail be kept below the level of the back, and an intense point, even with the tail at this level, is an inspiring sight. There is something which seems unnatural in the absolute flagpole tail, and the squirrel or sickle tail curled over the back presents an even worse appearance. Whether the tail is high or low is not, however, vitally important as far as a shooting dog is concerned. Some dogs wag or wave their tails, especially the tip, while on point. Sometimes this denotes a certain kind of game or it may show indecisiveness on the dog's part, or be merely a habit.

Some dogs sit down on point. This is generally frowned upon, but it is a fact that dogs with this habit are usually very steady. It is an especially common habit in certain strains of setters. Indeed, the name "setter" suggests this habit. In early times the setter was sometimes referred to as the "sitter."

A dog may lie down on point because he has held it a long time and is tired, or as the result of an exaggerated crouch, adopted for fear of flushing birds, the latter especially when he has stumbled on birds at close range. If he drops at the approach of his handler, obviously through fear of punishment, it is a disagreeable sight and a black mark for his trainer. Field-trial judges sometimes mark a dog down for dropping on point. Before shooting became popular, dogs, especially setters, were taught to drop in order that a net might be drawn over them and the covey of partridges which they were pointing, or, as it was generally called in those days, setting or crouching. Blaine mentions a setter which was trained to the net in 1555. In any event, dropping on point makes the dog hard to find. This is its chief disadvantage. Like the dog which sits down, the dropped dog is apt to be very steady and rarely flushes birds after the point is established. While on point dogs will frequently turn their head cautiously or roll their eyes in order to see if their handler is approaching. Immobility, intensity, an appearance of restrained keenness, a high head, and moderately high tail, standing four square or with one foot lifted, is the most desirable attitude on point.

Steadiness is of two kinds, the steadiness to wing, and to shot. Field-trial men and most sportsmen require both. Personally, I teach my dogs both, but in their second season teach them to break shot to retrieve. This occasionally loses a shot at a laggard bird, but greatly speeds up the retrieve and results in the loss of few cripples. With wing-tipped pheasants, especially in heavy cover, time spent in getting to the fallen bird, particularly if the fall is at a distance, is of great importance. The wing-tipped pheasant will be off like a shot and the dog cannot get to him too quickly. Delay, even with a good dog, may readily mean a lost bird, and this is true to a lesser extent with all game. A crippled grouse may hit the ground running, and at best is often a difficult job for the dog to retrieve. Breaking shot to retrieve has a tendency to make dogs unsteady on point, and this is why it is worth while to instill steadiness for the first season.

The handler who has proper control of his charge, however, need have no fear of his dog chasing. The dog should break shot only after it is seen that the bird has been hit. This is the hard point to teach, but it can be done. Sometimes the dog is so situated that it cannot see the bird. Under this circumstance, the dog should remain steady. However, no great harm is done if the dog breaks and hunts for the dead bird. The fact is that only if chasing develops is control required. Breaking shot to retrieve has a tendency to make companion dogs unsteady. This is a distinct drawback and most sportsmen prefer their dog to be steady at all times.

The dog should realize that flushing is a crime. Breaking shot encourages chasing, and this must be strictly checked; however, it is not usually difficult to prevent. I know that, for me, breaking shot to retrieve has resulted in securing many wounded birds which otherwise would have been lost. Some experienced dogs can tell better than the gun when a bird has received a mortal wound.

It is the experience of every sportsman occasionally to have birds retrieved which he believed missed.

The teaching of dropping to wing and shot has been largely discontinued in this country. For those who desire absolute steadiness, however, it is a certain method of preventing chasing. It was especially desirable in the days of muzzle-loading guns, as it permitted time to reload. Dropping to a sitting position has some advantages over a complete drop, in that it enables the dog to mark the fall better, gives him more air and, on wet ground, is not so hard on him. Occasionally, if the dog is on point and cannot see his handler, and the latter does not come up to him, he will develop the habit of backing out, finding the handler, taking him to the bird, and resuming his point. This is sometimes called reporting. It is a sign of intelligence, and like circling or heading a running pheasant, is something which the dog thinks out for himself and is not taught. The term reporting is also often used to describe a grouse dog which, in quartering and working out the ground to the sides and in front of the gun, may be frequently out of sight. He, however, reappears or reports at fairly regular intervals in front of his handler. I have seen two or three dogs that, instead of backing out of a point and reporting to their handler, would bark a few times to attract attention.

*Flushing on Order:* It is preferable for the handler to do the flushing, but there are occasions when flushing by the dog to order is of great advantage. Often a bird may be found in a high hedge, with the dog pointing from one side and the gun on the other. Under these circumstances, if the man attempts to flush the bird, it may break cover on the dog's side and a shot may be impossible. A somewhat similar situation may develop in thick cover. Often the bird is between the gun and the dog. A loud order may cause the bird to flush away from the shooter and in the dog's face. Hence the dog should be taught to obey a low command—a cluck of the tongue is a good one. It is easy to teach some dogs to flush to order, and others are difficult. The dog should flush by taking two or three sudden jumps toward the bird, and stopping the instant the game takes wing. It is sometimes the stopping which is hard to enforce. It is generally better not to try to teach a young dog this trick.

The level-headed, experienced dog which has been well grounded in stopping on "Whoa," can usually be taught without much difficulty. Some intelligent dogs acquire the trick themselves. It should be definitely frowned upon unless the order to flush has been given. It is somewhat like playing with fire, as the practice is prone to result in unsteadiness, but it is well worth while for those dogs to whom it can be safely taught. There are many dogs that it is unwise to attempt to teach this to.

*False Pointing:* Any point from which a game bird cannot be produced is, strictly speaking, a false point. It must be remembered that the differentiation of game birds from other birds, such as larks, is one of education. All dogs will point rabbits until taught to blink these animals. Furthermore, even experienced dogs will frequently point turtles and occasionally snakes. Dogs may occasionally point where game birds have recently been, and sometimes when there is no indication that game has been present. It is commonly supposed that false pointing is the result of an inferior nose. This is not necessarily the case. False pointing is more likely to occur when the dog is tired, or may result from severe punishment having been administered for flushing sometime in the past. At times dogs develop false pointing as a sort of show-off. Such points should be ignored by the handler or the dog given a slap and ordered on. The trouble with the former plan is that it is not always possible to distinguish a "vanity" point from a real one. If a real point is ignored it is bad for the dog's education to pay no attention to it, quite apart from the fact that a shot may be lost. It is well not to condemn a dog too quickly for false pointing. He may have an off day, scent conditions may be poor, or many other factors may be present. Certain strains exhibit a tendency to false point. Many of the English setters that are rich in Count Noble blood have a tendency toward this defect. For the frequent and confirmed false pointer there is no remedy, and the fault probably results from inability to distinguish between scents or is an abnormal development of the pointing instinct.

*Class and Style:* Class is something which can easily be recognized but which is difficult to define. It is an attractive and often inherited way of doing things. A trainer may educate his dog to the nth degree, but he can hardly give the dog class. On the other hand, a wild, half-broken dog may exhibit great class. Class dogs possess great nervous energy, and, as a result, are more difficult to control than more phlegmatic animals. When properly trained they are the great gun dogs and the type which enhances the pleasure of shooting over them. The desirability of style on point has been mentioned, but class and style also mean the manner in which the dog conducts himself while hunting. A dead tail or a low head, for example, give a poor impression. However, the dog with little tail action is less likely to get a sore tail as a result of cuts from briars. Keenness, speed, method of going, and generally the way the dog handles himself in the field are the determining factors.

*Backing:* A dog may honor another's point either at sight or at command. Refusal to do this often results in a flush. It can easily be taught, but is mostly a matter of experience. Many dogs back naturally, and will often back solidly before they are steady on their own points. Others despise it. Some fail to back because of ambition or jealousy to steal the point, and others may do so because of their training. Some trainers do not object to their dogs stealing the credit of a point. The backing dog is rarely intense unless he actually has bird scent.

*Retrieving:* All shooting dogs should retrieve, otherwise many birds will be lost that cannot be found or secured by the sportsman. Some trainers fear that retrieving will make their dogs unsteady, and for this reason do not require it of young dogs. In the British Isles, it is common to utilize one of the retriever breeds for this purpose. However, their methods of shooting are different from ours in this country where bags are smaller and most of the shooting of a different type. Some trainers think that the scent of a dead bird, filling a dog's nostrils as it must while retrieving, tends to impair his scenting ability for a time at least. It is not uncommon, however, to see a dog point with a dead bird in his mouth, and this when a sight point would have been impossible. Pointing dead is a poor substitute for retrieving.

With the present scarcity of game, every lost bird counts not only from the bag—for the gun may go on and fill his limit without it— but especially from the standpoint of conservation, even if one ignores the other unpleasant aspect. The retriever may be either force-broken or may retrieve quite naturally. The return should be to hand and not merely to bring in and drop. The bird should not be given up by the dog until he receives the order, "Give." A test of good retrieving is that the bird may be received with one hand. The return should be prompt—the faster the better. If the handler stoops and extends his hand the dog usually makes the retrieve rapidly. There should be no mouthing or chewing of the bird. Incidentally, hard mouthness can be detected better by feeling for broken bones than by examining the bird for tooth marks. If a dog gets badly scratched, it will often develop the habit of killing all wounded birds by giving them a quick bite across the back before retrieving. These dogs are not otherwise hard mouthed. This form of hard mouthness is especially likely to develop in experienced dogs that are used for pheasant shooting. The spurs of an old cock are formidable weapons, and the habit is therefore excusable. From a practical standpoint, it is especially important that the dog should retrieve from a distance. This some dogs will not do, though they may bring in birds from 40 or 50 yards perfectly. A wing-tipped pheasant may cover 200 yards, or even more, before the dog finally comes up with it, and all such runners are sure to be lost, unless the dog retrieves them. If after the delivery of the bird there are any feathers sticking to the dog's lips these should be removed. It is doubtful if they would affect the dog's scenting powers, but their removal certainly makes him more comfortable. The entire act of retrieving, including the return and delivery, should be done cheerfully, with no evidence of fear or being cowed. The natural retriever may refuse at any time, while the force-broken retriever is more reliable, and a little schooling can be given at the first failure.

Force-breaking to retrieve is not difficult, and can be taught any dog. Briefly, it consists in taking the dog into an enclosure where there is nothing to distract his attention, and placing a training collar on him, attached to a short leash. Dogs seem to like to retrieve the personal property of their handlers—probably because of the scent. It is also likely that an old hat or glove is more easily found on account of its scent. If, during training, the dog shows a tendency to be hard mouthed, the use of a hard object, which is wrapped in twine, to retrieve, often discourages this fault. I have taught retrieving as follows:

(1) Open dog's mouth and insert corncob, making him hold this in mouth; (2) take cob from hand—after this the job is half over; (3) gradually lower hand until he takes cob from hand on floor; (4) take cob from floor; (5) gradually get dog to take cob farther and farther away, until cob can be thrown to extreme confines of room, at the same time substituting training cord for leash; (6) outdoors and repeat, keeping dog on leash; (7) same, but take off leash; (8) hide cob or a glove and make dog hunt for same, and retrieve; (9) finally kill bird, preferably in open, where he can see the fall.

Sometimes the dog accustomed only to the corncob will refuse to retrieve the bird. If this is the case, pick up the bird and toss it away, as was done with the cob during training. The dog will then usually bring it in. Always make the dog sit down to give up cob or bird, and use the word "Give." Do not let the dog drop the cob or bird until told to give. During the course occasionally use an old glove or some other soft article, instead of the cob, and praise the dog for doing it properly. Give the dog some tidbit at the end of each lesson. Do not make the lesson too long. Twice properly performed is enough and constitutes one lesson. Make the dog understand it is work, not play. Training generally takes from ten to fifteen lessons, although some trainers teach retrieving in much less. Start each lesson by repeating the preceding one, thus, in teaching point 4, first make the dog take from the hand on the floor (3) and then start 4. There is an excellent detailed description in Lytle's book, *How to Train Your Bird Dog*.

There are many good natural retrievers. When once taught, most dogs delight in retrieving, whether they have been force-broken or possess this natural skill. It is sometimes a great advantage to have a dog which will retrieve from water, and dogs should be so taught. It is much easier to teach a dog to retrieve or cross water if he has been accustomed to swimming. All adult dogs can swim, but until they become accustomed to it many have a fear of water. A pond, having a gradually sloping bank, and one which is free of weeds and obstructions, is the best place to get a dog accustomed to swimming. A companion dog which is accustomed to water acts as an incentive. If the swimming dog encounters weeds he is apt to be thrown off balance. Equilibrium and the horizontal position are necessary; if weeds or other obstructions throw him in the upright position he will sink, and may even drown if he cannot regain the horizontal position.

Some trainers teach their charges to retrieve by a wing or by the head. Either exposes the dog to scratches from the bird's feet or spurs. The important thing is that they shall not mouth or chew the bird, and that the job shall be done promptly.

I have seen one smart old setter, when he was tired and wanted to go home—if he thought he was not observed—rapidly bury the bird or cover it with leaves, perhaps in the hope that if unsuccessful, the party would give up and cease shooting. He always had a comical appearance even if the mud, which was often on his nose, had not been equivocal to a confession of guilt. He would come in wagging his tail with a self-conscious, ingratiating manner which seemed to say, "I have made a thorough search, gentlemen, and the bird cannot be found." Persuasion and threats were useless, and, unless he had been seen in the act, it was often difficult to locate the site of the interment. The dog was handicapped by a broken leg, which had been badly set, and for this reason was never worked hard, but when I knew him he was a handsome, old-fashioned type of setter, and could do a splendid job on both woodcock and grouse. With the exception of an occasional lapse toward the end of the day, he was a reliable retriever. He was owned by the late H. V. Gates, of Yarmouth, Nova Scotia.

Spriggs records an instance of a retriever burying a grouse, which he attributes to atavism; and a correspondent of *The Field and Stream* of August, 1944, mentions an Irish setter which developed the habit. It is always curious how a dog's mind functions. I once saw a young southern dog which, when a covey of quail was flushed, would dig most energetically at the site from which they had taken off, apparently in the hope that he might unearth more birds.

A hard mouth can be corrected by inserting wires in a dead bird and requiring the dog to retrieve. A badly shot bird is more apt to be chewed, probably because of the blood and juice which have exuded. It hardly seems necessary to warn that a dog should never be permitted to retrieve a hawk or an owl. However, I have seen this done. While these birds have even a spark of life remaining they will contract their talons on the slightest touch, and may severely wound a dog about the mouth, or even the eye; and, apart from the immediate injury, may impair the dog's future willingness to retrieve. Herons and cranes are among the most dangerous of all birds. A single stroke of their dagger-like bills may destroy an eye. These interesting and handsome birds should not be shot unless they are found on a trout stream or raiding a hatchery. Dogs that are taught to break shot to retrieve are particularly likely to be exposed to these hazards.

*Conformation:* It is always a pleasure to own a handsome dog, and show dogs are apt to be superior in this respect to field dogs. Performance is more important than appearance, but there is no reason why the field dog should not possess good looks. The field dog is often lighter and built more for speed than the show dog. It is well for every owner to acquaint himself with the breed standards, as laid down by the American Kennel Club.

*Color and Coat:* The advantages of a dog which is easy to see have already been mentioned under the heading, "Dog or Puppy." A really distinctive or unusual mark, providing it is not unsightly, is sometimes of service as an identification. The character of the coat is important and is more or less a criterion of health.

*Courage and Gameness:* These are attributes which enable a dog to take a severe and perhaps undeserved thrashing, then cheerfully go on hunting. They keep a dog out in front at the end of a long, grueling day, when his companions have folded up and quit. They force him on determinedly when he has nothing left but his big heart. Together with the desire to hunt and find birds, his game spirit sends him into the most punishing cover. Gameness in well-bred setters and pointers is so common that it is generally taken for granted, but without it a dog is not worth training. A dog may be timid around the kennel, but be as courageous as any in the field. Gameness and courage can only be proved by test, but usually an accurate guess can be made as to their presence by the dog's general behavior.

*Car Broke:* For transportation a man with many dogs will probably use crates on the running boards or back of his car. These, if fairly draft-proof and provided with plenty of straw, are excellent. The car itself is often filled with tobacco smoke, which probably does not help the dog's scenting powers. However, to put a wet setter in a drafty crate on a cold day for a long drive home is, to say the least, not advisable. It seems unnecessary to state that care should be exercised to insure the exclusion of poisonous gas from the exhaust. Recognized hazard that this is, every year dogs are killed by neglecting this precaution. The baggage compartment of a motor car, if closed, may suffocate a dog, and lids which are propped up may fall down. A station wagon with a compartment in the back for dogs offers an ideal means of transportation. Some old rugs or straw can be placed on the floor, and are easily removed when the vehicle is used for other purposes. The man who expects to transport only one or two dogs will probably often employ the back of his sedan. An old blanket on the floor makes the dog comfortable. Dogs should be trained to lie quietly on the floor and not to get on the seat. The seat gets every draft there is, and muddy feet do not improve upholstery.

Car sickness is much like seasickness. It is well to get dogs accustomed to the car before they reach maturity. When carrying dogs in a car be careful in closing the door. This may seem an unnecessary warning, but I have seen dogs' feet, legs, and tails injured by carelessness in this respect. Dogs should never be chained in a motor car or wagon, and then left alone. I have seen one dog strangled in this way. Be careful in letting them out when on a highway.

*House Broke:* Although shooting dogs are better kept out of doors, there are times when it is convenient or necessary to bring them into the house. Adult dogs are, usually, naturally clean, and young ones can be taught to be so. Dogs are moderately regular in their habits, and a little attention to their needs is, generally, all that is required. In buying a dog it is an asset to get one which knows how to behave himself indoors.

*Yard Breaking:* This used to be more insisted on than it is today. All dogs should come to call, follow at heel, down charge, and stay put. They should also slow up when cautioned, and stop on "whoa" or order. It is preferable to teach all these things thoroughly before taking the dog afield. Being accustomed to control facilitates the field training. Forced retrieving is a part of yard breaking, but, as previously stated, its teaching is sometimes postponed until after the dog has been thoroughly steadied on point. Some trainers prefer to defer yard training until the dog has had field experience. The chief advantage in giving field work first is that if the dog does not show promise, he may be discarded, and the trouble of yard training thereby avoided. It is possible, however, to take a young dog afield before yard training is seriously started. By so doing it is often possible to hazard a fairly accurate guess as to its desire to hunt, and other field qualities.

*Summary.* It is impossible to get all the virtues embodied to their highest extent in any one animal. Dogs, like men, are often outstanding in one particular and lacking in another. Some dogs are naturally more biddable, more intelligent, more willing, and retain their training better than others. However, the desirable qualities resulting solely from education can be taught with sufficient patience. The natural qualities (such as desire to hunt, conformation, style) have to be present, and cannot be instilled by training, though some may be developed by it. The latter group of qualities are largely the result of judicious breeding and, to a lesser extent, to sheer good luck.

Despite the smaller number of game birds and shorter seasons, which result in lesser experience for dogs today, the general quality of pointing dogs has improved. Bench shows have done much to improve the appearance, and field trials have been of immense value in developing a high standard for field performance. It is to be hoped that those in charge of arranging standards for judging the now popular shooting-dog stakes will continue to bear in mind the practical requirements of the shooting man. It is obvious that different types of dogs are required for different terrains, and that the requirements for shooting dogs in the South are quite different from those needed in the coverts of the North. The winner of a shooting-dog stake should be a well-trained, easily handled dog of great natural aptitude, one which can be used with pleasure for a day's shooting. Although of secondary consideration, there is no reason that the shooting dog should not be a handsome, well-bred animal and conform to the standards of his breed.

In 1919, the president, J. M. B. Reis, and the secretary, H. H. Cahoon, prepared a standard for the ideal grouse dog which was to be used in the Pennsylvania Field Trial Club. This criterion follows, and may well be used for any class of shooting dogs to be employed for upland game in the northeastern states:

A high-class grouse dog is one whose every action denotes great interest in his work, which is full of animation and which is at all times searching for birds, in an independent and intelligent manner. He should be under such control that he will do his work with the minimum amount of handling, by either voice or whistle. He should keep the course and hunt to the gun, and within reasonable distance; in a fast, snappy manner work out all the likely cover in front of his handler. He should not cut back, but should consume his speed by working out his ground on each side of the course taken by his handler. When the cover is heavy and the course full of briars, he should not hunt the easy footing and pass up the likely objectives. He must pay little attention to the scent of fur; occasionally pointing a rabbit could be overlooked, but under no condition should he chase one. He should accurately locate and point his birds and be perfectly stanch on point until the birds are flushed, when he must be steady to wing and shot. He must back at sight of a pointing dog and not approach close enough to interfere with the dog or to disturb the bird. After the bird has been killed over a point, and the dog has been steady to shot, he must, on being ordered, go for and retrieve the bird in a prompt manner and without dropping it deliver it to his handler in an unruffled and undamaged condition. A dog is classable according to the manner in which he performs these requirements. (*American Field.*)

For grouse and woodcock there is also quite another type of dog used by many hunters. This is the slower, old-fashioned sort, which travels at a canter or fast trot, is extremely careful, and has an excellent nose, which enables him to point grouse at a long distance. He points on the first scent of the bird. The gun then walks up, and man and dog advance together. When the bird finally flushes, a shot is usually obtained. This type of dog does not find so many birds as the faster, wider, modern dog, but the proportion of shots obtained from birds found is greater. Grouse do not lie particularly well to any dog, and while it is true that the slow dog does not actually pin so many birds, he does enable shots to be secured from many which would flush out of range of the fast dog. He may not produce the thrills, but may be handsome and stylish on point, and the handler does not have to carry a training cord in his pocket every time he goes grouse shooting. He is often a big, heavily feathered setter. I have had too many pleasant days and killed too many grouse over these dogs not to respect them, and if I hunted nothing but grouse and cock would be glad to give a good one of this type kennel room at any time. He is a specialist on grouse, and usually deadly on woodcock, and will unerringly point bird after bird with almost machine-like regularity. He is too slow for pheasants and quail, and is generally a product of the grouse country.

I prefer the faster dog, but am not at all sure that more grouse and cock cannot be killed over the old-timer. Furthermore, the latter is not quite such a *rara avis* as the really good, modern-type grouse dog. All good grouse dogs are not good woodcock dogs, but most of them are. Since cocks are so frequently found in grouse country, experience with the latter usually means experience with the former, but the reverse is not always the case, and many dogs can handle woodcock quite satisfactorily and make a poor job of grouse. It is true, however, that many grouse dog specialists prefer to hunt the larger bird.

The shooting man who is contemplating the purchase of a dog will do well to bear definitely in mind that the chief function of the dog is to provide shooting. The dog that makes ten points in a morning is twice as useful as the one that makes five points. If the dog is handsome and well bred, so much the better. Speed, range, and training are means to an end. Class and style add greatly to the pleasure of watching the dog, but in the final analysis it is the dog that will give the greatest number of productive points that is the most important asset. For the novice, who is perhaps purchasing his first shooting dog, and who has little experience in handling, it is especially important to secure a well-broken dog. Often an old dog is best—certainly not one that is high strung or hard to control.

To refer to the shooting dog as "only a shooting dog," as if he were of an inferior race in comparison with the field-trial animal, is adopting an unwarranted attitude. The shooting dog may readily possess better style and all the other desirable attributes to a greater extent than the trial dog. The difference between the two may be merely a matter of training, and, in the shooting dog, bird work is generally stressed even more than it is in field trials.

To summarize the fundamentals—the pointing breeds should *Find, Hold* and *Retrieve.*

*In the whole history of the world there is but one thing that money cannot buy—to wit, the wag of a dog's tail.*
—Henry Wheeler Shaw (Josh Billings), quoted in Kate Sanborn's *My Literary Zoo.*

HANDLING. Improper handling will spoil any dog. The young dog is more easily spoiled than the older one, whose training is likely to be better grounded. To get the best out of a dog, the handler must know the individual dog. Each dog has his own peculiarities and strong and weak points, as to disposition and training. The handler may well start upon the basis that dogs which have been properly treated generally desire to please. When they err they usually do so for one of two reasons: either excitement, or lack of understanding of the order given. The handler should look on things from the dog's viewpoint and remember the animal's limitations. The latter statement is so self-evident that it seems superfluous. Lack of realization of it and loss of self-control are, however, two of the commonest faults in handling. Be fair and just.

The inexperienced man, perhaps more or less excited or unsure of himself, is prone to forget that even a well-trained dog understands only a relatively few words, and is generally guided by the manner of his trainer and the tone of his voice, as much as by the actual word spoken. Hence words of command should be short, distinct, and always the same. Furthermore, provided the dog is within hearing, nothing is gained by loud orders. The voice should be kept just loud enough for the dog to hear and the tone of voice such as to imply obedience. A loud-shouting man rarely has tractable or well-trained dogs. The trained dog should be kept always in control, both in and out of season.

Absolute control is the requirement of all successful training and handling, and it is vital to remember that, despite the willingness of the dog, he should obey because he recognizes that he must do so. He must know who is master. This does not mean continuous training or nagging, but is intended to convey the idea that dogs should not be allowed to disobey or get slack when orders are given. This is especially apt to occur during the off-season or in the excitement of shooting. Thus, a dog may be taken for a walk and allowed to frolic to his heart's content, but should he come on a game bird and deliberately flush, or chase fur, he should be warned or punished exactly as if this had occurred during the shooting season. However, dogs seem to recognize the difference between an exercise walk in the off-season and actual training or hunting, so it is not necessary to be too severe with them.

Give as few orders as possible but see that they are obeyed. Nothing will undermine a dog's education more than unenforced orders. Often he will want to do something other than obey, and if he is permitted to "get away with it" it will be harder to enforce the order the next time; but, in case of doubt, give the dog the benefit. For a deliberate fault, punishment should be administered immediately, but the trainer should make sure that the dog knows what he is being punished for. The trainer should go to, and catch the dog and administer the punishment or the reproof. It is a bad principle to call a dog and then whip him after he has obeyed the trainer by coming to call. Some headstrong old dogs require moderately severe punishment; for others, a sharp rating is sufficient. The bad old days, when dogs were often brutally flogged for a minor mistake, are gone as far as the intelligent handler is concerned, and are on a par with the idea that a pat on the head or a meat diet was ruinous. A little encouragement is excellent and dogs appreciate it immensely. There is no doubt that dogs appreciate justice.

Constant hacking leads to misunderstanding, fear of punishment, or more or less ignoring of orders. In many respects the mind of a dog works much like that of a child, though the dog understands fewer words. Most dogs have a good memory, but are relatively slow learners, and acquire knowledge only through constant repetition. It takes time. Actual punishment in the way of flogging is not often needed. This is particularly true with the young dog which is being trained. It is a different matter for the trained dog which deliberately transgresses. No trainer, however, can know with certainty how much punishment a dog will stand without spoiling him, and, once spoiled, the damage is done.

The amateur who does not do much training or handling is apt to punish too much or to be too lenient. He is especially likely to be too censorious of an occasional flush. He often does not differentiate between mistakes and sins. As far as effective work is concerned, "there is no more useless adjunct in incompetent hands than the whip" (Ripley). The most important thing is to check faults in their very incipiency. Some men seem to anticipate a fault and prevent its commission. These are the really gifted handlers.

A frequent example is found in the act of a dog jumping up on its master. Almost all untrained dogs will do this. It probably results from excitement and an effort to show their pleasure. If a pup is checked the first time he offends, and each and every time thereafter, three or four such experiences will prevent a repetition; but the habit once established is hard to eradicate. When a dog jumps up, I have heard it advised to hold his front paws and tread lightly but painfully upon the hind feet. Anyone who has seen an X-ray photograph or a skeleton of the delicate anatomic arrangement of the feet would hesitate to adopt this form of punishment. A sharp rating for the first offense and a smart cut of a switch for subsequent offenses is preferable, and will, if administered before the habit is formed, be all that is necessary.

Another example is seen in the reprehensible habit of chicken killing. If a pup is brought up with chickens and early checked at the first inclination to chase, this annoying tendency can be easily stopped, but the confirmed chicken killer is a totally different proposition, and no amount of leather or hanging a dead chicken around his neck is a certain cure. Farm-raised pups are usually immune to this temptation. A reprehensible form of punishment is the pinching or twisting of the ears. This may cause permanent injury, and at best is decidedly less effective than the whip. If a dog is to be flogged it should be on the back and hind quarters, never under the belly. The latter may result in injury to the genitals. Nothing but a whip or switch should be used. Kicking is outrageous. It is sure to bruise and may break a bone or do other serious injury.

The high-strung, intense individual, packed with nervous energy, must be treated differently from the dog of a more phlegmatic disposition. The trainer and handler must enforce obedience, but should do it in such a manner as not to take too much out of the dog. Often a high-strung dog has to let off steam. "To know when to punish and when to spare, to a large extent measures the qualification of a good handler" (Lytle).

Beginning deafness is difficult to detect. Deafness and, consequently, inability to hear orders, may be readily mistaken for obstinacy. When a dog that is known to be an honest, reliable worker fails properly to respond or errs in various respects, his character should be taken into consideration. Such a dog should be treated with indulgence. He is probably merely suffering from an off-day.

I do not employ a spike collar, but recommend a simple broad training collar. In my opinion it is inadvisable to use clogs, heavy drag ropes, and the like. The best training cord is that recommended by Foster, and is made of a braided tiller rope, with a flexible wire core and jib snap.

The trainer should remember that the dog's intelligence is lower than that of man, and that he absorbs learning only from repeated experience, and, furthermore, that dogs, like men, make mistakes. I have often been reminded of an old and successful trainer with whom I used to shoot in Maryland. His humor was often of a somewhat caustic type, and on one occasion a sportsman was rather severely and unjustly censuring one of his young dogs. The trainer bore this for some time, but finally turned on the critic, who was a notoriously poor shot, and said, "How would you like it, if that dog bit you every time you made a mistake and missed a bird?"

The importance, when handling a new dog, of knowing the methods of training, the words of command, and the signals to which he has been accustomed has already been mentioned. The usual whistle signals are: (1) a single long blast for "Come." Dogs generally obey this readily, and, if not, a check cord drill can be instituted. (2) Two short blasts indicate "Go On." This is taught by giving the signal every time the dog is sent away. In a short time they learn to interpret a couple of taps from the whistle properly. I sometimes use a single, short lip whistle to attract a dog's attention, if it is desired to wave him to the right or left. Whistle signals are easily taught and are better than shouting. There is a whistle on the market called the "Thunderer," which is a good one. At all events, it should be capable of producing a loud blast. It is easy to develop the habit of overusing the whistle.

Almost everyone with the ability to pull a trigger thinks he knows enough to handle a dog. As a matter of fact, to get the best work from a dog requires a good deal of judgment, patience, experience, and knowledge of dogs, birds, cover, scent. The less experience a dog has, the more important is good handling. The old experienced dog, hunting in familiar territory, will probably do better if left entirely alone than with an overanxious, inexperienced handler. This is another way of saying that well-trained, experienced dogs, especially if working for their owner, require relatively little handling. Overhandling is a common fault. Constant hacking may be a sign of a poorly trained dog, but more frequently of an inexperienced handler. To train properly, the handler must know more than the dog. He must keep cool, not lose his temper, and be steady himself. The man who runs excitedly to a crippled bird is not helping the retrieve. The man who loses his temper is sure to have cowed or bird-shy dogs. A little self-analysis on the handler's part is a good thing.

A dog is greatly handicapped by a strange handler. The manner, tone of voice, signals, method of hunting are all new, and even the words of command may be different from those to which the dog is accustomed. Furthermore, the handler is probably ignorant of the dog's idiosyncrasies and individual peculiarities. Allowances should therefore be made for the dog. On the other hand, a dog may sometimes attempt liberties with a new handler, and such tendencies should be guarded against.

The handler can do much to assist his charge in finding birds by paying attention to the wind, position of cover and by other measures. He should call the dog to heel when approaching highways or in birdless areas and arrange the course of the hunt so that water is available. If a game dog is beginning to tire, a rest and water are better than tapping him on with the whistle. Consideration for the dog and conservation of his energy mark the intelligent handler.

One word of advice to the guest gun: Never forget that a man will stand any form of criticism better than that directed against his dog.

*Lost Dog.* If a dog becomes lost in the field, he will usually cut his handler's trail and follow up from the rear. It is advisable, therefore, not to wander around looking for him and mix up the trail, but to walk a short distance in the direction in which the dog was last seen, if possible to an eminence which will command a view, and there wait. A shot will sometimes bring a dog back from a long distance. If the dog does not turn up in a reasonable time, it is likely that he has returned to the car, or, if it is not too far away, has perhaps gone home.

One thing is certain: before nightfall the dog will try to find some human habitation. It is well, therefore, to notify not only those living near the point at which the hunt was started, but also any farmers living near the place where the dog was last seen, and perhaps to post notices of a reward in the local post office, inn, or the like, and to advertise in the local papers. If the dog does not turn up by nightfall, he is almost certainly in trouble: stolen, tied up somewhere, hooked by his collar to a limb, or fallen into a pit from which he cannot escape. Sometimes he can be heard barking. If the dog is an intelligent, experienced animal, it is not a matter for delay.

The ideal way to hunt a dog is without a collar. But this is not usually practicable. Many states require that the dog carry a license at all times. The owner's name, address, and telephone number should be on the tag and will aid in the return of many lost dogs. While working the dog, the collar should be so loose that if the dog gets hung up he can pull his head out without difficulty.

BLINKING AND GUNSHYNESS.

*I beheld the wretch—the miserable monster whom I had created*
    —Mary Wollstonecraft Shelley, *Frankenstein.*

These are man-induced defects and closely allied to manshyness.

In the cases of some dogs there is an underlying timidity, often merely a soft spot which is brought out by the ordinary requirements of training. In others, the dogs are normal dogs that have been abused by ill-advised or brutal methods. Blinkers, or gunshy dogs, are not necessarily timid, and may be as bold as any, in other respects; and it goes without saying that many extremely timid dogs do not exhibit either defect in the slightest degree. Since both blinking and gunshyness are man-induced, they are not hereditary. Both are very serious defects. There are various phases and degrees of both. They are akin to each other and, to some extent, have the same causes. Sufficient ill treatment will probably make a blinker out of any dog.

*Blinking.* The well-trained setter or pointer which shies off from or ignores a rabbit is blinking fur, and has been taught to do so. The setter that drops on point as his trainer approaches may do so from the old inherent habit taught the early setters when they were used in conjunction with a net for taking the covey, or it may be from fear of punishment if the birds flush prematurely. In the latter case it may be a premonitory symptom to real blinking.

The confirmed blinker gets some misunderstood idea which associates the bird with punishment, and, consequently, works out that the best way to avoid punishment is to avoid the bird when his handler is in the vicinity. I have seen a confirmed blinker point birds perfectly when he thought he was alone; but all will not do so. In fairly mild cases the blinker establishes his point properly, but circles the bird as the trainer approaches. Sometimes he continues to trot around the bird in a circle, or may establish a new point, often opposite the trainer. Either of these forms of blinking often results in a flush. This is not to be confused with the clever, experienced dog, which widely circles a running pheasant in order to check the bird and give the gun time to come up, or with the dog that moves a little in order to secure better scent.

Another type is the dog which will leave his point on the approach of the handler and slink back to him or come to heel, often exhibiting unmistakable evidence of fear. This may be a form of gunshyness and not true blinking. Still others may road, or even establish their points, but, before the handler can reach them, will start hunting again, leaving their bird unflushed. In the more advanced stages of blinking the dog deliberately avoids the bird for fear of punishment if the bird flushes, or for other reasons. One may hunt all day in a good bird country with a confirmed blinker of this type and not see a bird unless one is walked up. Such a dog may appear to hunt excellently, but if he is watched closely he will be seen occasionally to alter his course suddenly, and if the gun walks to this point he will find a bird. The confirmed blinker turns off at sight of the bird, or at the first whiff of bird scent. Sometimes the blinker will be seen to sneak off a few yards, sulk, stop, drop his tail, or hesitate before changing his course. Blinking may develop at any age after training has begun. I have seen a seven-year-old dog develop the fault. Brown records the case of a dog that always blinked the first bevy of the day, but performed faultlessly thereafter. Mr. Coleman tells me that he has seen a shooting dog that would point coveys, but would often blink single birds.

*Gunshyness.* Blinking is due to fear of punishment; gunshyness to fear of a gun or the sound of a shot. In an advanced case of gunshyness, the dog will run at the sight of a gun, or even of a stick which he believes to be a gun. In mild cases, the dog will cringe or come to heel after the shot and may in a little while go out again and hunt. In still more advanced cases the dog will return to the car, go home, or actually bolt.

Almost everyone has had the disagreeable experience of having a shot fired too near his head and having his "head rung." Something of this sort is probably what starts most of these cases. Others may develop from having a salvo fired over their heads, when, perhaps, they have never previously heard a gun fired. Shooting at a dog for chasing may induce gunshyness. One case I know of was caused by the trainer, who was in the habit of shooting a blank 22-caliber cartridge into the ground in front of the young pointing dog, in an attempt to staunch him.

Both blinking and gunshyness are much easier to prevent than to cure. Much depends upon developing in the dog the love of bird hunting before restrictive measures are started, or any shooting of game is attempted. Real confidence in the trainer will go a long way to prevent the development of either blinking or gunshyness, and is of the utmost importance in attempting to cure both conditions. Blinking or birdshyness is a sign of improper training; generally, of severe punishment inflicted for some fault not realized by the dog. Prevention requires judgment. To prevent gunshyness the pup should be made accustomed gradually to the sound of a gun—first a shot from a 22-caliber rifle fired at a distance, preferably at mealtimes; then small loads from a shotgun, gradually working up to full loads. Pups will soon learn to interpret the sound of a 22-caliber rifle or pistol as a signal for meals. Later the trainer and sportsman should avoid blasting close to the head of the dog. It is a good general principle to try to get level or ahead of the pointing dog before shooting. Sometimes a step or two to the side will answer the same purpose. Shooting, especially at low-flying birds, over a dog's head cannot fail to "ring his ears." It is inadvisable at any time and particularly so if the dog is a young one. This point is often forgotten by even the experienced dog handler. With the gunshy dog it is worth while to have its ears examined by a competent veterinarian. There may be a diseased condition present which is at the bottom of the trouble.

Confirmed blinkers or gunshy dogs had usually better be discarded. With rare exceptions, they are not worth wasting time on, but they may make good house dogs or pets. They are often good dogs with the exception of this one weakness. Once definitely established, these faults are almost impossible to eradicate. The cure is certainly not a job for the average amateur. It is a case for encouragement, not punishment; for the more of the latter the worse the habits become. In their incipiency, one improperly timed whipping or shot may confirm the habit. The gifted, patient trainer may be able to cure these faults, but at best it is a tedious procedure. The celebrated Jay R's Boy was cured of blinking by Ed Farrior, and numerous other instances of the eradication of both blinking and gunshyness could be cited. If the habits are definitely established, however, it is not usually worth attempting, unless the dog possesses unusual quality. In their incipiency it is a different matter, but even here great care and judgment are necessary.

Some interesting observations on gunshyness have been made at the Cornell University Farm by Drs. A. V. Jensen and O. P.

Anderson. Jensen and his associate believe that gunshy dogs are neurotic and lack nervous and emotional control, and that the malady is similar to war neurosis in the human. Thirteen gunshy dogs were studied with two normal dogs used as controls. Two outstanding signs of abnormal behavior were noted—one the fearful attitude and the other an apparent absence of normal curiosity. The latter is probably dependent upon the former. A normal dog brought into a strange room, for example, shows immediate interest by exploring each corner and sniffing at objects in the room. The gunshy dog crouches in one spot and does not move. The pulse rate is apt to be raised, often running from 150 to 200 per minute, the normal rate being from 60 to 90. Jensen suggests, among other secondary causes, a ductless-gland imbalance. He found a high proportion of his gunshy animals were spayed females. Certainly there seems a close analogy between gunshyness in dogs and so-called shell shock as observed in some soldiers.

*Bolting.* True bolting is the act of running away; the dog has no intention of returning, and the handler has lost all control. It is caused by gunshyness, fear of punishment, or wilfulness. Some forms of self-hunting are, to all intents and purposes, true bolting. Often the runaway bolts as soon as put down; others may wait until they get behind a screen of bushes or over a rise of ground out of sight of their handler. The confirmed bolter is practically useless and his cure difficult to accomplish.

As a final word in regard to the shooting dog—it should be remembered that he is not a machine, but appreciates good care and kindness. Different dogs require different methods, although the underlying principle is the same in all, i.e., control, without taking too much out of the animal. The man who makes a companion of his dog will not only get more out of him, but will have greater enjoyment in shooting over him. The dog is a fine fellow and should be so treated.

*The careful ways of duty.*
—John Greenleaf Whittier, "Among the Hills."

IF A DOG is to be kept, he is entitled to proper care. If a man does not wish to accept this responsibility, he should not keep one. Justice, as well as common sense, demands that he be given adequate attention.

In the hands of a keen sportsman, harder work is required of the setter or pointer than of any other breed of dog. The fact that dogs can stand a great deal of ill treatment is no justification for lack of care. Proper care is insurance for good health, and no sick or ailing dog can do his best work. Strict cleanliness of the dog and of its food, water, and living quarters is essential to health. Dirt, dust, and lack of care regarding hygienic details favor the development of infectious diseases, parasites of all kinds, and many other evils from which the dog is a frequent sufferer. The clean dog is apt to be a healthy one. Furthermore, the dirty, smelly dog is an unpleasant companion.

*Food.* The dog is one of the carnivora, as an examination of his teeth will show, but generations of association with man have enabled him to withstand many dietary abuses. If given the choice dogs will nearly always select meat which indicates that it is their natural food. A dog may look quite healthy, or do well for a time without meat, but under the added stress of hard work or disease he will fail to exhibit stamina. The same is true to a lesser extent of a diet containing an inadequate amount of muscle tissue. Dogs that were used in the armed forces were given an allowance of two pounds of meat daily.

The best meat for the dog is fresh moderately lean beef or mutton, but almost any kind of meat is better than none. Beef

68

contains about 18 per cent protein and 9 to 20 per cent fat. Liver is good occasionally, but it has a laxative tendency. A little added to the meat is often beneficial, but straight liver is not advisable. If the sharp spicules which are often present in beef hearts are removed, these are also a satisfactory and cheap food, and almost any of the glands may be utilized.

Most dogs like fish, and it is an excellent occasional diet. It is best when cooked and the bones removed. Large cod and halibut heads contain a considerable amount of meat and are cheap. If thoroughly boiled, the meat can easily be removed. Tinned meat or fish is good emergency ration. An occasional change of diet often helps poor feeders, as dogs, like people, sometimes get tired of the same thing day after day.

In theory, horse meat is excellent, but practically, horse meat is generally derived from old, thin, worn-out horses, and is often devoid of the normal amount of fat. A little suet or kidney fat, or real lard added to horse meat should help matters. Fat is indispensable, and its total or even partial absence from the diet may cause a scaly skin, loss of hair on the back, face, and neck, and sometimes hemorrhagic spots and sores of the skin (Lentz). State or federal inspection is not always required for horse meat, and even animals that have died from disease may be utilized. Hence there is no guarantee of the health of the horse or even of the freshness of the meat. Furthermore, the horse may have been treated with enormous doses of drugs before its death. The mark "Veterinary Inspected" means little. Cooked fresh pork is a moderately good food, but is less satisfactory as a routine diet than beef or mutton. A variety of tapeworm may be transmitted by raw pork.

The dog's diet should consist of a minimum of two-thirds, by bulk, of meat, though three-fourths is better. Tainted meat may make a dog sick. It is a mistake to ask the butcher for dog meat, for if this is done the quality is sure to suffer. It does not matter how tough the meat may be, provided it is fresh. So-called soup meat is satisfactory. Good meat is best fed raw, and most dogs prefer it this way. If horse meat, or other kinds of doubtful origin, has to be utilized, it is safer to boil it for ten minutes in a covered pot, using just enough water to cover it. This largely sterilizes and so is more or less a safeguard, but it does not prevent ill effects from tainted meat. The water in which the meat was boiled can be utilized on the supplementary food or roughage which is to be added. Meat can be almost completely digested and results in a small, firm, dark, normal stool.

Commercial dog foods may be used for a supplementary diet, but in my opinion if fed alone without a meat supplement they are poor food, and their extended use may cause many ills. Lentz states that "no one factor is more responsible for skin trouble than the indiscriminate feeding of dog biscuit, wheat bread, improperly cooked cereals or any too highly carbonaceous food." Most commercial foods contain meat in some form, as well as other ingredients. The catch is that, in their advertisements, the makers do not always state the amount of each ingredient.

Cereals, dry bread crusts, well-cooked vegetables such as spinach, cabbage, celery, greens, onions and carrots (preferably mashed), provide roughage and are useful as a supplementary diet. Onions, while valuable as food, do not prevent worms, a common superstition to the contrary. Food should be moderately dry, certainly not souplike.

Bones are unnecessary, provide little nourishment, wear down teeth, are apt to become covered with dirt or even parasite eggs, and may cause perforation or obstruction. In summer they attract flies. Dogs digest bones fairly well and may eat them happily for years, though the danger from sharp spicules lodging in some part of the digestive tract is always present. The occasional giving of a well-cooked knuckle bone is not particularly risky, but is best fed to the dog on grass or a clean floor. It should never be left in the kennel yards to collect dirt and flies. Sharp bones or those which will splinter should never be given.

Milk or buttermilk is an excellent supplementary diet and supplies calcium. Unskimmed milk is best. It is especially valuable for pregnant or nursing bitches and dogs which are underweight.

Dogs are proverbial beggars. Most house dogs are fed too often and too much. A fair criterion of condition is that one or two ribs should be plainly visible in the short-haired breeds. However, many shooting dogs may be leaner than this when in top condition, for like men, they vary, some appearing bony, but all having a hard, muscular look and usually being thinner than the well-conditioned show dog. A dog weighing forty or fifty pounds has a stomach capacity of about six or seven pints—more than twice that of a man. Furthermore, it takes a dog much longer to digest food. Food remains in a dog's stomach for from four to twelve hours. It is obvious, therefore, that nature intended the dog to eat large amounts at a meal and to be able to fast for long periods.

Hard-working dogs should have a light breakfast—about a half to three-quarters of a pound of meat—and their main meal in the afternoon, after their work is over and they have cooled off. Dogs go better if they have a light breakfast, this being especially noticeable if they are required to work all day. For these reasons the healthy adult dog should not be fed too often, and during off-seasons, one meal a day is sufficient. Most of them do not eat well in the morning and are best when fed regularly in the afternoon. At that time, the average dog may be given nearly all he will eat. But dogs vary, some being gluttons and the amount for them must be regulated. Others are poor feeders, and should be coaxed. The average, hard-working forty-five to sixty pound dog will require a minimum of one and a half or two pounds of meat per day. The big sixty-five pound dog will naturally need more food than a little bitch that weighs perhaps half as much. Also, dogs when working hard require more food than during the off-season. It is bad for the dog and poor kindness to overfeed it or let it get fat. It is preferable to keep off fat by exercise, though during the off-season this is a difficult thing to do with some dogs. It is a sign of overfeeding if the healthy dog does not lick his pan clean. A little salt should be added to the diet.

No matter of what the diet consists, some dogs exhibit a tendency toward constipation. Probably this is largely the result of lack of exercise. It is rather rare and is most likely to be noticeable in old or sluggish dogs. Giving laxative drugs is a poor way to treat such a condition. Generally, it can be disregarded. If it persists, a tablespoonful of moistened bran added to the food will usually rectify this tendency. The bran may be given daily, or two or three times a week, as thought best. A handful of stewed prunes from which the seeds have been removed, when well mashed and mixed with the food, often has a laxative effect. They should be only slightly sweetened. What would be called constipation in man is natural in healthy dogs. The stool is normally more or less hard and a certain amount of straining to effect its passage is natural. Dogs possess anal glands in the lower end of the large intestine, which secrete a lubricating material that facilitates the passage of hard feces, and to a large extent they prevent constipation.

Each dog should have his individual shallow pan which is washed clean after feeding and preferably used only for him. Give him time to eat his meal. Some eat more slowly than others. Often, when half through his meal, he will stop to get a drink of water. However, do not leave uneaten food, and see to it that no dog eats another's food. This latter rule should be strictly enforced from puppyhood or from the time individual pans are used. It is normal for dogs to bolt their food and swallow relatively large pieces. Their teeth are not adapted to chewing and mastication in the ordinary sense of the word.

Grass eating is common among all dogs. This provides roughage and perhaps possesses other desirable features. It is not a sign of illness. In winter, when no green grass is available, dogs sometimes will eat the reddened leaves of honeysuckle. In eating grass, etc., they exhibit considerable choice and select only certain leaves. The eating of soil or dirt is a sign of dietary deficiency or ill health. It is often due to lack of minerals or to acidosis.

Without proper food, and this means meat, dogs cannot be expected to stand the hard, grueling work often required of them. Some years ago I purchased a three-year-old setter from a trainer in a near-by state. The following year, the dog was taken back for a day's shooting. The trainer was a good man and certainly took better than average care of his charges. On the day in question, he took out four of his dogs, using two in the morning and two fresh dogs in the afternoon. My dog worked all day. Except for the first thirty or forty minutes in the morning and after lunch he was on the outside practically all of the time. When we took up, late in the afternoon, he was running with almost as much punch as when first put down. The trainer's dogs at the end of the morning had shortened markedly, and, of the afternoon pair, one was at heel and the other scarcely out of gunshot. This difference in stamina was due, I am sure, to nothing but diet. My dog had been fed almost exclusively on meat, while the other dogs had had very little. They were good dogs that had plenty of work, but they lacked the staying qualities which come from an adequate diet.

During the last fifty years I have seen similar examples many times. As a dog food there is no substitute for plenty of good, fresh meat. Its only drawback is its expense. A man will get more satisfaction, have less sickness, and get more work out of two meat-fed dogs than out of four that are improperly fed.

The problem of proper feeding is really a simple one. Give a sufficient quantity of good meat and about a quarter by bulk of some supplementary food, such as Gaines' meal or some other commercial food moistened with milk or soup, or make up the supplementary food from table scraps or with a cereal or a few dog crackers such as those manufactured by the National Biscuit Company. The crackers promote the flow of saliva, which in itself aids digestion. A little dry food, such as a crust or biscuit every day, acts also as a dental cleaner and keeps the gums in good condition. Incidentally, discoloration of the teeth is not always the result of a soft diet, but may be due to many other causes.

If meal is used, dampen it some time before feeding, so that it swells before, rather than after, being eaten. Vary the supplementary food as is convenient for you; one day using one type and next day, another. In winter add a teaspoonful of a vitamin-proven codliver oil, such as Squibb's. Feeding is so important that it should not be entrusted to anyone except the handler or owner. If the owner cannot or does not wish to do it himself, he should at least be present to see that it is properly done. This is especially true when dogs are being worked or are away on shooting trips with their masters. They have worked hard and have earned this care. Furthermore, feeding and handling in the field are the two best ways of securing a dog's friendship.

Dietary deficiencies, especially insufficient meat, form one of the common causes of fits, fright disease and many other ailments.

I believe I have worked my dogs a good deal harder than the average, but have found they thrived upon it. I am convinced their stamina has been due largely to meat diet.

All dog owners should read the excellent article on canine dietetics by Edwin R. Blamey, M.R.C.V.S., which may be found in *The Complete Dog Book*, The Official Publication of the American Kennel Club. This book also contains good advice regarding general care and a description of the common canine ailments.

*Water.* Dogs require an abundance of fresh, pure water at all times. Many dogs will drink almost any sort of dirty water. This is no more of a sign that it is good for them than is the fact that they will eat dirty food. Running water is ideal for the kennel yard, but lacking this, one may use a bucket. Give fresh water twice daily in summer and once during the cold weather. Drinking receptacles should be kept clean and wiped out each time the supply is renewed. White-enamel buckets are the easiest to keep clean. When working dogs in a dry country a supply of water should be taken along for them.

*Bathing, Combing, and Grooming.* Regular bathing is unnecessary for shooting dogs. If for any special reason a dog is to be bathed, tincture of green soap is the best cleansing agent. This is a liquid soap made up in alcohol, and it is preferable to the ordinary dog soap. It can be secured at any drugstore. A warm day should be selected, and the dog should not be allowed to become chilled subsequently. The morning is best as it insures plenty of time to dry off. If the dog is dried off a bit and allowed to run in a grass field, he will soon dry. During warm weather a good soap and water bath is often beneficial and makes the dog more comfortable. If routine washing has to be done often, plain water should be used and all soap omitted.

The long-haired breeds should be combed sufficiently often to prevent their hair becoming tangled or matted. Mats of hair are especially prone to develop back of the ears and in the feathers and upper rear part of the hind legs. If these are present they should be cut off close to the skin; subsequent combing will prevent re-formation. To prevent undue pulling and consequent struggling on the part of the dog, hold the hair to be combed close to the skin with one hand and comb with the other. Large burrs can be broken up and combed out piecemeal. Combing is useful only to prevent tangles and to remove dead hair.

Grooming with a good, clean, long-bristled brush will keep the dog clean. It also improves the appearance and quality of the coat and is far better than bathing. The beautiful coats often seen on show dogs are due largely to frequent grooming. A dog does not have sweat glands, except on the pads of the feet and along the side of the nose, but the skin contains many sebaceous or grease glands, which keep it healthy and the coat in good condition. Grooming stimulates these glands, and, in reason, the more brushing a dog gets the better is his coat. Grooming removes the dead hair and is especially important during the shedding periods in spring and fall. However, shedding is irregular in many dogs, and house dogs often shed more or less all the year round. For working setters, it is generally advisable to trim off most of the feathers on the front and hind legs, leaving about three-fourths of an inch of hair. This saves time in deburring; most of it would be pulled out anyway by the end of the season. Some men also trim off an inch or two of the feathers at the root of the tail. This is a good plan with some dogs. If the dog gets wet during his work he should not be placed in a cold kennel, but dried off as well as possible and kept in a room having some heat until thoroughly dry. Deburring is difficult when the hair is wet.

*Exercise.* Dogs need exercise to maintain their health. Statistics show that the small-sized dogs live the longest. This is probably because dogs of about terrier size are generally left free and not penned, and hence get more exercise. Most shooting dogs are confined and get far too little exercise except during the training and shooting season. Even in a large pen most adult dogs do not take much exercise.

Without preliminary exercise it is folly to take out a dog the first day of the season and expect him to work well all day. He is like any other athlete: his physical condition has to be gradually accustomed to what is required. In a state of nature, the dog had to take exercise to obtain his food. With the modern dog this situation is altered, and he is prone to become lazy and soft. Apart from preparation for field work it is better for his general health to give him a daily run. Half an hour every day will keep a dog well, and when pre-season work starts he is far better prepared for it. The title of "Doctor" has sometimes been jokingly conferred upon a dog. If his owner takes him for a daily half-hour walk, the dog may earn the sobriquet, as certainly he is not the only beneficiary. In warm weather, if suitable water is available, it makes an excellent objective for a walk, and the dog will enjoy and benefit by a swim. As mentioned elsewhere, it is a good plan to get dogs accustomed to swimming. Not only is it good exercise, but it makes retrieving from water more easily taught.

Pre-season work for the shooting dog generally should aim at developing stamina rather than speed, though dogs differ in this respect. It is better to work them on game, as even the most ambitious dogs tend to lose interest if worked day after day in a birdless country. Early morning is generally the best time of day for workouts, although in the cool weather it is not so important. Late in the afternoon is also an excellent time. The work should be regular, not once or twice a week, and should gradually be increased according to the response of the dog's condition.

Exercise also prevents constipation and the need of giving laxatives. Usually the first thing a dog does on being taken out for exercise is empty his bladder, and after a preliminary canter his bowels usually move. Regularity in these respects goes a long way to promote health.

Properly worked up to by preliminary conditioning and correct care, dogs thrive on the hardest kind of work. I have never spared my dogs in this respect. At the end of a season they are lean and hard. I have worked them in rain, cold, snow, and freezing sleet, and have had setters jingle from icicles. I have, of course, dried them off when wet, and put them in a warm car for their homeward journey, but have never seen any ill effects.

*Care of the Feet.* Unless the feet are in good condition, the dog cannot work. The soles of a dog's feet are covered with a firm, leather-like tissue. Without exercise this becomes soft, just as do the palms of the hand. Work hardens and promotes growth of this tissue, but, if the dog has not had regular exercise, the work must be gradual or he will become footsore. Burrs lodge between the toes, especially in the long-haired breeds, and cuts from broken glass are not uncommon.

It should be part of the routine to examine the dog's feet at the end of each day's work. Lacking anything better, whiskey makes a good wash for minor abrasions. It is cleansing and antiseptic. Small thorns are often hard to find. Clean the foot well and secure a good light. A pair of tweezers helps in the removal of thorns. The use of boots and the treatment of cuts are mentioned under the heading of "Sore Feet."

*Kennels.* Shooting dogs are best housed out of doors. If a little heat can be secured, so that the temperature in the house does not fall below 35° or 40° F., so much the better. One has only to look at even a "long hair" to see that he is uncomfortable on an extremely cold day, and a dog in confinement suffers more than one loose, as the latter gets more exercise. If some heat in the kennel is not arranged for, then it is necessary to have the sleeping quarters made as tight as possible. Even in the coldest weather dogs will do splendidly out of doors without heat, if they have a well-built kennel.

There are various types of housing. One which I have found satisfactory for two dogs is as follows: a concrete foundation, 5 feet by 5 feet square, 4 feet high in front and 3½ feet high in the rear, with the floor made of boards and raised an inch or two above the concrete. (If dogs sleep regularly on concrete, they are likely to develop a rheumatic condition.) The entire front is a tight-fitting, sliding door which can be opened or removed in hot weather, and which permits easy cleaning, changing of bedding, etc. There is an opening 18 inches square on one side, and leading to this is an enclosed entryway 3 feet broad, 3 feet high, and 3 feet deep, with a doorway 2 feet square. On the floor, in the summer, are two upright boards 1 foot high, arranged in a T-shape. This makes a corridor and two enclosures. The latter are the sleeping quarters. The T-shaped boards fit in slots, so they can be removed for cleaning the floor and removing the bedding.

In the winter the upright, T-shaped boards are removed, and

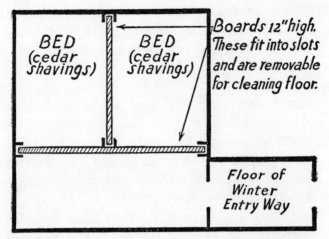

*KENNEL, interior viewed from above. During cold weather partition boards are removed and summer beds replaced by barrels. During winter all doorways are covered with flaps of carpet.*

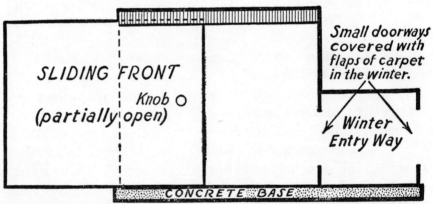

*KENNEL, viewed from front. Lower groove of sliding door is flush with the floor. When the sliding door is removed for cleaning the house an accurately fitting square piece of wood 5 ft. long by 1x1 in. is placed in the groove. Floor boards are laid pointing towards the sliding door.*

two whiskey barrels, placed in cradles and held in firmly by a three-by-four, are installed. The front of each barrel is closed, except for an opening just large enough to permit the passage of a dog. Over each door is hung a piece of carpet, which can be tacked up and out of the way when not required.

In extremely cold weather it is a good plan to nail a piece of carpet on the upper and inner side of the door and another on the outer side. Thus, if one is displaced by the passage of the dog, the other is almost sure to fall in its proper position.

The outside house is made of interlocking one-inch boards, covered with tar paper, and given two coats of weatherproof paint. A test at 10° F. outside showed the following temperatures: inside the entryway 12° F., inside the house 21° F., inside one of the barrels 41° F. This was with two dogs in the kennel and all four carpet-curtains down.

The weak part of this house from the heat standpoint is the large sliding door, hence this should be carefully fitted. Such a house costs about $10, not including labor and barrels. Boxes can, of course, be substituted for the latter. It is important to have everything tight and waterproof, and to remember that small quarters are more easily warmed by body temperature than large ones. In a big house the dogs are sure to suffer in cold weather.

*Bedding.* In winter, plenty of wheat straw is the best. Oat straw or hay may be substituted, but they are inferior. It has been claimed that alfalfa hay has an inhibiting quality against fleas and lice. In summer bedding can be dispensed with and the floor of the sleeping compartment covered by newspapers or a scanty bedding of cedar shavings. I prefer the latter. Bedding should be changed and boxes and sleeping quarters swept out every two weeks in winter and every week or ten days in summer.

*Yards.* Dogs which can be let free generally keep themselves more or less fit, but such freedom is inadvisable in most localities. The danger of being run over by motors, of fighting, contracting contagious diseases, self-hunting or destroying young game birds or nests, and chicken killing, are, in most areas, sufficient to require confinement. Furthermore, in some states it is illegal to keep dogs at large during certain seasons, so that some means of confinement must usually be adopted.

Chaining a dog is the worst way to keep him. He gets practically no exercise, and is apt to be dirty and unhappy. However, much depends upon conditions. If the chained dog is given adequate daily exercise, he may be healthy. Chaining to a small kennel has one advantage. That is, the kennel can easily be moved and the danger of infection from parasites in the soil thereby limited. It is also a convenient way to keep dogs while in quarantine and when treating for parasites, as it permits easy isolation. A chain attached to a ring which runs on a long overhead wire is bad enough. But if a chain is used it is well to remember that it may get twisted or caught, or, if there is a near-by fence, the dog may jump over the obstruction and thus be strangled. Only recently a well-known field-trial dog is reported to have lost his life in this sort of an accident. Many dogs have been hung by jumping out of a motor car or wagon to which they have been chained. Puppies should never be chained and dogs unaccustomed to the chain should be watched or they may injure themselves. A fenced yard is the best. I had one 90 by 90 feet built by a fence-building firm, which cost $250. A few years later I had occasion to require another. This time I got extra-heavy chicken wire and iron posts from Sears, Roebuck and Company and built one of similar size, which, without labor, cost $16. This included setting the corner posts in concrete.

If space is available, the larger the yard the better, provided it is not too big to keep clean. About 90 by 90 feet square is a satisfactory size for two or three dogs. This permits room for a little exercise and is not too large to keep easily clean. It is better to get eleven-foot wire and fold the lower 2½ or 3 feet inward in a shallow trench about 6 inches deep and cover with stones and dirt. This prevents digging out and involves less labor than a deep trench. It is the way many fox farmers build their runs. A solid board fence helps to prevent barking, but requires either a stone foundation or a hem of buried wire, since wood soon rots underground. Furthermore, with a wire fence it is possible to see at a glance what is going on inside. Personally, I prefer wire and believe it to be better and cheaper than wood. Some dogs are great diggers, and if a dog once manages to escape he is subsequently hard to hold.

If possible, select a site for the yard which is sunny, well drained, sheltered from the north wind, and with shade available in summer. Although much can be done to discourage barking, it is well to select a site not too near a bedroom. On the other hand, extreme isolation is an invitation to thieves and is unfavorable in the event of dog fights or other disturbances. The ground of the dog run should be cleared of rubbish and be at least moderately smooth. A patch of grass is an asset, as dogs will eat some of this and benefit thereby. Do not place the doghouse near the fence, else dogs may use it to help them jump over the fence. A low, open shelter in the yard will be appreciated by the dogs in hot weather, or when the ground is wet, and it can be used as a place for feeding during rain. Keep a shovel in the yard and remove all droppings every day. Some form of incinerator in which to burn used bedding should be placed near at hand. One made of wire 3 or 4 feet high is satisfactory and may be placed near the yard gate. If a little care is exercised in regard to the direction of the wind, ashes will not be blown into the dog yard.

In addition to this yard, a somewhat sloping concrete run 50 or 60 feet long and 10 or 12 feet wide, built extra strong, with an enclosed wire top, is well worth while. This involves the construction of a second kennel. It is preferably placed some distance from the regular run. It can be used for bitches in season, as a quarantine, or in deep snow. Snow is easily swept out and the concrete dries quickly. In addition, it is valuable for use during treatment for intestinal parasites. If droppings are promptly removed and the concrete swabbed with boiling water containing an antiseptic, parasites and their eggs and larvae cannot survive. Reinfection is one of the chief problems in the treatment of dogs for hookworm, and is especially difficult to prevent in dirt or grass yards.

*Medicine and Surgery.* The sick dog has a worse chance than the ill man. He cannot tell his symptoms, and, as a result, disease is apt to get more of a start before the diagnosis is made and

treatment instituted. Furthermore, whereas veterinary medicine
has made definite advances in recent years, it has hardly kept
pace with medicine as applied to man. Surgery is often crude and
the equipment far from modern. Dogs and men are subject to
many of the same diseases, and their treatment, whether medical
or surgical, does not differ markedly. The writer is not a veterinarian,
and hence is not in a position to treat the subject of dog ailments
authoritatively. As in all medicine, prevention is better than cure,
and the proper care in feeding, exercise, and housing will prevent
many ills. If a dog is ill, the best advice to the owner is immediately
to call a competent veterinarian. This gives both dog and veterinarian a better chance. It is best to isolate the ailing dog at once.
The condition may turn out to be contagious and in any event
the animal should be at rest.

The ailing dog is apt to lose appetite, be listless, and alter his
habits. Contrary to Arthur Guiterman and to popular opinion, a
cold nose is no certain criterion of good health. The use of the
thermometer is the only sure method of determining the presence
of fever. Pulse rate is of equal importance; it usually rises with
the fever. The pulse is best taken at the upper and inner aspect
of the thigh. The normal rate is 60 to 90 per minute and the
normal temperature 99° to 102.5° F., the average being about
101.6° F.

Like physicians, some veterinarians are more competent than
others, and the average owner has little to go upon to guide him
in his selection. A man of good reputation and character in his
community who is a graduate of a good school is obviously desirable. It is preferable to select one who specializes in dogs. An
ailing dog should have a thorough examination, and this is not
a matter of a moment or two. In his examination of the dog the
veterinarian should give the impression of thoroughness and care.
It is no sign of incompetence if he is unable to make a positive
diagnosis at his first visit. Honesty in this respect is a far better
sign than an effort to impress the owner with his competency. The
average owner wants the best treatment he can get for his sick
dog. Plainly incorrect or improbable statements regarding the

dog's illness or the required treatment only hurt the reputation of the veterinarian in the opinion of the intelligent owner.

No man can practice veterinary medicine properly without the aid of modern laboratory methods. The microscopic and chemical examination of stools, blood, and urine, as well as other procedures, is often absolutely necessary. It is well to bear in mind that improperly applied tests are worse than none, as they lead to incorrect diagnosis and thus to improper treatment. As an example, one has only to think of the heartworm, the recognition of which depends upon finding the immature worm in the blood stream. If the worms are present, and examination of the blood fails to disclose or recognize them, the disease will continue to advance, whereas the report of a positive finding, when the disease is absent, is likely to result in the administration of a treatment which, while called for by filaria, is itself quite severe and not without hazard.

This is not an argument against the employment of laboratory methods, but an effort to point out the necessity for selecting a competent veterinarian and one thoroughly trained in modern methods. There are a number of sound books on veterinary medicine, and a little knowledge will help greatly in the selection of a veterinarian. The indiscriminate and often meddlesome use of drugs by either owner or veterinarian is a dangerous procedure. Some veterinarians seem to believe that the owner will feel that he is not getting his money's worth unless a prescription is given— many times other things than prescriptions are more important. Thus, the dog which is suffering from constipation will generally get more benefit by regulation of diet and regular exercise than the routine administration of a laxative.

Some owners are forever dosing their unfortunate dogs with condition powders and other advertised nostrums. Particularly pernicious is the practice of frequent and unnecessary worming, which may lead to liver or kidney disease and the ultimate death of the dog. Patent medicines generally imply a secret formula and their use is poor economy. They may do more harm than good. A good rule is never to employ any drug unless its administration has been advised by a veterinarian.

*Distemper.* Probably every owner is more or less familiar with this scourge. The disease is produced by a filterable virus, which, translated, means that no causative agent can be demonstrated by the ordinary microscope. It is common to dogs, wolves, foxes, and ferrets. It is highly contagious, and, it has been claimed, can even be carried by clothing.

Practically all unprotected dogs of any age are susceptible, although young dogs are especially so. Second attacks are infrequent and prone to be less severe. In many respects the disease resembles influenza in man. Complications are common and it is these which generally produce the mortality: pneumonia, meningitis, and gastro-intestinal conditions are among the most frequent. Severe complications often develop after apparently mild attacks. No attack should be considered trivial. Sequelae following apparent recovery are frequent, of which chorea or twitching is one of the most common. Nephritis is also frequent. Pustules on the skin, especially on the abdomen, often occur during various stages of the disease. Even light attacks weaken the dog's resistance to invasion by many other pathologic micro-organisms. The presence of complications largely explains the diversity of symptoms.

The disease is usually ushered in by discharge from the nose, followed, a little later, by discharge from the eyes due to the development of conjunctivitis, cough, lack of appetite, dullness, fever, elevation of the pulse, and an increased respiratory rate. The fever rises rapidly at first, is followed by a remission lasting a day or two, and then rises again and remains moderately elevated throughout the attack. Unusually high temperature is an ominous sign. Diarrhea, vomiting, and other gastro-intestinal symptoms are prone to develop. The diagnosis may be difficult. When the nervous system is involved, salivation, champing of the jaws, convulsions, paralysis, and coma may follow. Deafness or visual disturbances are not uncommon. Pneumonia or meningeal symptoms are ill omens—even in the mild case the prognosis should be guarded.

*Treatment.* This should be undertaken only by a competent veterinarian. In the early stages large doses of homologous canine anti-distemper serum are called for. As of all biologic products, it is important that these be fresh and the product of a reliable laboratory. The serum is administered subcutaneously or intravenously; the dose is 1 to 2 cc. per pound of body weight of the dog. It should be repeated at twelve to twenty-four hour intervals, according to the dose used and the indications. The "sulfa" drugs are of special value in the pneumonia cases and in those of the mixed infections, especially of the streptococcic varieties. The mortality from pneumonia in man has been reduced by two-thirds from its former rate by the use of the "sulfa" drugs. Penicillin is equally valuable. If the dog can be placed in a good veterinary hospital, his chances are improved. No hard work, little exercise, and the best of food should be given for two or three months following recovery.

*Prophylaxis.* Distemper is one of the most common and serious of canine diseases. Gun dogs are particularly apt to develop distemper because they are so frequently sent to training quarters, containing large groups of dogs where they are exposed to the infection. Formerly the only protection against the disease was secured by a previous attack. Modern science has, however, perfected a method which protects against distemper in the vast majority of cases, and which carries little risk: inoculation. Even in those infrequent cases in which complete protection is not secured, subsequent attacks are likely to be mild. Laidlaw and Dunkin are responsible for much of this work, which was fostered by *The Field* (London). Various methods are employed. I prefer that of Laidlaw and Dunkin. Virus, especially, is sometimes unreliable, and for this and other reasons a modification of the original Laidlaw and Dunkin technic is at times employed. Some veterinarians recommend substituting Virogen for the virus.

All dogs should be protected. Puppies can be safely treated when about four months of age. It is important that the dog be in good health and free of parasite. This involves a thorough examination and a laboratory investigation of the blood and stools. Failure to do this is to court trouble. The principle involved is that the dog's resistance to distemper be built up, and when this reaction is at its peak he is then inoculated with virus. One of the drawbacks to the treatment is that for a time after the inoculation with the virus, unprotected dogs associating with the patient may contract true distemper. Hence it should be a rule to protect all dogs and not select only one or two. Prophylaxis is not work for a layman, but for an experienced veterinarian. As stated before, the biologic products should be fresh, properly prepared, and from a reliable manufacturer. Lack of care in these details is likely to lead to unsatisfactory results. One has only to read the results secured in the many large series of cases recorded in *The Field* (London) to be convinced of the efficacy and harmlessness of the treatment when properly carried out and when employing good biologic products.

*Intestinal Parasites.* These are the curse of dogdom and for reasons previously mentioned are particularly common in gun dogs. Parasites may actually kill; but, except in the case of puppies, this is unusual. In most cases they reduce the dog's strength and open the door for infections and other ailments. A heavily infested dog is like a sailing ship dragging a sea anchor. In young dogs and puppies the parasites produce more severe results than in older animals. The blood-sucking worms, especially, find ready victims and bring about severe results in a short time particularly among dogs which are not fed meat. Many dogs carry a few worms without showing definite symptoms. This is particularly true in old, well-fed animals.

*Treatment.* There are four varieties of parasites frequently found in the gastro-intestinal tract: namely, hookworms, roundworms, whipworms, and tapeworms. It is important for the dog owner to know that no one type of treatment is efficient against all parasites. It is, therefore, necessary to recognize the variety of parasite present before effective treatment can be instituted. The old "shotgun" prescription or patent medicine, which claims to expel all parasites of whatever kind, either is compounded of a number of ingredients or is, more often, a fake. In the former case, the patient is being administered some useless and unnecessary drugs. In the latter, either the formulas or the amounts are secret. In any case, the owner has no redress if they kill or injure his dog. All effective vermifuges are powerful drugs and their indiscriminate use is often followed by ill effects. The drugs employed may destroy the parasites, but they may also shorten the life of the dog by injury to the liver or kidney.

Occasionally, some worms may be seen in the stool and identified. Even this form of diagnosis does not exclude the presence of a second type. When worms are seen in the stool a heavy infestation is generally indicated. Conversely, the dog may be loaded with worms, yet none may be observed. The only certain method of determining the presence of intestinal parasites is the microscopic examination of the stool. In this way the type of parasite present can be identified with certainty, and the proper treatment started. By microscopic examination, the degree of infestation also can be fairly well estimated, and the presence of more than one variety of parasites can also be determined. Even with the most careful laboratory technic, only a very small portion of the stool is actually examined, so that in doubtful cases a second examination may be required.

The sugar technic, whereby a portion of the stool is dissolved in a glucose solution in which the parasite eggs float to the surface, the surface fluid collected, centrifuged and examined, is more reliable than the simple smear. In sending a specimen for examination about an ounce of fresh-passed stool is required.

If dogs have been regularly parasite-free, show no physical signs of infestation and presumably have not been exposed, an annual routine examination of feces is desirable. It is wise to test all ailing or unthrifty dogs at once. All new dogs should be tested, and if a dog has once been infested and found negative after treatment, tests should be made at monthly intervals for a period of six months. It is advisable to have a test made on all bitches before breeding. The pregnant bitch is not a good subject for treatment, and indeed it is sometimes advisable to delay treatment until after parturition.

*Prophylaxis.* Prevention is far easier than cure. Once parasites have gained entrance into a kennel, their eradication is an extremely difficult undertaking. Just when the owner has carried out careful and repeated treatments, changed yards, and done everything possible, believing he has eradicated the trouble, he will frequently find he gets a positive from one or perhaps more of his dogs and the entire procedure has to be repeated.

The practice of routine worming regardless of the condition of the dog, and without a fecal examination, cannot, in most cases, be too severely condemned. The unconsidered use of vermifuges may do more harm than the parasites themselves. There is no vermifuge that can be depended upon to rid a dog of all parasites by one dose. Generally, the treatment has to be repeated at least once or twice. Frequent fecal examinations are required after discontinuing treatment, to determine whether or not all parasites have been eradicated.

In some kennels, especially those located in the South, all dogs are wormed with tetrachlorethylene periodically. This is done because of the prevalence of hookworms, the difficulty of eradicating the larvae from the soil, the number of dogs involved, the difficulty of securing individual fecal examinations, and other factors. This method, although by no means ideal, is sometimes, perhaps, the most practical. It does not eliminate the parasite, but tends to reduce the number in the dogs, and in some instances it is about the only method possible. No matter how effective the treatment, it is of no permanent avail unless arrangements are carried out to prevent reinfection. Old kennel yards that have harbored parasite-carrying dogs are generally teeming with larvae, and unless the patient's surroundings are changed, reinfection will take place in a short time. This is a point often overlooked or not sufficiently stressed by the careless veterinarian. Some parasites may perhaps be transmitted to the puppies *in utero*, but parasites do not develop spontaneously.

*Hookworms.* Formerly confined to the South, hookworms are now found everywhere. There are three species of hookworm that may attack the dog. The most common is known as *Ancylostoma canium*. All are destructive, all possess the same general characteristics, and all require similar treatment. The hookworms vary in size from about three-eighths to nearly an inch in length, the female being the longer. Their diameter is about that of a pin. They are grayish white, but, when filled with blood, have a reddish tinge. Under the microscope it may be seen that the bell-shaped mouth contains a cutting arrangement, with which the parasite bites into the mucosa of the small intestine, where it hangs on and sucks blood.

Single hookworms may consume 0.8 cc. of blood in twenty-four hours, and perhaps average nearly 12 minims, and this does not take into account the hemorrhage from the wound left by the parasite after it lets go its hold. A dog may readily harbor two hundred to three hundred hookworms.

The worms secrete a substance which prevents normal coagulation of the blood, and facilitates its extraction from the host. This secretion also promotes hemorrhage from the wound. Many eggs are produced, and these pass out with the feces. Under favorable conditions they hatch in about twenty-four to forty-eight hours. The resulting larvae undergo two or more molts.

It is while in the encysted stage that the microscopic parasite is able to enter the body of the dog. During this stage, the larva is capable of passing up or down through the soil to secure its necessary moisture or to avoid freezing. Also during this stage the larvae may live for a year or more in the soil. They may gain entrance to the dog via the mouth from dirty bones, etc., or by boring through the skin—often of the feet. From the site of entry they reach the blood stream and then the lungs, hence to the air passages and via these to the mouth, where they are swallowed, finally reaching the small intestine, where they bite into the intestinal mucosa, lay eggs, and the cycle starts all over again.

*Symptoms.* The onset is gradual. As might be expected, many of the symptoms are the result of the anemia which is produced by the loss of blood. Blood may be visible in the stool. This may be either bright red or more often dark blackish brown. Diarrhea is common. The patients lack life, tire easily, exhibit a poor coat, and are generally unthrifty. The animal may eat dirt or gnaw on foreign substances. He often coughs occasionally, due to the passage of the parasites through the lungs. Light infestation, especially in old, meat-fed animals, may result in few and mild symptoms, or the animals may appear even normal. Nursing puppies often succumb rapidly. Infected bitches may be sterile or may abort, and stud dogs may become sterile. The microscope is the only certain means of diagnosis. The hookworm is one of the worst intestinal parasites that can afflict a dog.

*Treatment.* To rid the dog of hookworms, tetrachlorethylene is probably the most effective drug. Caprokol Veterinary, Buchlorin, or hexylresorcinol are sometimes employed. As soon as the disease is suspected, feed the dog well, especially with meat and liver, and immediately have a fecal examination made by a competent veterinarian. Do not give any vermifuge until the diagnosis has been made. Dogs suffering from distemper or other severe illness as a rule should not be treated. Give no oils or fats in either meat, milk, or butter, for thirty-six hours preceding treatment. Lean meat is the best diet.

Starve for ten hours preceding the administration of the tetrachlorethylene. The dose is about 0.1 cc. per pound of body weight of the dog. The drug is not purgative, therefore it is necessary to follow it with a cathartic. One of the best is Epsom salts given in a saturated solution. The dose of the solution is 1½ ounces and should be given three to four hours after the administration of the vermifuge. Milk of magnesia, 1½ to 2 ounces, may be substituted. Do not give castor oil. A low saline enema, of not more than a pint, often helps matters. Give slowly by gravity, and do not elevate the enema bag more than three or four feet. Discontinue if the enema evidently causes pain. After the administration of the vermifuge the animal should be confined in a box stall or small pen until the laxative is given. This is advisable because it is then possible to see if the tetrachlorethylene has been vomited. If it has, the cathartic should be given and the entire treatment repeated a week or ten days later. It has been estimated that the first treatment should remove at least 90 per cent of the hookworms present.

Tetrachlorethylene is a powerful drug, possessing properties potentially injurious to the liver. In weak animals it is sometimes advisable to reduce the dose to permit the patients to regain strength for subsequent treatment. The treatment is best given in the morning. In order to aid the action of the cathartic the animal should be allowed a little exercise. Tetrachlorethylene is given in a capsule. Care must be exercised in administering the capsule for if it should break in the mouth and the tetrachlorethylene get into the lungs, it may kill the animal. The capsule should, therefore, be administered by an experienced person. It is best to give three doses of the tetrachlorethylene, each eight or ten days apart. Follow this by three fecal examinations at two week intervals; the first, two weeks after the last dose of the vermifuge and a fourth final examination, three or five months later. If any one of these is positive the entire course of treatment should be immediately repeated. Hookworm victims are being bled by the blood-sucking parasites as severely and surely as if they were bled externally every day by severing a vein. For this reason it is doubly important that, after treatment, the patient should be fed liberally with blood-making food, such as fresh red meat, to which a little liver has been added. After the eradication of the hookworms an occasional blood examination should show a steady rise in the hemoglobin content.

*Prevention of Reinfection.* All treatment is futile unless reinfection is prevented. This is much more difficult than the treatment of the animal. To prevent reinfection, cleanliness and sanitation are necessary. Various methods of ground sterilization have been attempted. Saline solution (1½ pounds of salt per gallon of water) soaked into every inch of the ground is one of the best. It requires at least 1 gallon per square yard. Preliminary removal, preferably by burning, of all débris, dead grass, etc., and loosening the surface soil by raking, facilitates matters. Repeat the salt treatment in ten days. Thereafter sprinkle the saline solution thoroughly over the entire yard using a large garden sprinkling-can. Do this twice a week. In addition, a box containing damp salt should be placed so that the dogs must walk through it on entering and leaving their sleeping-quarters. This tends to prevent infestation through the feet and, as a by-product, hardens the pads. Remove all droppings twice daily and continue the sprinkling with the salt solution until the microscopic examinations definitely prove the dogs are free from hookworms. Spading or plowing up the ground has been recommended. The spading should be repeated one or more times at ten-day intervals.

Even the most conscientiously and thoroughly performed sterilization of soil in runs is uncertain. Flooring small runs with wire, so that the dogs' feet are kept off the ground, has been tried, but this has many drawbacks and is difficult if the run be of adequate size. However, it is valuable for small runs. The best plan is to keep the dog on concrete until a cure, as proved by at least three negative fecal examinations performed at monthly intervals, has been effected. By removing all stools as soon as possible, thoroughly scrubbing the stool-soiled area with a brush, and flushing with a strong antiseptic, such as lye or one of the phenol products, together with liberal daily flushing of the entire concrete yard with a saturated saline solution, concrete can be kept fairly free of larvae. Concrete prevents the larvae from burrowing in the ground and dries quickly. Thorough desiccation kills the larvae. The success attained will depend upon the thoroughness with which the work is carried out. It is hard to make the average kennel man appreciate the meticulous care required in these procedures. If the owner has the use of two concrete runs, it facilitates the work. In addition to the above, all kennels, beds, and inside floors must be sterilized daily by scrubbing and flushing with saline solution.

If it was practicable to keep boots on dogs while they were in their pens the practice, combined with moderately efficient ground sterilization, would go far to prevent infestation. The wearing of shoes has done much to eliminate hookworms among humans.

After the dog has been proved definitely free of hookworms, he is then best placed in a previously unused and uninfected run of adequate size, and the old dirt yard discarded. If space is available, this is the quickest and safest plan. Attempts to eradicate larvae from dirt runs are difficult. It is often better to discard the old run at once and not use it again for at least a year and a half. Kennels and concrete runs are more easily sterilized.

In a chapter of this character it is hardly necessary to review in detail the treatment of other gastro-intestinal parasites. The best advice to the dog owner is that previously given—to consult a competent veterinarian if his dog is ailing and to do this without delay.

There are many excellent reviews on the subject of parasites available to the layman. That already referred to by R. Blamey in *The Complete Dog Book* is extremely useful. Without wishing to appear presumptuous, I may say I particularly like his advice regarding the treatment of tapeworms. I have seen unfortunate results follow the use of arecaline hydrobromide, so popular with some veterinarians at present. Its purgative action may be imagined, when it is known that it may act violently within fifteen minutes of its administration. Oleoresin of male fern (1 minim to each 2 pounds of body weight) and kamala (1 gram to each 2 pounds), followed by Epsom salts, is preferable. The tapeworms are the only parasites that can often be recognized without the aid of the microscope. They are frequently seen as white or grayish-white segments, suggesting somewhat a maggot in appearance, in the first part of the stool passed, or they may be observed in a partially dried state in the hair surrounding the anus. Prior to treatment, when parts of the worm are seen in the stool, they vary in size, but are generally about ¼ to ¾ inch in length. A number are often present. If examined closely it can be seen that they are segmented, and, as the name indicates, they are flattened or tapelike. The flattening is not noticeable unless a careful examination is made. Immediately after being passed the segments may exhibit movement. The tapeworm-carrying dog may pass many stools without segments of the worm being observed. The eggs may be demonstrated in the stool by the use of the microscope, but they are comparatively few in number. Tapeworms are generally transmitted by fleas or lice, and perhaps other external parasites. The flea eats the tapeworm eggs which are prone to collect around the anus of the infested dog. The fleas may then get on another dog. Because the dog will bite at an irritated area he gets the insect in his mouth and swallows it. Thus the parasite is transmitted. Occasionally other varieties of tapeworms are acquired by eating infected raw meat, such as rabbit, pork, or fish. Thorough cooking safeguards the meat. Broken-off sections of tapeworms may be mistaken for pinworms. They often cause irritation in the region of the anus. Dogs may carry tapeworms for years without presenting symptoms. A dog may harbor one tapeworm or many, and as long as a single head of a worm remains in the intestinal canal a cure has not been effected. Long segments, or the entire worm, may be passed after treatment. These should be examined by the veterinary, to determine if the head has been passed. As in all worming, it is not so much what is passed as what remains behind that is the important point. Hence the advisability for subsequent fecal examinations.

*Roundworms or Puppy Worms.* As the name indicates, these are especially common in puppies, but may occur in dogs of any age. They are two to four inches long and pointed at both ends. Tetrachlorethylene is effective and requires the same precautions as previously described under the treatment of hookworms.

*Whipworms.* The worm somewhat resembles a whiplash in shape. The adult worm is found in the large intestine and especially in a blind pouch—the cecum—from which they are difficult to eradicate. As a rule, whipworms do not produce very severe symptoms.

*Treatment.* Blamey recommends santonin, ½ to 2 grains, and thymol, ⅛ to ½ grain, according to the weight and condition of the patient, given in enteric capsules, in a series of doses, morning and evening for seven to ten days. After the last dose is given the dog is fasted and tetrachlorethylene, followed by a saline cathartic, is administered. Owing to the situation of the whipworm in the cecum, drugs that are given by mouth tend to by-pass the parasite; hence oral treatment is often ineffective. The surgical removal of the cecum is sometimes advised, but it is a formidable operation.

*Coccidiosis.* This is due to a protozoa. Heavy infestation causes diarrhea, general weakness, and sometimes the passage of blood. The diagnosis is made by microscopic examination of the stool.

The coccidia-infected dog or pup is the most common source of infection. Chickens and animals other than dogs are minor sources. Kennel runs become infected from the stools. The cocyte or protected forms of the coccidia may remain viable in damp earth for months or more. When in the soil they are fairly resistant to chemicals. Dryness and heat destroy them, but such destruction is usually difficult to accomplish.

*Treatment.* There is no effective specific treatment, which is therefore symptomatic and aimed at sustaining the patient's general health. Recently a preparation containing 5 per cent silver oxide and 2 per cent copper oxide has been used successfully in the treatment of coccidiosis (Allam).

Strict sanitary measures and the keeping of dogs, especially puppies, out of infected kennels or chicken yards, will help to prevent infection. If reinfection is prevented, many dogs recover spontaneously. Good care, sanitation, and proper feeding are definite aids. If distemper appears, the combination of the two diseases is often fatal.

*Filariasis.* For reviews upon filariasis recent publications should be consulted. In passing, it may be said that filariasis, or heartworm disease, is not uncommon and can be positively recognized in the living dog only by a microscopic examination of the blood. It is transmitted by mosquitoes and its treatment is not without risk and should be entrusted only to an experienced veterinarian. The common symptoms are: lack of stamina, shortness of breath, general unthriftiness, poor coat, cough, irregular heart action; sooner or later it is possible that dropsy may develop. Sudden death may occur. The symptoms are usually mild in the early stages. The fact that the dog gets out of breath and tires easily are often the phenomena first noticed. In their early stage the larvae are microscopic in size, and as many as a dozen or two may be carried in a single mosquito. The adult parasite is a worm sometimes as long as the finger and inhabits the heart or adjoining great blood vessel. Here the filaria multiply and an immature form, microscopic in size, may be found in vast numbers in the general circulation. It is these latter which the mosquito extracts, and, after certain changes that take place in the body of the insect, may be transmitted by it to another host (dog).

*Convulsions or Fits.* Prevent the dog from injuring himself. Call a veterinarian. Fits are symptoms and it is necessary to find the cause before a cure can be effected.

*Fright Disease or Running Fits.* The cause must be determined. Dietary deficiencies, generally lack of sufficient meat, and parasites, especially hookworms, are among the most common causes. The fits usually develop while the dog is being worked. Hold the animal until the convulsion is over. Take him up at once and give no more work until treatment has been instituted as suggested by the veterinarian.

The most common cause for fright disease, running fits, or canine hysteria, is, as stated, some dietary deficiency. Feed ½ to ¾ pound of good raw meat in the morning, and 1½ pounds in the afternoon. To this add one teaspoonful of Squibb's codliver oil and about one-quarter by bulk of roughage (see "Feeding"). Permit no exercise except in the yard or on a leash. If the condition is due to lack of protein, improvement should be shown in about a week, but it will take six weeks or two months to effect a cure, and there should be no work for this length of time. Have a fecal examination made at once, and treat for worms if the report is positive.

*Canker of the Ear.* This is a rather loose term. The condition is generally due to an infection by pathologic microörganisms, or sometimes by a small parasite. If not causing much discomfort, the condition may be treated by daily instilling into the ear one tea-spoonful of a 2-per-cent phenol solution made up in glycerin. This should be continued for a few days after apparent cure. If this treatment does not produce beneficial results in a short time, a veterinarian should be called. He should examine the ear with an otoscope, to determine the exact condition and cause of the trouble. If it is known that the trouble is due to ear mites, a preparation composed of 10 or 12 per cent sulfur made up in olive oil may be applied daily to both the inside and outside of each ear for a week. Burn old bedding and wash the sleeping quarters thoroughly with one of the phenol preparations, in order to eliminate mites from the kennel box. Repeat the course of treatment and the sterilization of the sleeping quarters in a fortnight. Cats are frequently affected and are a common source of infection.

*Fleas.* Fleas do not originate spontaneously. Apart from the ordinary annoyance resulting from a flea bite, there is reason to believe that certain intractable forms of so-called summer eczema result from flea bites (Crowe).

By a few dippings repeated at weekly intervals, fleas may be removed from the dog. But fleas multiply with great rapidity. The dog flea (Pulex serraticeps—Gervias) deposits its eggs upon the infected animal—these are not fastened to the hair or skin, and as a result drop off when the dog moves about or scratches. The eggs ultimately find lodgment in cracks or crevices. Under favorable conditions they hatch in from two to four days. The larvae are white, slender, and elongated. They feed upon dust, fragments of cuticle, and perhaps hair fibers. The larvae cast their skins twice. The entire cycle required to develop a new generation takes about a fortnight (Howard).

To get rid of fleas, their eggs and larvae must also be destroyed. Lewis's lye used according to directions makes an excellent dip. This is usually made up in a large container and the dog dipped, being careful not to permit the solution to get into his eyes, nose or mouth. The dip may be used many times.

The formula usually used is as follows: Dissolve three pounds of Lewis's lye in three quarts of boiling water, using a wooden or earthenware vessel. When the lye is dissolved, stir gradually into it five pounds of powdered sulfur, stirring until the sulfur is dissolved. Pour this compound into 45 gallons of water and stir well. Then add 8 ounces of sulfuric acid, and again stir well. Keep this dip out of the dog's eyes, ears, mouth and nose, and do not immerse for longer than thirty seconds. This dip may irritate the skin of some dogs. I have found it rather strong and prefer to reduce the lye to 2 pounds, the sulfur to 4 pounds, and the sulfuric acid to 4 ounces, and immerse for not more than one minute. When only one or two dogs are to be treated, and perhaps requiring only one or two treatments per summer, sheep dip or any of the other phenol or cresylic preparations manufactured for the purpose may be diluted in a bucket to the strength recommended by the makers, and thoroughly applied with a sponge, soaking the dog thoroughly to the skin but avoiding eyes, mouth, nose and the inside of the ears. The dip does not need to be washed off, but I prefer to do so, with a hose, after which the dog can be dried or turned loose. Most of the phenol preparations are cleansing, and if the dog is given a good scrub it will clean him as well as if soap were used.

For the living-quarters thorough scrubbing and soaking with almost any of the phenol preparations, using the dilution recommended by the manufacturers, will destroy the adult flea. The eggs are probably more difficult to destroy, and for this reason, the allowing of sufficient time for the eggs to hatch, plus repeated sterilization, are necessary. All dogs, before being installed in a kennel, should be inspected for fleas and dipped if necessary. Fleas are not particularly difficult to eradicate in kennel dogs, and their presence should not be tolerated. From house dogs they are harder to get rid of because of reinfestation. Flea powders are not so certain in their effects as the method previously recommended. The free use of pyrethrum powder is, however, moderately satisfactory. How valuable and safe the new insecticide D.D.T. will prove about the kennel has not yet been determined.

*Car-Sickness.* This is a nuisance and is analogous to seasickness or motion-sickness in man. It is commoner in young than in more experienced dogs. In some individuals it is never totally eradicated. To prevent car-sickness it is advisable to get the young dog accustomed to the car, and, for obvious reasons, not to feed victims before being taken out in a motor. Experience usually results in a cure. Bromides and other sedatives have been recommended as preventives, but in my experience they are of little avail. It was reported (December 15, 1943) that the United States government has developed a formula that will largely prevent seasickness among men. The formula was a war secret, but it will be made public. Seasickness and car-sickness are so similar that it seems likely that a remedy for the one may readily be valuable for the other.

*Cut or Sore Tail.* This may develop in any dog, but is especially apt to do so in long, low-tailed animals that possess excessive tail action. Bold, hard hunters are particularly likely to develop this trouble. The large bluish gray briars are special offenders. It is a condition which should be treated at once, for if allowed to develop, permanent loss of hair over the affected area may result. Quite apart from the unsightliness of the dog's appearance it will then be difficult to prevent a subsequent recurrence of the trouble. I have seen a dog's flanks almost red from blood because of this. The injury nearly always occurs near the tip of the tail. In mild cases the use of a small piece of clean gauze or muslin wet in boric-acid solution and covered with a dressing of tire tape is sufficient. I have experienced with a short leather sheath which I had had made, but this was difficult to keep in place. A home-made sheath cut from the armpiece of a lady's long kid glove was an improvement. In bad cases the best treatment is to have the last two or three joints of the tail amputated. This is a more humane and more certain method than any other and does not materially affect the appearance of the dog. The operation should be performed under local or general anesthesia. It does not put the dog out of action for more than a few days.

*Sore Feet.* Footsoreness is almost unknown in dogs that have received proper preliminary work. It is usually a sign of lack of regular exercise. A treatment which may be temporarily beneficial is to wash the feet in 70 per cent alcohol, allow them to dry, and then apply a dressing of tar. Permit the tar to harden before exercising the dog. I have seen leather or canvas boots used on dogs in the Southwest and these seemed to serve the purpose fairly well. Two or three coats of New Skin, which can be secured at any drugstore, are also beneficial. The surface to be treated should be cleansed with alcohol before its application.

True footsoreness is due to wearing away of the leathery covering of the feet. Time is required for this tissue to renew itself. Cleanliness and some form of protective dressing, together with the reduction or discontinuance of work, are all that can be done.

*Long Nails.* Old or chronically sick dogs and those that take little exercise frequently develop long nails. Old pensioners often need their nails cut four or five times a year. In all others it is an unfailing indication of lack of exercise. On dew claws, the nail, if not attended to, may grow into the flesh. All long nails should be cut, the horny part being removed about ¼ inch from the quick. The quick grows down into long nails and recedes as the nail is naturally worn down. A pair of canine nail-cutters can be secured from any veterinary supply house. Ordinary scissors are not suited to this operation and are apt to split the nail.

*Split Nails.* Cut off on the proximal side. If the quick is involved, cut off as low as possible without invading the sensitive area. Apply tincture of iodine and protect the wound from dirt by means of a boot or bandage. Do not repeat the iodine application. One must not allow the split to develop farther. Time is required. As soon as it can be accomplished painlessly, cut off beyond the split.

*Wounds.* Cuts on the feet are not uncommon. They should be cleansed thoroughly, making certain that no foreign bodies, such as dirt or bits of glass, remain in the wound. This is most easily accomplished by separating the cut edges and syringing the wound vigorously with a mild antiseptic solution, such as 10 per cent boric-acid solution. A wet dressing, held in place by a gauze bandage reinforced by adhesive plaster, is all that is generally necessary. A severe cut may be treated in this manner and the dog subsequently taken to a veterinarian for stitches if these are found necessary. An immediate suture of all cuts of the foot which are of any real depth usually results in the quickest recovery. The same general treatment can be used with wounds in other parts of the body, except that it is generally best to remove the adjacent hair with scissors. Indeed, this is advisable with any severe cut.

Hemorrhage can often be checked by pressure. If the hemorrhage is from a wound on an extremity and does not yield to pressure, a tourniquet may be applied above the injury. This should be loosened for a minute or two every ten minutes, or it may cause severe injury. The dog should be immediately taken to a veterinarian who will treat the wound and, if necessary, administer salt solution through a vein to make up for the blood lost. The intravenous solution, after a massive hemorrhage, may be life-saving. Plasma is preferable but is rarely obtainable. Whole blood is excellent, but a rigid technic in transfusion is required. The principles in the treatment of any recent wound are cleanliness, asepsis, coaptation of the edges of the wound throughout its depth, and checking hemorrhages. In cases in which there is likely to be infection or the possibility of the presence of a foreign body, drainage or permitting part of the wound to remain open may be advisable.

EUTHANASIA, OR MERCY DEATH.

> When the fourteen years which Nature permits
> Are ending in asthma, or tumor, or fits,
> And the vet's unspoken prescription runs
> To lethal chambers or loaded guns,
> Then you will find—it's your own affair—
> But you've given your heart to a dog to tear.
> —Rudyard Kipling, "The Power of the Dog," *Actions and Reactions*.

A dog's life is all too short. It has been the unhappy experience of nearly every owner to be forced to end the suffering of some old or hopelessly ill, faithful servitor. This is a wretched business, especially to the one- or two-dog owner, for whom the dog is often a valued member of the family. The fact that the dog is old and its useful days over are not in themselves, in my opinion, indications for euthanasia. Most shooting dogs have more than earned a pension. The only reason for euthanasia is to end suffering due to some incurable condition. Then it is definitely called for.

Various methods of destruction are employed, of which the following are some of those frequently used:

*Strychnine.* This method involves the thrusting of a long needle into one of the heart cavities and the administration of a fatal dose of strychnine. It has the one advantage of making death quick, provided the needle is properly directed. This can readily be messed up by the dog's struggles or inexpertness on the part of the operator. Strychnine poisoning is extremely painful. This method was formerly popular with many veterinarians, but in my opinion it should not be tolerated. Most veterinarians now employ nembutal.

*Lethal Chamber.* This is moderately quick and probably not very painful. One disadvantage is that lethal chambers are not always available. Many dogs appear to anticipate what is coming, due probably to their sense of smell and the strangeness of the surroundings. Some of the humane societies have enclosed cars which contain a lethal chamber to which the exhaust pipe is attached. It may be pure sentiment, but I believe that with some dogs, if the owner is willing to be with them to the last, their passing is made easier, although this generally entails a tough ordeal for the owner. I have had old pensioners, for whom I would have done anything to make their death more tranquil and peaceful.

*Shooting.* This sounds like a brutal business, but I believe when properly performed it is instantaneous. It has been recommended in the Correspondence Department of *The Field* (London). I have never seen it deliberately practiced. I was once shooting quail in the South with a big pointer who had the habit of jumping up to mark the fall of dead birds. The dog pointed near an old stone wall, jumped up at the shot, and received the entire charge from a 12-gauge gun in the occiput at about four or five yards' distance. The shot entered in a somewhat downward and forward direction just below the occiput, blowing a hole in the back of the head and severing the spine at its junction with the skull. The wound was about three inches in diameter. My companion who shot the dog was naturally greatly concerned, but, as far as I could determine, the dog was dead before he touched the ground.

Shooting is not a method that would appeal to the average owner, and it might readily result very painfully to both dog and owner if the animal moved suddenly or if for other reasons the shot was not accurately placed.

*Chloroform.* This was commonly employed in the past. Anesthesia by chloroform is not particularly disagreeable for man to take, but results in a good deal of struggling and choking when administered to an animal. For these reasons it is not entirely satisfactory and if enough is not given the animal may revive.

*Nembutal-Chloroform Sequence.* Some years ago I had a setter bitch who was suffering from recurrence of a malignant tumor of the mammae with involvement of the bladder. I had owned the bitch since her puppyhood, having trained her myself, and she had lived in the house practically all her life. It was plain that euthanasia was called for, and because I was so fond of her I made a rather extensive study on what had been written on the subject and consulted a number of veterinarians, dog men, and physicians who had charge of experimental work on dogs. None of the methods recommended seemed entirely satisfactory.

Any physician would naturally think of morphine. In the human this is an invaluable drug which temporarily relieves pain, and, if given in excess, produces a deep sleep which passes into unconsciousness and death. However, it acts differently on dogs and is unsuitable for them.

At the time I speak about I had charge of the Maternity Service in the Hospital of the University of Pennsylvania—this comprised about 1,800 births annually. In an effort to secure painless childbirth we had been employing nembutal extensively and with considerable satisfaction. This drug produces deep, painless sleep. It occurred to me that its use, followed by chloroform after unconsciousness was produced, might result in ideal euthanasia. I felt that it would be easier for the bitch if no strangers were about, and the following technic was employed:

On an empty stomach 9 grains of nembutal in capsule was given. In ten or fifteen minutes the bitch went quietly to sleep, the sleep deepened into coma, and in a half-hour she was barely breathing and the end was accomplished with chloroform. As a matter of fact, the chloroform was probably unnecessary, as death would probably have occurred from the nembutal alone. Of course, any other method which would insure against the possibility of revival could be utilized at this stage. There was no semblance of struggle and apparently death was absolutely painless. Since then I have seen this method used upon four other dogs, with identical results.

When nembutal is given in small doses to the human, there is a small proportion of cases in which there is a stage of excitement, which, however, the patients have no memory of having experienced. If this method of euthanasia were employed in a large series of dogs it is possible that some might develop such a reaction. If so, the owner may be assured that the animal is not suffering. However, for this reason it is safer to keep the dog on a chain or in a confined space. It is quite likely that this method may have been employed for years by veterinarians and I happened to stumble upon it accidentally. In any event, it is the best method of euthanasia with which I am familiar.

Many laboratory men now use intraperitoneal nembutal routinely as the most humane method of destroying dogs. The intraperitoneal administration involves the use of a long hypodermic needle and the introduction of about one ounce of fluid. It can also be given intravenously. The effect of the drug given in either of these ways is quicker than if taken by mouth, but otherwise it has no advantage and does have some obvious disadvantages. I prefer the oral administration. The dog should be quiet and unapprehensive at the time the nembutal is given. Nembutal requires a veterinarian's or physician's prescription to purchase.

*How to Give Medicine.* Very often medicine can be given with food. A powder may be mixed with food, provided that it is not distasteful. The same is true of certain liquids, such as codliver oil, to which most dogs do not object. Milk of magnesia can be given in milk. A pill or small capsule may be concealed in a small piece of meat, which the dog will probably swallow whole. Sometimes, however, a sick dog will not eat, and the medicine must be administered in another way.

It is important that the dog be not apprehensive or frightened. For capsule or pill, grease this with a little butter or oil (omit grease when administering tetrachlorethylene), and place it far back on the center of the tongue, close the jaws and raise the muzzle, holding them in this position until the dog is seen to swallow. The presence of the pill on the posterior part of the tongue sets up a reaction whereby it is swallowed. It should not be dropped or tossed into the mouth. If the pill or capsule is too far forward the dog will refuse to swallow and will attempt to eject it. If forced too far back it may get into the windpipe. An applicator for this purpose can be purchased from the veterinary supply houses, but this is not necessary except in the case of vicious dogs. Usually there is no difficulty in administering a pill or capsule. As previously mentioned, in giving tetrachlorethylene, disastrous results may follow if the capsule is broken in the mouth, and for this reason the drug should not be given by an inexperienced person.

To give a liquid drug, hold the dog's head up, separate the skin from the underlying jaw at the angle of the mouth, and pour the medicine into the pouch thus formed. Close the lips and continue to keep the head elevated. The liquid gravitates between the teeth to the back of the throat and the dog will swallow. Continue to hold the dog's head up and the mouth closed until all the liquid is swallowed. The administration of liquids is facilitated if the dose is placed in a small, clean, long-necked bottle and passed into the cavity between the lips and teeth from the receptacle. Give slowly. If, for example, an ounce of liquid is to be administered, pour about two or three teaspoonfuls into the skin pouch at the angle of the mouth. Keep the dog's head up and mouth closed until the patient is seen to swallow; then repeat at intervals until the full dose has been given. If the liquid is given too fast the mouth becomes flooded and a considerable quantity of the medicine is sure to be lost.

*How to Secure a Specimen of Urine.* About two ounces is usually sufficient. Fasten a clean receptacle somewhat the shape of a dog's feed pan, on the end of a stout handle about three feet long. Walk the dog or bitch on a leash and catch the urine when it is voided.

Pour into a clean bottle, cork and label. It should be kept cool and examined within twenty-four hours of being voided. Veterinarians often prefer to catheterize, and this is mechanically a simple procedure in either the male or the female. Unless the operation is performed with rigid aseptic technic, it is likely to cause infection of the bladder, and the simpler method previously referred to is decidedly preferable. There are conditions for which it is necessary or advisable to catheterize, but these are infrequent.

*How to Secure a Specimen of Blood.* To secure blood for hemoglobin estimate or for blood counts, only a few drops are required and a small puncture on the inner aspect of the ear is all that is necessary. When more blood is required, as in the examination for possible filaria, a vein must be punctured and the blood withdrawn with a large hypodermic needle. Veterinarians usually select a vein on the front leg. Anyone who has seen this small operation performed at the bend of the elbow of a man by a skilled technician knows that it is a simple procedure involving little more than a pinprick. However, the vein of a dog is somewhat smaller and an inexperienced veterinarian may have trouble getting the syringe point into the vein and the operation may cause a sore leg. It is preferable to utilize a vein in the ear. If there is trouble getting the needle into an ear vein a small puncture, not more than an ⅛ or ¼ inch in depth and length may be made with a knife point, from which an ample supply of blood can be secured. A small pad usually checks bleeding after the specimen has been secured. The ear is the site selected by most physicians who do research work upon dogs.

*Taking Temperatures.* This is taken per rectum with an ordinary clinical thermometer. Insert the thermometer inward and slightly upward, but use no force. Do not permit the dog to sit down or struggle, lest the instrument be broken. Allow one and a half to two minutes for it to register. The normal temperature of the dog is about 99 to 102.2° F.

*We're creepin' on wi' each new rig—less weight an' larger power.*
—Rudyard Kipling, "McAndrew's Hymn," *The Seven Seas.*

THE GUN. The choice of a gun is like the choice of any other equipment for shooting—a personal matter. A man should have the gun he can best shoot with; in addition, he wishes a handsome and sportsmanlike weapon and one whose cost will suit his bank account. Next to the dog, the gun is the most important item in equipment. Shotguns are of many kinds and sizes, and made for various purposes.

The gun for upland shooting should possess the following qualities: (1) It should shoot well for a distance of from 20 to 35 or 40 yards; (2) it should be of such weight that it can be comfortably carried; and (3) the stock and general make-up should be selected with the thought in mind that it will often have to be shot rapidly and not infrequently from a poor stance. Beauty, durability, and cost should also enter into its selection.

*Gauge.* With the measurement being taken behind the choke, the standard shotgun-bore diameters are as follows:

8 bore, 0.835 inch
10 bore, 0.775 inch
12 bore, 0.729 inch
16 bore, 0.662 inch
20 bore, 0.615 inch

Gauge and weight are intimately associated. The 10-gauge is too big and clumsy for fast shooting and need not be considered even if the weight were not prohibitive. The normal load for a 12-gauge upland gun may be placed at 1⅛ ounces of shot. No gun, shooting less than this, is so effective. To put this another way, let us suppose that the size shot selected contains 200 pellets to the ounce. The

106

1⅛-ounce load will therefore contain 225 pellets. If we imagine an ideal pattern in which there is distributed 1 pellet per square inch, the 1⅛-ounce load will give a killing circle which will contain 25 more square inches than the 16-gauge, shooting 1 ounce (200 pellets); 50 square inches more than the 20-gauge, shooting ⅞ ounce (175 pellets); and so on down to the 410, shooting ½ to ¾ ounce (100 to 150 pellets).

With adequate charges of powder all will shoot with sufficient penetration. Furthermore, the larger gauges mutilate a relatively smaller proportion of pellets. This is true even when using chilled shot, and doubly so when soft shot is employed. Mutilated pellets are prone to fly wild of the main pattern and string out behind the main shot charge. For these reasons a good 12-gauge will throw a better pattern with 1 ounce of shot than will any smaller gauge shooting the same load. For the same reason large chilled shot tend to make a better pattern than small and soft shot. In theory the gun shooting the larger shot charge should throw a larger or thicker pattern. In practice it generally does both. An average 12-gauge with normal loads will outshoot an average 20-gauge by about ten yards and has greater power throughout every yard of its killing range. This is largely because it shoots 12.5 to 25 per cent more shot. The size of the pattern is chiefly dependent upon the shot charge and degree of choke rather than actual gauge. In endeavoring, however, to step up the small-gauge it is well to remember that to shoot heavy loads from the latter comfortably, the gun must possess extra weight. The reason small-gauge guns often get a reputation for hard shooting is that they are usually bored a little closer than the twelves. However, there is another side of the problem, as proved by the popularity of the small gauges. In the old days of muzzle loaders the 12-gauge was of such diameter that a round lead ball weighing 1/12 pound would just slip down inside the barrel, a 16-gauge would accommodate a ball weighing 1/16 pound, and so forth down to the 28-gauge taking a ball weighing 1/28 pound. However, such rough-and-ready methods would be unsafe in the modern shotgun.

*Weight.* The usual weights for field guns of the different gauges are about as follows:

12-gauge—6 lb. 4 oz. to 6 lb. 12 oz.
16-gauge—5 lb. 13 oz. to 6 lb. 6 oz.
20-gauge—5 lb. 4 oz. to 6 lb. 4 oz.
(American 20's are usually slightly heavier)
28-gauge—4 lb. 14 oz. to 5 lb. 4 oz.
410-gauge—3 lb. 14 oz. to 5 lb.

Some of the 410's are practically diminutive, streamlined mag-nums—beautiful little guns that shoot a 3-inch cartridge containing ¾ ounce of shot. With the ½-ounce load they are little more than toys and great cripplers. Indeed, any gun shooting a very small amount of shot is more or less open to the same criticism.

At present there is considerable interest in the 12-gauge built to handle a 2-inch cartridge, shooting 20-gauge loads. These guns weigh from 5 pounds to 5 pounds, 7 ounces. For ladies and elderly shots they possess some advantages. I do not like them and, since they weigh about the same, I prefer a 20-gauge.

The 16-gauge makes a fine gun. Relatively, it is infrequently seen nowadays, probably because it is more or less of an in-between—that is, it does not possess quite the shooting qualities of the 12-gauge nor the real lightness and handiness of the 20-gauge. It is an excellent ladies' gun or suitable for a man not quite up to the weight of a 12-gauge. Arguments regarding the advantages and disadvantages of different gauges and weights are unending, gen-erally running somewhat as follows: Small-gauge enthusiasts claim that the small-gauge shoots an adequate load, is easier to swing and point, and consequently the wielder can get on his target quicker and does not require such a large pattern as with a gun of large gauge. The small-gauge is lighter, and therefore is less fatiguing to carry and pleasanter to shoot than a large-gauge gun. The shooter, due to absence of fatigue, is, at the end of a long tramp, more efficient and able to shoot better than if he had been loaded down with a heavier weapon. The cartridges for the small-gauge weigh less. However, with the present small-bag limits, this last argument is not particularly important.

Twelve-gauge shells are probably a little easier to obtain at out-of-the-way stores than are the 20's, and the chances of getting 28's or 410's in the average village shop are almost nil. The small-gauge gives a narrower sighting plane than the large ones. Some men, however, prefer the broader tubes. The small-gauge gives less recoil and is a more sportsmanlike weapon. This contention, however, seems to be entirely unsubstantiated. The smaller load of shot requires more accurate centering; it also cannot fail to result in a slightly greater proportion of crippled birds and to cripple is far from sportsmanlike. Furthermore, sportsmanship is not dependent upon the gun but upon the way in which it is used.

That small bores shoot well there is no doubt—one has only to examine the skeet scores made with them to be convinced of this fact. To contend that they shoot as well as the larger gauges is, however, without basis of fact. If I were a better shot than I know I am, and if my shooting were to be confined to grouse, woodcock, and quail, I should select a 20-gauge. However, since in most of the Middle Atlantic states the ringneck bulks large in the game list and gives promise of continuing to do so I do not use a 20-gauge.

The pheasant is a thick-feathered tough bird which, unless it receives a vital wound in the head or neck, will carry off considerable shot. It requires a hard blow to kill. I suppose there is no upland game bird in the East that requires so much killing or one in which a higher percentage of cripples is lost. I do not think that small-gauges are suitable for pheasant shooting, and if only woodcock and grouse are likely to be found, the 1⅛ ounce of shot can be reduced to 1 ounce in the 12-gauge.

Possibly there are some men who can shoot one gun one day and switch to another the next without loss of shooting ability, but I do not think this is true of most people. It must be remembered that in upland shooting speed is often at a premium. Nothing can make up for a gun to which a man is thoroughly accustomed. It is for these reasons that I personally prefer a 12-gauge. There is perhaps some basis for the statement that if a man cannot carry 6¼ pounds he should not go afield. Six and a half pounds is a nice weight for the average 12-gauge field gun, and 6¾, or at most 7 pounds, the maximum. To a certain extent the shooting man must choose between taking the recoil or toting the weight. I find that with a very light gun, such as a 28-gauge, swing is not so smooth and steady.

Since I gave up a muzzle loader, recoil has not bothered me, as I have learned to take a good deal of this with the arms. However, overloaded light guns undoubtedly tend to produce flinch, slow the use of the second barrel, and make the muzzle kick up. Therefore, in light 12-gauge guns of 6 pounds 4 ounces, 3 drams and 1⅛ load is about the maximum load. If it is intended to use larger loads, it is preferable to employ a gun weighing a little more, such a gun should be chambered for the 2¾-inch case, and if the work is properly done it will shoot the 2⅝-inch case entirely satisfactorily. However, it should be remembered that open-bored barrels do not handle high pressures well and tend toward irregular patterns. If it is decided to get a small bore, a 20 is probably the best. It is a delightful gun to handle and it shoots remarkably well. Many boys start with a small gauge, graduate to a 12, and later return to the smaller weapon. If the 20 is to be used for all purposes, it is advisable to get one that is not too light and one that is equipped to shoot an ounce of shot. If it is to be a second gun and to be employed only for small-bird shooting, ⅞ ounce of shot is sufficient and the gun may be lighter.

If the buyer has a 12-gauge which suits him, let him send this to his gunmaker at the time the 20-gauge is ordered, with instructions to make the latter as nearly the same in balance as the old gun. It is not necessary to designate the amount of choke—indeed, it is preferable to request that the right barrel be bored to give an optimum pattern at 25 yards and the left at 35 yards, stating the load intended to be used. What follows elsewhere regarding stock, fit, length of barrel, balance, etc., of the 12-gauge, applies also to the 20.

Too heavy a gun is sure to be a sad failure and a distinct detriment to fast shooting, however, it sometimes has a steadying influence on nervous shots. With too-heavy guns the tendency is to shoot low. Undoubtedly the weight of the gun should suit the physique of the shooter. Lieutenant-Colonel Hawker, in his admirable book, *Instructions to Young Sportsmen,* suggests the following test: The man of average physique should select a gun which he can throw to the shoulder thirty times without undue fatigue, the strong man about forty times, and the athlete perhaps fifty times. The man of middle age will often find that he can perform better with a gun weighing a bit less than the one he used when he was twenty-five years of age.

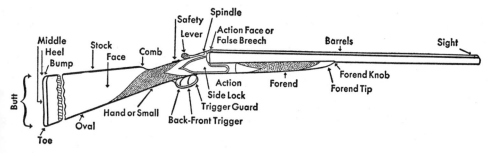

12-Bore Hammerless Ejector Shotgun

*Barrels.* With the modern smokeless powders there is no practical advantage, as far as actual efficiency is concerned, in extreme length of barrel. Barrels are generally made from 25 to 32 inches in length, but for field work 26 to 28 inches is a good choice. Short barrels are, perhaps, easier to point, but due to the shorter sighting plane they are, theoretically at least, more difficult to align accurately. It is said that for men taking up shooting late in life the short-barreled guns are easier to handle. It is my opinion, however, that short barrels give a gun a stumpy appearance, and their advantage when shooting in thick cover has been overstressed. The short sighting plane and increased tendency toward powder blast are disadvantages. A tall man shooting an extremely short-barreled gun presents a somewhat incongruous appearance, as does a short man with a long-barreled weapon.

Barrel lengths are a matter of usage. If a man is accustomed to long barrels, short barrels will seem unhandy to him, muzzle-light, and the muzzle will tend to wobble around the target and be unsteady. Short-barreled guns feel lighter in the hand than those of similar weight with long barrels.

Whether the barrels shall be side by side, or one above the other, is a matter of personal choice. The over-and-under is more complicated to manufacture, and therefore slightly more expensive. From a mechanical standpoint, the over-and-under from a good maker is reliable and is not likely to give trouble. It is particularly adapted to the man who has been accustomed to using a pump gun or an automatic because of its single-barreled sighting plane. Mr. Nichols, the able gun editor of *Field and Stream,* believes that some over-and-under guns have a tendency to shoot high. Because of their construction, the over-and-under must open much more widely in order to load and unload the under chamber. The deep frame necessitated by their superimposed construction tends toward canting of the barrels, particularly if one is shooting from a poor stance, and canting itself is then more difficult to recognize. Personally, I like best the side-by-side arrangement.

Some light guns are made without a rim. This, I think, is a disadvantage, as is the sway-backed type. However, it is a matter of choice, and some prefer barrels without a rim. The absence of rim certainly gives a neat appearance, and it may be argued that the rim is not of much use. It is all largely a matter of what one is accustomed to using. If a rim is desired, it should be glare-proof and taper rather quickly toward the muzzle. Ventilated rims are hard to keep clean and are rarely used on field guns. The sight is not very important. A rather large, low, white sight is perhaps the best. A high sight has a tendency to produce low shooting. Old-fashioned stub twist and Damascus barrels are not safe with modern powders, and this type of material has now been superseded by tougher and stronger steel.

*Choke.* Barrels which have a little constriction at the distal end shoot better. There are various ways of producing the choke, the details of which are in many cases trade secrets, and in any event not very important to the average shooter. The constriction varies from about 3 to 40 thousandths of an inch. The chokes differ in shape and length, according to the pattern to be obtained. If 3 or 4 inches are removed from the end of the barrel, these generally contain all the choke and the barrel will then be a cylinder.

A true cylinder barrel will place approximately 40 per cent of the shot charge in a 30-inch circle at forty yards.

An improved cylinder will show about 50 per cent
¼ choke will show about 55 per cent
½ choke will show about 60 per cent

¾ choke will show about 65 per cent

Choke will show about 70 per cent

Full choke will show about 75 per cent

A properly loaded, well-made, improved cylinder barrel should give about a 50 per cent pattern at forty yards. However, all do not, and the pattern may fall as low as 35 per cent.

The center of the 30-inch circle from which the estimates are made is placed in the thickest part of the pattern. Experience has shown that for the average 12-gauge field gun the most satisfactory boring is an improved cylinder for the right and a half choke for the left barrel. Some shots prefer left barrel to be three-quarters choked. The killing pattern of an improved cylinder barrel at 20 yards is slightly smaller than that of a full choke barrel at 40 yards. An approximate guide for the number of pellets which should be found in a 30-inch circle at 30 yards is 140 per cent of the number which are found in the gun's 40-yard pattern; 119 per cent at 35 yards; 100 per cent at 40 yards; 82 per cent at 45 yards, and 67 per cent at 50 yards. With true cylinders, patterns beyond 25 or 30 yards or under tend to become irregular, even with normal pressures and with moderately heavy loads this is doubly the case. The chief effect of a slight constriction, such as is found in a loose improved cylinder boring, is to ensure regularity of pattern.

With an improved cylinder the killing circle should be approximately 20 inches in diameter at 20 yards, and 30 inches at 30 yards, with a half choke about 16 inches at 20 yards, and 26 inches at 30 yards. With walked-up game the bird is usually a more or less out-going shot. Under ordinary circumstances, the second barrel will be used before the bird travels more than 8 to 14 feet, and hence the half choke gives ample leeway. Closely choked barrels are a distinct handicap at the distance at which the average shot at upland game is presented. Probably 90 per cent of all grouse, quail, and woodcock are killed at ranges of 25 or 30 yards or under. Pheasants perhaps average a few yards farther. To insure a thick enough pattern, small-gauge guns shooting less shot are often more choked—that is, the killing circle is reduced in size in order to maintain the thickness of the pattern. There is obviously a limit to which this can be carried. Hence the smaller bores shooting less shot have a more restricted range.

The upland field shot is not generally required to shoot much beyond 40 yards, and the best plan in ordering a gun is to state that the optimum pattern is required for 25 yards for the right barrel and 10 yards farther for the left. This means a moderately loose improved cylinder for the right barrel and a half choke for the left. Quick shots can shoot a slightly more open barrel with more advantage than can those using a more deliberate method.

If a man routinely shoots over spaniels he will probably average a little greater range for his shots than over pointing dogs, therefore, he may well use a little closer choke than he would otherwise. Barrels which are cylinder or improved cylinder give better results with cartridges which produce moderate or relatively low pressures. Even distribution of shot is quite as important as percentage. It is a matter of boring and loading and can be determined with certainty only by test. True cylinder barrels often give somewhat irregular patterns. Often they can be recessed choked. This tends to improve their shooting. It is common to hear of a particular gun shooting unusually hard. The gun usually gets such a reputation because it shoots a close pattern. Hard shooting, i.e., velocity and penetration, is almost entirely the result of loading. In ordering a new gun, it is advisable to inform the maker of the size of shot mostly to be used, for it is well known that certain methods of boring shoot better with fine than with coarse shot, and vice versa.

*Stock.* The fit of the stock is more important in the upland-game gun than in any other arm. A fine shot may shoot wild fowl well with almost any sort of stock, but his shooting will suffer if he is forced to perform in covert with a poor-fitting gun. With a good fit the gun is a natural pointer. Most guns will shoot well enough to make a good showing, but fit and balance are very difficult to secure. It costs no more to get a good than a bad fit. Poor-fitting stocks increase recoil and tend especially to prevent effective use of the second barrel and fast shooting. Men may, and many do, learn to accommodate themselves to ill-fitting stocks to a considerable extent. This is especially true during youth, when the muscles are more supple.

When I was sixteen years of age, I made what was, for me, a phenomenal run of consecutive kills of birds in the field during three days' shooting, using a gun which had a 3½-inch drop. Shortly afterward I was given a new gun, which had a drop of a scant 2¼ inches. Within a month or so I had an equally long run on live pigeons, using the new gun, during two days' shooting. During these two days I won one match of twenty-five birds and won or divided every stake I entered. I remember coming home with my pockets bulging with dirty five-dollar bills. These scores are cited only to show that youth can and often does accommodate itself to an ill-fitting stock. However, the live-pigeon shot often needs a straighter stock than when shooting in the field.

The importance of perfect fit and balance is not generally appreciated. The really good shots and those of wide experience almost invariably go to great trouble to secure guns which suit them and which possess properly fitted stocks. If the purchaser was buying a gun from a London maker, the question of fit was usually easily solved. He was sent to a shooting grounds equipped with targets, variously placed clay-pigeon traps, a tower, and try guns of various gauges fitted with single and double triggers. Here he was met by an experienced stock fitter, who in a short time would determine his most suitable stock measurements.

The professional coach and fitter is not always one hundred per cent correct, but he is more likely to be right than are those who have had less experience. Bob Robertson, of Boss & Co. Ltd., London, W.1, England, is one of the best. To show how accurate these men are, one of my friends was fitted by three different London professionals, and the stock measurements recommended by them were practically identical.

It is perhaps needless to state that a try gun is one equipped with a stock which, by means of screw adjustments, can be changed to any length, bend, or cast-off. It is invaluable in securing a proper fit. One of the London firms employs a try gun not only possessing an adjustable stock, but so arranged that when the trigger is pulled a spot of light is projected to the exact point at which the gun is aimed. This arrangement not only aids the fitter, but also permits the shooter to see any fault in alignment. By its use a fairly accurate idea of stock requirements can be arrived at before the purchaser goes to the shooting grounds.

An adept shooting coach will also detect various faults, such as checked swing, raising the head after the discharge of the first barrel, improper stance, incipient flinch, canting, and other errors which lead to poor shooting—errors which the shooter may have been practicing unknowingly for years. The good coach will also be able to suggest remedies. Some such fault is likely to be present even in the expert shot, and especially so in the average or poor performer.

Nothing can make some men shoot well, but even the worst can be helped. A well-fitted and properly balanced gun should come up dead on the mark and need little or no correction. Merely pointing the gun, in distinction to actual sighting, should place the barrels in the desired alignment. A low, soft collar and the usual shooting coat should be worn while being fitted. An unduly thick coat or one that bunches at the shoulders will make it appear that a shorter stock than need be is required. A starched shirt or suspender buckle may also interfere with securing a proper fit. The joking excuse for bad shooting, that a man was wearing his cold-weather clothes and shooting his summer gun, has some basis in fact.

There are some try guns in this country, and a few professional fitters. Abercrombie & Fitch, of New York City, formerly maintained a shooting grounds for coaching and fitting just outside of New York City. To anyone interested, Mr. Krug, the manager of the gun department of this firm, would, I am sure, give information. Probably there are other similar places.

It is difficult to get a good fit by merely going to a gun store and aiming a number of guns. The average clerk is more interested in making a sale than in properly fitting the customer. Consequently his advice is likely to do more harm than good. Almost anyone who has ever pulled a trigger thinks he knows all about fit. An experienced shot can probably help, as can some of the target shooters, although the man who wraps himself around a big pigeon gun is a far cry from the field shot.

Skeet requires a well-fitting gun, but because the target has a tendency to be falling it calls for a trifle more drop than is required in the field gun. No satisfactory directions can be given for fitting by the written word. Too straight a stock tends to overshooting; too much bend to undershooting. A long-armed man requires a long stock; the opposite, naturally, is needed by a short-armed shooter. The possessor of a long neck or the man who holds his head high requires more drop than the short-necked individual or one who drops his head low on the stock. The gun which points constantly to the right or left will be helped by a lateral bend, i.e., cast-off or cast-on. The great majority of guns manufactured in this country are made without any lateral bend, while the English gun-makers nearly always recommend some cast-off. Our best shots compare favorably with the best of any country, and most of them do not use any cast-off, but it is undoubtedly of help to some men.

The shape and angle of the butt should be such that it comfortably and accurately fits the shoulder. Moderate depth from heel to toe is generally the most desirable. Pitch is the divergence from barrel inclination to the right angle of the butt. Obviously, if the measurement from the center of the front trigger to the toe is unnecessarily long it will have a tendency to throw the muzzle up; the reverse is, of course, true. If the shooter has a gun with a butt plate this can be loosened, and packing may be placed underneath in order to test greater length of stock or different degrees of pitch. With an otherwise properly fitting stock moderate divergence of pitch is perhaps not vitally important, although opinions differ regarding this point. However, it is best to test carefully. Err on the side of the stock which will make for high shooting.

The pitch and shape of the butt should be such that when the gun is properly mounted and pointing straight ahead at a point corresponding to the height of the shooter's eye, the entire butt, from heel to toe, should press evenly upon the hollow of the shoulder. The required thickness of the comb should be dependent upon the shape of the face and the method of mounting. It should be such as naturally to place the right eye directly in line with the center of the rim. Thus, a thin-faced man will probably shoot best with a moderately thick comb. Much, however, depends upon the position in which the head is naturally held during the act of shooting. A Monte Carlo comb provides a full-rounded comb and for some shooters is advantageous in holding the eye at its proper level. To an extent, this type of comb prevents cross shooting or lateral divergence. They are more commonly employed by trap than game shots.

A full pistol grip, while necessary for steadying a heavy rifle, is an abomination on the field gun. I do not think it matters much whether or not a small pistol grip, sometimes called a half- or a quarter-pistol grip, is present. Most American guns have them, while most English guns are made with a straight grip. More American guns than formerly are now made with a straight grip. For one thing, a pistol grip of any kind prevents easy slipping back of the hand for the pulling of the rear trigger, and thus tends to displace the aim and slow the use of the second barrel. No change of grip is, of course, necessary when single-trigger guns are used. The use of a pistol grip perhaps tends to keep the muzzle low. They do not add to the beauty of the gun. If, however, a man can shoot better with a small pistol grip, he should by all means have it.

With the straight grip, the stock should generally be about ⅛ to ¼ inch longer than if a half pistol grip is employed. This extra length in itself has some advantage and makes for more accurate estimate of elevations. I prefer a straight grip, and believe that it has a slight advantage when shooting rapidly rising, overhead, or passing birds, especially those going to the right. For a one-armed man a pistol grip is an advantage, because of the greater leverage which it offers. A gun for a man so handicapped had best be light, with little weight forward, short-barreled and certainly fitted with a single trigger. Careful gunmakers will ask for an outline or in some other way determine the size of the shooter's right hand and the length of his fingers, in order to make the grip or "small" of proper dimensions. The grip should be oval. A comfortable grip makes considerable difference. A thick, round, or badly shaped grip is clumsy and awkward and has a tendency to tire the hand. The surface of the grip is roughened, but if the checkering is too coarse or sharp it soon becomes uncomfortable. Most high-grade field guns are now made without a butt plate and this seems to answer satisfactorily. A rubber recoil pad may be applied if desired. This is generally unnecessary on the field gun, in which large charges are not required. It may, however, sometimes be placed upon a lady's gun. If a recoil pad is to be placed on a stock which has already been fitted properly, care must be exercised lest its application alter the measurements. The pad should be so shaped and adjusted that it fits the shoulder accurately when the gun is mounted since pads may change the balance of the gun.

Various methods are employed to test fit and balance. One of the most useful is to hold the gun in the usual manner and throw it quickly to the shoulder with the eyes fixed on the target. The target should be some yards distant and at the level of the shooter's eye. If, without the slightest correction of aim, the sight is found to be dead on the target; or, better, a few inches above, the gun fits properly.

Most English guns are sighted to throw their charges a few inches high at 40 yards. Naturally this test should be repeated a number of times, for no fitting or balances can make the gun respond one hundred per cent. If this test seems to show a fairly good fit, then take the gun to a testing ground and use exactly the same technic in shooting light loads at a large target placed 30 yards away and head high.

The target should be extra large: not less than 6 feet square. Shoot a dozen shots and then examine the target. Even if the gun fits well, there will be some shots wide of the mark; but the bulk should be fairly on the bull's-eye. Both of these tests are useless if there is any attempt to aim or fit yourself to the stock. They must be true snap shots. Another way to test fit is to stand off a few yards from a mirror and aim quickly at the reflection of the right eye. This also will show errors in stance, grip, tendency to cant the barrels, and the like. A rough and ready guide for length of stock is to place the butt on the right arm just above the elbow. If in this position the trigger finger comes to rest properly on the forward trigger, in the case of a two-triggered gun, the length is about right, or perhaps ⅛ inch short.

To attain proper fit it helps greatly if the shooter is able to mount his gun in exactly the same manner each time, for it follows that if sometimes the butt is high on the shoulder and the next time too low, it is more difficult to appraise the necessary amount of drop required; the same is true, but to perhaps a slightly lesser extent, in lateral deviations. It is equally difficult to fit the man who has formed certain bad habits of which he may be uncon-scious. As men get older they often require a little more drop and a shorter stock, and certainly at this time of life absolutely correct fit is most important. Naturally, the lanky youth will require a different stock as he fills out and becomes heavier. Beware of the near fit. With a bad fit the shooter will take pains to align properly.

If the choice lies between two stocks, it is better to select the longer and straighter one. As a man gains experience he will generally find that he can shoot better with a straighter and longer stock than seemed required during his beginner shooting days. Both have a tendency to keep the muzzle high. The tendency for most men is to shoot low, and nearly all game shots are rising. The final and most important test of fit is to determine which gun can be shot best at moving objects. A round or two of skeet or with the hand trap should help. The stock measurements that are correct for one gun may not be entirely satisfactory for another which is of different balance and construction. This is another reason why it is preferable to shoot only one gun or to have a pair of similar weapons. For trap shooting or wildfowling different types of guns are desirable and these will probably require different stock measurements from those of the gun for upland shooting.

The preceding brief description of fitting the shotgun stock presupposes that the shooter is right handed; also that the right is the master eye, or that the shooter closes the left eye during the act of shooting.

It is preferable to shoot with both eyes open. Closing the left eye is only a habit, often acquired when first learning to shoot.

Rifle shooting often starts it. Even if the habit is established, most men can learn to shoot with both eyes open without much difficulty. If this cannot be done, it is of no vital importance. One of the best shots I ever saw as well as many old-timers always closed the left eye. At present, however, most good coaches advise the binocular method. Some men close one eye during the preliminary stage, but, unknowingly, open it before shooting and, therefore, unconsciously employ the binocular method. If both eyes are kept open it is essential to determine the master eye. This can be accomplished as follows:

Use the point of the finger or a lead pencil, and with both eyes open sight with this upon some small object about 10 feet distant. Then close the left eye. If the sight remains true on the mark, the right is the master eye. If, on the other hand, the sight jumps to the right, the left is the master eye. Repeat this test a number of times.

Another test is to sight a gun at some object, keeping both eyes open, and then close the left eye. If the sight remains accurately on the object first aimed at, the right eye is the master. Some individuals do not have a definite master eye; in these the sight will sometimes move to the right and sometimes remain true on the mark. If this is the case, there is no need to worry, and fitting can continue as if the right were definitely the master eye. If, however, the left is really the master eye, one of six things can be done:

1. The shooter can accept the condition and merely close the left eye when shooting.

2. He can use a disk fitted on the gun, so that the right eye alone can look along the barrels.

3. Sometimes the shooter can be taught to grip the barrels in such a way that the thumb of the left hand blocks out the sight of the left eye.

4. He may have a "cross-eyed" stock made. This stock possesses an excessive cast-off so that when mounted in the ordinary manner on the right shoulder the barrels will be aligned to the left eye. I have seen men shoot very well with these awkward-looking stocks.

5. According to Mr. Nichols, arms and ammunition editor, *Field*

*and Stream,* Mr. L. Smith of the Lefever Division of the Ithaca Gun Company has devised a stock which works well for left-eyed men. The comb is cut away. This permits the shooter to place his head over the stock until his left eye comes into proper alignment.

6. When the left is definitely the master eye, the shooter may switch over and shoot from the left shoulder. This is not a very difficult thing to do, especially for the youth. In baseball, many men who are right handed, in all other respects, bat left-handed. This is often the most satisfactory answer, and is usually so for the man or boy who is learning to shoot and has no established habit. For the right-handed man who has lost the sight of his right eye, the cross-eyed stock, or the L. Smith stock, or the switchover are about the only methods. I have known one man who could shoot equally well from either shoulder, but this type of ambidexterity is extremely rare. In *Shooting* it is recorded that in 1885, Sir Victor Brooke killed 740 rabbits and one woodcock in a single day to his own gun. Sir Victor expended exactly one thousand cartridges and shot from his right shoulder for one half of the day, and from his left shoulder during the other half.

The best stocks are made from fine imported walnut and are oil-finished. There is no more comparison between a fine oil finish, and varnish than there is between a fine old walnut table, smooth and soft as a result of two or three generations of loving polishing, and a cheap article glistening with many coats of varnish. Furthermore, varnish shows up every scratch or dent.

*Balance.* Balance is the point, generally a little forward of the trigger guard, upon which the gun will be in equilibrium. However, it is really much more than this. It is intimately associated with length of barrel, distribution of weight, general make-up, and that almost intangible something which enables the experienced wielder to handle, mount, swing, and aim the gun with accuracy, speed, and ease. Well-balanced guns feel lighter than they are and are a pleasure to handle. They are neither muzzle-light nor muzzle-heavy.

A well-balanced gun is more pleasant to use and appears to give less recoil than one of the same weight which is poorly balanced. The reverse is true of an ill-fitting stock. In the latter case the apparent excess recoil is largely due to less satisfactory mounting. A badly shaped stock may bruise the jaw and an ill-balanced gun is apt not to be placed uniformly and properly against the shoulder.

Finally, when you get a gun that is satisfactory in fit and balance, stick to it. The more practice, the better. No amount of fit and balance can produce one hundred per cent accuracy. Do not let shooting friends persuade you that you need some alteration in the stock or other dimensions. If your tests have been thorough and satisfactory, the rest is dependent upon practice and your ability. Further attempts at alteration only throw you off your shooting. Some men are forever tinkering with their gun stocks. This destroys confidence and impairs that thorough familiarity with the gun that comes only from long practice.

*Lock.* Locks are of two main types: (1) the side lock, and (2) the Anson and Deeley type of box lock. Both are efficient, strong, and durable. The side lock is more complicated and expensive, and it is claimed that it is a little faster than the box locks. It can be more easily removed. The side lock is placed on all high-grade English guns except those of extremely small bore. Most American guns are provided with box locks. The reason box locks are generally placed on small bores is that the side lock necessitates the cutting away of considerable wood, and in the small gun results in the stock being weak at this point. I doubt if there is much practical difference between the two. The side locks make for more symmetry. The Smith guns are one of the few American makes equipped with side locks.

*Trigger.* Whether the trigger is to be single or double is your only choice. The former is a little more complicated, but it has the obvious advantage that no change of grip is necessary in shooting the second barrel. Single triggers are usually placed in the position of the right-barrel trigger in a two-triggered gun, but they can be placed farther back if desired. Early single triggers were not always reliable, but the modern ones by good makers are now satisfactory.

In theory, the single triggers should permit a little faster and more accurate shooting of the left barrel, as its use requires no change of grip. As a matter of fact, I doubt if many experienced shots are aware of any change in grip when using two-trigger guns. A single trigger sometimes prevents bruising of the trigger finger, but this can be prevented in other ways—a spring blade fitted to a double-trigger gun is a certain cure. All high-grade single triggers are of the selective type.

The advantage of two triggers is the instant selection it furnishes if the right and left barrels possess different degrees of choke. This is often of considerable practical value, and for this reason alone I prefer double triggers. It is true that with a single trigger the user can accustom himself to adjust the mechanism quickly in order to shoot either barrel first, but at best there is a certain amount of time lost. With practice, however, it can be done fairly rapidly. Any pause is, however, fatal to good shooting. Irregular or heavy trigger pull can spoil shooting. It is best to have the right-barrel trigger fixed at 3½ pounds and the left at 4 or 4½ pounds. The rear trigger pull is made a little heavier than the right because of the better leverage which can be obtained on it. Trigger pull is so important that it should be tested occasionally. It is also a safety measure. A pull less than three pounds is dangerous, and if too light may even be jarred off by the recoil from the first barrel. In even the best of guns the sears may wear and if poor material is used this wearing is of course more likely to occur. Pulls may increase or decrease. If the pull increases it is sure to spoil accurate shooting and if it decreases it is dangerous. A rough-and-ready test for trigger pull may be made by attaching two pieces of twine to the trigger, carrying one back on each side of the stock, and then fastening them to an ordinary spring balance such as used for weighing fish. So-called creeping pulls are rare nowadays, but are sure to interfere with good shooting. The gun should fire instantly the trigger is pulled.

Some years ago I was shooting a borrowed gun. It seemed to fit well, but my shooting was atrocious. In the evening I examined the gun and found the stock measurements almost identical with those of my own field guns, but when the trigger pull was tested, it was found to be between 6½ and 7 pounds. A hard pull is certain to result in undershooting, and this is not always recognized in the field.

*Quality.* It is sometimes argued that a good gun will last a lifetime, and hence is cheap at almost any price. So it will, but by that time it will probably be somewhat of an antique. Many sportsmen believed the ultimate had arrived with the advent of the detonating gun. The last fifty years have seen the muzzle loader disappear and the breech loader become universal; the advent of the hammerless; the barrel shortening due to the use of smokeless powders; automatic ejectors becoming routine equipment; selective single trigger becoming frequent, and many other minor improvements. Whereas it is difficult now to visualize many improvements for the modern field gun, the next fifty years probably will bring them. I am an advocate of a man's getting the best gun he can afford, and I believe he will never regret money so spent. A gun is like a cigar and many other things; if a man becomes accustomed to the best, he will never be quite satisfied with anything else.

Without regard to price, the best guns I know are those manufactured by the London gunsmiths. A man cannot go wrong if he gets a Purdey, Boss, Woodward, or any gun made by perhaps three or four other London gunsmiths. These guns have a beauty, finish, smoothness of action, balance, and a snakelike symmetry that are unequaled. My own dealings have been chiefly with the Purdey firm. They have carried out my wishes with the greatest care, down to the smallest detail. The used-gun market is a fair guide in the selection of a maker. There is nothing better than a best-quality London gun, unless it be a pair. If a pair of guns are ordered, they should be identical, except that number two may well be bored so that it will give optimum patterns 5 yards farther than number one. Such a gun is ideal for late in the season pheasant shooting, and for use over spaniels. After the leaves are off it is also useful for grouse shooting and can, at a pinch, be employed for marsh ducks over decoys. It is also adapted for certain forms of prairie shooting.

In England the 2½-inch case is standard on field guns, so, when ordering English guns, it is well to specify the length of chamber desired. For the light 12-gauge, 2⅝ inches will accommodate the 3-dram and 1⅛-ounce load, and 2¾ inches most of the heavier charges. Instead of drop at heel, the English sometimes substitute drop at the "bump," which is a point 15 inches back from the face of the action or false breech and consequently slightly forward of the heel. Drop at the bump is often a small fraction of an inch less than drop at the heel.

All English guns are submitted to two proofs. The first is the "Provisional" proof, which is applied to the uncompleted barrel. The second is termed the "Definite" proof, and is applied to the finished gun or to a gun in "the white," which latter is, from the safety point of view, a finished weapon. The gun is subsequently marked with proof marks and the bore and length of cartridge case impressed on each barrel. Definite proof mark is the letters G. P. interlaced in a cipher surmounted by a crown. Foreign proof marks are confusing, and the prospective buyer who is considering purchasing a gun from a doubtful source would do well to familiarize himself with the various proof marks. *The Shot Gun*, by Purdey, contains illustrations of the various proof marks.

The chief drawback to London guns is that they are expensive. The best cost about £130, and by the time they are imported to the United States they will average about $1000 (pre-war price). Good guns can sometimes be obtained secondhand, but even then the cost is high, and a certain risk is entailed. A new stock will probably be required; this will average from $50 to $100. A really superior gun is something like a high-grade motor car. Let a man drive a $2500 car for a time and he will realize the difference when he comes back to the cheaper grade.

For $200 to $400 a fine gun, made in the United States, can be purchased. This gun will shoot as well and be as safe and as durable as any gun made anywhere. One advantage of the arm made here is that the purchaser does not have to pay the excessive import duty charged on English guns.

With the exception of pumps and automatics, most of my American guns have been Smiths. I bought my first Smith forty years ago—a field grade. Except that the metal in the muzzle of the right barrel is worn, due to the thousands of rounds that have been shot from it, the gun is as tight and almost as good as it was the day it was purchased. It was sold recently at a loss of only $10 from the original cost. I have had five Smith guns; all have shot well, have never become loose, and have been entirely satisfactory. They have had hard work but good care. Doubtless many sportsmen could relate similar experiences with Parkers and other makes of American guns. Dollar for dollar, there is more value in an American gun than any sporting arm I know.

Guns should open and close easily. A stiff gun is a nuisance and a good "self-opener" a luxury.

Engraving adds to the cost of a gun. Personally, I do not admire heavy, elaborate engraving or gold inlays, but fine, smooth, well-executed engraving does add greatly to the gun's appearance and beauty. Unless otherwise ordered, all high-grade guns are engraved, and it is only a question of the type desired.

*Pumps and Automatics.* These are hard-shooting, durable, fine guns for wild fowl and certain other types of shooting, but in my opinion they are not comparable to a fine double gun, for upland work; nor do they possess the advantage of the selective choke. Those interested in the mechanism of modern shotguns should read Major Burrard's excellent work, *The Modern Shotgun.*

As previously stated, purchasing a shotgun over the counter of the average store is a poor way to buy. This, I think, is true when one is buying even the cheapest grade. It is far better to take a little time and trouble and order direct from the maker. This insures getting exactly what is desired, presupposing that the buyer knows what he wants. If one has an old gun that suits, this can be sent as a copy, or an outline can be cut out of light board or cardboard, which can then be cut into convenient size, and sent to the factory. However, the latter gives the maker little idea of balance, and should only be done as an emergency measure.

*Case.* A good, strong, sole-leather case is an insurance against injury to the gun. It is often convenient to carry a gun without taking it down. For carrying it in this way an extra case is necessary. The ordinary canvas case is inferior to one of sole leather. In an automobile, guns are often crowded and especially likely to get knocked about, and a case with some stiffness is decidedly worth the additional initial cost.

Good sole leather is hard to get nowadays. There is a cheap imitation on cardboard, but it is worthless. The occasional application of Propert's saddle soap or meltonian cream will prolong the life and improve the look of leather, and soon eliminate any unpleasant new appearance. Saddle soap is, I think, better than oil. Have your initials stamped on gun cases. A damp gun should never be cased.

*Test for a New Gun.* It is well worth while to test the shooting qualities of a new gun. For this purpose get a number of sheets of thick paper, about 5 or 6 feet square, and test the right barrel at 25 measured yards, and the left at 10 yards farther. Use the loads expected to be employed in the field. Be sure there is a safe background. A good plan is to start with 3 drams and 1⅛ ounces of No. 6 shot, and later 3 drams and 1 ounce, No. 9. (A really better load for woodcock, grouse, and quail is 2¾ drams and 1 ounce, but this is not a standard load and can be secured only in 500-cartridge lots.) The 2½ drams and 1 ounce standard load is inferior. The theory has been advanced that with the 3 drams 1 ounce load the pellets at the edge of the pattern are more effective and there is less stringing of the shot than with the 3-1⅛ cartridge. At all events, it is an excellent load for upland game shooting, especially if fairly fine shot is used. Whether the 3-1 or 2¾-1 should be the choice depends largely upon the degree of choke and can be determined by test. It is well, also, to test the desired loads in different makes of cartridges.

The tests should include percentage of shot within a 30-inch circle, the center of which is taken from the thickest part of the pattern; penetration; and, of equal or even greater importance, uniformity of distribution. Do not be disturbed if there is occasionally a hole in even the best patterns. Modern guns and cartridges shoot better than the average man can hold. The tests should include a series of about five or six shots from each of the best loads and from each make of cartridges. These tests are best made with an elbow rest. This is a time-consuming job, but it is worth the trouble. For a 12-gauge gun the aim should be to secure the best cartridge for a 1⅛-ounce load and the same for a 1-ounce load. Thereafter, when possible, use only those loads which have proved most satisfactory and those cartridges manufactured by the firm which has given the best results.

*Cleaning the Gun.* It is best to look after the cleaning of the gun, personally, since others may be rough, careless, or not understand the mechanism of a fine gun. Despite advice to the contrary, the gun should be cleaned every day after shooting. There should be *no* exception to this rule. Separate forearm barrels and stock and dry thoroughly with a clean cloth. Buy a new soft toothbrush, slightly oil the bristles and use this for crevices otherwise inaccessible. If the gun has been wet, place it in a warm room to dry after having removed all the moisture possible. Run a dry swab through the barrels to remove most of the powder residue. Then swab out the barrels with clean patches wet with solvent until the patches come out clean. Swabs should fit snugly, but undue force may bulge a barrel. In order to economize on swabs, a wad of dry newspaper may be substituted for the first swab used through a dirty barrel. Hoppe makes a convenient patch for cleaning. Run a Thomlinson cleaner through a few times, follow with a dry patch and finally a patch soaked in Hoppe's No. 9 or some other good solvent. Efficient as it is, it is safer not to depend too much upon the solvent. Mechanical cleaning or "elbow grease" is more reliable. Clean all metal work and oil lightly but thoroughly. Do not use an excess of oil. This is all that is required if the gun is to be used again in a few days.

If it is not to be used for a week or more, swab out the solvent from inside the barrels, and when the patches come out clean run through a patch soaked in good oil.

If the gun is to be put away for six months, leave the solvent in the barrels for twenty-four to forty-eight hours. Then use the Thomlinson cleaner again thoroughly, follow with a dry patch, and finally coat all metal surfaces with a good grade of vaseline or gun grease. Any grease will answer, provided it is not too thin and is free of salt. Most animal fats contain salt, which in itself promotes rust.

Most hammerless and ejector guns should be stored, dismounted.

Some men like to keep their guns assembled; this has advantages. In this case the guns should be uncocked. Some guns can be decocked by pushing forward the safety, pulling both triggers simultaneously, and at the same time slowly closing the breech. Dummy or "snap" cartridges slightly greased can be inserted and the hammers snapped. Do not snap the locks on an empty chamber. It is a good plan to keep an old pair of gloves in the gun cabinet, for even a slight amount of perspiration on metal will produce rust.

The difficulty with the oil is that it gums; this is true, in time, of all oils. Real sperm oil—the grade sold for clockmakers as chronometer oil—is by far the best in this respect, but it is expensive and some of it has an unpleasant odor. The Hoppe or 3-in-1 oils answer most purposes. Some gunmakers recommend nothing but grease, but even grease will gum in time, hence the advisability of regreasing guns that are in storage every six months.

I use plenty of solvent and oil inside the barrels, but if this is done the barrels should be wiped out before the gun is put together, for if held in the upright position the excess fluid may gravitate down and get into the plunger holes, where it gums. For the same reason care should be exercised not to let excess oil get into the ejector or cocking mechanism. In old or ill-made guns, or those which have been badly treated, an unsuspected opening sometimes develops under the rim. If this occurs, moisture may get in and rust develop to such an extent as to finally cause a burst. These bursts may occur in an apparently well-kept arm. For this reason the side of the rim should be carefully cleaned and kept well lubricated. Needless to say, if any aperture develops under the rim, or if the latter gets loose, it should be repaired immediately. Occasionally a little linseed oil, well rubbed in with a soft cloth or with the palm of the hand, will keep the woodwork in good condition. Do not use too much or leave the wood soaked in it. If too much oil is used, or if free oil is left on the woodwork, the latter soon becomes very dark. This is a common fault.

With high-grade guns it is worth while every year to return them to their makers or to some first-class gunsmith for a general check-up, cleaning, and lubrication of parts, such as locks and ejector mechanism. The check-up should include testing the trigger pulls. This latter requires skill and should not be attempted by anyone except the expert. Do not send a high-grade gun to any but a competent gunsmith. Defaced screwheads are the least that can be expected from the incompetent.

If a gun falls overboard into water, it should be taken to a gunsmith immediately. If this is impossible, kerosene liberally applied to the ejector and cocking mechanism may help, and, if the owner has the proper tools, the locks and other parts may be removed, dried, and oiled, and the gun taken as soon as possible to a gunsmith. Blotting paper often helps to dry crevices. Generally speaking, the removal of locks and taking apart of the ejector and cocking mechanism is a job for the gunsmith, for the amateur is very apt to mar screwheads and do other damage.

If the gun is to be used in rainy weather, a light coat of grease, instead of oil, is a great protection. In doubtful weather, a greased rag can be carried in the pocket of the shooting jacket. A little prevention is well worth the trouble entailed. Apply the grease especially over the locks and engraving, along the rim, and the upper end of the firearm where it comes in contact with the barrels. If the woodwork gets wet, rub thoroughly until dry and then rub in linseed oil. Raindrops may spot a stock, especially if it is a new one. Canton flannel is an excellent cleaning material. Clean the inside of the barrels from the breech.

*Dents:* If the barrel has been dented, send the gun to a competent gunsmith—preferably to the maker. The local man may be little more than a blacksmith. A good gunsmith can easily repair the barrel. If the dent is a bad one, do not on any account shoot the gun until repaired. A swelled barrel is really serious and should never be shot under any circumstances.

*Storage:* Guns should be stored in a place that is dry and, preferably, of moderate, equable temperature. For long storage remove old grease and apply new every six months.

*Bursts:* The following are some of the common causes for bursts:

The breech or barrel may be originally defective, badly made or made of steel not suitable for modern powders, such as Damascus or other old steels.

Rust may form inside the barrels in the form of excessive pits.

Rust may form outside the barrel. This is plainly noticeable in the ordinary form. As previously stated another type of outside rust is due to a defect under the rim, which permits the entrance of moisture, and in the course of time excessive erosion may occur. If the entrance defect under the rim is small and the gun otherwise in good condition, you may not observe the condition. The burst which may result is usually longitudinal.

Obstructions may be in the barrel. As elsewhere mentioned, a 20-gauge shell may become mixed with those of 12-gauge, and inadvertently inserted in the chamber of the larger gauged gun, into which it disappears, lodging in the barrel. When an attempt is made to shoot, only the snap of the falling hammer is heard. The breech is then opened, found to be empty, and a proper sized cartridge inserted. The same thing may result if a 28-gauge shell is inserted into a 16-gauge gun.

A piece of cleaning rag may be left in the barrel. This type of burst occurs in the first shot of the day.

A defective cartridge may result in a wad, or even other parts of the load, becoming stuck in the barrel and not expelled. Such bursts follow a misfire or some abnormal sound of the report of the previous shot.

Mud or snow may get into the barrel. This burst occurs after a slip on a muddy bank or on slippery, muddy, or snow-covered ground. It is not necessary for the mud or snow to occlude the entire bore. If the obstruction is in the extreme end, a burst may not result, but if it is three-quarters of an inch or more from the muzzle, a burst is apt to occur. Obstruction from mud and snow often causes a bulged or a "swelled" barrel.

Excessive pressure may result from defective loading, but is very unusual with modern factory-loaded cartridges.

The use of properly kept, good guns and cartridges and the habit always of looking through the barrel before loading or after a slip or stumble, particularly on muddy or snow-covered ground, will prevent most bursts. If the expert is provided with a history of the case, the burst gun, remains of the shell, and the remainder of the unused cartridges, he can usually determine the cause of the accident. Burrard has examined 120 different bursts since

1920, and only four caused any serious hurt to the shooter. His book contains an excellent résumé on the subject of bursts.

*Ammunition.* In this country cartridges are now largely standardized. For the 12-gauge gun, loads usually used for upland shooting run about as follows:

> 2½ drams or its equivalent and 1 ounce shot
> 3  drams or its equivalent and 1 ounce shot
> 3  drams or its equivalent and 1⅛ ounce shot
> 3¼ drams or its equivalent and 1⅛ or 1¼ ounce shot

As previously stated elsewhere, special loads can be secured in lots of five hundred cartridges.

Different manufacturers use different cases, wadding, and crimp. This makes some difference in their shooting, recoil, etc. For example, one company uses a dumbbell-shaped wad, instead of the black-edged wads employed by another. It has seemed to me that those cartridges loaded with the dumbbell-shaped wads shoot as well and have less recoil for the same loads than those of some other manufacturers. This is probably more apparent than real, however, since recoil is dependent on the weight of the gun and the momentum of the ejecta, and certain other factors.

All charges are more or less standardized, to develop about the same ballistics and the velocity of the shot charge, and are therefore not greatly, if at all, affected by the individual powder. Hence, the commonly employed term of a "quick" or "fast" powder has usually little meaning. However, as previously stated, it is well to test all cartridges and then, as far as possible, to stick to those giving the most satisfactory results. The cartridge and powder companies in the United States have done a vast amount of work on the ballistics of shotgun loads and now produce excellent ammunition. This can be proved to the satisfaction of anyone by the study of scores made at the traps. A hundred straight breaks is not very unusual, and scores of well over 95 ex 100 are of daily occurrence. In 1938, J. F. Hiestand, of Hillsboro, Ohio, made a record run of 1,434 straight breaks from the 16 yards rise, and there are a number of five hundred straight scores at both trap and skeet.

Cartridges, good enough to smash 95 ex 100 of such a small

target as presented by even a stationary clay pigeon, are impossible with anything but good ammunition. Indeed, present-day cartridges are so excellent that it is difficult to imagine great future improvements. All field shots would like to eliminate stray pellets outside of the killing circle, in order that all birds would be either killed instantaneously or completely missed. However, the old excuse for misses due to poor ammunition is usually without foundation. Misses nowadays are nearly always the result of inaccurate holding or shooting at birds which are at too great a distance.

Much is written about pattern. The three things in cartridges chiefly affecting the pattern are: (1) pressure, (2) velocity, and (3) crimp, or, as the English term it, turnover.

Pressure is caused by the combustion of the powder. If too weak, there will be lack of penetration and low velocity; if too high, a "blown" or irregular pattern results, especially when fired from openly bored barrels; if very excessive, pressure may burst the barrel.

Cartridges for 12-gauge upland shooting, i.e., 3 drams or its equivalent, and 1 or 1⅛ ounces of shot produce pressures, just ahead of the chamber, of from 2½ to 3 tons per square inch. When pressure falls to 2 tons, velocity and penetration suffer. Three and one-half tons is excessive, and four tons is dangerous. The velocity of an average game load at 20 yards is about 1,050 feet per second. If below 800 feet per second, it is weak, and if above 1,150 feet per second, it is apt to result in "blown" patterns. One of the most recent innovations in cartridges is the elimination of the overshot wad, its place being taken by the crimped end of the cartridge case. For a long time there has been a theory that the shot wad occasionally produced "cartwheel" patterns. This new method is claimed to result in a 5 per cent improvement in pattern.

The late Captain Paul A. Curtis, former gun editor of *Field and Stream*, author and enthusiastic student of everything pertaining to guns, believed that overloading was one of the three cardinal reasons for poor shooting. One thing is sure, and that is that a light gun will produce more recoil with similar cartridges than a heavy one. In other words, the combination of a light gun and light recoil is impossible, and heavy recoil is detrimental to good shooting, apart from robbing the sport of its enjoyableness.

We, in America, generally shoot heavier loads than the English. In England, the tall driven pheasants are harder birds to kill than are ours, when shot over pointing dogs.

There is a fairly large class of men, generally composed of the inexperienced, who go on the theory that the heavier the load the greater the range at which they can kill, and who ignore or are ignorant of the many disadvantages attendant upon its use. On the same theory, very often the same type of shooter employs the closest shooting gun he can lay his hands on. Day in and day out, 1⅛ ounces of shot is plenty for upland game birds and, for some shooting, 1 ounce is decidedly preferable. Apart from other ills, excessive loads mutilate game and make it unfit for the table. One used to hear a good deal about stringing of shot. Of course the load of shot while traveling through the air does not move as a wall, but as an oblong body. Using modern ammunition, shot-stringing with an ordinary game gun and load is not often of practical detriment, nor does wind or gravity play much part in upland game bird shooting.

In order to secure a wide pattern from a closely choked barrel, scatter loads may be employed. These may be made by placing four to six cardboard wads between the shot load, i.e., 1/6 ounce of shot and then a wad, and so forth. Sometimes such loads produce rather irregular patterns.

Cartridges should be stored in a cool, dry place of equable temperature. Dampness, changes of temperature, and especially high temperature are detrimental and prone to result in variations of pressure. Under high, dry temperature the paper case dries too much and the moisture content of the powder is decreased, which tends to violent ballistics. Under favorable conditions, cartridges keep well for at least two to three years, or even longer. However, freshly made cartridges are preferable.

Investigations by W. H. Coxe, ballistic engineer of the Du Pont Company, have shown that when No. 6 shot is fired from a gun held slightly above the horizontal, the pellets cover an area of approximately 400 feet in depth, the nearest being about 300 feet and the farthest 700 feet. When the gun is fired at a 40-degree angle, the area covered varies from 400 to 900 feet. No. 7½ shot from trap loads has an extreme range of about 900 feet. The standard specification of the official skeet field allows 300 yards of safety area.

The Remington Arms Company has made the following estimate showing the purpose for which cartridges are used in this country: 26.9 per cent on rabbits, 14 per cent on squirrels, 13.9 per cent on quail, 10.5 per cent on wild fowl, 9.5 per cent on pheasants, 7 per cent on dove, 3.5 per cent on other game, and 12 per cent for trap and skeet.

*Tracer Cartridges.* Tracer or rocket cartridges are, as the name indicates, so constructed that the course of the shot can be followed with the eye. They are more expensive than ordinary cartridges but can be bought at some of the large ammunition houses. They are not intended to be employed on game but are for determining why certain shots are missed. Used in conjunction with clay pigeons, they possess value for such a purpose. The only tracers I have ever used are the Eley Rocket cartridges. These contained a pellet about the size of a buck shot, which has a range of 200 to 300 yards, so care must be taken in its use. If shot low into inflammable material, this pellet may cause a fire. Game hit by the pellet should not be eaten, as the pellet is more or less impregnated with barium oxide and barium carbonate. At best, the tracer is none too easily seen and sometimes was invisible. The use of rocket cartridges cannot injure the gun.*

The following is a comparison of the shot sizes standard in the United States, Great Britain, Belgium, France, Italy, and Germany:†

* For those interested in the study of ammunition, *Ammunition,* by Captain Melvin M. Johnson and Charles T. Haven, is recommended, as well as the previously mentioned work of Major Gerald Burrard, *The Modern Shotgun.*

† U.S., Belgian, and German figures from *Field and Stream,* September, 1942. Figures in re French and Italian shot from Burrard, Major G.: *The Modern Shotgun,* II, 113.

| Size Shot | Pellets per Ounce | | | | | |
|---|---|---|---|---|---|---|
| | *U. S.* | *British* | *Belgian* | *German* | *French* | *Italian* |
| 1 | 73 | 100 | 104 | 75 | 74 | 79 |
| 2 | 88 | 120 | 122 | 91 | 85 | 96 |
| 3 | 109 | 140 | 140 | 112 | 99 | 120 |
| 4 | 136 | 170 | 172 | 140 | 113 | 175 |
| 4½ | ... | 200 | ... | ... | ... | ... |
| 5 | 172 | 220 | 218 | 178 | 170 | 220 |
| 5½ | ... | 240 | ... | ... | ... | ... |
| 6 | 223 | 270 | 270 | 231 | 221 | 270 |
| 6½ | ... | 300 | ... | ... | ... | ... |
| 7 | 299 | 340 | 340 | 308 | 260 | 340 |
| 7½ | 345 | ... | ... | ... | ... | ... |
| 8 | 409 | 450 | 450 | 422 | 402 | 450 |
| 9 | 585 | 580 | 580 | 601 | 680 | 580 |
| 10 | 868 | 850 | 850 | 897 | 963 | 850 |

Shot is of three kinds: soft, chilled, and copper-coated. The hard or chilled is generally preferable. It has less tendency to lead the barrel than soft shot, and there are fewer malformed shot as a result of passage through the barrel, hence it gives about 5 per cent better pattern. Chilled shot is usually used for clay-pigeon shooting; in field shooting it is more apt to break bones.

Soft shot is a little heavier, and some men prefer it, especially for soft-feathered birds. There is probably little practical difference and both soft and chilled are satisfactory.

Copper-coated shot is not so widely employed as either soft or chilled, but excellent patterns can be made with it. According to Major Burrard, the first patent for plating shot was taken out in England in 1878, the idea being to prevent contamination of game. He further states that the thickness of copper plating is about 0.00001 of an inch.

*Balled Shot.* This is a term used to describe a condition in which all or some of the shot charge adheres together and shoots more or less like a ball, instead of separating and spreading as it is intended to do. True balling, i.e., the holding together of relatively large quantities of shot, is fortunately very rare, for it may travel far beyond normal range and may inflict serious damage. Fine shot, fired from a small-gauge gun, predisposes to balling. Loose wadding and high pressures are also factors, as are perhaps cylinder-bored barrels. I have seen patterns which showed that two, three, or four pellets had adhered together, but large clusters are probably of very rare occurrence. I have never heard of copper-coated shot balling. Most ballisticians believe that heat developed by the friction of the passage of the shot through the barrel, plus the jamming together of the shot cause the fusion. That there is considerable leakage of hot powder gases ahead of the over-powder wads and into the shot charge has been proved by spark photographs. Perhaps both or either may be etiological factors. In this connection, Burrard states that balling is due either to welding together of the pellets or to fusion of the shot. The former is caused by violent impact of the pellets, the result of high pressure, while the softer the shot the greater the liability to welding. Anything which favors the escape of hot powder gases past the wads tends toward fusion. M. A. Robinson and Nichols are of the opinion that chilled shot is definitely more liable to ball than soft or drop shot, because as antimony is added to lead, the melting point of the alloy is reduced.

*To ride, shoot straight, and speak the truth—*
*This was the ancient Law of Youth.*
                    —Charles T. Davis, "For a Little Boy."

THIS chapter is for the beginner. I am such an indifferent performer myself that I have great hesitancy in attempting it. However, perhaps the novice may learn from it some of the fundamentals and theory of the art of shooting. As a matter of fact, many fine shots have never heard of lag, time, stance, and much else that the experienced coach believes to be of vital importance. Such men have learned by experience; they have good eyesight, nerve control, and excellent coördination. They invariably know how to approach the pointing dog in order to get the best possible shot when the flush occurs. They know from experience the places which game birds "use." They have learned the hard, but practical, way to kill birds regularly, and to do it without book learning. Many of them are fine companions and are able to walk from dawn to dark. They are often "natural" shots, but even the best of them could probably be helped by a coach, and certainly their apprenticeship could have been shortened.

Successful shooting must be almost automatic, hence practice is the only way to become a good shot. Much can be learned as to correct methods and causes of failure, but only prolonged and repeated practice can insure satisfactory performance. The necessity of practice is well recognized in all exercises and games requiring skill, coördination, nerve control, and speed; but it is often overlooked when applied to shooting. To go afield, before a certain degree of skill is attained is not only unfair, but is sure to result in unnecessary wounding, wastage of game, and dissatisfaction to the sportsman.

139

The quickest and best way to learn to shoot is to secure the service of a good coach or an experienced friend. Even the professional coach as found in the English shooting schools (or, as they are now often termed, shooting grounds) may err. In this case, however, he has probably been selected originally for his ability and knowledge, and in addition has had a vast experience, perhaps extending over years, with every variety of shooter, and his proportion of error in regard to advice to his pupils is likely to be correspondingly small. In England shooting grounds are used extensively by experienced shots for pre-season practice, as well as by the novice who is learning to shoot. In this country valuable advice may often be secured from the representatives of arms or ammunition companies.

Not only will the coach demonstrate the proper form (which is only another way of saying the most efficient and easiest way of doing things, as proved by the long experience of others), but he will also prevent the development of bad habits. Bad habits once acquired are hard to overcome and are often unconsciously a cause for poor shooting for the remainder of a man's shooting life. The novice is apt to concentrate on trying to hit the target and to forget all else. To learn by demonstration is far easier than to learn by word of mouth.

To start from the beginning, the good coach will instruct by word and demonstration upon the following:

*Safety.* Never permit the loaded or unloaded gun to point at any living thing which is not intended to be killed.

*Assembling the Gun.* This should be done with firmness but without force, and when the gun is closed one should note that the top lever lies in the long axis of the barrels. If the top lever has not returned to its proper position in the long axis of the stock, the barrels may not be securely bolted in position. A minute portion of foreign substance or even gummed oil may impede the action of the lever.

To assemble:

Take the stock in the right hand and the barrels in the left hand, the former under and the latter overhand, guard and lump downward, and holding them at right angles to one another, as close as possible to action and lump respectively, place the hook of the lump of the barrels on the cross-pin of the action, and keeping it there firmly, turn the barrels to their place. A little vaseline on the sides of the hook will assist the operation with a new gun. Then put on the forepart, taking care to snap it well, however. Guns fitted with an ejector should always be permitted to eject the fired cartridge case, as, if the barrels are only partly dropped and the empty cartridge case removed with the finger and thumb, it may not be possible to fire the gun as the internal hammers will only have been partly raised and will rest in the inside safety catch until the gun has been opened again and the barrels properly dropped to their full extent.—Purdey's Instruction Book.

A common fault is to hold the barrels too far away from the breech end and at too acute an angle, when adjusting the hook to the forward lump. Once the hook is seen or felt to engage, pull strongly away from it, and at the same time raise the stock. It will save wear if, at the same time, the top lever is pushed over.

*Stance.* Good shooting is dependent upon good balance. Good balance is dependent upon good footwork and proper stance. Proper stance is therefore vital. With practice, it becomes, as it should be, entirely unconscious in its performance. Let the pupil imagine that he is standing upon the dial of a large clock and that the expected target is at twelve o'clock. For the average man, the feet should be about 12 inches apart from heel to heel, the left foot slightly in advance of the right. This should lead to a comfortable, well-balanced position, with the ability to swing easily to the extreme right or left without altering the position of the feet. In the swing to the right the left heel will be raised; in the swing to the left, the reverse will hold. A natural pivot, not a sway, results in the smoothest swing. Feet too far apart, awkward hips or bent knees—all act unfavorably on the balance, and hence on the smoothness of the swing. If the feet are reasonably close together, there is less necessity for raising any part of them when turning to take shots to either the right or left. Smooth, even, comfortable pivoting is dependent upon the position of the feet. The method of changing stance in order to shoot toward the rear will be postponed to later lessons.

For shots far to the right it is advisable to turn well around, often placing the left foot to the right and perhaps pivoting on the right foot. At all events, turn well around—"face the shot," in the parlance of the trap shooter. This brings the bird more in front and permits the use of the second barrel without hurry. Very often a bird will flush at the side as the gun is walking past. If the bird flies to the rear it can, especially if on the right side, be easily missed if the shooter does not turn well around and face the shot. By turning well around a difficult shot is converted into an easy one. Everyone will turn around; the important thing to do is to turn quickly, and well around. The inclination is to locate the bird first and not turn far enough. Mount the gun while turning and locate over the barrels. Too much swing from the waist tends to result in canted barrels. In shots to the extreme right it may be necessary to shorten the grip of the left hand. For a shot well around to the left, with the target crossing from right to left, raise the right heel while pivoting on the right toe, keeping the left foot flat and taking most of the body weight on this foot. Unless the left foot is in the general direction of the target, the tendency is to shoot behind, because of the cramped position. Whereas these movements sound complicated on paper, there is actually nothing difficult about them. Most people would perform them naturally without instruction.

The importance of proper stance can hardly be overestimated; it is, however, generally underestimated by the inexperienced. Burrard believes that footwork and stance amount to nearly 70 per cent of the total importance in shooting.

It is almost impossible to shoot well from a poor stance. It is well worth while for the beginner to cultivate an easy, comfortable shooting position. This, like so many things in shooting, soon becomes a habit. Queer postures are sometimes adopted by clay-pigeon shots, but the clay-pigeon gun is a very different arm from the field gun. The level ground and the more or less known point of fire also account for the awkward position often assumed by the latter. The stance assumed by the good live-pigeon shot is much nearer the desired attitude of the game shot. However, even with the live-pigeon shots, the stance varies considerably. Roberts, who was one of the finest amateur live-pigeon shots in Europe, stooped forward as if he were almost trying to place the gun butt on top rather than in front of his shoulder, and instances of many other celebrated pigeon shots who assumed awkward attitudes could be cited. However, most good trap shots use a good stance. It is a pleasure to watch J. E. Heistand shoot.

When facing twelve o'clock the body is upright, with a little greater weight on the left foot and with perhaps a slightly forward inclination, but this should not be at all exaggerated. Too much weight on the right foot tends toward leaning backward and over-shooting. This is doubly true with the second barrel, as the recoil of the first barrel had probably pushed the shooter still farther back-ward. Slightly "leaning into the gun" helps in taking recoil, hence helping in an accurate second barrel, but do not overdo it, and for shots in front avoid lifting the right heel. The whole poise should be easy and alert.

The game shot often cannot assume a definite stance, but he cannot shoot well off balance. He must know stance and footwork, so that he can assume as good an attitude as possible under existing conditions. Indeed, it is upon the ability to assume instantly the best stance possible that much of the success of game-bird shooting de-pends. This is true at all times, and is particularly so when shooting in covert or from uneven ground. I knew one excellent quail shot who invariably advanced to the pointing dog by edging forward, left foot advanced. This is, of course, unnecessary, but it is advisable to take a look at the ground and to endeavor to select as smooth a foot-ing as possible. Many good game shots shoot from a partial crouch, with knees slightly bent, but an upright posture is more natural and usually preferable. For birds high in the air and overhead shots a crouch is a distinct handicap. Physique, weight and balance of the gun may require alterations in stance as may different types of shots. Endeavor to be comfortable, easy, and on the *qui vive*.

*Grip of Gun.* This should be natural, but do not carry the right hand too far around the top of the stock. This is a common cause for a bruised finger. The right forefinger is on the trigger guard. The left hand should grip the barrels just forward of the end of the fore-arm, or include the tip of the forearm in the ring and little fingers. Long-armed men may grip a bit farther forward; the reverse may be followed by short-armed men. If one is forced to shoot a gun with too short a stock the situation can be helped by gripping farther out on the barrels with the left hand. Those with extremely square shoulders may find it more convenient to bend the left arm a little more. An exaggeratedly straight left arm is to be avoided as there is a certain stiffness connected with its use, but the extremely short grip is even worse.

The gun is to be raised by both arms, and should balance comfortably and come up naturally pointing at the target. The pointing of the gun is chiefly the function of the left arm. The right helps to maintain the balance of the gun, places the butt properly against the shoulder, keeps it there, regulates the time of firing, and coöperates with the left in pointing the barrels. If anyone will test for himself, he can determine that a moderately straight left arm points more easily than it does if there is nearly a right-angle bend at the elbow. If the left hand is too far back, there is a tendency for the muzzle to sag. A fairly straight left arm also permits better swing.

Grips should be light and easy, but tightened the instant before the trigger is pulled, in order that some of the recoil may be taken up by the arms, especially the left. This is usually done involuntarily, but it is worth cultivating as a habit and aids in the use of a fast second barrel. Fred Kimble believed that half the misses were due to too tight gripping and tense muscles.

*Mounting.* Before mounting, the barrels are pointing forward and to the left, but sufficiently high to clear any near-by dog if an accidental discharge should take place. Immediately before mounting the gun, the butt of the stock should be kept close to the body and, more or less, pressed against the ribs. This assists in accurate placing of the butt in its proper place in the hollow of the shoulder and is of especial help when birds are about to be flushed in front or to the left of the gun. Nichols, in an excellent article entitled "Butt-End Control," particularly emphasizes this point. Butt-end control is easily accomplished with a well-balanced good-fitting gun. In mounting, the whole gun should be brought up level and then pushed tightly to the shoulder just before the trigger is pulled. It is vitally important that the butt be properly placed exactly in the hollow of the shoulder. Failure to do this is a common cause for misses, generally resulting in slow shooting and often in a bruised shoulder or upper arm. It is a common error. In mounting do not square the elbows. Let the act be natural and easy. The right elbow should be somewhat below the level of the shoulder. A black-and-blue mark on the biceps is not so much an indication of excessive recoil as it is of improper mounting. It often results from attempts to shoot too far to the left without turning around sufficiently and properly facing the shot. Practice before a mirror is really worth while, as it shows errors in mounting and cant and many other mistakes. During mounting, too high a muzzle may cut off the sight of the rising bird. The act of mounting should be practiced repeatedly, in order that it may be a uniform, smooth, fast, automatic movement. There should be nothing nervous or jerky about it.

"Dry" practice indoors, such as aiming and swinging at various objects, is of much more value than is generally supposed. One gets the feel of the gun, develops coördination, and hardens the necessary muscles. Next to actual shooting, ten or fifteen minutes' dry practice of this kind every day for a week or so before the season opens is about the best preliminary work a man can perform. It is valuable at all times, but especially so for those who are not shooting much. Practice before a mirror is especially valuable for the novice, because it shows up various errors. The experienced man generally is aware of his mistakes and "dry" practice is needed chiefly in order to reëstablish coördination and dexterity.

*Loading.* It is important to acquire the habit of looking through the barrels before loading. A bit of cleaning material, snow, mud, or a stuck wad from an imperfect cartridge may cause a burst barrel. Every year accidents occur from small-bore cartridges becoming mixed with larger shells. A 20-gauge shell will disappear in a 12-gauge barrel and lodge somewhere in it, and when the gun is opened the breech is empty and the proper-sized cartridge may be inserted. The same thing may happen with a 28-gauge cartridge in a 16-gauge gun. After glancing through the barrels and finding them clear, the gun is loaded by dropping in the cartridges. Ill-fitting cartridges should never be crammed in, but discarded.

When closing the breech bring the stock up to the barrels with the right hand, not the barrels up to the stock. This is done by an easy, smooth movement, with no jerk or jar. An easy way to insure doing this properly is to grasp the toe with the right hand and then raise the butt. This method of closing the breech keeps the muzzle pointing to the ground and the cartridges drop easily into the chambers.

Major Burrard describes a novel way of loading. The open gun is held with the left hand. The right hand is brought under the grip and around the stock, and the cartridges dropped in from the outer side. In order to close the gun it is only necessary to raise the right elbow. This method, like the preceding one, insures keeping the muzzle pointing downward. The latter is a safety procedure and guards against injury from a premature explosion. As a matter of fact, premature explosions from this cause are extremely rare when using factory-loaded cartridges and good guns. In the old days, when reloaded cartridges were frequently used, occasionally a cap would be left projecting beyond the base of the shell and these offered a definite hazard. A plunger which has not returned to its proper place may also offer a risk. In any event, bringing the stock up to the barrels is just as easy and quick as the ordinary method of bringing the barrels up to the stock, and, like many safety measures, should be developed into a habit. Neither bullets, concentrators, nor wire cartridges should be used.

*Releasing the Safety.* This is often called cocking. Unless they have been decocked or the trigger pulled all loaded hammerless guns are cocked at all times when closed, and if the safety mechanism is defective may be discharged at any time. Pushing forward the safety merely relieves a mechanism which prevents the fall of the hammers or the pulling of the trigger. When in the field, some men carry their gun with the safety off practically all the time. This is a dangerous practice, especially when shooting in company, but is perhaps not so hazardous as would at first appear. It is better than the constant pushing back and forth of the safety which may readily result in an accidental discharge through a mistake resulting from the belief the gun was at safe, when really it was ready to fire. Men who carry their guns at ready are naturally extremely careful in the direction in which their barrels point.

The best way for the beginner to learn is to push forward the safety during the act of mounting the gun. Thus the gun is "safe" at all times except when it is about to be fired. It is easy for the beginner to acquire this habit, which soon becomes as automatic as putting one foot in front of the other, or avoiding a stone when driving a motor car. Once acquired, it is the safest method and eliminates balks which occasionally result when a bird flushes unexpectedly. Who has not seen some companion nearly pulling the trigger off in an effort to fire a gun with the safety on? Indeed, the pushing forward of the safety after the flush has for some men a steadying influence, and thereby benefits their shooting.

*Trigger Pulling.* It is questionable if many men know how they pull the trigger, or, in fact, if they have given much thought to it. Certainly there should be no tendency to "squeeze" in the rifleman's sense. Generally, the index finger is placed around the trigger and quickly contracted. Some trap shooters bend the finger from a straight position along the trigger guard and not in actual contact with the trigger when the movement is begun. This is called "slapping" the trigger, in contradistinction to the ordinary method of pulling. Whichever technic is adopted, the movement should be a rapid and firm one, and performed instantly the proper alignment is made. The shotgun adept must be familiar with the amount of force necessary to release the sear, as well as know exactly when the release will occur. Hence the necessity for a good mechanism and not too heavy trigger pulls. Delay in trigger pull spoils time and results in "riding out" the target. Burrard states that bad trigger pressure causes more birds to be missed than any other single fault, except perhaps checked swing. He believes trigger pressure is a more descriptive word than "pull" for what should be done. Anything in the nature of a pull is likely to jerk the muzzle downward. The pull should be a quick and absolutely smooth movement. Faulty trigger pressure can be tested with dummy cartridges, by having someone else load the gun, and by occasionally slipping in a dummy and then closely observing the muzzle of the gun when the effort to shoot is made. Practice with dummy cartridges is the best cure for faulty trigger pressure.

So much for some of the preliminaries. It may not be generally known by the amateur that under good conditions an experienced coach can see the shot in the air, regularly, and that anyone can see it occasionally. Given a clear bright day with good visibility and background, and by standing almost immediately behind and slightly to the right of the shooter, the shot can be seen as a slight cloud which instantly disappears near the target. The shot looks like a little puff of cigarette smoke which evaporates almost as soon as seen. Under certain circumstances a pistol bullet can also be seen. To see the shot, stand in the position previously indicated and concentrate the vision on the clay pigeon. It is more likely to be seen if the target is missed. The man who shoots cannot see the shot. The shot cannot often be seen in the field, and never unless almost back of the shooter. The ability to be able to say, "You were under that clay pigeon," or over or to the right or left, as the case may be, is obviously of inestimable value to the pupil. Tracer cartridges may be used, but they are not altogether satisfactory.

In order to make the subsequent discussion somewhat plainer, it may be well here to describe certain methods of shooting:

*The True Snap Shot.* This is one in which the eyes of the shooter are centered on the target, the gun quickly mounted, and discharged the instant the butt touches the shoulder. There is no correction of aim. Very few men can accomplish this shot successfully with any degree of regularity. It is required very rarely, and if the average shooting man could totally eliminate it from his repertoire, I am convinced he would kill more game. The shot is often used when a bird is flushed unexpectedly. As a result of the loud whirr of wings there is a fraction of a valuable second lost; the reaction in the hunter, that the bird is getting away, sets in; and a hurried snap shot, that usually results in a miss, is made. Many men think they use this method but are unconsciously adopting the corrected snap.

*The Corrected Snap.* In this the gun is quickly mounted, but a well-spent small fraction of a second is taken to correct errors in alignment. There is no dwelling or aiming. The entire procedure appears to the onlooker as one rapid, continuous movement, with the butt reaching the shoulder and the discharge occurring, almost if not synchronously. This is a deadly method and is often the only one possible when shooting in cover, with the exception of the aforementioned true snap. It is so superior to a true snap that there is no comparison. It is preferable to shoot over the back of the bird, i.e., high. All snap shots are emergency shots—to catch a grouse as it dashed through an opening, or a woodcock topping an alder. They are speedshots when there is not time for anything better. Snap shots should not be used when there is time for more accurate alignment. The method employed is largely a matter of habit. It is a bad principle to get into the habit of using snap shots unnecessarily. Needless hurry causes more misses in the field than any other single cause. This is particularly true of quail shooting.

*The Intercepted Shot.* This may be a snap or a corrected snap, but it is generally a slightly more deliberate method than either of them. A point ahead of a crossing bird is selected, an instantaneous calculation of distance, angle, speed of flight, etc., is made, and the shot delivered from the almost stationary barrel at such a point that shot and target meet. In other words, the shooter deliberately fires at some point ahead of the target. This is a safe method in that it eliminates the swing, which may carry the aim back to a companion walking in line. Many good shots use this method. It is fast, and great accuracy can be developed with it. It is the method generally adopted for absolutely straightaway shots, for those straightaway birds which are descending, and often for quartering shots.

*The Swing.* In this the muzzle swings past the crossing bird, and when sufficient lead has been acquired the shot is fired from the forward-swinging barrel. Even in snap shooting there is often more or less swing. Payne-Gallwey refers to jerking the barrels ahead of the target. This is particularly descriptive of the best method of killing high oncoming birds, in which case the target is blotted out by the muzzle. Because the swing is almost involuntary and unconscious, it is hard to describe. There is the mental image of the moving muzzle and the space ahead of the bird, and the bird itself. Exactly how the muzzle gets ahead is hard to determine. Certainly there is no "muzzle chasing," which is fatal to good results. There is no consciousness of the gun, except the muzzle. The swing should start during the act of mounting. Nothing must interfere with its smoothness. The proper swing during mounting will bring the muzzle in the line of flight of the target with almost the necessary lead. The brain transmits the order to pull the trigger as the muzzle passes the target, and the "lag" is converted into lead, as the muzzle continues traveling faster than the object aimed at. If the bird alters the direction of its flight, the eye automatically follows it and the gun muzzle follows the direction of the vision.

It should be explained that "lag" is the reaction time of the shooter—the time consumed while the eye telegraphs to the brain, the brain to the trigger finger, while the hammer falls (lock speed), and the charge leaves the muzzle of the gun—and is almost inappreciable but is sufficient for the fast-swinging barrels to convert this time into lead. According to Foster, recording instruments have shown that it takes various people from 0.018 to 0.030 of a second to pull a trigger after the decision to do so has been made.

When time permits, as it usually does, this is probably the best of all methods, and for most men is far easier of successful accomplishment than the intercepted shot. It is applicable to all angles. The swing is made with the legs and body, as well as with the arms, the body starting to swing as the gun is being mounted. It is hopeless to start the swing after the gun is at the shoulder. It is essential to keep the shoulders level. In shooting to the left, the tendency is to drop the left shoulder, and the right shoulder, in aiming to the right. Unless the shoulders are level, the barrels tend to tilt and canting is a common cause for defective alignment. Good stance, comfortable balance, acquiring the habit of swinging from the waist, knees, and ankles—all have much to do with keeping the shoulders level. Often it is advisable to change the position of the feet in order to more nearly face the target.

A good coach and dry practice before a mirror help materially. The whole secret is to shoot from a swinging barrel. With the fast shot the onlooker hardly sees any swing, so quickly does the shot follow. Follow-through is absolutely necessary. Any checking of swing will result in failure and in shooting behind the flying target. Indeed, checking of swing is one of the commonest of all causes for missing. Checked swing also slows the use of the second barrel. Swing does not, to any practical extent, alter or affect the shot charge or spread out the pattern. Tests have been made at a target moving 30 miles per hour. These showed a lateral spread of four inches. It is to be understood that in all these methods there is no dwelling on the aim or the actual sighting, in the way which may be used when shooting at a stationary object; and, indeed, the fast swing of the upland shooter is quite different from the more deliberate method often employed by the wild fowler. The fact is that most men develop a technic, or combination of technics, which they have found by experience to be the most efficient for their qualifications. Many good shots do not know how they shoot.

Walter O'Neal and his brother were formerly market shooters and rated among the best shots in Ocrakoke—that Mecca of ducks, geese, and brant. One day during lunch we were discussing the question of lead. Both insisted that they invariably aimed at the bill, regardless of the distance or angle of flight. This is obviously impossible. No one can regularly kill fast-crossing ducks—as both these men could do—without more lead than this. It takes a charge of shot about 1/7 second to travel 40 yards, and during this time a bird, at 40 miles per hour, moves forward about 8 or 9 feet. Without doubt, these men unconsciously swung ahead of their ducks. They pulled trigger as their fast swing was about to send the muzzle of their gun ahead of their target, but the lag permitted the unconscious attainment of the proper forward allowance.

The pointing-out method is described in the *Handbook on Shotgun Shooting* as follows:

Begin swinging the muzzle at exactly the same rate or pace as the apparent speed of the target, at exactly the same time. Begin mounting the gun without checking, or altering the swing, with the object of bringing the line of sight to the path of the target at the proper forward allowance, now initiate the pressure on the trigger which will cause the gun to be discharged while in full motion, maintaining its proper forward allowance. The forward allowance consists only of the distance the target will move during the time of flight of the shot charge, all other factors being eliminated by the swinging motion of the gun.

Correct lead is something a man has to determine for himself. Distance, angle, and personal nerve and muscle response must be considered; the two latter vary with the individual and, indeed, somewhat from day to day. One used to hear a great deal about fast and slow powders—as a matter of fact, there is little difference. Even the so-called high-velocity loads require practically the same forward allowance as do the standard loads. The 3–1⅛–6 game load requires a flight time of 0.060 second over 20 yards, 0.097 second over 30-yard range, and 0.137 second over 40-yard range. The heavy 3—3¾—1¼ No. 6 duck load, with 1,444 feet-seconds average muzzle velocity, requires a flight time of 0.053 second over 20-yard range, 0.084 second over 30-yard range, 0.120 second over 40-yard range, and 0.159 second over the 50-yard range (Nichols).

Figures mean little in calculating lead. It is a matter of experience. However, it may help to remember that a bird traveling at 40 miles per hour advances about 8 or 9 feet in the 0.138 second required for shot with a velocity of 1,070 feet per second to traverse 40 yards. Pollard quotes investigations by Nobels which show that from the time the order to pull the trigger is given by the brain, to when the shot arrives at its mark 40 yards away, is 0.212 second. During this period the bird moves 20.41 feet. Muzzle swing, however, converts time into lead and considerably reduces the enormous forward allowance which would otherwise be necessary. In any case, it is apparent why most misses are caused by shooting behind or below. Most game shots are at rising targets, and one is far more likely to kill cleanly by shooting a little too much ahead and high, rather than too far in the rear and low. It is better to err on the side of too much rather than too little lead. Who has not shot at the front bird and seen a bird in the rear fall? It is hard to estimate lead in feet, but a cock pheasant is about three feet long, and one bird's length ahead of him for near crossing shots and two for more distant ones will, for most men, generally result in a clean kill.

The necessity for adequate lead can be demonstrated if the shooter will fire point blank from about 30 or 40 yards at some object floating in a rapid stream. Sometimes a bird is going faster than it appears. I have seen crossing live pigeons missed which had been crippled with the first barrel and were barely able to fly; the gun almost invariably shooting behind because, on account of the slow flight, he feared to lead too much.

*Crossing Shots.* With crossing shots, take the bird while it is still coming on. When two or more birds are approaching or passing it is usually best to take the leading bird first and thereby have more time for a double. Most men wait too long and take the shot when the bird is opposite or has passed, and as a consequence, if they miss, they have to use the second barrel at long range. There is usually plenty of time. The thing to do is to get started early and turn well around. Do not face where the bird is, but where it will be at the time the shot will be fired. Probably most good shots shoot more or less similarly but interpret their actions quite differently. Thus, Churchill, in *How to Shoot*, states, "Your barrel must always be aligned precisely where your eye is looking—apparently you are shooting straight at the bird, but unconsciously you will be making all necessary allowances." And again: "So the shooting man must keep his eye on the bird and ignore his gun." Churchill needs no bush. He is a fine gunmaker and an experienced coach, and, as might be expected, his book on shooting is a valuable one.

Adam Bogardus was one of the foremost live-pigeon shots of his day. For years, when game was plentiful, he was a market hunter, shooting day in and day out through long seasons. Probably no one in this country has killed more upland game. He was of the opinion that most birds were missed by shooting either too low or too far behind.

Leslie Sprake says that there are "in my opinion three details of technique the observance of which is almost essential to the possibility of straight shooting: correct stance, with consequent comfortable balance; continuity and regularity of swing; and instinctive (rather than conscious) aiming." Personally, I like "Middle Wallop's" description immensely, and believe it embodies all the essentials for good shooting.

Lancaster in *The Art of Shooting* describes in detail the mechanics of shooting. His book contains many illustrations depicting stance, grip, lead, and other technic. It is well worth studying. Lancaster is a maker of fine guns and a coach of wide experience.

Curtis stresses the importance of proper timing, lack of gun consciousness, and automatic aiming, rather than sighting or poking, and, in some instances, dwelling on the alignment. The gun should not be tied down to any one system. His chapter on "How to Hit 'em with a Shot Gun" is an excellent one.

Askins stresses stance, mechanics, form, and, especially, timing and confidence. Captain Askins has had an extremely wide experience, and his advice is excellent.

Smith summarizes: "There is usually plenty of time after the game flushes to mount the gun and shoot without hurry, provided we do not unnecessarily waste time at the initial stage of the proceeding. The secret of good field shooting is a combination of deliberateness and speed, timed and blended into synchronized action reduced to a habit which, when boiled down, simply spells timing." Both the novice and the postgraduate can read Lon Smith's book, *Shotgun Psychology*, with advantage. It is one of the best and will repay a second and even a third reading.

This is all good advice, particularly that which refers to unnecessary loss of time during the initial stage. This time is extremely important. If the shooters reaction time is slow he may lose nearly a second from the time the bird flushes to the time he starts to go into action. During this time, if the bird is flying at the rate of 20 to 25 miles per hour, it will travel about 14 yards. At the completion of the second, the shooter decides to accept the shot, takes a stance, brings his gun to his shoulder and fires. This probably requires one-half to three-fourths second. In the meantime, the speed of the bird has increased to perhaps 30 miles per hour and it has traveled an additional 10 yards. If the bird has flushed at 8 or 10 yards it is therefore about 32 to 34 yards away at the time the shot is fired. Of course no one should let a bird get a lead of 14 yards and these figures are only approximate but are given to show the importance of getting started without a delay. There is no way of speeding up reaction time except to be calm and alert. One of the reasons pigeon shooters make better scores at the traps than in the field is that they are keyed up and as a consequence lose less time in the initial stage. For the same reason a man is likely to be quicker when shooting over a point than when a bird flushes unexpectedly. From any viewpoint the time between the bird's leaving the ground and the shooter's going into action should be reduced to the minimum. Let anyone analyze his last half-dozen misses and he will almost certainly find that faster shooting—not necessarily hurried shooting—would have resulted in easier shots. The need for speed depends upon the distance at which the bird flushes and other conditions but slow shooting should be avoided.

Fast, clean kills generally mark the expert. Live-pigeon shooters used to have a saying that "anyone can be fast on a slow bird and no one can afford to be slow on a fast one." From the foregoing quotations the reader can appreciate that there is a general similarity in the advice given. Short quotations are often unfair to an author, and the student of shooting will do well to read the originals *in toto*.

*Time.* Time is closely associated with rhythm. It means a smooth, fast, uniform movement, and firing instantly upon its completion. There has been no delay and no undue hurry. All similar targets are fired at, at about similar distances. Overanxiousness or lack of confidence spoils proper timing. A good coach would prefer to see his pupil shoot, in good time, and miss, rather than poke and hit, in poor time. Uniform good timing is the sign of a finished shot. Men vary in their individual reactions and hence vary somewhat in their time. Individual reaction time (sportsman's time) often varies from day to day. Proper timing is also dependent upon surroundings and may be speeded up or slowed down, according to requirements. Different varieties of game birds possess different speeds, and this sometimes has a tendency to disturb the time of even the most experienced shot. In the Northwest one may shoot Huns for a few days, and find his time far off if he switches to the larger and slower chickens.

After the fundamentals are understood, the rest is a matter of practice; and, as stated, much can be gained by dry practice. This can be done indoors with an unloaded gun, and with discharged cartridge cases, or, better, a pair of dummy cartridges. Do not snap the hammers on an empty chamber. Practice not only at a stationary object, but also swinging at various marks. Be on guard for uneven barrels and faults in stance. Use good style. Remember: the man who misses but does so in good style only needs practice; but he who develops bad form and habits is forever handicapped. This is where practice before a mirror or with a coach is so very valuable.

Clay pigeons in one form or another offer excellent practice. It should be remembered that clays and game differ in one respect— the clay starts fast and tends to slow up, and game birds do the reverse. In all clay-pigeon practice it is well to set the trap so that the target will be thrown fast. In shooting, do not wait for the clay to lose momentum. Try to shoot it while it is rising, for most game is rising. Keep the butt below the elbow until the trap is sprung. The regulation arrangement of the traps is all right to start with, but use a short rise. The so-called "joker" trap, especially if the shooter walks toward it and the latter is sprung unexpectedly, affords excellent practice. The trap may be placed so the target will be thrown among trees or over a bush. Much the same end can be accomplished with hand traps which can have the advantage of real unknown angles. They are inexpensive and available to any-one. Have someone walk with you and throw an unexpected target at unknown angles, deliberately trying to make you miss, and prac-tice those shots which you know you are weak on. This latter may be of great advantage to even experienced shots. Occasionally have clays thrown low over the surface of a pond. By watching where the shot strikes the water, it is possible to determine faults in alignment.

Skeet also offers good practice, but, on account of the necessary speed, is apt, for the beginner, to engender the habit of snap shoot-ing and is not always conducive to a good stance.

Hammond, in his excellent little book, *Hitting vs. Missing*, ad-vises practice at skimmed stones, for the same reason. Sometimes there is a boathouse or other building on the shore. If so, the shooter may stand in the doorway, and, as he gains speed and accuracy, retreat from the door, thus getting low crossing shots, which have to be taken quickly. Practice and more practice is the only key to good shooting. Do not depend on practice in the field, for seasons are too short and game too scarce. Study all misses and try to determine their cause. Wait a moment after a miss and think it over.

Never permit yourself to get sloppy or careless in form and funda-mentals. Try to shoot in good time and style. When in the field do not be satisfied with anything but clean kills. The bird should be centered, not merely knocked down, wounded. Learn to measure distance and do not take shots out of range. It may be a sign of good holding to pull down an occasional bird at a great distance, but for one bird so secured there are a dozen wounded, and good sportsmanship and conservation are unutterably opposed to such practices. There is nothing creditable, but quite the reverse, in shooting at birds which are beyond the killing range, which should previously have been determined by targeting the gun and learning to estimate distances. A cock pheasant is a big bird and often looks nearer than he actually is. As said before, he also takes a lot of killing.

In shooting in the woods the question of distances is not nearly so important as in the open, because most birds that can be seen are in good range. The tendency in thick cover is to overestimate distances, and if the bird can be seen it is generally in range. Over water or against a clear skyline, the reverse is generally true. In all going-away shots the bird is getting out of range fast. In crossing shots this is not the case to the same extent. In crossing shots some men have a tendency to raise the gun to the line of flight and then lower the muzzle before firing—either from too strong a trigger pull or other causes. This so-called "rain-bowing," of course, results in undershooting. It is often the result of a bad stance. In quartering or curving birds it is well to direct the shot to the inside wing, or a bit farther in, in quick-curving or small birds.

*The Second Barrel.* Beginners are apt to be slow with the second barrel. Good time and a fast, accurate second barrel mark the finished shot. Few could equal the old-time live-pigeon shot in the use of the second barrel. Generally speaking, the second-barrel shot is at a greater distance than the first shot, therefore more difficult of successful execution. Hence the importance of the unhurried speed. There is a great difference in being quick and in being hurried. The muzzle is swung from the carry-through of the first shot. There should be no check in this swing, nor lifting of the head, for lifting the head is inimical to good shooting. The cheek should be kept glued to the stock while shifting the alignment. The gun should not, of course, be taken from the shoulder. In its proper place the use of the second barrel should be developed into a habit almost automatic in its performance. If it is not so automatic, and the shooter has to stop and think, valuable time is lost and good shooting time is spoiled. When it is automatic, it is not only faster, but there is less tendency to check swing, raise the head, or displace the gun butt. When two or more birds rise simultaneously, or when a covey of quail is flushed, the more or less subconscious knowledge that a second bird should be killed often spoils the accuracy of the first barrel. This is the place above all others to do one thing at a time. Practice in using the second barrel can be obtained when shooting clay pigeons by loading both barrels and using the second on any large fragment which remains intact. Or two clays may be thrown simultaneously.

Using the second barrel is largely a matter of habit. If a bird is missed with the first barrel, especially avoid any effort to make sure or to dwell on the aim. Increase the swing, force the muzzle ahead, and pull at once. If the first barrel is ineffectual, do not hesitate—always shoot the second. This should be developed to a habit. If good judgment is used in shooting the first barrel, the bird will be in range. If a second bird flushes, ignore it; stick to the bird first shot at. There may be a few exceptions to this, but it is a bad general principle to change birds. In using the second barrel at a stationary target on the ground, such as a cripple, aim at the feet or legs unless the bird is at extreme range. This is especially advisable if the stock is straight. Never hesitate to use the second barrel on a cripple, particularly if it be a pheasant. Use it while the bird is in the air or on the ground, as seems best. Be quick but do not be careless. A bird on the ground can be easily missed.

The preceding advice may be of some assistance, but no one can shoot well without confidence, for confidence in himself, his gun and load is almost half the game. This is another reason why practice at clay pigeons is valuable, for the man who knows he can break a fair proportion of clays has a certain amount of confidence when a bird flushes. A series of misses may throw a man off his form, or a lucky shot or two may help him. Some men develop a sort of stage fright and are never able to do their best in company. It is well worth while trying to develop confidence. Much depends upon temperament. Some good shots are naturally phlegmatic; but the majority key themselves up and develop a kind of alert coolness. *Handbook on Shotgun Shooting* gives valuable advice regarding shotgun shooting at both skeet and trap, and afield. A last bit of advice: shoot with good shots and observe their methods.

*Common Causes for Missing.* This is a subject which I feel particularly qualified to discuss. Misses may result from many causes. It may be that an otherwise good shot is weak in some particular angle or type of shot, perhaps due to an unconscious bad habit, or an ill-fitting, badly balanced gun. If such a man knows his fault, he may force himself to correct it. Most experienced men can generally "call their shots," i.e., can say, "I saw that rising bird over the rim and of course shot under it," or "I checked swing and shot behind." In regard to seeing the rising bird over the rim at the instant of trigger pulling, the foregoing is undoubtedly true, for in order to secure the proper lead and center the steeply rising bird, the target must be blotted out by the muzzle of the gun.

For a gradually rising target some men depend upon a straight stock to throw the center of the charge sufficiently high. The latter is the method employed by many clay-pigeon shots. Much depends upon the angle of the rise and how low the head is dropped upon the stock, as to whether complete blotting out is necessary. It is generally preferable to shoot a bit high rather than low, and hence blotting out or aiming over the back of the bird is usually the better method. However, the amount of upward allowance is like the forward lead—a thing which must be worked out, to an extent at least, by the individual shooter.

Much more hopeless than the man who can call his shots is the individual who thinks he is aligning properly but who always misses a certain shot. Here the capable coach can be of the greatest service.

What causes the average man to miss is often an entirely different problem. Cold, fatigue, a bad night's sleep, mental irritation, headache, worry, improper gun mounting, overanxiousness, lack of confidence, or an ill-fitting gun—all may be factors. But there are many misses which cannot be accounted for on such a basis.

Psychology enters largely into the matter. If it were possible to substitute clay pigeons for the game birds, undoubtedly the scores would improve. Perhaps the most frequent cause for missing is somewhat as follows: The covey roars out, the grouse explodes, or the cock ring-neck gets up making a great fuss and to-do. This startles the sportsman and is worse if the flush is unexpected. Perhaps seconds are lost in locating the bird, after which the shooter loses another instant of vitally important time—eyes protruding and mouth probably open. He suddenly realizes that the bird is escaping, and that something must be done and done in a hurry. He is in a poor stance and off balance, but no matter—a hurried snap shot results. Likely enough the recoil has jarred him from his poor stance, and he is off balance more than before, but, nevertheless, he must make sure with his second barrel. He pokes with this, dwelling on his aim or actually attempting to sight. Swing is checked and an easy shot missed. In short, he has done everything wrong because he let the bird rattle him.

I think something like this accounts for more failures than anything else. Let the man put in a couple of exploded shells and snap them at the next bird or two, and he will see how easy it is to cover them accurately. Some men never get over being more or less disconcerted by the flush of a game bird. Very few, and usually only those having had long experience, can shoot at a hurtling grouse as coolly as at an inanimate target. Note how easy the birds appear during the pre-season, dog-training period, when you do not have a gun. Every marking of the plumage is distinct and plainly visible. Who has not been impressed with the fact that there is usually plenty of time when he has been watching someone else shoot?

Scarcity of game, overanxiousness to kill—both facts militate against straight shooting. If an experienced shot is shooting badly and does not know the cause, it is a good general policy to speed up his shooting time and take more lead, but especially to speed up his time. Attempts to hold more accurately result in dwelling on his aim and worse failure. If an experienced shot is available and will stand back of the man who is shooting badly, he can generally determine the cause. Do not trust an inexperienced man; he will be sure to make matters worse. Many slumps are due to improper timing, and this in turn may result from nervousness, overanxiety, and many other causes. Bad shooting may be due to defects in vision. This defect is particularly likely to develop in men over forty years of age. Correct glasses may rectify the trouble. A consultation with a good ophthalmologist is often rewarding. Lack of practice, too, accounts for many misses. In no game requiring speed or coördination would a player expect to exhibit his best form without preliminary practice, yet the sportsman often goes afield at the beginning of the season—perhaps scarcely having handled a gun for the best part of the preceding year—and expects to perform well.

Although men have different weaknesses, it is well to remember that most birds are missed by shooting behind or below. My own experience with straightaway birds is a case in point. I used to miss this apparently easy shot with almost clocklike regularity. Of course I would occasionally get a bird with the edge of the pattern. Two or three people, who should have known better, told me I was overshooting. It finally got so bad that I came to dread the shot. I was shooting a fairly straight stock, but it did not matter how low I held, the result was a miss.

More or less in despair, I decided to get a new stock, and fortunately was able to obtain the advice of Bob Robertson, the expert coach of the Boss Company and one of the best of the London professional fitters. I told him of my trouble. He fitted the try gun to the measurements I had been shooting. Of the first six straightaway targets I think I knocked a piece out of two, whereas they should all have been mashed to powder. Robertson told me that on every clay I had shot about 18 inches to 2 feet too low. He recommended a little straighter stock, and, incidentally, gave me a little cast-off. This was the best stock I ever had. Here my trouble ended, for, while I still miss plenty of straightaway birds, the number is not out of proportion to my general average. It is not so much the straighter stock but the fact that I now try to hold high on these shots that has cured the matter.

The fact is that straightaway birds are not so easy to shoot as they appear to be. The bird presents its smallest diameter and the vital parts are pretty well protected by the backbone. Most important of all, the shooter is apt not to realize that almost all these apparently straightaway birds are really rising, and, if the aim is on the bird, a low shot results. A low-passing, grass-skimming bird, especially if going to the right, and a grouse diving out of a tree are about the only shots commonly missed by shooting too high. To center all rising targets, the target must be blotted out by the muzzle of the gun. Unconscious swing and lag may result in centering, in the same way that some men kill ducks, by aiming at the bill. If this is not done and the bird is visible over the top of the rim, at the time of firing, it will be missed or perhaps hit by the top of the pattern. As stated previously, it is therefore axiomatic that if a steeply rising bird is seen over the rim at the time the trigger is pulled it will probably be undershot.

If a man gets in the habit of shooting too fast or using snap shots when a more accurate method should be employed, the fault can often be overcome by the temporary use of a heavier gun and one possessing somewhat longer barrels than his regular field piece. However, a little study of the cause of missing, self-discipline, and practice will often overcome too fast shooting. It is a common cause of failure. Fast shooting is desirable, the faster the better, but it should not imply, as it often does, total disregard for alignment.

It may not be generally known that one of the earliest symptoms of slight deafness is the inability to locate the direction of sound quickly. Such a man is greatly handicapped when shooting in cover. At best the interval between the moment when the bird's feet are heard running on the dry leaves as a preliminary to flight, or when one hears the whirr of wings, and the moment when the sportsman goes into action, is short and of the utmost importance. Anything which increases this interval is seriously detrimental to a successful shot. Another thing which often causes delay is bad light. If a man has to wear what are called "distance" glasses, these cut off a little light, and on dark days, especially with a bad background, cause delay in locating the bird and necessarily diminish the time for an effective shot.

To recapitulate, some of the common causes for missing easy shots are: rattles, hurry, snap shooting, poor balance, bad stance, checked swing, slowness in locating the bird, improper mounting of the gun, lack of alertness, incipient flinch, raising the head, attempting to sight, bad time (too fast or too slow), lack of confidence, too much anxiety to kill, and shooting behind and too low. To quote again that excellent instructor, Leslie Sprake, as a parting shot I would advise the novice to be prepared, constantly on the alert, to concentrate, not to lose time, to hold the barrels level, not to check swing, to develop confidence, and be optimistic.

*Cant or Uneven Barrels.* This is one of the bad habits which one may acquire without being aware of it. A canted barrel will throw the center of the charge of shot 3 to 6 feet off the target at 40 yards. Improper grip, poor stance, bad balance—all tend to produce dropping of one shoulder, resulting in uneven barrels. Level shoulders do much to prevent cant, and level shoulders are dependent upon level hips. Smooth, even pivoting depends on the position of the feet. The method of mounting may cause this defect, but is most often developed in an attempt to shoot too far to the right or left, without sufficiently turning the body. Many men swing too far from the hips. If necessary, it is better to move the feet so that the target may be more squarely faced and there is no strain or undue twist of the body—another way of saying that uneven shoulders are at the root of the trouble. Hence, proper footwork and an effort to face the target more definitely often effect a cure. Canting is less frequent in straightaway shots. The important point is to recognize its cause, and this the experienced coach can usually do at once.

*Raising the Head.* During the act of shooting, the pupil of the right eye is immediately in line with the center of the rim and a fraction of an inch above it. Any divergence from this position contributes toward inaccurate shooting. Raising the head has a tendency to cause overshooting. It is also likely to cause the eye to diverge laterally from the line of sight down the center of the rim, and hence to cause cross-firing. As the shooter sees only the muzzle of the gun the necessity of automatically placing the butt in its proper position against the shoulder is apparent. Raising the head may be caused by anticipation of recoil, a form of flinch, or may be done involuntarily in an effort to see the result of the shot. If the former is the case, a change of stance and the adoption of a somewhat forward stooping crouch will often correct the fault, as from this position it is more difficult to raise the head. Other procedures commonly utilized to prevent flinch may be worth trying. A bruised jaw, the result of a badly fitted stock or improper mounting, may cause this trouble. It is usually involuntary and can be detected at once by an experienced onlooker.

*Flinch.* This is a common cause for missing. Even an incipient flinch is fatal to a straight holding. A man may and often does flinch badly without being aware of the fault. The most common cause for flinch is being overgunned. The conscious mind may not fear the result of the shot, but the subconscious mind may dread it. It is not often actual fear of recoil or powder blast, although with some individuals this may almost result in gunshyness. It has been likened to lifting the head while playing a stroke at golf. For diagnosis of this fault, get someone to load your gun without your seeing it, occasionally placing a dummy cartridge in one barrel, and try the result on clay pigeons. A few rounds of this kind will show whether or not there is a tendency to flinch. This is a more severe test than one might think.

The onlooker can usually detect a flinch. Flinch may be caused by overloading, excessive recoil, or powder blast, plus lack of nerve control. The cure is either a heavier gun or lighter loads; a better fitting stock may help and the use of a smaller gauge will often correct the trouble. Powder headache, also, tends to promote flinch.

*Powder Headache.* This is probably an extremely mild form of concussion of the brain. The rapid firing of an unusual number of shots may cause a powder headache, especially if the loads are heavy ones. Overhead shots are particularly likely to produce the trouble. Poor health, a bad night's sleep, indiscretions in diet or drink are all more or less causative agents. Recoil probably plays a part. Powder headache is especially common among wild-fowl shooters. A change of powder is sometimes beneficial. Anything which increases powder blast, such as short barrels, predisposes to the condition.

*Recoil.* Excessive recoil is noticeable when using loads out of proportion to the weight of the gun; heavy, hard, tight wadding and long and tight crimps are also factors. Theoretically, the tendency to recoil is greater when one is using choke bores and small shot. It is always more noticeable when shooting at a stationary target, and when the butt is not held firmly and properly placed against the shoulder. A rubber recoil pad sometimes helps.

The recoil from an ordinary field gun and average load is about 16 to 26 foot-pounds. Cartridges loaded in the United States usually give greater recoil than those manufactured in England, and our loads are generally heavier than those used abroad.

RECOIL IN FOOT-POUNDS OF 12-GAUGE DU PONT SMOKELESS LOADS *
*Recoil in Foot-pounds with Guns of Different Weights*

| Load | Muzzle Velocity Ft. Sec. | 6-lb. Gun | 6¼-lb. Gun | 6½-lb. Gun | 6¾-lb. Gun | 7-lb. Gun | 7¼-lb. Gun |
|---|---|---|---|---|---|---|---|
| 3 -1 | 1218 | 20.5 | 19.9 | 19.0 | 18.2 | 17.6 | 17.2 |
| 3¼-1 | 1314 | 24.0 | 23.0 | 22.2 | 21.0 | 20.4 | 19.8 |
| 3½-1 | 1424 | 28.0 | 27.2 | 26.0 | 24.8 | 24.2 | 23.5 |
| 3 -1⅛ | 1180 | 24.0 | 23.0 | 22.2 | 21.0 | 20.4 | 19.8 |
| 3¼-1⅛ | 1278 | 27.9 | 26.8 | 26.0 | 24.8 | 24.2 | 23.5 |
| 3½-1⅛ | 1376 | 32.3 | 31.2 | 29.9 | 28.9 | 28.0 | 26.8 |
| 3 -1¼ | 1148 | 27.6 | 26.2 | 25.2 | 24.2 | 23.5 | 22.9 |
| 3¼-1¼ | 1240 | 32.3 | 30.9 | 29.5 | 28.6 | 27.6 | 26.8 |
| 3½-1¼ | 1338 | 37.4 | 35.8 | 34.5 | 33.3 | 32.2 | 31.0 |

RECOIL IN FOOT-POUNDS OF 12-GAUGE DU PONT SMOKELESS LOADS *(Cont.)*
*Recoil in Foot-pounds with Guns of Different Weights*

| Load | Muzzle Velocity Ft. Sec. | 7½-lb. Gun | 7¾-lb. Gun | 8-lb. Gun | 8¼-lb. Gun | 8½-lb. Gun | 8¾-lb. Gun | 9-lb. Gun |
|---|---|---|---|---|---|---|---|---|
| 3 -1 | 1218 | 16.5 | 16.2 | 15.6 | 15.2 | 14.9 | 14.4 | 13.7 |
| 3¼-1 | 1314 | 19.0 | 18.9 | 18.3 | 17.7 | 17.2 | 16.7 | 16.0 |
| 3½-1 | 1424 | 22.5 | 22.0 | 21.4 | 20.8 | 20.1 | 19.6 | 19.0 |
| 3 -1⅛ | 1180 | 19.0 | 18.6 | 18.0 | 17.2 | 16.7 | 16.4 | 16.0 |
| 3¼-1⅛ | 1278 | 22.5 | 21.6 | 21.0 | 20.4 | 19.7 | 19.2 | 19.0 |
| 3½-1⅛ | 1376 | 26.0 | 25.0 | 24.4 | 23.6 | 22.9 | 22.2 | 21.9 |
| 3 -1¼ | 1148 | 21.8 | 21.0 | 20.4 | 19.9 | 19.6 | 19.2 | 18.6 |
| 3¼-1¼ | 1240 | 25.6 | 24.7 | 24.1 | 23.4 | 22.8 | 22.1 | 21.5 |
| 3½-1¼ | 1338 | 30.0 | 28.6 | 28.0 | 27.0 | 26.6 | 25.8 | 24.8 |

* Reproduced from *Field and Stream*, April, 1944.

The du Pont ballisticians who recorded the above recoil data are of the opinion that "recoil heavier than 28 foot-pounds cannot be endured for any considerable time"—an opinion that experience proves reasonably conservative, we'd say (Nichols).

Major Burrard states that long experience has proved that a velocity recoil of approximately 16 feet per second is about the maximum that the average man can withstand. This estimate is based upon practice and not upon theory, and upon English standards, in which more cartridges are fired—sometimes five hundred or more in a single day. The late Lieutenant-Colonel John Cobbold is said to have shot 40,000 cartridges in one season. In shooting walked-up game, as is done in this country, comparatively few shots are usually fired, and a little more "kick" is not so noticeable. Men also vary considerably in sensitiveness to recoil. Quite apart from physique, a good deal depends upon stance and method of grip, as well as the nervous make-up of the shooter. As soon as recoil becomes unpleasantly apparent, accuracy is almost sure to suffer. It is particularly important that boys and those learning to shoot be not exposed to excessive recoil. If, even subconsciously, the shooter develops a dread of recoil, all pleasure is gone, and flinch and checked swing tend to develop. Under these circumstances, means should be instituted immediately to reduce it. A better-fitting gun, lighter loads, a heavier weapon, smaller gauge, or better form will usually accomplish this end. A well-established flinch once developed may take some time to overcome, and is fatal to good shooting.

*There is always a best way of doing things, if it be to boil an egg.*
— Ralph Waldo Emerson, "Behavior."

A FEW scouting expeditions before the season opens are useful and are invaluable to the man who depends upon near-by free shooting.

Make all plans beforehand and do all packing the night before. By so doing, things are not likely to be forgotten and one can start off calmly and without hurry or worry. Do not let weather influence you too much. Many an ominous morning is followed by a pleasant day and one can always return if the weather gets too bad. Unless conditions are evidently very unfavorable it is generally better to go.

An extremely early start is not generally advisable; indeed it may do more harm than good. By it both sportsman and dog are often tired before the best of the shooting has started. There is nothing gained by the very early start, so far as quail and grouse are concerned, since these birds do not move around much until the cover has at least partially dried off. Pheasants, however, are early risers, and one can hardly be too early for them. As a rule, woodcocks do not move much during the daylight hours.

The best time to start, however, depends considerably upon the weather and season. During clear, warm spells, when there is little moisture, the early morning is often a favorable time, but, taking the seasons through, from about nine to twelve o'clock and the two or three hours before sunset are the times when quail and grouse are most apt to be feeding and are the best periods for shooting. Pheasants, while feeding a little earlier in the morning, usually feed again late in the afternoon; indeed, both grouse and pheasants often feed more or less all day.

There are many other things besides straight shooting that help to fill the game bag and increase the average per cartridge. Knowledge of the habits of the game sought—their preferred cover and their food at different seasons and times of day—as well as dog handling and the ability of the sportsman to cover ground, are all important factors. A shooting trip should be so arranged that it is a pleasant outing. Everyone likes to get game, but the head of game killed is, alone, a poor criterion. Good weather, fine dog work, straight shooting, pleasant companionship, and attractive surroundings all enter into the enjoyment. A knowledge of natural history, not only of the game sought but of other live things which are likely to be seen, adds immeasurably to the interest of a day afield.

However, the primary object of going shooting is to shoot. Presuming that there are at least a few game birds known to inhabit the terrain selected, and that, if necessary, arrangements have been made or permission secured to shoot on the ground, the following points may help in getting a few of them. Incidentally, in a country strange to the sportsman, information regarding game can often be secured from the country-store which sells ammunition. Inquiries at this source are often well worth making.

Arrange the course as much as possible so that the dog will have the advantage of the wind. In shooting over a restricted area, hunt first around the edges, and endeavor to drive the game toward the center of the preserve rather than over the boundary. In general, work away from the cover rather than toward it, for thus the birds are likely to turn back toward the cover and offer a chance rather than flush wild and fail to present a shot. Furthermore, shots are more likely to be quartering. When working toward cover the birds may run into it and escape.

See to it that all good cover is investigated. There is no sense in walking miles and passing by half the birds. Neither is it good policy to loiter in what is evidently barren country. A slow or moderate pace is generally best. Hunt good areas thoroughly, which generally means slowly. Every man has what might be called his optimum pace, which he can comfortably keep up; but if he goes beyond this he will tire rapidly, and a tired man does not have much pleasure. To the youth it is not so important as to the older man, but even to him there is much in learning to walk afield. The pavement-trained man will tire quickly on rough country. Watch the experienced woodsman slipping through heavy cover: unconscious balance is his secret. He is rarely off center and consequently slips through openings and over obstructions which check the inexperienced.

Get into the habit of looking for "signs." The presence of quail is indicated by the "roosting rings" of white droppings and dusting places. Pheasants leave rather large formed droppings not unlike those made by chickens, or an accumulation of droppings where they have roosted. Woodcock leave characteristic borings and "chalk marks." A few stray feathers are often seen, especially around dusting sites. Footprints may be seen in moist areas or in light snow. Learn to keep a constant eye on the dog, and this will soon become a habit. The dog will find most of the birds, not only because of his sense of smell, but also because he travels much farther than the gun and investigates all the good covers. Give him time to do so, and, if necessary, direct him to spots he may have overlooked. Good handling can do a lot to help him find birds. Get to the dog without delay if he is seen making game. If the dog shows evidence of game and after a thorough search cannot locate it, look over the ground. A hawk, cat, dog or other sportsman may have disturbed the birds. If the quarry has not been killed it is probably in the nearest cover. This hold true especially for quail.

All noise disturbs game, a fact which is often overlooked. The human voice is probably the worst offender. It is a common practice to shout: "Here is a point." If anything is needed to attract a companion's attention, a low whistle, followed by a gesture to indicate the pointing dog, is far preferable.

It is impossible to walk through a long day holding the gun at the ready, but it is possible to carry the gun in such a manner that it can be brought into action without undue delay if one happens to walk up a bird. Even more important is constant mental alertness. No matter how good the dog, the gun will occasionally stumble on an unexpected bird. Try to keep the feet free, and maintain balance at all times, for no one can shoot well when off balance. Quite apart from the discomfort involved, upland shooting is not generally worth while in heavy rain or deep snow. Birds do not travel, but hole up in thick cover. Immediately after a rain is a favorable time. Scent is usually good, the wind has gone down, and birds begin to move about. After a heavy rain pheasants often get on a low branch of a tree or on a fence to dry themselves. In cover, leaves are less noisy and grouse especially can generally be approached more readily. Heavy wind makes for bad scenting conditions, and game is generally wild during it. A soft rain or mist, if not too dense, is often good shooting weather.

When the dog points, get to him as soon as you can. No matter how steady the dog, the longer he is on point the more chance there is for the bird to run or flush prematurely. This is particularly true of pheasants and grouse. In going up to the pointing dog, do so quietly and make as little noise as possible. The properly trained dog needs no orders; he knows you are coming and will remain steady. I stress this because so many handlers, when approaching a point, seem to think it necessary to caution the dog. This may be good policy with a Derby, or half-trained animal, but it is certainly ill-advised with a properly trained dog. It is, of course, a different matter if the dog shows signs of unsteadiness. Constant cautioning may finally result in the dog being unsteady unless spoken to. It is useless and may cause the bird to run or flush prematurely.

With quail or woodcock it is best not to crowd the dog who is working on scent. When using a well-trained dog these birds will usually lie well, and it is preferable to let the dog work out the scent until the point is established. With grouse, and even more so with pheasants, it is of the utmost importance to keep up fairly well with the dog. Even in good holding ground pheasants are prone to run and flush wild. If the gun is well up, a shot is likely to be obtained, but if the sportsman is some distance behind the dog when the bird rises, the latter is apt to be out of range, or at best offers a long shot. Grouse, also, often resort to this trick, but are not as a rule such fast runners as pheasants, and, as a consequence, the dog is easier to keep up with. Of course much depends upon the dog and the cover. It is worth remembering that if the gun stops, or, sometimes, even slows his pace while approaching game, a flush often results. Probably the crouching bird hopes the man will pass, and loses its nerve or believes itself discovered when the stop occurs. This is particularly true of grouse, but it is a habit common to all game birds. It is advisable, therefore, if a stop is to be made, to select a point from which a probable shot is likely to be secured in the event of the bird taking to the air, and to be ready. This habit also accounts for the frequency with which birds flush while the shooter is negotiating a fence or lighting a pipe. A stop on the near side of the fence before climbing over may make all the difference between an easy shot and an impossible one.

To summarize: Walk quietly and promptly to the pointing dog. Do not attempt to sneak up to him. If shooting with a companion, signal him where you wish him to go. Select the best path, so as not to be caught off balance if a premature flush occurs. Endeavor to pick a favorable site from which to shoot. Conditions vary, but it is generally best to come up back of the dog or a little to one side. This is likely to result in a quartering or outgoing shot; however, birds in the open generally head for cover. Carry the gun well up and the barrel level. Be on the alert. Concentrate all attention on killing the bird. The situation is analogous to that of the trap shooter on the score; every pigeon shot recognizes the importance of absolute concentration. Do not talk or encourage your companion to talk. Remember game birds often flush if the approaching gun suddenly stops or even alters his pace, so if a stop is to be made, select a favorable place from which to shoot. The bird is probably watching you and your dog. If your course is one that will take you past the bird on one side it is more likely to sit tight and let you pass and perhaps flush in the rear. In the case of a direct approach, especially if the cover is sparse, it is more likely to flush wild. In thin cover all game birds get under way much faster than when it is thick. If the dog is rigid and intense the bird is probably where he is looking. If the dog appears uncertain, he may not have located accurately or the bird may have run. Sometimes a wagging tail is an indication of uncertainty. Dogs vary in their manner of pointing, and it is an advantage to know the habits of the individual dog.

It is of the utmost importance to locate the bird the instant it flushes. This may mean the difference between an easy shot in good range or a hurried shot at extreme range, or indeed no shot at all. The sportsman generally hears the bird before seeing it—a whirr of wings or the patter of its feet on the dry leaves. Pheasants frequently take a preliminary run, grouse occasionally, quail rather infrequently, and woodcock rarely.

At the first intimation of a flush turn toward the expected bird, if necessary changing stance. At the same time bring the gun to the firing position with butt to the shoulder and locate the bird over the barrels. Do not wait to locate and then mount the gun. If the bird is missed with the first barrel, or more than one bird rises, keep the gun at the shoulder with cheek pressed against the stock, continue to follow the flight of the target, or select a second bird and fire the remaining barrel the instant the alignment seems to be correct. Switching birds is not generally advisable. Concentration, mental calm, alertness, and unhurried speed are the desirable things.

When a bird is known to be in a piece of particularly heavy cover, the "smart" companion will sometimes maneuver so that his partner will have to be the one to go into the thicket, while the schemer stays outside and has an open shot when the bird tops the cover. In practice this is often a good method of getting birds, but it is sometimes a little irritating if you are the one who has to play dog too often, or if the scheme is too obvious. Apart from any selfishness as to who gets the shot, and contrary to the general belief, I think the man who goes in often has the advantage. Even if he does not see the bird when it flushes, or if he misses, he has the satisfaction of not having been beaten by a bit of thick cover. If he will go very slowly, keep on the alert, shoot if necessary at the flash of a wing where he thinks the bird ought to be, it is surprising how often the dog will bring in a dead bird.

The thing to do is to make up your mind that you will not wait for a clear definition, but fire instantly; you cannot be too quick in firing in what appears to be the line of flight taken by the bird. Even in cover so thick that it is almost impossible to get through, such shots can frequently be brought off. Years ago I used to try shooting from the hips. I never could do any good with this method, and I have given it up entirely. Unless the barrels are caught in a vine or other obstruction, it is generally possible to get the gun to the shoulder some way, even if from the kneeling or stooping position. Indeed the old trick of dropping to one knee is often well worth employing. In this sort of work it is important not to accept low shots and to keep an accurate track of the whereabouts of your companion and your dog. This going in, rather than sending a companion, is more apt to result in a shot in the case of woodcock and quail. Grouse and pheasants are more likely to run or go out on the "other side," and this is where two men have a great advantage. In general, the man who handles the dog should be the one to go in, and I suppose because I have usually shot over my own dogs and have shot a good deal alone, I have gotten into the habit of doing so. Of course in some covers the dog can be sent in and the gun or guns work on the outside; but there are other types of cover in which this is not advisable. Furthermore, a dog generally works better and will face the worst kind of cover more readily if his handler is with him. At all events the man who goes in is not always at a disadvantage, and, if his shots are harder than if he had stayed outside, he probably has more of them.

Woods-walking has been mentioned. The man who is constantly choosing the easiest way will not get the greatest number of shots. When walking through thick cover, endeavor to select a path from which it is possible to shoot at any moment. This means freedom from vines and branches, especially from the waist up. It is entanglement of the upper half of the body which interferes most with shooting. Some men seem always to get the greatest number of shots. This is particularly true of covert shooting. It is largely because these men know the habits of game birds, and are willing to face cover and keep their arms free. Be he dog or man, the seeker of the easiest way is not apt to encounter game birds. However, in certain types of grouse cover, an old woods road is often well worth traveling.

Lieutenant Colonel Hawker advised lifting the feet high to avoid disturbances when approaching the pointing dog, and this is not bad counsel. Also, keep the feet free and maintain balance, and be on the *qui vive* for a premature flush. The bird will generally be where the dog is looking, but the best dogs sometimes fail to locate accurately. The importance of selecting a clear path, free from débris, and one which will result in an unobstructed shot, cannot be overestimated. In hunting hedges the experienced dog will work on the lee side in order to secure the advantage of the wind. As a consequence the birds are apt to flush on the windward side. However, apart from an innate habit, the dog is often down wind. If so all game birds are likely to fly away from the dog and hence into the wind. This is especially worth remembering when pheasants or quail are being hunted. It is also worth taking note of the presence of near-by cover. Both these varieties of birds are apt to head for dense cover, and will often break for it despite the presence of the pointing dog.

When shooting with a friend an arrangement should be made early in the day as to which shots are to be taken by each man. When shooting a covey each man shoots on his own side, but on single birds many like to alternate, and I think this is the best plan. A shared bird is always unsatisfactory. When shooting in cover it is often advantageous to separate, so that a shot can be secured no matter which way the bird flies. At all events, make a plan early in the day and do not wait until the dog is pointing to decide what shall be done, or who shall mark. Walk quickly, quietly and without delay, to the point. Often from one side of the pointing dog the shot will be easy, but perhaps almost impossible from the other. The probable course the flushed bird will take must be guessed at, but frequently this can be predicted with considerable certainty. When more than one man approaches the pointing dog or place from which it is thought birds are likely to be flushed, they should keep level. Apart from greediness, this is a safety measure. Furthermore, one man far in advance of the other may prevent his companion from securing a shot. Proper sizing up of a difficult situation is often more important than the actual shooting. The experienced shot will so place himself that he can cut down birds which would have been impossible from another point, or at best have presented a very difficult shot. Pay attention to the sun, so that it will not be necessary to shoot into the glare. I may seem to stress these rather obvious points, but they are factors which will make a great difference in the size of the bag.

As a general rule, the gun should flush the bird. There are exceptions to this with certain kinds of game, but it requires an especially trained dog. If the bird does not flush, the gun should walk ahead of the dog and endeavor to put it up. Pheasants often run, in which case the dog should advance. Keep well up with him. Be on the alert for a wild rise or a bird which may have been passed. It is a hard, and, in the case of quail, an almost impossible feat to head them off from cover, and coming up from the rear is likely to result in the most favorable shot. Occasionally a running pheasant may be circled by a quick run, but the gun has to be careful to get far enough around or the bird may be in the rear.

When shooting alone, if two birds rise, both of which are within range, shoot the one farthest off first. The inclination is to shoot the nearest, which is obviously incorrect as it often results in a long shot at the second bird. Get into the habit of accurately marking all dead birds, and especially birds which are not cleanly killed. Mark the line of flight by some conspicuous object. The distance is more difficult to estimate. One has only to watch a good pusher on a rail marsh to see to what a point the accurate marking of dead birds can be developed. Get the dog to a cripple as quickly as possible. This is the situation in which the dog that breaks shot to retrieve has an advantage, for time lost may readily mean a lost bird.

Attend to securing cripples first; a clean-killed bird may be marked by a broken limb or some other landmark, and picked up later. If a bird is apparently missed, watch its flight. It may be wounded, and in any event is probably worth following. Especially watch any bird which seems to flinch or change its flight at the shot. A small feather floating in the air usually indicates a body shot; these birds should be followed as soon as possible. Good marking, both of cripples and of missed birds, is a habit worth cultivating. Never leave the marking of your bird to your companion, who, likely enough, will be busy with his own affairs.

As soon as the shot is fired, reload at once. If the gun is an ejector take the cartridge or cartridges from your pocket and have them in your right hand before opening the breech. This permits quick loading if there is a laggard. In any event, if you do not acquire the habit of loading immediately, you may find yourself trying to shoot an unloaded gun at the next bird. If the dog fails to find a dead bird at once, give him a little time. The bird falling stone dead has just had an "air wash" and may not give off much scent. Do not walk around too much and disturb the scent—at least until the dog has had a fair chance to find it. If the bird is really dead and you have marked fairly well, it will almost certainly be secured; but it may not be as dead as it looked and may have run.

If the dog fails to find an apparently dead bird in a reasonable time, it is a good plan to start where the bird appeared to fall and to walk in widening circles. If the bird has run, it is better to depend upon the dog. The man has not much chance of finding it. Always keep the gun in hand; a wounded bird may get up and fly.

Try and keep the dead birds' feathers smooth and free from blood. They deserve this much and, furthermore, draggled birds, apart from being unsightly, do not keep so well. There is something distasteful, or almost disrespectful, in the sight of a mass of bloody, rumpled birds being dragged out of a coat pocket. Of course they cannot be kept as smooth as wild fowl, but at least some effort can be made to maintain their original beauty. If there is someone along who is not shooting it may be possible to have him tie up and carry the dead birds instead of placing them in a pocket. This not only keeps feathers smooth, but helps cooling. In fact the pocket is a necessary evil. It is a good plan to lay out game birds in the shade during the lunch hour and to remove them from the pocket for the journey home. If game is to be shipped it will keep better if each bird is wrapped separately in paper. Wet birds should be first dried and all should be cooled by being hung a few hours. Dry ice is excellent for shipping.

Last, remember that shooting is a sport and not a business. Do not let a few misses spoil your day. Everyone misses occasionally. Except for trying to determine the cause and in future correcting the error, forget the misses. Frequent misses undermine confidence, which is vital to straight shooting. We cannot all be experts. From personal experience I can vouch for the fact that it is not necessary to be a very good shot to enjoy field shooting. For the ordinary shot a run of ten or twelve straight quail is something to remember for a long time, while a few misses tend to spoil the day for the man who has a reputation to sustain. Do not make excuses for misses, no matter how valid the reason may have been. Every excuse is worn threadbare and they only bore a companion, even if they are accepted at face value. Excuses are of no interest except to the teller. People soon learn whether you are a good or a bad shot, and nothing you can say will make any difference.

Do not spoil birds for the table by shooting at too close range. If it is necessary to shoot at very close range, use the edge of the pattern. Do not count cartridges. Take advantage of every reasonable opportunity. No one can learn to shoot well by accepting only the easy shots. Do not shoot birds out of range or at birds that belong to a companion, and shoot on your own side of a covey. If a bird is going toward a companion and there is a chance that he does not see it, shout at once "mark right" or "left," as the case may be. This is often very helpful, especially in cover. If he plainly sees the bird, keep quiet.

There is an old rhyme to the effect that a pheasant shared were better spared. Shared birds are always unsatisfactory, and usually indicate greediness or bad judgment on someone's part. Birds are sure to be shared or doubled occasionally, but if it happens frequently it is apt to engender ill feeling, even if nothing is said openly. Never accept a shared bird, certainly not the first—insist on your companion taking it. In case it is doubtful who should shoot at a bird, the best plan is to shout at once: "Your bird!" This prevents all confusion as to who shall shoot, and should eliminate the "shared" and "spared" birds.

Years ago, in Maine, I witnessed an amusing incident. My companion was one of the best and fastest covert shots I have ever seen. Our guide was old John Morton, a fine dog trainer and a reliable, though rather slow, shot. My friend, for some unexplained reason, missed his first two or three birds, and old John, who had never seen my companion before, got the idea that he could not shoot, and, purely in the goodness of his heart, explained to me that at the next opportunity he would shoot synchronously with my friend, and then pretend that he had not shot. It was none of my business, and I held my tongue. Every experienced man knows how sometimes a bird will be shared without either party being aware that the other has shot. John worked this plan successfully on the first bird, winked at me, loaded without being seen by my friend, and tossed him the retrieved bird. Wonder upon wonders, he succeeded in doing the same thing on the next woodcock; but the third time he tried it he was a fraction of a second late and my companion evidently realized why John had been crowding upon him when he shot.

Nothing was said, but I could see my friend was much irritated at John's attempting to steal his shots. For the next hour or two he cut down every one of John's birds, blowing some of them to pieces, before old John could get a chance scarcely to mount his gun. Finally, John lost his temper, and remarked that the next day he would leave his gun at home. My friend then asked John why he had shot his birds when we first started out. John did not like to own up to the reason why he had done so. It was evident that the joke had gone far enough, and that considerable friction was developing on both sides, so I explained. Both were fine fellows and had a good laugh over the matter, but I do not think there was another shared bird during our entire week's shooting.

If a companion shoots, and you cannot see the result of the shot, do not shout, "Did you get it?" Nothing is gained, and if the bird has been missed it does not lessen the discomfort to have to own up to a failure. If shooting with a friend, give him every advantage. This is doubly true if he is shooting over your dog, or if he is a novice. A greedy shot is the worst kind of companion and soon gets a bad reputation and is on a par with the chronic "claimer." If at the end of the day you have more birds than your companion, insist on dividing the bag equally, and if there is a question, make him take the major share. Practice safety at all times—in short, conduct yourself in the best sense of that much abused word, "sportsman."

Do not disregard the rights of landowners. Trespass signs mean just what they say. Permission to shoot can generally be secured if a little tact is used in approaching the landowner. He has definite rights. Place yourself in his position. Do not damage fences, leave gates open, or shoot near stock or building. Farmers are generally coöperative if they are shown consideration. Disregard of their rights leads to the erection of more "no trespass" signs.

When you have arrived home you can look after your own needs and comfort. Your dog cannot. See that he is freed of burrs; carefully examine his feet for thorns, burrs, cuts, and injury to his nails; if wet, see that he is rubbed off and kept in a moderately warm place until he is dry. Give him his food, fresh water, and a pat on the head, and see that he is comfortably bedded. Then see to yourself and your gun. I have no patience with the pseudo-sportsmen who neglect their dogs after a hard day's work.

*Where the snow powdered hillside rings hard to the tread:*
*He is not for the pick-up,*
*Hark, there is his hoarse hiccup*
*Afar mid the twilight, blue jowled a chill,*
*The splendid old rascal who laughs at us still.*
—Patrick Chalmers, *Green Days and Blue Days.*

COMMON NAMES. Ring-necked pheasant; ring neck; Chinese pheasant; Denny's pheasant; Oregon pheasant; rooster or hen.

*Field Marks.* "This is the largest of the New England game birds— the only one with a long, streaming, folded, tapering, pointed tail. The head of the male appears black, the breast bronze, the sides yellow with black spots, the tail barred blackish. The female is brown, slightly scaled on the back, and lighter below, with a shorter, barred, pointed tail; flight is noisy, but not so much as that of the ruffed grouse" (Forbush). On being flushed the cock frequently emits a series of loud cackles. The hen weighs 2 to 3 pounds and the cock from 2½-3½ pounds. There is on record a cock that weighed 5 pounds, 14 ounces, and Sharp in *The Gun: Afield and Afloat,* mentions one an ounce heavier. I have killed a wild cock that weighed a full five pounds—an unusually large and very fat bird. Weights vary somewhat in different sections. Birds are heaviest in the fall.

The ring-necked pheasant of today is somewhat of a mixture of various strains. For those interested in the natural history of the pheasant, William Beebe's standard monograph is recommended. The pheasant is a bird of ancient lineage and is mentioned in the works of Martial, Aristotle, Pliny, and Aristophanes. In *The Forme of Cury* which is stated to have been compiled by the chief master-cook of King Richard II, is a receipt "fare to broile

180

Fesant, Plruch [partridge], capons and curlew" which carries back to 1381.

In 1790 Governor Wentworth and Richard Bache, son-in-law of Benjamin Franklin, introduced pheasants on the former's estate in New Jersey. George Washington is believed to have liberated several pairs at Mount Vernon. These and other early attempts to establish them in America failed. The first successful stocking was done in 1881. These Chinese birds were secured by Judge O. N. Denny, American Consul-General at Shanghai, and liberated in Oregon. His shipment consisted of twenty-eight ring-necked pheasants. They were pure, or nearly pure, *Phasianus colchicus torquatus*. Others were introduced later. From the first the birds did well. Eleven years later, the first day of the first open season was estimated to have yielded 50,000 pheasants.

The first English pheasants stocked in the East were introduced by Rutherford Stuyvesant in 1887, and were finally established, after several unsuccessful attempts. In 1894, S. Forehand, of Worcester, Massachusetts, secured some birds from Oregon. These pheasants were used as a breeding stock by Mr. Brackill, Chairman of the Massachusetts Commission of Fisheries and Game, and their progeny later liberated.

It was soon recognized that pheasants were desirable game birds, and that they thrived in this country. Other importations, mostly from England, followed; state and private game farms sprang up, until at the present time the pheasant is well established in most areas in which it is likely to thrive. According to a survey made by the Fish and Wildlife Service in 1940, there were 2,029 licensed breeders of pheasants in North America.

Since its introduction into this country some sixty-odd years ago, the pheasant has steadily increased in numbers. Today in many states sportsmen kill more pheasants than all other species of upland game birds combined. There is an open season in 18 states. A single state has reported an annual kill of more than a million. In Pennsylvania some of the state is mountainous, and not all of it is suitable for the pheasant. However, the state kill in 1941 was 537,990 pheasants, and in 1942 (despite the cartridge and gasoline shortage and the fact that many men were in military service) the state bag was 463,794 compared with a kill of 337,969 of all other upland game birds combined. Records from the Dakotas and other parts of the West show even larger bags.

The English pheasant is usually a hybrid. The pheasant was originally an Asiatic bird and was introduced from Asia into Europe and then the United States. It is thought to have been brought to England by the Romans. It is recorded to have been introduced into Europe 1,250 years before the Christian era (Daniel's *Rural Sports*), and into Britain in A.D. 1299, during the reign of Edward the First (Echard's *History of England*). Forbush states that probably the first to be acclimated in Europe was the English pheasant, which, a native of Transcaucasia, is said to have been brought from the river Phasis in Colchis by the Argonauts of Jason's expedition in search of the Golden Fleece, hence the name *Phasianus colchicus*, derived from its nation's river and country. The pheasant now found on the bank of that river (now known as the Rion River) is the Rion Caucasian pheasant *(Phasianus colchicus)*, which closely resembles the original English pheasant and gives color to the tale of its origin.

Among those most frequently brought to this country were the so-called English pheasant *(Phasianus colchicus)* the Chinese pheasant *(Phasianus torquatus)*, and the Mongolian pheasant *(Phasianus versicolor)*. These have now more or less interbred, with the result that a purebred bird is rarely observed. Mongolians are the largest and the English black-necked is supposed to lie a little better to a pointing dog.

Pheasants thrive in a moderately mild climate, provided there is adequate food and cover. They are not sufficiently hardy to endure the hard winter of some of our northern New England states and other areas where prolonged snows and extreme cold are likely to occur. During severe sleetstorms pheasants have been found frozen to the ground by their tails, a phenomenon which suggests that during the winter they sometimes roost on the ground. They thrive in a farming country, and, perhaps more than any other of our game birds, are adapted to semi-civilization. They have done well in the Northwest, but, so far, have been a failure in the Deep South.

In most areas pheasants are increasing in numbers. The Chinese variety seems to be more easily acclimated than the English birds. In its native land of Asia the pheasant is a dweller in river valleys, marshes, low level grounds and low, rolling, scrubby country and forested hills. It thrives best in a similar terrain here. The bird likes grain fields, especially corn, wheat, and oats. Pheasants frequent small woods with briary undergrowth, swamps, grassland, and moors, but are not often found in deep woods. They must have gravel, and, as a consequence, are often found around overgrown disused gravel pits. They like water, and frequently are discovered near small streams or on the overgrown banks of ponds or small lakes. When necessary, pheasants can swim well.

In summer and fall, pheasants roost chiefly on the ground, but in cold weather they are prone to resort to trees. They roost lower in stormy, windy weather. Young conifers are often selected. In some localities tree roosting is more common than in others. Occasionally a flushed bird will light on a tree, and if followed by a dog may be seen turning its head and watching the animal. Pheasants also light in low trees or on fences in order to dry themselves after rain; but, as a general rule, they keep to the ground. When the ground is covered with snow, pheasants have been seen "budding" in trees. In hard winters they may come to the barnyard and feed with chickens. The pheasant is a handsome, intelligent, aggressive bird, and quick to learn how to care for itself and adapt its habits to its environment. During the shooting season old cocks especially may be found hiding in all sorts of odd places, sometimes deep in the woods or in cover near some dwelling house.

*Voice.* During the mating season the cocks are especially brilliant, and their loud, raucous crowing is frequently heard. In southern Pennsylvania crowing is heard most frequently during the latter part of May. Cock pheasants crow more or less all the year around but especially during the spring and early summer. Cocks also crow during periods of excitement—when flushed, the cock often gives voice to a loud, raucous, machine-like cackle, which continues for several seconds. Old cocks are more likely to cackle on being flushed than young ones and their voice is louder and more metallic. Hens do not cackle on being flushed. In captivity, both hen and cock have been heard to emit other notes—a sort of crooning has been described as indicating satisfaction and is often heard at feeding time, and while dusting. Cocks also make an inquiring "putt-putt" while walking from place to place. There is also a sort of grunt which expresses anger. Hens cluck to their chicks, and cocks frequently crow on going to roost. At the mating periods, cocks conduct themselves somewhat in the manner of the domestic rooster, strutting and flapping their wings.

*Courtship.* The cock pheasant is polygamous. Breeders usually allow four or five hens to each male, but under some conditions the bird may acquire a much larger harem. During the breeding season fights between the cocks are frequent. These do not usually end fatally; but I have seen wild birds with blood on their heads and necks, exhausted, but so intent on their fight that it has been possible to approach them in an open field within easy gunshot. This, however, is unusual, and I doubt if many birds die as a result of these mating fights.

Encounters between cock pheasants and domestic fowls have been observed. Old cocks on a shoot are a mixed blessing. If they survive two or three seasons they become extremely crafty and difficult for a dog to handle. They usually develop long, sharp spurs and are bad fighters. When one happens to be shot it is inferior for the table. However, they provide breeding stock and are valuable in this respect. During the winter the sexes separate to a large extent, although mixed groups are sometimes encountered. Among adult pheasants gregariousness is least common during the late summer. During the mating season, the cock, like the domestic rooster, often calls up a hen, when he finds a choice bit of food. Cock ring-necked pheasants have been known to mate with domestic fowls, pea fowls, gray-hens, even the turkey, and will breed readily with many other varieties of pheasants. The progeny of a pheasant and a domestic hen is called a Pero.

*Nesting.* The nesting site is usually under some rank vegetation, but sometimes is on fairly open ground, often at the edge of a wood, under a hedge, in the shelter of a bank or in a hayfield. Pheasants are especially fond of alfalfa fields and bushy pastures. The nest is sometimes placed against a tree trunk. Instances have been recorded of nests in trees, and, sometimes, in the deserted nest of another species, but these cases are unusual. Roadside nests are frequent. The nest is a shallow saucer-shaped depression in the ground, sometimes scantily lined, and surrounded by dead grass, the leaves of coniferous trees, and other débris.

In Pennsylvania egg-laying occurs from about mid-April to late June. The incubation period is from twenty-three to twenty-five days, and is accomplished by the hen, although instances have been recorded in which the male has performed this function. Unless the nest is destroyed, there is usually only one laying a year. The eggs are from eight to sixteen in number. Larger clutches have been recorded, but they have probably been the product of two hens. The eggs are ovate, olive brown, pale blue or bluish-green, and average about 1.41 by 1.18 inches. The purebred Chinese ring-necked pheasant is said to lay pale bluish-green eggs, spotted with a deeper tint.

The chicks are covered with down and can run almost as soon as they are hatched. They are buff or rufous buff to dark yellowish-brown above, with dark stripes on the back and head, and a dark spot on the ear region. Below, they fade gradually to yellowish and white, with more buff on the breast, sides, and flanks. Some have a dark spot on the thighs.

*Molts.* Juvenile plumage, which is acquired by complete postnatal molt, is completely shed (beginning before the young are grown) excepting the two outer primaries; and the first winter plumage, with the exception of the two outer primaries (which are pointed), is like that of the adult. Adults have one complete molt annually, finished in September or October (Forbush). Pheasants have the reputation of being indifferent mothers; but I agree with Leslie Sprake that this is not true of wild pheasants. In captivity, however, it is a different story. The care of the young rests with the hen, but on two occasions I have seen it taken over by the cock bird. In both instances the young were half grown, and being molested by dogs. The hen was not seen in either case, but the efforts of the cock to divert the dog from the young birds was unmistakable and persistent. If birds ever looked distressed and worried, these two cock wild pheasants did. Occasionally, old sterile hens will destroy eggs and young chicks. This is not uncommon in captivity, but probably less frequent in the wild state.

The young chicks cannot fly, but by eight to ten weeks of age they are capable of short, rather weak flights, and at three months they can fly with fair strength. At the latter age, or somewhat before, the male and female poults can be differentiated by their plumage. By mid-October, or somewhat earlier, the birds have assumed adult plumage. Occasionally old hens or those that have reccived a wound in the region of the ovaries may assume male plumage, and instances have been recorded in which cocks have assumed hen plumage. The former is less rare, and the latter metamorphosis is more complete than the other phenomenon. Under such circumstances a clue to the correct sex may be found in the smaller size, shorter tail, and difference in head plumage. The only instance that I myself have seen was in a young hen bred in captivity. The resemblance to a male was, however, striking, and, if the bird had been seen in the field, it would almost surely have been mistaken for a cock.

*The Melanistic Mutant or Black Pheasant.* These are dark birds, more or less covered with greenish and bluish iridescence. According to Leslie Sprake these are a new type of pheasant, bred from English birds, and were first noticed by Lord Rothschild, at Elveden, in 1888, and recently have become common in England. They are not a cross between two species. The young are black and brown chicks. The soles of their feet are white. The melanistic mutant is said to lie well to a dog, and to rise high on its initial flush. It is also claimed that they roost in trees more frequently than the common ring-necked. I have had no experience with them.

*Food and Economic Status.* Pheasants are known to injure some farm crops, especially corn and tomatoes, and occasionally peas, fruit, and potatoes. Pheasants are omnivorous feeders. The food varies in different sections and at different times of the year. According to J. Pearce, in McAtee's *The Ring-Necked Pheasant,* pheasant food in the Connecticut River Valley, Massachusetts, consisted of wild seeds, 32.5 per cent; grain, 26.3 per cent; insects, 19.6 per cent; leaves and grass, 11.6 per cent; fruit, 10.0 per cent. Most of the grain was waste; of the wild seed much was from injurious weeds, and large proportions of the insects were harmful. Cutworms were found to be a favorite food. Dalke in the same book reports that, in Michigan, 92 per cent of farmers stated that injury done by pheasants was of minor importance. As a matter of fact, harm done by crows is often attributed to pheasants, especially the pulling of young corn. It is significant that those states which contain the greatest number of pheasants are among those yielding the heaviest grain crops. Miss A. F. C. Eveshed investigated the crops of 303 pheasants, and found that while grain was present in 10.69 per cent (much of it waste grain picked up in the stubble), 16.41 per cent of the food was insects. After four years' study, and the examination of 188 birds, Collinge states that "apart from their value as game, they merit the protection of all interested in agriculture." From the West have come a number of reports of damage done to crops by pheasants, but there the birds are present in unusual numbers. Most scientific studies of this problem show that pheasants do far more good than harm, and that in the aggregate they are highly beneficial birds.

A special report of the Massachusetts Board of Commissioners on Fisheries and Game reported finding the following injurious insects in the crops of pheasants: coddling moth—adult and larvae; apple maggot—adult and larvae; tent caterpillar—adult and larvae; tussock moth—adult and larvae; cherry lice; plant lice; June bug; tree borer; curculio on plum, peach, and apple; elm-leaf beetle; mosquito; house and blow fly—adult and larvae; Gypsy moth—larvae; brown-tail moth—adult and larvae; and rose bug.

Pheasants are great insect eaters, devouring caterpillars, worms, and slugs. They also like roots, acorns, beech mast, young clover, alfalfa, berries, grains, and weed seeds. In the fall they eat a great deal of grain, but chiefly the droppings after harvesting. At certain seasons weed seeds constitute a large part of the pheasant's diet. Pheasants seem to like sphagnum moss. Whether they eat the moss or seeds, or insects which may be present, I do not know. While shooting, I have often found birds in a bed of this plant and it is worth remembering that such spots should always be investigated. The first hour after sunrise is spent in moving about and in search for food. The birds then feed for about two hours. They start again two or three hours before sunset and continue until roosting-time. In bad weather, feeding time is often irregular and upon occasions the pheasants may feed off and on all day.

There is a belief that pheasants occasionally kill young rabbits. It is, however, a fact that many heavily populated pheasant ranges in Pennsylvania and New Jersey contain a great number of rabbits.

*Stocking Pheasants.* Pheasants are roamers, and it is useless to attempt to stock them unless the area contains adequate cover and, of even more importance, food. Without a liberal supply of food, pheasants will leave. At least three hundred acres should be under control, for less than this is certain to result in a high percentage of loss due to birds going over the boundary. From four to six hundred acres is preferable, permitting more frequent shooting and a smaller proportion of loss due to straying of the birds.

Presupposing that there is plenty of suitable food, a roosting swamp and cover, there are three chief methods of stocking:

1. Old birds, in the proportion of one cock to four or five hens, may be liberated two or three weeks before the egg-laying season. This is about, or a little after, the time the new grass becomes noticeable in sheltered locations. Birds can be secured for this purpose from any reliable game farm. It is important to make sure that the birds are breeders, not too old, and that they can fly properly. Place the crate near and facing cover, let the birds settle down, and then permit them to walk out. Great care should be taken not to frighten or to force them to fly. In the latter event, the bird may fly until exhausted, and fall an easy victim to a predator. It is advisable to scatter a little food near the cover three to four times a week, at least for a time.

Birds should not be liberated during bad weather. The morning is the best time. It is better to hold the birds over night rather than liberate them late in the afternoon, when predators are likely to destroy them before they become oriented. There are many mishaps which may occur to the breeding stock, nests and young, before the next shooting season, and some will roam away but with ordinary luck twelve hens should produce about twenty to twenty-four cock birds for shooting, and a like number of hens. Much depends upon weather, vermin, and other factors. I have had fairly good success with this method. Doubtless a proportion of the breeding stock is destroyed as pen-raised birds are particularly easy prey to all sorts of vermin. However, the chicks have the advantage of a mother, and the birds available for shooting are wild birds.

*The Pheasant Breeding Manual* gives some valuable hints for the amateur breeder of pheasants; also *Upland Game Propagation*, and Bailey and Nestler in *The Ring-Necked Pheasant*, edited by McAtee.

2. Twelve- to fourteen-week-old poults may be secured and planted, generally from mid-August to mid-September. Grasshoppers and other food are usually plentiful at this season. At this age, the young birds should be able to fly well. They should be fed regularly after they are released. The feeding tends to hold the birds, and if they once acquire the habit they will return regularly to the place at which they are accustomed to find feed, and this despite the fact that natural feed may be abundant. Young pen-raised poults are particularly vulnerable to all vermin, and a fox or cat will return time and time again as long as a young pheasant remains. Poults cost about a half or two-thirds the price of adult birds. Personally, although this is a recognized method of stocking, my own experience has not been so satisfactory as it should have been. With a gamekeeper to protect them and provide food this is doubtless an excellent method, but if turned out and forced to shift entirely for themselves, my impression is that many poults fail to survive or fall victims to vermin. When poults have been put down, the birds killed are young ones, and therefore preferable for the table.

3. The third method is to turn down adult birds during or just before the shooting season. This is rather artificial, but despite captivity the pheasant always maintains its innate wildness. However, much depends upon the quality of the birds that are liberated. If the environment and food are good, and the birds are given a sporting chance, i.e., not shot for a few days after being turned down, there should be about a 40 to 60 per cent return or better. In one large public shooting grounds, when pheasants were liberated twice weekly, there was a return of 77 per cent. In another,

in which birds are liberated each morning, the return is 84 per cent. From a shooting club in New York where the pheasants are liberated the night before, there is a return of about 70 per cent, and in a Pennsylvania club, at which pheasants are liberated early in the morning of the shoot, the return is about 73 per cent. The above figures refer to shooting over a dog and are seasonal averages. It is obvious that the longer the birds are at liberty, the greater is the loss. It is best to liberate a few each week or at shorter intervals. There is no need to waste sympathy on the dropped bird. It can look after itself quite adequately in a day or so, or even immediately after the liberation. It is definitely a mistake to turn them all down at once and expect them to provide shooting throughout the season. Recently planted pheasants lie better to a dog than birds raised in a wild state, and the shooting is apt to be at a little closer range. However, while recently dropped pheasant shooting is not in a class with shooting wild birds, it may have to be this or nothing, and, as a matter of fact, it is more sporting than the inexperienced would imagine. When pheasants are to be shot shortly after planting, they are best scattered over the preserve, a bird or two being put down here and there. If the cover is thick and food and water available, they tend to stay near where they were planted for a few days at least. It is a good plan when shooting to take a couple of quarts of feed and scatter it in suitable places. At all events they should be fed regularly.

In addition to these methods, eggs may be secured and hatched under a domestic hen, and the young liberated as either poults or adults, or poults may be purchased and raised to maturity. Banding of stocked birds should offer a means of determining the best method of stocking. If this were carried out by a state game commission, in a few years data could be accumulated which should be conclusive as far as the best method is concerned. There seems to be a growing opinion among sportsmen that the putting down of ten- to twelve-week-old poults is on a par with stocking small fry in a trout stream—a large proportion fail to attain maturity. In 1945 the New Jersey Fish and Game Council advanced the age of young pheasants which they liberated to sixteen weeks and reported improved results. The question of pheasant-raising is not a difficult one. Of all our game birds they are the easiest to raise, and are quite hardy after they have arrived at maturity.

Both the Mongolian and the English black-necked are good for stocking purposes. Smith states that it is more economical to buy mature or half-grown birds than to attempt to raise small lots, i.e., less than one thousand. However, with fifty or one hundred birds the expense is not great, and it is a good plan to start the first year in a small way. If eggs are to be hatched, engage the eggs early from a reliable game farm. Also arrange to get some setting hens. These should be healthy, and well dusted with insect powder at least twice. All broodies should be set on dummy eggs for a day or two before being given pheasant eggs. This is to make sure they are setting properly. The average hen can accommodate fifteen to eighteen eggs.

The nest should be disinfected previously and should be on the ground. Place an inverted sod in the bottom of the nest and cover with a little short hay. Nest boxes should be well ventilated. A few days before hatching, disinfect and clean the coops and set them out on the rearing field, in order that the ground under them shall be dry. Never use ground on which chickens have been raised. In selecting a rearing field, bear in mind the fact that insects are an important item in the diet of the young pheasant, hence a moderate growth of grass is preferable. Sunshine plays an important role. Some time before setting out the coops, eliminate all vermin, especially rats, weasels, skunks, cats, and crows. Coops should be rainproof, and arranged about 50 to 60 feet apart. The chicks should be dry and active before being transported to the coops. Surround the coops for the first few days with a small run of fine-mesh wire, in order to prevent wandering. Provide a few branches for shade and cover. Coops should be moved to a new site every day.

Sprake recommends the following (Leslie Sprake's directions, as well as those of Lawrence Smith and W. W. Bailey and R. B. Nestler, should be read in detail by those contemplating the rearing of pheasants):

For the first week: hard-boiled eggs, chopped very fine, with scalded biscuit meal slightly impregnated with codliver oil, made and given four times a day. After the first week the same as before; but a little meat added, and dried off with whole ground barley meal, with a little spice to make it attractive in flavor—made and given four times a day. When the third week arrives, a little boiled rice can be added and the meat proportion gradually increased—but the droppings of the birds must be carefully watched, and if there is any sign of scouring, the meat proportion must be reduced. Similar feeding can be continued for the rest of the time on the rearing field; but boiled wheat and ribbled maize can gradually take the place of the egg allowance. This mixture should always be well dried off with whole ground meal, so that it is tacky.

The more insects that the young pheasants get, the better. I have had good success with this feeding, but have always had trouble with vermin, and for this reason have recently purchased poults or grown birds as needed. It has been suggested that incubator-raised pheasants are not so well fitted to look after themselves when liberated as are those hatched in the wild. As indicated previously, my experience has been that all artificially raised pheasants rapidly revert to the wild when put down.

Pheasant shooting is largely a matter of money, and there is no reason for not shooting them down to the last bird if so desired, as more can always be purchased. If no hens are shot there should be a fair proportion of these left for breeding stock during the following spring. When one has enough birds to provide sport "cocks only" is a good rule and is of course necessary in most states unless a special license is obtained.

Much can be done to improve cover. Clean farming is an enemy to all game. A little uncut grain or grass along the fences and in the corners, undrained swamps, briar and honeysuckle patches in otherwise useless land all help. Brush piles may be left, instead of being burned. Toward the edge of a wood a few small or medium-sized trees may be felled, so that all fall inward. This pile may be planted with honeysuckle, or, even without this, it soon becomes covered with weeds and berry-producing vines, and makes a fine shelter for pheasants and grouse. Pheasants especially like honeysuckle.

Corn and small grain scattered under bits of cover help immensely to hold pheasants. Corn goes much farther if cracked, and is not so apt to be carried away by squirrels, rats, and mice. Another

P. T. Jones

A good shot in open country.

P. T. Jones

Irish Setter Champion Bryan of Tyrone.

P. T. Jones

Gordon Setter Champion Brownside Bonnie of Serlway.

English Setter Field Trial Champion Beau Essig's Don.

Champion Maro of Maridor. Best of English Setters, Westminster Kennel Club Bench Show, New York, 1940.

English Springer Spaniel Field Trial Champion Fleet of Falcon Hill.

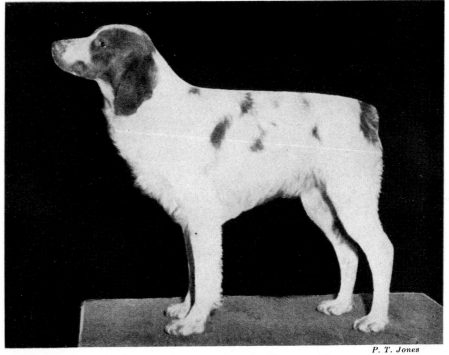

Brittany Spaniel Brit of Bellows Falls.

Nice dog work by a pointer and a setter.

Lebanon Tim owned by the Lebanon Kennels and winner of many field trial championships. A fine type of the modern working pointer.

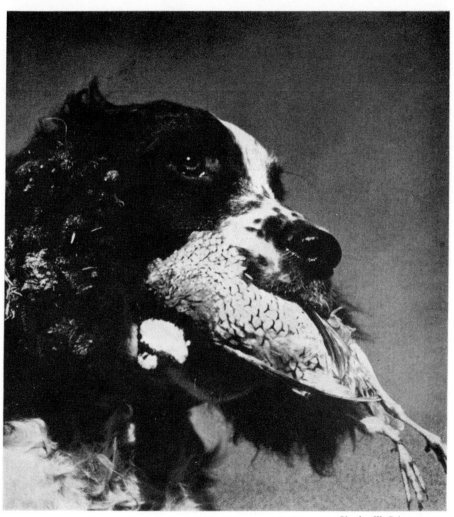

A case for de-burring.

Twenty-third Annual Dog Show of the Tuxedo Kennel Club, 1941.

A clean kill of a quartering bird. Note moderately extended left arm and the position of right elbow. Good shooting form.

Demonstrating good form and a clean kill.

P. T. Jones

Two pheasants have been flushed almost simultaneously. This picture demonstrates two important details: (1) the bird farthest away has been shot first and (2) it has been killed without undue delay. As a result, there is ample time for a double. Note the conspicuousness of the white ring around the neck of the cock.

It is a target at which to aim rather than the center of the body.

P. T. Jones

German Short-haired Pointers in varied poses.

Cock Ring-necked Pheasant. Showing an excellent method of providing corn in winter. (*See page 193.*)

A rocketing pheasant. The long tail is prone to result in shooting below and behind. In order to center the head and neck, the bird must be blotted out by the muzzle of the gun.

The fast-going Maryland Dan has literally slid to a stop. However, before the gun could get up, the pheasant started to run.

The dog follows the running cock pheasant for a hundred yards.

As a result of faultless dog work the bird is finally forced into the air in the open, providing an easy shot. The pointing dog is behind the brush on the right.

Ruffed Grouse.

*Courtesy of "Field and Stream"*
Drumming Grouse.

*Above:* Night flashlight photograph. Note the "Venetian blind" effect of the drumming wings. The line of the breast is distinctly visible through the primaries. The widely spread tail does not show in the picture. Photograph by Mr. S. W. Reese, Wisconsin Conservation Department and by courtesy of *Field and Stream.*

*Below:* The camera stilled the action of the drumming wings. Photos by S. W. Reese, Wisconsin Conservation Department.

Bobwhite.

*Photo by Captain Nelson Page. Courtesy of "Field and Stream"*

Quail Eggs Hatching in an Incubator.

Note the neatness and symmetry with which the eggs have been opened. In the wild, hatching is a critical time for the chicks and many are destroyed by vermin or ants. Considerable odor is emitted from the nest and this facilitates detection by dogs, cats, skunks, etc. The cheeping of the newly hatched chicks also tends to attract predators.

An eight-bird covey.

Bobwhite cock incubating eggs in a domed nest.

A single quail and a promising young English Setter. Owned
by Mr. E. M. Queeny of St. Louis.

Dr. Norris with Lad and Sadie. Abernathy Farms, February, 1930.
*(photo use courtesy of George Bird Evans)*

"The Little Purdey." Willed to author's friend George Bird Evans.
*(photo use courtesy of George Bird Evans)*

excellent way to supply corn is to take a number of sticks, each about eighteen inches long, sharpened at both ends, and thrust one end into an ear of corn and the other into the ground. This method is easy, preserves the grain, and is particularly useful when there is snow on the ground. It is best to place feed under some cover (honeysuckle, briars), since, if placed in the open, it will be eaten by the crows. A little grit should be added to the feed when snow is on the ground.

Self-regulating feed boxes are inferior to placing the feed on the ground, because so many animals and birds, other than pheasants, steal the feed. Automatic feeders are excellent in deep snow, however, or shelters may be made and feed placed under these. Shelters are necessary for winter feeding and it is vitally important that feeders be kept free of snow. Shelters should be open at both ends, in order to permit escape in the event of a predator suddenly appearing. Feeding, especially winter feeding, tends to result in concentrations of game birds. These concentrations draw predators of all kinds, so if feeding is to be carried out, predator control is doubly necessary. The planting of small patches of suitable feed, preferably near good, natural cover, is the best of all ways to supply an adequate quantity of feed. What to plant should be governed by the soil, climate, and length of season. The local Farm Bureau will supply information regarding adaptability. Corn, barley, alfalfa, sweet clovers—all are excellent. Buckwheat is liked by pheasants and quail, and can be grown on poor soil. It is an early crop and very nearly gone by the shooting season. Corn is good, but if cultivated assiduously leaves little cover underneath.

L. B. Smith in his *American Game Preserve Shooting* recommends 1 bushel of oats, 1 bushel of barley, and 16 quarts of sweet clover to the acre. This provides cover and food.

Smith's is an excellent book, and should be read by everyone interested in the subject. It contains detailed instructions regarding raising pheasants, quail, and ducks; vermin control; creating a preserve; legal matters, as well as much valuable information for game management as required for this country.

The Western Cartridge Company recommends the following mixture, which is sufficient for one acre, but is often best divided into smaller patches: Kaffir, 3 pounds; Sudan, 1 pound; Black Amber, 3 pounds; Buckwheat, 2 pounds; Orange Amber Cane, 3 pounds. Giant Japanese millet has been recommended. The large variety of sunflowers produce excellent feed, but are apt to be eaten by blackbirds before they fall to the ground.

Good land breeds game is a true saying. Soil improvement and soil conservation is often an important factor in game management and in the long run may be more valuable than stocking.

Pheasants have been known to live more than eight years but among wild birds the average life is much shorter. In some localities three-fourths of the cocks are killed during the first week of the shooting season. The highest mortality among hens occurs during the reproduction period, mowing causes the greatest number of these fatalities.

*Predator Control.* Shooting disturbs Nature's balance. It is ill advised to spend time and money, only to have a large proportion of game destroyed by predators which have no season, since they work day and night throughout the year. The destructiveness of different kinds of predators varies in different locations and at different seasons of the year. In some localities, the fox may be the chief offender, and in others it may be stray dogs or cats. No unselfish person would wish to destroy all the red foxes in a hunting country, but, on the other hand, when those animals get too numerous and destroy large quantities of game, something must be done to regulate their depredations. Foxes have a special predilection for pheasants, and in a non-hunting country should be destroyed by every legal method. In southeastern Pennsylvania, gray foxes have increased greatly during recent years, and now outnumber the reds in many localities. They are quite as destructive to pheasants as the reds and seem to possess a special appetite for these birds as well as for rabbits, grouse, and quail. They are not popular with fox hunters and there is no reason why they should not be destroyed by every legal method. Audubon saw a gray fox quartering a field and utilizing the wind like a pointer. On encountering scent the fox drew to the covey and leaped on the quail, one of which was secured.

Cats are bad offenders, and this is not limited to the semi-wild variety. On many farms, cats are kept out of doors or in the barn, for the purpose of killing rats and mice. Many, however, prefer birds, and young game birds are particularly frequent victims. Stray dogs, especially those containing some bird-dog or hound blood, also often develop the habit of destroying nests, eggs, and young. Skunks, raccoons, minks, and weasels are evil neighbors, and in many places rats are a menace, especially to ground-nesting birds, and particularly to birds in confinement.

Even the most ardent bird lover has little good to say for the great horned owl. Fortunately, the great horned owl is not particularly plentiful, but when present in a game country is sure to be destructive. Migrations of snowy owls occur occasionally, during severe winters, to New England, and when this occurs these birds are very destructive to grouse, and will take pheasants if they are available. The same may be said for the Cooper's and sharp-shinned hawks. The goshawk and duck hawk are destructive, but they are relatively uncommon in many localities. Large flights of goshawks sometimes occur as they did in the winter of 1906-07. When present these birds do great damage to game birds. I have seen a female marsh hawk take a full-grown wild hen pheasant, and it is probable that all hawks will occasionally kill game birds. Forbush cites conclusions arrived at after an examination of the contents of about 2,700 stomachs of eleven varieties of hawks collected in New York. Of these, five were admittedly injurious, namely, the goshawk, the Cooper's hawk, the sharp-shinned hawk, the duck hawk, and the pigeon hawk. Two others, the red-tailed hawk and the marsh hawk were doubtful. Of the four remaining, three were found to have eaten either poultry, game, or other birds.

The results of stomach analysis of hawks and other birds of prey may be misleading. How long parts of a game bird remain in the stomach in a condition which can be identified is not known. Feathers and bones are usually disgorged as a ball or pellet. It is common to read the report of a series of stomach analyses of a certain species which, perhaps, showed that only 1 or 2 per cent contained game birds. Such data are usually furnished without reference to the abundance or scarcity of game in the area from which the hawks were collected. Stomachs negative for game-bird remains means nothing if the predators have been secured in areas barren of game, and are of little significance if collected where game is scarce. To prove that the hawk is not a game killer one must know that it has been killed where game is abundant. Even large series may not average up.

The subject of bird predators is one requiring careful study. Abroad, nearly every bird that, even occasionally, destroys game birds is liable to be destroyed by keepers, but even there the more intelligent sportsmen recommend sparing certain species, sometimes on account of their rarity or handsomeness, or because their beneficent qualities counterbalance their injury to game-bird life. However, conditions abroad are different from those obtaining here. Furthermore, aside from the fact that some of our hawks and owls have been proved to be genuinely beneficial, some are protected by law, and their indiscriminate destruction would soon get the overzealous game-bird protector in trouble.

Far from being an enemy to wild life, the true sportsman is its defender. It is surprising how large a number of song, and other interesting, birds will soon collect on a preserve in which vermin are controlled. A hawk or owl may be beneficent at one season and destructive at another; in one locality it may be valuable, yet do great injury to game in another. Thus, while the Buteos may take young pheasants—or even in some cases adult birds— on the other hand, in the South on game preserves where cotton rats are particularly destructive to quail, these hawks more than counterbalance the occasional quail they kill by their destruction of rodents. It is commonly claimed in extenuation for these birds that the chief food of the larger Buteos is the rabbit. However, the latter is the chief game of the majority of those who buy shooting licenses.

Again to refer to the southern preserve, Stoddard, who has given the question of quail preservation most intensive study in his *The Bobwhite Quail,* strongly and properly recommends the elimination of the domestic cat. Doubtless cats kill cotton rats, but it is a question of the study of large groups of so-called predators to determine whether their activities are chiefly for good or for evil. Pheasants, particularly around game farms and in heavily stocked preserves, are particularly vulnerable to the attacks of predators of all kinds. Such areas attract predators. In general, when game birds are plentiful, predators are numerous, so that some means to check their serious inroads into the game supply must be taken.

During the egg-laying and chick season, game is destroyed by crows, jays, and snakes, as well as by many animals. The pole trap is one of the most practicable methods of destroying birds of prey. The trouble with pole traps lies not only in their cruelty, but also in the fact that they destroy many harmless and some-times valuable birds, and, thereby, lay the owners of such traps open to legal action. Indeed, some states have passed laws against their employment. They are especially useful around breeding pens or rearing fields. They should be so placed that all can be inspected from a convenient central point. The catch should be filed "hard," so that only heavy birds will spring the trap when lighting on the pan. By wrapping the jaws with hard cord some leg-breaking of larger birds can be prevented, and small birds, unless injured or killed when the trap is sprung, may escape. Traps should be inspected frequently, but this can hardly be done at night.

Indeed, all steel traps which do not kill should be frequently inspected, else needless suffering will result. I confess to a dislike of the pole trap, and indeed to the steel trap in general and greatly prefer shooting when this is possible. However, sometimes all methods have to be resorted to. I do not like the use of poison, and moreover its use on bait may destroy a dog. Even when placed in a tree or under ground, there is danger of its being displaced or dug up.

An egg is an excellent trap-bait for crows and jays. Tunnel traps are effective for weasels. These consist of a tunnel made from three pieces of old board about two feet long and six inches wide. The steel trap is set inside. No bait is necessary. Large box traps are effective for cats. Foxes are best caught with steel traps. Two or three should be concealed around the remains of any kills which are found, or near the earth. A fresh rabbit skin nailed to the trunk of a tree at such a height that the fox has to stand on its hind legs or jump to reach it, is an excellent bait. One or two steel traps are placed on the ground immediately under the skin. If steel traps are employed care must be exercised to ensure that all the traps are sprung or taken up before shooting commences. A dog caught in a steel trap is extremely difficult to release, especially so for the lone handler. It must be done quickly or in his struggles the dog is sure to injure himself and under these circumstances the best of dogs may bite. Sometimes the shooting jacket can be thrown over the dog's head and a muzzle improvised by wrapping a necktie or a belt around his muzzle and tying the end at the back of the neck.

Skunks, raccoons, opossums, black and water snakes are all injurious to game. In addition to trapping, a vigorous crusade by shooting is advisable. A good, small-caliber rifle, equipped with a telescope sight, is an excellent weapon in the hands of a good shot. A duck gun loaded with super X also makes an efficient weapon for this purpose. One method of killing crows is by the use of a stuffed owl as a decoy. Place the owl on an upright pole, in some favorable locality, and build a blind nearby. This, in conjunction with a crow call, is one of the most effective methods of destroying these pests. Shooting is unfortunately ineffectual against the many night predators.

Pheasants frequently nest in hay fields. When this is the case a very high proportion of nests, eggs, and young pheasants are sure to be destroyed by the mower, it being not uncommon for the hen to be killed with her brood or on her nest. Unfortunately, the hay-cutting season coincides with the nesting period. In many localities the mower does more to decimate the pheasant population than all other factors combined. In a single field adjoining my farm six pheasant nests were destroyed in a single morning. A game protector of Lehigh County, Pennsylvania, reported 1,500 pheasants' eggs recovered from 123 acres of alfalfa as it was being mowed (quoted by Smith, *American Game Preserve Shooting*). Bennett reports that acts of man, chiefly mowing, were responsible for 56.6 per cent of destroyed nests. He further adds that 30 per cent of nest destruction was caused by predators, the skunk and crow being the chief offenders.

The destruction of nests and eggs by mowing is difficult to prevent. Various types of flushing bars have been invented, the idea being that when the bar flushes the hen, the knives are lifted, leaving an uncut strip which contains the nest. I have experimented with flushing bars, and whereas they do good, those I have used have by no means been entirely satisfactory, for despite every effort some nests and even birds have been destroyed. Unfortunately, hen pheasants sit tight, especially toward the end of the incubating period, and the modern tractor-mower combination travels at considerable speed.

The bar on the flushing apparatus should be arranged well in advance of the knives, and should not bend down the grass and so entrap the hen that she cannot escape. Flushing bars would probably be quite effective with a horse-drawn mower, but the horse is rapidly being displaced by the tractor. Furthermore, many farmers do not like pheasants, and most will not take the trouble to use or go to the slight expense of securing a flushing bar. From my observation I do not believe one farmer in five hundred uses a flushing bar, unless he has been paid to do so by someone interested in game protection. This is a subject which might well be studied by game commissioners.

A small bonus to farmers for each successful hayfield nest would seem to be an excellent investment and a cheap way of obtaining pheasants. Successful nests could be checked by the local warden. Perhaps some plan whereby an efficient flushing bar could be made available to farmers at cost price could also be worked out in connection with the bonus system. Furthermore, such a plan would stimulate farmers to secure a head of pheasants on their land. Any scheme, to be successful, must show the farmer a worthwhile profit. An increase of twenty-five cents to the cost of each shooting license would probably finance such a project.

If the nest is destroyed and the hen is not injured by the mower, she generally lays a second time. Second clutches are usually smaller than first. However, the pheasant possesses a strong nesting instinct—probably stronger than that of any of our native birds. This is an important factor in their survival, especially in farming districts. Moreover, there is evidence to show that second or even third nesting attempts are made with little delay. This is true of most game birds, whether the nest is destroyed by dogs, mowing, or weather conditions. Research has demonstrated that about 75 per cent of hen pheasants will produce young before the season is over. However, late hatching may increase the mortality among the young birds. If the eggs are hatched and the entire brood perishes, the hens do not usually lay again the same season. It is on the theory that a second clutch of eggs will be laid that some game preservers in Europe remove the first set and hatch them artificially. Cold weather and heavy rains destroy many young birds. Floods and severe winters have occasionally nearly exterminated the pheasant population in certain areas. Dry weather during the nesting and rearing season favors a good crop and excessive rain usually results in a subnormal number of young birds in the shooting season. Studies by P. E. Randall, of the Pennsylvania State College, show about 20 per cent of nesting success among wild pheasants. This does not take into consideration second nesting. Randall places the average at 9.7 per cent chicks per each successful clutch. In the area studied by this investigator, 25 per cent of nests were in wasteland, 22 per cent roadside nests, 27 per cent in hay fields and 29 per cent in grain fields.

Spraying with arsenate of lead, D.D.T. and other insecticides in beetle-infested and other areas doubtless takes a toll of pheasants. It is difficult to strike a true balance in these ecologic problems. It is a common practice to burn brush and weed patches. This destroys cover, and, if done late in the spring, is likely also to destroy many nests. If burning must be done, it should be minimized and performed prior to the nesting period.

The entire question of private stocking and game protection depends upon how deeply one wishes to go into it and how much money one is willing to spend, for, after all is said and done, it is largely a matter of dollars. One or two men may rent two or three adjacent farms and get fair shooting at the expense of a small outlay, by judicious stocking and some form of recompense to the farmer for his work—which may be much or little, but should certainly consist of posting against trespassers and an honest endeavor to keep off poachers, often the chief problem. Run-down farms are best and they can also be rented more cheaply. The area should contain cover and natural food; if there are marshes or an overgrown stream, so much the better. If the area contains some wild pheasants, it is a good sign, and if it contains a few quail, woodcock, or grouse, naturally this is an additional asset. Areas barren of game generally indicate insufficient cover or feed, or may mean an abundance of vermin or much poaching. Areas in which there have been much free shooting and no attempt to keep trespassers off are much harder to control. A nearby speed highway is destructive to game, dangerous to dogs and an invitation to poachers.

Much depends upon the character of the landowner. It should be made plain that the owner must give up all his own shooting privileges and coöperate with the lessee in improving the shoot. A written lease should be drawn up. Sometimes the farmer has a son who can be utilized to trap fur-bearers or some scale of recompense can be arranged for vermin destroyed. Another method is to pay the farmer for each head of game killed on his property. The entire problem is largely a matter of money to the farmer, and it has to be made worth his while.

I shot last year on a preserve which was run as follows: one dollar was paid the farmer for each head of game killed on his farm by the lessee; one dollar was paid for each predator killed on the farm, and two dollars were paid to the farmer for each hayfield nest which hatched out. The farm was 400 or 500 acres in extent. The first year the plan was in operation the money paid for predators was the chief item. Now this bulks small and the other two items have increased enormously. In addition, the farmer now raises a few pheasants each year. Judging from results, it seems to have been a successful plan.

The ideal farm is not too modern. Clean farming means little game. Fallow fields, overgrown rail fences, briar and weed patches, swamps—all offer good covers. A small stream is an asset, as is the pond or small lake. Small grain and corn are favorable crops. A more satisfactory plan is to establish a licensed preserve. This involves the payment of a fee to the Game Commissioner, whereby, if certain rules and regulations are carried out, longer shooting seasons may be had, hens may be shot, and state limits are not enforced. Game Commissioners would do well to encourage such preserves, as they are a splendid method of securing free stocking of adjacent territories. The twenty-fifth biennial report of the Connecticut State Board of Fisheries and Game proves this statement conclusively. During the season of 1942-43, 5,475 game birds were released on preserves operated under state regulations. Of this number only 47.4 per cent were killed on the preserves. The longer the season permitted for shooting on such preserves, the more pheasants will be put down, and consequently the greater will be the number escaping to adjoining territory. Furthermore, the more favorable the regulations formulated by the state game commissioner covering the establishment of such preserves, the more frequent they will become. Some state game commissioners recognize the value of private preserves, but apparently others do not. This applies to both private preserves and public shooting grounds, at which a fee is charged for the shooting privilege.

The California game management plan seems to be working out well (K. M. Bradford in *American Field,* June 10, 1944). This plan embodies many of the features found in the pay-as-you-go public shooting preserves of New Jersey. I have heard the argument used that a certain number of state-raised wild pheasants are killed in such preserves. This may be true as far as a few birds are concerned, but a preserve which is putting down even a small number, such as a hundred or two, is losing many times more than it gains, and if it is liberating some thousand or more birds per season, will lose many hundred per cent more than it gains. Far from being undemocratic, the private preserve is the best means of stocking adjacent territory and insuring good free shooting in the neighborhood.

When renting ground for a preserve, a long lease is desirable, provided the grounds are suitable. Under proper management, the shooting should improve each year. Although it is a never-ending conflict, a large proportion of the predators should be eliminated during the first year. It takes time for poachers to learn that they will be strictly dealt with. If hens are spared, and food and cover available throughout the year, in a few seasons a supply of hens should be built up and, if shooting is not too heavy, it may be necessary to put down only a few cock birds in the spring. On lands where free shooting is permitted probably 75 per cent of the cock birds are killed in the first week of the season. The alternative to making a private preserve is to join a shooting club. This is often the easiest and most satisfactory solution.

State game laws are now necessarily so restrictive, both as to length of season and bag limits, that there is a definite desire among shooting men to secure more liberal bag limits and a longer shooting season. If sportsmen are willing to pay for this privilege, and at the same time to improve the shooting for others, they should be encouraged and not hampered in doing so.

Every year more land is posted. Indeed, many farmers look on game as a nuisance, as it attracts unwanted trespassers. Furthermore, no matter how efficient the Game Commissioner, the sportsman cannot expect much return for two dollars, which is the price of the average state shooting license. In England, the climate and many other conditions are different, but in a recent issue of *The Field* (London) there is a report from a 500-acre shoot which for the last four years has averaged over 1000 head of game per season, including pheasants, partridges, hares, and various other game. This report demonstrated what can be done on relatively small acreage.

It is a great mistake to shoot a small preserve too frequently. It is better to shoot a preserve thoroughly once or twice a week than to potter around with a gun and dog daily. The latter plan is sure to result in driving the game off the preserve. Pheasants especially will not stand being disturbed too frequently.

*Shooting Pheasants.* Pheasants are plentiful in many localities. They are hardy, wily, adaptable birds, and, given proper environment, can survive heavy shooting. In some ways the pheasant takes the strain off our higher-class native game birds. On the other hand, the increase in pheasants undoubtedly tends to bring more gunners into a field, and this militates against the latter. At all events, the bird is here to stay, and is popular with most gunners. The pheasant quickly learns to take care of itself and shortly after the season opens, old cocks are often found in queer places, sometimes deep in the woods or in thick cover, where they lie most of the day. Old overgrown gravel pits are a favorite location.

Mention has been made regarding the type of cover in which pheasants are most often found. In some years, there is considerable standing corn left during the early part of the shooting season. When this is present in a pheasant range, it is almost sure to hold birds. It is a generally poor place for pointing dogs to work. Ground cover is often ·sparse; dogs are soon lost sight of; and pheasants do not hold but tend to run and flush out of range. Sometimes, when two or more guns are shooting together, a gun may be stationed at one end of the field and the field beaten toward the stationary shooter. For choice, the gun should be placed up wind, in order to give the approaching dogs the best chance. However, while standing corn often holds birds, it is often not a very satisfactory type of cover in which to shoot. Thick cover adjacent to corn or other grain fields and swamps, especially if, in the latter, there are some small trees or bushes, or good holding grounds for pointing dogs and almost sure places in which to find pheasants if any are in the neighborhood. Owing to the running proclivities of the pheasant, always hunt every cover out to the extreme end. It is often at the far edge of a cover that the running bird will be found.

In common with many game birds, but especially quail, pheasants in cold weather, after filling their crops, love to rest in some sunny spot that is protected from the wind. Often a ditch bank, the foot of a hill, or a warm slope is chosen. In order to get the full benefit of the sun, the site selected is often comparatively free of low ground cover. Two or three pheasants are frequently found together in such a place. When two or more pheasants are found together they are usually wild, and hard for a pointing dog to handle. On flushing, there are not likely to be any real laggards, but there is sometimes a slight interval between their taking-off. They generally scatter and each bird takes its own course. Occasionally, especially with stocked birds, two may fly off together.

As with most game birds having a wide distribution, methods of hunting vary in different localities. As in all shooting, knowledge of the habits of the game sought is necessary if any degree of success is to be hoped for. Pheasants are early risers, and tend to be found feeding in the open for two to four hours after sunup; they then usually return to cover and come out to feed again in the middle of the afternoon. This is particularly true of cock birds, in a hard-hunted country, and late in the season. Sometimes they feed more or less all day.

As frequently stated, pheasants prefer to give "leg bail" rather than to fly, and usually, while on the ground, follow cover during the course of their movements from place to place. It is not uncommon, however, for them to fly to and from their feeding grounds. Hedgerows are favorable avenues of travel, especially so if they connect feeding grounds and cover. Giving due consideration to the direction of the wind, it is, other things being equal, best to direct the hunt away from, rather than toward, a swamp, and if cover tends to become narrow, to hunt toward the small end.

Early in the fall, cocks and hens are frequently found together; later they often separate. Under certain circumstances pheasants will leave a field long before the man and dog enter. A few years ago three of us were shooting in a strip of woods bounded on one side by a single-track railway line. Occupying this tract were one or two grouse which usually got up wild and flew across the railway. In an effort to circumvent these wily birds, a gun was stationed on the railway track, while another gun and myself went through the woods. My friend who went through the woods with me had with him a young dog, and, as a consequence, there was considerable noise. No grouse were seen, but no less than one hen and three cock pheasants were observed sneaking across the rails. These birds were far ahead of both men and dogs who were working the woods.

A few days later, in the same place, the performance was repeated, except that in this case only two pheasants were observed. In neither instance were any pheasants found in the woods. All had escaped by running, long before gun or dog had approached them. I have seen similar behavior under different surroundings a number of times. A certain proportion of wily old cocks will regularly run as soon as they are aware of the approach of man or dog, and if they do this early enough, the dogs become confused, and this despite the fact that pheasants give off a strong scent. Pheasants can run fast and far—another reason for quiet while hunting.

At best, wild pheasants do not lie very well to a pointing dog. A moderately fast and intelligent dog which is well broken on quail will usually handle pheasants and soon become accustomed to their peculiarities. I do not believe that it is harmful to the dog's training to work him on pheasants. To a dog out of control, of course, the running proclivities of pheasants often end in exciting the animal, making him harder to handle. Young pheasants lie better than old birds, and in September these birds are satisfactory for training purposes. The ideal pheasant dog depends chiefly on body scent, but if the bird runs and the scent begins to wane, he will move on and relocate. Many excellent fast dogs will slide in and pin the bird, but if the bird starts to run will follow, but not closely enough to cause a flush. This permits the gun to keep up and usually results in a shot being secured which would be lost by any other type of dog work, except circling, and it is not every dog that will run around a running bird, and fewer still that can do it properly. If the dog follows too fast and will not slow on order or the gun does not keep up, a flush at a distance almost invariably results, usually within range of the dog and out of range for the shooter. The pace at which the pheasant runs is to some extent dependent upon that of the dog.

The moderately fast dog is apt to come on the bird suddenly, and may force it to squat or hold, but the slow trailer pins fewer birds. It is true that, with the latter, the gun may follow alongside the dog and get a shot, often at long range, when the bird finally takes to the air. It is on this principle that the slow-trailing beagle is sometimes employed. Some of these dogs become very adept in handling pheasants in this way. The well-trained springer is to be preferred for this kind of shooting. Whether or not a pheasant will lie to a pointing dog depends much upon the cover in which it is found. On bare ground they will never lie, and rarely if the cover is sparse. However, it is surprising in what thin cover a pheasant can hide. Corn fields often look thick, but many are really quite bare on the ground. The same is true of some briar patches. Heavy marsh land and thick weed patches are usually good holding cover. Stubble is moderately good holding cover but is more favored by hens than cocks. A bird, running ahead of a trailing dog, may squat if it comes to a heavy bit of cover, but once started it is apt to run until it puts considerable distance between itself and the gun. It is almost sure to flush if it comes to a patch of bare ground.

As stated, the pheasant that definitely starts to run is rather infrequently pinned. If the trailing dog, who to all intents and purposes is pointing every step of the way, attempts to dash in and make the bird squat, it generally has the opposite effect and puts the bird in the air. Most of the pheasants that are pinned are come upon suddenly by the dog while the bird is in good holding cover and can sometimes be seen crouched in a clump of cover ahead of the rigid dog. If the bird happens to be found on fairly bare ground, it is prone to run, and if pressed unduly by the dog will almost surely resort to flight. Both sexes are apt to run, but cocks, especially late in the season, are particularly likely to do so. The running pheasant is generally sneaking off and not by any means putting its best foot forward, as it does if wounded. A man traveling at a fast walk can keep up with it and with the trailing dog. However, the behavior of the bird varies, and probably depends upon a number of factors. All pheasants are prone to flush wild, but are much more apt to do so on the approach of a man than a dog. Dropped birds that have been free only a short time, while exhibiting the same general tendencies, are more likely to hold and are easier for a dog to handle. The moral of all this is that, if the dog is trailing, it is of the utmost importance that the gun should try to keep up so that a shot can be secured, and to be on the alert for a raise some distance ahead.

Why a game bird allows itself to be pinned or holds for the pointing dog is an interesting problem. Some species hold much more readily than others. Some men think it is due to a sort of mesmerism on the part of the dog. Certainly some dogs seem to get a higher proportion of productive points than others. However, this can be explained on other grounds. Another more likely theory is that the bird crouches in the hope that it has not been seen, and remains immovable in order to escape detection. This idea is strengthened by the fact that the bird is more likely to "freeze" if it is in cover which more or less conceals it, while on bare ground it does not so often resort to the trick. Fright caused by the dog's sudden appearance and close approach also probably play a definite part.

A running pheasant often makes a preliminary run in order to get up speed before taking flight, or may momentarily pause on coming to the edge of a bare spot. In the former event, if in the woods, tne bird can often be heard running on the dry leaves. At all events, the sportsman should be prepared for the flush when a bare place is approached. The bird generally raises diagonally. If the pheasant is pinned he may raise diagonally, or, if at the edge of a wood or in a covert, may rocket up almost perpendicularly. I have frequently stated that I believe most birds are missed by shooting behind or below. A cock pheasant is almost three feet long, and about two-thirds of his length is made up of his tail. The temptation is to shoot at the center of the target, and hence behind; and in the case of a raising bird, below. If the tails were cut off or absent there would probably be a higher proportion of clean kills. Try to eliminate the tail and body from the vision and shoot at the head and neck.

The pheasant can carry quite a lot of shot. He is strong and thick-feathered, and from the rear his body is especially well protected. Hence, in pheasant shooting it is doubly important to shoot well ahead and high. A shot through the head or neck is the desirable point. If hit here, there are no runners. The white ring around the neck is conspicuous and makes an excellent mark at which to shoot, and tends to prevent aiming at the center of the bird, which in the case of the cock pheasant means insufficient lead. Owing to its size and brilliant plumage, the cock pheasant looks nearer than it is.

The chief problem, however, with the pheasant is to get within range. Although the pheasant's rise is noisy, it is not fast, and it takes the bird some time to get under way. If the bird is within a reasonable distance, there need be no particular hurry, and the shooting is not difficult. When a pheasant has risen to the highest point in its flight, it is prone to make a gradual descent, by alternate flapping and sailing, until it finally planes to its landing site. Its flight is sometimes slightly curving, but generally moderately straight. It may be influenced by the wind. The pheasant rarely flies level, i.e., it is generally either rising or descending. It probably takes a pheasant 50 or 60 yards to attain its maximum speed, which is about 35 or 40 miles per hour, or perhaps a little more. (An easy method to approximate feet per second is to take one and a half times miles per hour. Thus, 40 miles per hour is, roughly, 60 feet per second.) With a strong tail wind, this speed may be considerably exceeded. Some years ago Mr. Griffith, of the Schultze Gunpowder Company, tried some experiments with pheasants which he flew down a tunnel and timed. The average speed was about 47 miles per hour, and this was believed to be a little in excess of the speed at which the bird would fly under normal conditions. During strong winds, pheasants are a little more difficult to flush than during mild weather. Under these circumstances they have, after getting well in the air, a tendency to fly down wind and make comparatively long flights. The average flight does not usually exceed ¼ or ½ mile. Occasionally, especially after having been shot at, pheasants will fly for a mile or more and may rise to 250 feet.

Occasionally pheasants are flushed at a distance by the dog or someone else. If so, the bird is as likely as not to pass or even fly directly overhead of a gun. These are generally really sporting shots, especially if the bird is fairly well up. They are going fast, and unless a good lead is taken, can be readily missed. The high incomer, perhaps with a wind back of him, is a particularly attractive shot. Take him well out—so far out that there is time for the use of the second barrel before the bird passes. Most men let him get entirely too close. The bird is coming fast, so go into action early. A very fast shot can get off two aimed shots in front in four-fifths of a second, but the average man will require nearly twice this amount of time. The incomer is presenting his most vulnerable aspect and a clean kill or miss generally results. If the bird passes, it is a more difficult shot requiring a quick change of stance, and often results in a wounded or missed bird.

To kill an incomer, face the bird and bring the barrels up in the line of flight. Pass the bird with the muzzle, and shoot the instant the target is blotted out. Checked swing or delay is fatal, but not to the bird. Shoot the choke barrel first, and reserve the cylinder for the nearer shot, which may be necessary in case of a miss. It is an easy shot once the knack is acquired and one learns to shoot before the bird gets too close. Most of us are accustomed to shooting walked-up game, and for this reason are sometimes weak on this shot.

The real crux of the situation is properly to time the going into action. Every experienced wild fowler when shooting over decoys knows the importance of selecting exactly the proper time to "rise on them." The situation with the incoming pheasant is quite similar.

The mounting of the gun, swing, blotting out of the bird, and trigger pull should be one synchronized action. Unless familiar with the shot, and perhaps because the bird is out of sight at the time the trigger is pulled, there is a tendency to hesitate and check swing or delay trigger pull. Any of these faults results in shooting behind.

Practicing on incomers, especially overhead incomers, from a clay-pigeon trap is a great help. Most shooting schools have traps placed on towers; these are particularly useful for this sort of practice. If a tower is not available, a trap may sometimes be placed on the top of a suitable building or a steep hillside. At the risk of repetition, let me repeat that the trick of this shot is properly to time the going into action, and the tendency is to wait too long. I have stressed the necessity for going into action early and that starting too late is a common fault.

However, sometimes the gun sees the bird approaching from a long distance and starts to mount his gun too soon. As a consequence the sportsman has to wait and "ride out the bird." This spoils the smooth, uniform, synchronized performance and usually results in a checked swing and a miss. When the range permits, kill the bird well out in front. If the bird is missed, swing fast past the target again, and use the second barrel. If wearing a hat, keep the brim well up and out of the way; in overhead shots it has a tendency to interfere with the vision. With very high incomers take them nearly overhead, but this shot is rarely offered over pointing dogs. It is a hard shot for most of us. The right foot must be farther back than usual, and the grip with the left hand somewhat shortened. Another way to handle the high incomer is to turn sideways to the bird's line of flight and take the shot as one would a high passing target. This plan has the advantage that the bird is in sight at all times. It works well for birds that are almost directly overhead and is the method often employed for high mallards in timber. Cant must be guarded against.

A clean-killed incomer comes down fast and hard, a cock pheasant weighing three or four pounds. To be hit by a falling bird would probably not happen in a lifetime, but it is, nevertheless, worth keeping an eye on him, for no bird falls harder than he. This is reminiscent of the oft-quoted remark of the Irish gamekeeper who, after his master had killed an especially tall cock which crashed to earth with the soul-satisfying thud that only these birds can produce, said, "Faith, I'm thinkin' you wasted a cartridge. The fall alone would've killed 'im!"

Attempts to flush pheasants a second time are often disappointing, even though the point of alighting may have been accurately marked. Of course this is due to the running proclivities of the bird, but often they seem to have simply evaporated. In attempting to flush ahead of the pointing dog do so boldly and rapidly. It is not usually necessary to thrash around too much under his nose, as one might do if a quail were expected. At all events be on the alert lest the bird has run and flushes from a distance. In following the dog which is working on a pheasant make as little noise as possible, and do not talk or encourage talk from a companion.

If a pheasant is wounded, and there seems any chance whatever of its being able to run, use the second barrel without hesitation, either in the air or on the ground. Get the dog to all cripples as quickly as possible. Wounded pheasants can run like quarter horses. A survey made by the Pennsylvania State College a few years ago showed that inexperienced hunters lost 35 per cent of wounded birds, and that those more practiced lost 15 per cent. I think this is an underestimate, and is certainly so, as far as wing-tipped birds are concerned, unless the sportsman possesses the services of a good retriever. Without a dog practically all the pheasants that can run are lost.

As previously mentioned, the dog that breaks shot to retrieve has a great advantage, for the quicker it can get to the point of fall the better. Wing-broken pheasants generally run straight away or quartering. They are apt to run in a fairly straight line, and if not too badly wounded, often travel for a long distance and at a fast pace. If the bird comes to an extra thick bit of cover, such as a dense honeysuckle tangle, it will often run into it and hide. To follow a strong runner a good spaniel or retriever is usually better than either a pointer or a setter, because they use foot scent more than do the pointing dogs. If the pointer or setter can catch even a glimpse of the escaping runner, the chances of securing the bird are excellent, but if they do not, they are less certain, although many such cripples are retrieved. The spaniel is a natural trailer and whether the pheasant is seen or not it is usually caught.

Probably more crippled pheasants are lost than all other upland game birds put together. Use nothing smaller than the No. 7½ shot; 6's are even more effective. An ideal load is 7's in the right barrel and 6's in the more closely choked left. However, many experienced shots prefer 7's in both barrels. The 3¼ or 3½-1¼ load is excellent for pheasants provided the gun is chambered for the longer shell and is not too light. However, it is rather heavy for most other upland game birds and the 3-1⅛ load is satisfactory and more suitable for most field guns. Do not be tempted to shoot at birds out of range, especially at those flying directly away from the gun.

With all his faults, John Pheasant is a pretty sporting bird; give him a chance. He ought not to be murdered from a car or on the ground.

In some places pheasants are shot by tracking them in the snow, a procedure that may be quite successful. Practically everyone has utilized this method on occasions of light snow. However, deliberately to go out for this purpose without a dog is a different type of shooting. In really heavy snow the thing to do is to take a bag of feed and leave the gun at home. In parts of the West, four men are placed at one end of a large field and the remainder of the group, perhaps eight or more, sweep the field from the opposite end. The end men of the line keep somewhat in advance of the beaters and, when the circle is completed, fast shooting is apt to be obtained. Large bags are often made in this way. Dogs are not usually used and it has been estimated that two of every seven pheasants shot down are lost. *The American Field* of January 16, 1946, quotes figures editorially which show that 40 per cent of the shooters in South Dakota who fail to secure their limit do so because dogs are not employed.

As has been mentioned, pheasants are not usually difficult birds to hit. Overanxiety or aiming at the tail rather than the head of the bird, and out-of-range shooting account for most of the failures. Under favorable circumstances they are much easier to hit than good live pigeons. If long-range shooting is eliminated, there is no game bird in the East, with the possible exception of the rail, that should be brought down more regularly. The official guns at the spaniel field trials miss few birds. The late Captain Curtis shot at Fishers Island trials and missed only one pheasant in two days' shooting. The late Adam Bogardus offered to back himself to kill one hundred straight Jacksnipe. Bogardus was an expert, but the man who could kill even 80 or 90 per cent of these birds could probably shoot pheasants over a dog all day with hardly a miss.

Shots over points or over spaniels, provided they are within good range and unless in extremely thick cover, should account for 75 per cent of pheasants with the first barrel, and this figure should be pushed up to nearly 90 per cent by the use of the second barrel. Taken by and large, a fairly good shot should grass about 70 to 80 per cent of pheasants that are within good range. The pheasant is the answer to the percentage shooter's dream. If a man wishes to pick his shots a miss should rarely occur. Practically the whole problem is to get near the bird. The preceding statements presuppose that the gun is fairly proficient and is shooting over a good retriever. If out-of-range shooting is indulged in it is impossible to make any estimate. It is shots at extreme range, where the pattern is getting thin, that cut down the proportion of kills per cartridge.

The cock pheasant is a big, handsome, brilliant bird, produces a lot of meat and is generally looked upon as more or less of a prize. Furthermore, he is often thought to be nearer than he actually is, hence the frequency of out-of-range shooting.

*Driven Pheasant.* Abroad, driving is the favorite method of shooting pheasants. It is dependent upon the fact that pheasants are essentially pedestrians and prefer to run rather than to fly, and can therefore be driven by the beaters. A volume could be written on this type of shooting.

Driving has the advantage that it is open to those who are unable, through age or other physical infirmities, to do much walking. An endeavor is made to collect the birds in a wood, from which they are driven over the guns. They fly better if they can be driven toward their home coverts. Every effort is made to make the bird fly high over the guns, and as fast as possible. Obviously, to drive pheasants successfully, the cover must be suitable, and to get this may require cutting of rides through a wood or some other arrangement. Often some obstruction such as netting is placed at the edge of the wood which is to be driven in order to get the birds well in the air.

Beaters must be under the orders of a man experienced in this type of shooting. To show good high birds is the aim of every experienced keeper. Drives are often progressive. They should be so arranged that the birds flush singly or in small groups, and not all at once. To prevent birds running out at the side, stops are placed. Drives may be large or small. The shooting itself is difficult and the man who can kill with any regularity high, perhaps curling pheasants, even without a wind back of them, can be counted a good shot.

The character of the shooting is not unlike our pass shooting of ducks. Driving is not resorted to much in this country, except on a few large estates, but it is destined to become more popular than it now is. It is a very attractive and sporting method of shooting as the birds are in full flight. The one disadvantage of all driven birds is the absence of dog work, which adds so much zest to field shooting. For detailed descriptions of the method of driving pheasants, the reader is referred to almost any of the modern English books on shooting. *Shooting by Moor, Field and Shore,* edited by Eric Parker, covers the field adequately. For driving in this country, see *Upland Game Bird Shooting in America,* edited by E. V. Connett, 3rd, and *American Game Preserve Shooting,* by L. B. Smith.

Pheasants easily can be trapped, snared, or shot out of trees on moonlight nights, while roosting. There is not much of this done in the United States, but on large estates abroad there is apt to be a good deal of poaching. In some localities here, a good many pheasants are shot from a motor car. Hens are protected in most states. Despite this many are killed. Every hen killed results in a reduction of next year's game crop by about five pheasants. In most states, too, it is illegal to shoot from a motor car or near a public highway. Not infrequently gunners, going or returning from shooting, kill a stray bird or two in this way. But there is another type of poacher who makes a business of driving along country roads and shooting every bird he can secure. These men make no pretense of hunting, do not wear shooting clothes, or own a dog. They often operate in the early morning and sometimes before the season opens. They have no regard for trespass signs and will shoot a pheasant as readily on a gentleman's lawn as anywhere else. Generally they work in couples, one man driving and the other watching for game or for the presence of a possible warden. This form of poaching is hard to break up, as, the instant the bird is retrieved and the gun concealed, the poachers become apparently good citizens driving upon their lawful occasions.

# THE RUFFED GROUSE
(*Bonasa umbellus umbellus:* Linnaeus)

*Sport royal, I warrant you.*
—Shakespeare, *Twelfth Night*, Act II, Scene 3.

NOMENCLATURE. The ruffed grouse is sometimes called partridge, "pa'tridge," drumming grouse, tippet, white-flesher, wood grouse, long-tailed grouse, and pheasant. It was formerly known in Pennsylvania as the pheasant, but since the advent of the ring-necked pheasant this name has been largely abandoned, although in some localities it is still referred to as the "native" pheasant. In the northeastern part of New England the bird is usually called partridge, a name commonly applied to the quail in many parts of Pennsylvania and the South. The term white-flesher was formerly not uncommon in the markets of Philadelphia and perhaps elsewhere—it probably was applied in an effort to distinguish the grouse from the dark-meated prairie chicken, which was often for sale at the same shop.

The Latin name *Bonasa*, a bison, may have been applied to this game bird because of the impetuous character of the flight, which suggests the headlong charge of a buffalo, or because a moving herd was said to produce a noise not unlike distant thunder, which itself is similar to the sound of the drumming. *Umbellus* was given because of the umbrella-like ruff that can be elevated and spread and from which the bird also derives its English name.

*Field Marks.* "The ruffed grouse is the largest brown native ground bird of the woodlands in southern New England. Its sudden spring from the ground with an extremely noisy whirring flight is characteristic. The female ring-necked pheasant resembles it somewhat in flight, but it has a longer, more pointed tail, and when rising in flight its wing beats are slower and not so loud as the grouse's. The drumming of the male is distinctive" (Forbush). The grouse ranges in weight from 16½ to 27 ounces. The male's weight is from 21 to 27 ounces. The latter is thought to average slightly more than the female, which usually averages from 18 to 22 ounces.

In addition to the usual black-ruffed type, there is a red phase in which the neck ruffs and the tail feathers are reddish brown. This so-called red phase is not uncommon. These birds may be part of a brood the greater number of which are marked in the ordinary manner. Adults, male and female, present the same general appearance. The hen is somewhat duller, her ruff is less pronounced and less brilliant, and her tail is slightly shorter than the male's. A hen's tail measures from about 4½ to 5½ inches; that of the cock about 6 to 7 inches. Some believe that the band across the tail is continuous in the male and broken in the female, but this test is not reliable. The extreme length of the adult female is from about 15½ to 17¾ inches, and that of the male from 17¾ to 20 inches. Dissection is the only certain method of distinguishing the sexes.

*Molts.* In the case of young birds wearing juvenile plumage, the sexes are also generally similar and resemble the adult female, but they are browner and the barrings are not so distinct as hers. Ruffs are absent. Chicks are a chestnut buff above and varied with pale buff. They are lighter on the top of the head, with a black line, sometimes broken, posterior to the eye. Their color is a lighter yellowish buff below. Chicks molt in the early summer, at which time the natal down is replaced by the juvenile plumage. The flight feathers develop early. Juvenile plumage is well developed when the bird is three-fourths grown. The first part of the juvenile molt occurs in the early fall; this is followed by the first winter plumage. The adult undergoes a prenuptial molt about the head and throat which is most marked in the cocks, and a complete postnuptial molt in the fall.

*Voice.* The ruffed grouse is generally a quiet bird. When alarmed, it may utter a "quit-quit," a sound made sometimes when on the ground but most often when the bird has risen well up and is in full flight. Passing birds, when uttering this note, may sometimes be seen to open and shut their beaks. The hen has a *"crut-crut-cur-r-r"* (W. Brewster) and a kind of clucking note used for the chicks. Grouse are said sometimes to utter a low soft "*coo-coo-coo-coo*" and a squirrel-like chattering and snickering (Forbush).

*Range.* "Ruffed grouse are found in the eastern United States from southern Minnesota, southern Wisconsin, southern Michigan, southern New York and southern Massachusetts, south to eastern Kansas (formerly northern Arkansas), Missouri (rarely), Tennessee, and Virginia, and in the Alleghenies to northern Georgia and northern Alabama" (Forbush).

The Northern ruffed grouse, Canadian ruffed grouse, partridge or birch partridge *(Bonasa umbellus togata)* has the same general appearance as the ruffed grouse, but is a little larger (occasionally weighing up to two pounds). It is darker and grayish above, but blacker and less reddish in color; brown markings below are very conspicuous. Like *Bonasa umbellus umbellus,* it also has a red and a gray phase. This bird is almost identical with *Bonasa umbellus umbellus,* but it can be distinguished from it by comparison (red-tailed birds are not considered as typical *togata*).

"The Canadian ruffed grouse range in the Canadian zone of North America from James Bay south to northern Michigan, central New York, northwestern Connecticut, northern and western Massachusetts, Vermont, New Hampshire, and Maine; and, in the mountains, south to North Carolina. Birds indistinguishable from the eastern form occur from east central British Columbia south to eastern Arizona and central Idaho. It is a common resident throughout most of Maine, New Hampshire, and Vermont in wooded regions, and south through the mountains of western Massachusetts and northwestern Connecticut. In southern New England many intermediates between *umbellus* and *togata* may be found, most of them approaching *togata* in coloration" (Forbush). This bird is the common northern grouse, and is similar in habits and breeding to the *Bonasa umbellus.* It is said to bud more than the *Bonasa umbellus.* But from the sportsman's viewpoint it is practically identical.

*Courtship.* The grouse is polygamous, but not to the same extent as the ring-necked pheasant. This is shown by the fact that the male frequently rejoins his family in the late summer. More than one hen, however, has been observed to accept the same male at a drumming place. During the season of incubation the cocks congregate together. During the courtship the male struts, spreads his tail, and with crest erect and dragging wings, attempts to woo the hen. The ruffs are raised sometimes so as almost to hide the head. He struts like a small turkey gobbler, moving about with mincing steps and often rushes at the hen, which, as likely as not, eludes him by flying to a near-by tree. Strutting is occasionally performed in the winter and is common in the early spring. Hens have also been observed to strut, but to a lesser extent.

*Nesting.* The ruffed grouse nests in upland forests or in low woods. Nests are usually located near the edge of openings, perhaps because of the increased number of insects available for the young in these locations. Ideal brooding cover is a low dense canopy adjoining openings. Ground cover is extremely important. Although such cover is utilized for only a short period by the young, it is necessary for their preservation, for it is during early life that the highest mortality exists. Heavy ground cover tends to save many young birds (King).

The nest is sometimes in dense cover, and often placed at the foot of a tree or partially concealed and protected by a log or rock. All the nests I have seen have been well hidden, although there are many records of an occasional nest in an open space. In rare instances, the nest has been found in a tree. "If the grouse is persistently molested when nesting on the ground, she may avail herself of the abandoned nest of a crow" (Samuels).

It is said that the hen avoids the cock when making her nest, and that the latter may destroy the nest if found. The hen, while incubating, sits close, and, in much the same manner as hen turkeys, often covers the eggs with leaves while feeding. Sometimes she places leaves on her back, which fall when she departs from the nest, covering the eggs. Some hens make no effort to conceal the eggs, especially if the nest itself is well hidden.

The nest is a shallow hollow in the ground, lined and surrounded by dead leaves. The eggs are seven to fourteen in number (larger clutches are probably due to two hens laying in the same nest). The eggs measure about 1.60 to 1.70 by 1.00 to 1.30 inches, are ovate and whitish cream, pale pinkish buff, or pale brown in color; sometimes they are faintly spotted or blocked with darker shades. Egg laying takes place in Pennsylvania usually from April 15 to early May. Incubation is for about twenty-four days and is performed by the female, who has one brood yearly but who often lays a second setting if the first has been destroyed.

The young can run and hide almost immediately after hatching, but they cannot fly. They remain in the nest for a short time, and, when they leave, do not return. They have a low, piping peep, which is rarely uttered. In ten days or two weeks the young can fly a short distance. Heavy rains and forest fires destroy many eggs and young. Adult grouse have been observed to fly directly into a forest fire.

From the time the young can fly, they and the mother usually roost high in trees. Until November or later there is a tendency for the broods to remain together. The hen is an excellent mother and will risk her life in defense of her young. If one disturbs a young brood, the hen utters a few warning clucks, and on hearing these clucks the chicks instantly hide. The hen will frequently advance toward the intruder, behaving in much the same manner as a domestic hen, ruffling her feathers and often feigning injury in an effort to draw off the enemy. I have seen a mother grouse advance to within 10 or 15 feet of a man and this in a country in which grouse were much hunted and wild.

Wilson relates a unique performance in his *American Ornithology*. He came upon a hen grouse and one young chick. The bird attempted to lead him off in the usual manner, but when this failed darted to her young, grasped it in her bill, and flew rapidly away. Toward the end of the summer the male rejoins them. From this time until spring the entire family often remain together, unless separated by persistent hunting or scarcity of food.

*Food and Economic Status.* The grouse's food is varied, and changes with the seasons and in different localities. During the summer and fall, large quantities of insects, many of them injurious, are eaten—grasshoppers, crickets, locusts, ants, beetles, cutworms, and leafhoppers. Later, apples from deserted orchards, apple seeds from fallen fruit, wild grapes, blackberries, rose hips, sumac, alders, haws, cranberries, huckleberries, Virginia creeper, and many nuts, seeds, buds, blossoms, clover, foliage, and other fruits are also eaten, as well as certain grasses, edible mushrooms, green fern leaves, hazelnuts, beechnuts, chestnuts, and acorns. Cow wheat is a favorite food.

The New England Ruffed Grouse Investigation Committee listed twenty-eight varieties, of which acorns, thorn apples, and grapes were most frequently found. Combined, these constituted nearly one-third of the total diet.

In winter, grouse sometimes eat the leaves of sheep laurel (*Kalmia angustifolia*) and mountain laurel (*Kalmia latifolia*)—the only time when it is eaten to any extent—both of which are known to be poisonous to man. It has been claimed that the flesh of such birds may be poisonous to man. Forbush questions J. Somers (in *Proceedings* of the Nova Scotia Institute of Natural History) who described being poisoned in this manner. Similar statements to the same effect are not uncommon by the older writers. I have been unable to find record of any fatal case, nor have I been able to find the report of any recent instance. It seems at least possible that the illnesses described may have been improperly diagnosed. In my younger days I have eaten many winter-killed grouse without ill effect, an experience I have shared with many others. Warren in *Birds of Pennsylvania* states that he has eaten freely of the flesh of the grouse, after emptying the crop of large quantities of laurel buds, without experiencing any bad effects. Bogardus and many others make similar statements. At all events, it is now illegal to kill grouse in the winter.

An adequate supply of winter food is most important, for in summer, because of its catholic taste, the bird can easily get along in most localities. In deep winter and early spring, food is likely to be scarce and grouse are often dependent upon buds. Birch buds and hard hack are much utilized in those localities where they are found.

As far as the economic situation is concerned, all who have made comprehensive studies of the birds are unanimous in agreeing that the grouse is most valuable. Occasionally, it is true that grouse, budding in fruit trees—particularly apple—may result in some loss of crop. C. J. Maynard records that at one time a bounty of twenty-five cents was placed on each grouse head in certain Massachusetts towns. However, Spiller, in his delightful volume, *Grouse Feathers,* states that the damage done to apple trees is oftentimes overestimated. He reports one instance in which five grouse budded in a single tree for almost two weeks, and in the succeeding fall that tree bore the largest and choicest crop it had ever produced.

W. Wheeler (quoted by Forbush) states that "for twenty years one or two grouse continuously budded an apple tree near my farmhouse window. The tree seemed to be their favorite. But notwithstanding the budding or because of it the tree bore a good crop of large apples every year, while other trees not budded by the grouse often bore none. Apparently the thinning of the buds by the birds was a benefit to the crop."

In former times, when grouse were much more abundant than they are at present, they may sometimes have done local injury, and in a few localities may do so at present. Even in these rare instances, however, it seems certain that in the long run they do much more good than harm, and the only pity from every standpoint is that the birds are not now more numerous.

*Early history.* Early in the history of the settlement of the eastern seaboard, the settlers found the Indians securing grouse by traps and snares and with blunt arrows. During the days of William Penn there was a ready sale for these birds in Philadelphia. The Puritans in New England found both grouse and heath hens in abundance. Wilson states (1829) that great numbers were brought to the markets and sold for from 75 cents to $1.25 per pair.

The grouse is essentially a woodland bird. Deforestation and other conditions which follow in the wake of civilization have done much to reduce its number and decrease its range.

*Habits.* Grouse are very adaptable and soon learn the advantages offered by abandoned farms, cut-over areas, and other changes instituted by man. They are also quick learners. Probably no bird, unless it be a black duck or a Canadian goose, exhibits greater ability to protect itself from the man with a gun than the grouse in heavily shot areas; while, on the other hand, in wild regions few birds show such a confiding nature or permit closer approach than does this same species. It is said that if undisturbed the grouse will live its entire life within a short distance of its natal spot.

R. T. King, professor of zoology at the University of Minnesota, marked numerous grouse in a certain section. As a result of his studies he is of the opinon that they have a definite cruising range of not more than half a mile, and that they will starve to death rather than go any farther for food or for any other reason. Furthermore, he thinks that the saturation point or carrying capacity of the land is about one grouse to every four or five acres. Certain it is that wherever a grouse is found on one day it is likely also to be found there the next and for a considerable time thereafter. If shot at or persistently hunted, it will sometimes leave. My belief is that grouse on occasion may go a considerable distance for food and usually do so by walking.

Grouse also move according to the season. They may be high on the hills in summer, but tend to come to the lowlands as winter approaches, during which season the normal mortality is about 17 to 20 per cent. Abundance or scarcity of food is also a factor. W. H. Foster thought that this home-loving instinct has been overestimated. My experience is also similar, but I believe that the grouse's tendency is to occupy but a small area, and that this is more marked in the wild than in the hard-hunted localities, such as New York, northern New Jersey, and northern Pennsylvania. When salmon fishing, on a number of occasions I have seen a grouse or family of grouse occupying the same locality for a month or more. I had no way of making sure that these were always the same birds, but that was my impression.

Until young chicks learn to fly, they are probably brooded by the hen at night and in bad weather. In November, I have seen grouse roosting both on the ground and in trees. It has been claimed that when occupying the former site the birds fly to the roosting place in the same manner as do quail, and perhaps for the same reason. Probably the choice of a roosting place depends upon the terrain, the weather, and the prevalence or absence of predators. During severe storms grouse often seek shelter well up in some thick conifer where they crowd against the lee of the bole.

In winter, grouse frequently fly into a snowbank, thus leaving no trail or scent, and here spend the night. I have seen grouse dive into the snow to escape pursuit during the daytime, and on one occasion as I approached I saw the head of the bird, with crest elevated, appear out of the snow some distance from the tunnel entrance. The head was almost instantly followed by the body of the bird, which seemed to come out in full flight. It is possible that some of the tunnels may be made in an effort to secure food.

My experience of shooting grouse in deep snow is limited. Many years ago I arrived at Wurtsboro, Sullivan County, New York, at about noon. While driving to my destination, a shack in the mountains ten miles distant, it started to snow, and by the time of my arrival, with one of the Reiner boys of Wurtsboro, there were 2 or 3 inches on the ground. By the time we got our duffel unpacked and the horses attended to, it was snowing hard, and despite the fact that it was November it gave every evidence of being a heavy storm. However, being young and enthusiastic, we took a short hunt which resulted in our killing two or three birds, mostly among heavy evergreens. It snowed most of the night, and by morning, when it cleared about ten o'clock, there were 8 or 10 inches on the level, and drifts many feet deep. We plowed through the snow, sometimes nearly knee deep. Curiously enough, quite a few grouse were found, all among evergreens and moderately well up on the hills. This was the first time I had seen grouse tunnels. I have often heard of catching grouse under the snow, and this may be possible in the wilds. These Sullivan County birds, however, needed no kicking out, but would burst forth often at a great distance as if the ground had been bare. Many flushed from trees. Some would flush from one tree and fly to another; others dived into snow banks. One of these birds was pointed while it was buried in a snow bank. Another was pointed while perched on a tree. On account of the deep snow the dogs could not range to any extent and were of little practical assistance. Reiner, who was an experienced grouse hunter, believed that the reason so many birds were found was because the grouse had left the lowlands and swamps and moved to higher ground on account of the heavy snowstorm. These incidents occurred at a period when game was still comparatively plentiful, conservation was in its infancy, and few sportsmen had awakened to the fact that in deep snow, game birds should be fed and not shot. I am reminded of the experience by an account of a similar one by Mr. Vinton W. Mason, of Lexington, Massachusetts, which was published in *The American Field* on February 5, 1944.

Grouse utilize only soft snow to dive into, but they are sometimes trapped when a crust forms subsequently. Usually they are able to break through, but unfortunately this is not always the case. Indeed, Samuels states that it is a common occurrence to find them dead, in the spring, having perished in this manner. The site at which grouse enter snow is generally one to which the sun has access, and it is possible that this selection is made with the view to melting any crust that might form.

Grouse may plunge into the snow at an angle, closing their wings just before they make contact. Criddle states in *The Field* (English) that sometimes while flying over snow they drop down, take a quick look around, and then force themselves into the loose drift. Tunnels vary in depth, but are usually about 16 inches long. Northern grouse and those inhabiting a range in which heavy snows are frequent are more likely to enter snow than are those birds living in a milder climate. Ptarmigan resort to the habit routinely. When a strong crust does form, thus preventing birds from securing shelter in the snow, they seek a harbor under some low-hanging dense cover, or in an evergreen tree, and there roost.

*Tameness and Wildness.* In locations in which the grouse is undisturbed it is one of the tamest of birds, and has well earned the name sometimes applied to it of "fool-hen." During moose-hunting trips I have frequently killed all that were required for food with a 22-caliber pistol. The birds might fly a few feet up into a tree, and generally permit an approach to within 25 feet or less. It is said that when a number of unsophisticated grouse are perched in a tree that the entire flock may be killed if care is taken to shoot the lowest one each time. This may sometimes be true but is not by any means always the case. However, the falling birds do probably have a tendency to scare the others.

In contrast to this tameness, in locations where the bird is hunted to any extent, it soon becomes wild, crafty, and difficult to approach. This is a fortunate trait, as otherwise this splendid game bird would soon be exterminated; indeed, this ability to protect itself is what makes grouse shooting one of the most fascinating of all sports. In captivity the birds become as tame as chickens.

If our Pennsylvania birds were as easy to secure as the birds in a naturally wild country, grouse-shooting would be little more than pot-hunting.

*Drumming.* Drumming was sometimes called "beating" by the older writers. For many years the question of how drumming was produced was a subject of conjecture, and various theories were advanced to explain the sound. Drumming seems to be the means of attracting the female, a challenge to other males, and sometimes, though less frequently, merely a "letting-off of steam." It is most often practiced during the mating season, but may occasionally be heard at any time of the year. It is least frequent during the winter. Drumming is most often heard during the morning hours, but it is common at any time during the day and is even practiced at night (Forbush, Schley, and others). Criddle believes that night drumming is more frequent during the full of the moon. It is said that young males do most of the autumn drumming.

The drumming site is usually a fallen log, or sometimes a rock. The cock returns again and again to the same place, sometimes year after year, so that eventually the drumming log may be worn smooth. Feathers and excrement may be present near an old drumming log.

The drumming starts with a few preliminary thumps, which become augmented, and are followed by the characteristic humming, muffled, throbbing sound. The sound is not unlike distant thunder, especially if, as is so often the case, the preliminary thumps have not been heard. Sandys likens the noise to that produced by a wagon being driven rapidly over a distant wooden bridge. The first few thumping sounds are quite regularly spaced and suggest the noise produced by the flapping of the wings of the domestic cock. When drumming is at its loudest it, as the name indicates, somewhat resembles the roll of a muffled drum. The drumming continues for a few seconds—perhaps five or ten—and gradually decreases in volume.

The drumming is produced by wing beats, and is completed by

the shortening of these rather than by diminishing the speed. The throbbing, ventriloquistic character of the sound of a grouse drumming makes him extremely difficult for a man to locate, either as to direction or distance. This is especially noticeable in a hilly country, as the sound tends to reverberate from hill to hill. Drumming is apt to be thought nearer than it actually is. On still days the sound may be heard for half or three-quarters of a mile—perhaps even farther. Many times I have attempted to stalk a drumming grouse. The general plan is to advance as silently as possible during the drumming, and to become immovable the instant it ceases. It helps considerably if the site of the drumming log is known beforehand. It is a mistake to believe that the bird is so taken up by the act of drumming that safety is lost sight of. The bird actually is on the alert at all times, and he will slip away or flush at the slightest suspicion of danger.

I have killed a number of drummers during the shooting season, but have witnessed the act of drumming only once. The bird appeared to stretch and stand almost upright; the tail was spread and trailing and the ruffs were raised. The wing beats were so rapid that only a blur was visible.

The noise is produced by the wing beat in the air and not against the drumming log. If, as has been suggested, the sound were caused by the striking of the wings against the drumming log, the wing feathers would soon be worn away. Old drumming sites show evidence of use, but their appearance suggests that this wear is produced more by the feet than the wings. The photograph of a drumming grouse reproduced in the text also indicates that the wing beats clear the log by a considerable distance and that they are on a plane well above the surface of the drumming site. It is possible that the wings beating against the breast may augment the sound; they appear to do so, but it seems improbable. The instant the drumming ceases the bird stands even more erect and apparently listens intently, looking around very carefully. This interval of silence is used by the bird to discover an approaching hen, a rival cock, or danger of any kind. During the entire time he is intently alert. If he is undisturbed, the drumming is repeated at frequent intervals. If a hen appears, mating takes place, but if another male arrives on the scene a fight frequently occurs. It is doubtful if these fights are ever fatal. Edwin C. Kent, in his delightful reminiscences, *The Isle of Long Ago,* describes one of these fights, which was all "fuss and feathers." As far as I know, no other bird in America resorts to drumming. Many other varieties of grouse perform various antics and produce curious vocal and other sounds during the mating season. Of note is the booming of the prairie chicken; but all these differ markedly both in tone and method of production from the drumming of *Bonasa umbellus.*

*The Crazy or Mad Season.* Many students of grouse habits believe that in the autumn the birds undergo a sort of crazy period, during which they may fly against houses or through windows, or even through the glass of moving motor cars, trolleys, or locomotive headlights. Forbush states: "So careless are they of obstructions that a high wire fence around a covert is likely to kill all the ruffed grouse within its confines. From September to November, whether hunted by man or not, some of them rush wildly about from place to place and some sometimes kill themselves by striking against buildings far from woods."

Some years ago, while I was camping in Michigan, it was necessary to walk about three-fourths of a mile beside a high Page wire fence, to get to a lake which we often fished. On a number of occasions some member of the party, on taking this trip, found a grouse which had killed itself by flying against the fence.

Almost every writer on grouse mentions the crazy period. The theory has been advanced that it is Nature's method of reducing the number of males. Certainly the grouse is, to some extent, polygamous. An examination of the sex of a series of birds killed by flying against obstructions might throw some light on the subject, but, so far as I have been able to ascertain, this has never been done. Moreover, most of the birds killed are destroyed by flying against man-made obstacles, so this theory seems hardly tenable inasmuch as grouse existed long before the country was settled.

I live in a gray stone house situated on the top of a hill. The house is almost surrounded by woods, and has many large plate-glass windows. During the last eight years ninety-one birds of various kinds have killed themselves by flying against these windows. This has occurred during both the day and the night—at night, especially during the periods of migration. Approximately about twice as many have hit against the windows but have been able to fly off either immediately or later. The varieties include a sparrow hawk, sharp-shinned hawk, screech owl, doves, thrushes (four varieties), woodpeckers (two varieties), purple finches, sparrows (three varieties), titmice, nuthatches, warblers (five varieties), and others. Whether these accidents are due to sun glare, reflection, or the appearance of an opening is impossible to determine.

On the causeway leading into Mauricetown, New Jersey, where I frequently go rail-shooting, there are a number of overhead wires. Almost any morning during the rail season a few sora, which have killed themselves by flying against the wires, can be picked up. Almost anyone who drives a motor car has had birds hit against it. The number of birds that kill themselves by flying against electric lights and lighthouses is enormous, but this probably can be explained on a different basis. However, these few facts are cited to show that it is of common occurrence for many varieties to kill themselves, during both day and night, by hitting obstructions; yet, despite their number, no one, as far I am aware, has attributed any "madness" to them.

The grouse, by reputation, is a strong, powerful, impetuous flyer. I have often seen a shower of twigs follow its line of flight. Forbush has seen a grouse strike a limb and fall to the ground. However, this particular bird had been shot at in a neighboring wood and may have been wounded. There is also record of a grouse which, in flight, collided with the broken end of a limb and drove this deeply into its body (Forbush). A number of similar instances of these birds injuring or even killing themselves by flying against obstructions have been observed.

All grouse hunters have had the experience of seeing a bird that has been flushed at a distance by a dog or a companion dart past them at close range without deviating in the least from its line of flight. On two or three occasions I have had them fly overhead so near that I could almost have struck them with my gun barrel. In addition to this, grouse generally fly low and with great speed, especially when covering open spaces. Personally, I question the existence of any crazy season and believe these accidents are not more frequent than can be explained on a basis of the character of the birds' flight. That close observer, Mr. Foster, was of much the same opinion. Furthermore these accidents occur at all seasons of the year.

The grouse is an extremely hardy bird, able to stand severe cold, and, if need be, will subsist on immature buds, small shoots, and even dead leaves. It is during these periods that laurel leaves are eaten. Forbush states that the stomach seems to digest the bark of twigs, leaving the twigs white and bare. During winter the feet of grouse develop feathers, which act the same as snowshoes do to humans. Grouse are non-migratory, in the usual sense, although local movements have been observed. Spiller records such an instance.

*Flight.* With grouse it is difficult to foresee the direction the bird will take. It is usually away from the gun, but, occasionally, the bird will come back, sometimes almost in the face of the sportsman, but more often to one side or the other or it may even rocket upward. One point is almost certain, and that is, that the grouse will head for the heaviest cover available.

Birds occasionally permit the sportsman to pass and later flush in the rear. The grouse is distinctly a fast flyer and gets under way rapidly. When frightened it appears reckless and, as stated above, dashes through minor obstructions with apparently little effort to evade them. In this way it differs from the woodcock and wood duck.

There is no other bird of similar size that can make such a loud whirr of wings. However, the grouse can rise almost noiselessly. Audubon was of the opinion that the loud whirr was caused by the bird being startled, and came from an effort at great speed so that it could escape. This urge to escape seems to be a logical explanation for the wing noise, not only for the grouse but for the same trait in many of the gallinaceous birds. Chapman has suggested that the startling whirr of a flushed grouse may have a certain protective value, as it alarms a predator about to spring. There is no doubt that it has caused many a load of shot to fly wild of its mark.

Generally speaking, the flight of the grouse is moderately low, often not rising more than 10 to 30 feet. Sometimes, however, it will rise to the top of the trees and go off on a long flight. In such a flight it may turn on reaching its elevation, and disappear at more or less of an angle. This is the time for a fast second barrel, if the first has failed. The flight is usually fairly straight and is not usually more than 200 or 300 yards. In young birds the flight is more restricted. The flight is also likely to be shorter early in the season and in those localities in which there is little or no shooting. I have seen grouse, while moose hunting, whose flight did not average 25 yards. If the bird is flushed on a hillside it is apt to go uphill. However, there is no definite rule to follow and the bird may pitch downward to some impenetrable swampy fastness, or go off level along the hillside.

Spiller kept a record of the flight of one hundred birds, and is convinced that by preference they rise against the wind. Grouse rarely alight in the open. It is said that if birds flush wild and are shot at they are apt to lie close after two or three such experiences. Thus they differ from the woodcock and many other birds which tend to rise farther away from the gun after each time they have been put up.

Sometimes, after being flushed, grouse will light on a tree, often a conifer. If the gun is near, he can often hear a sort of thud or flap made by the alighting bird. This flap may disclose the fact that the bird has alighted in a tree, and be more or less of a guide to the alighting site. The thud or flap is not always heard, but is most often produced if the bird has been flying fast before alighting. I have, however, heard it when the bird has risen silently and has made only a short flight. The noise appears to be made by the closing of the wings, but may perhaps be caused by the heavy bird striking against its alighting site. Very low-flying birds are not apt to tree. The perching site is not likely to be low and may be at a considerable elevation. If it is thought that the bird has treed, ex-amine each suspected tree carefully and be on the *qui vive* for the hardest shot offered to the upland hunter. Grouse usually alight near, or even crowd against, the bole. They stand immovable, except for an occasional cautious turn of the head. Their attitude is extremely upright, and they may be readily mistaken for a natural knob or limb stump. On leaving the tree—and they invariably seem to select the time most favorable for them—they dart downward and away with incredible speed. The man who can kill such grouse can be rated an expert grouse shot.

I have twice flushed grouse from hollow, fallen logs. On both occasions the weather was good and both birds were being pointed by a dog. It is possible that the birds ran into the log to escape the dog. Mr. Kent tells of a similar experience, except that, in his case, six or eight birds had sought shelter in a single log and "poured out like water from a hose." On a number of occasions I have seen wounded grouse enter a hollow log or the hollow base of a tree in an effort to escape, but I think it is unusual for uninjured birds to do so. The above habits refer, of course, to grouse in areas in which they are hunted fairly hard.

*Enemies.* The abundance of any game bird is due to a number of factors, one of which is food. As grouse are omnivorous in their diet, they are less affected by this than many other birds. Other factors are cover, the habits of the species, capacity for reproduction, and their ability to withstand severe weather and local conditions.

*Weather.* Heavy or continuous rains frequently destroy many nests, eggs, and young; unusual or prolonged cold spells during the breeding season also produce a definite mortality. In regard to mortality, King states that the greatest single loss is juvenile mortality. This is an annual loss, separate from, and in addition to the periodic cyclic losses. Juvenile mortality accounts for normally at least 75 per cent and includes nest destruction, accidents to the young, etc.

On August 12, 1933, *The American Field* published the following from the Progress Report of the Ruffed Grouse Invesigation carried on by the Division of Fish and Game of the New York Conservation department. Contributors to the report were Dr. Gardiner Bump, superintendent of the Bureau of Game; E. C. Edminster, Jr., R. W. Darrow, game research investigator, and Dr. A. A. Allen, professor of ornithology at Cornell University. An analysis of the facts collected gives the following conclusions:

1. Food does not seem to be a controlling factor in grouse abundance.

2. Ideal grouse cover is made up of four types: spring nesting grounds, summer feeding grounds, fall feeding grounds, and winter shelter.

3. In coverts composed largely of hardwoods, a scattering of clumps of evergreen makes them much more desirable. Large areas devoted solely to conifers are not desirable, and serve mainly as reservoirs for predatory species.

4. The proportion of male to female grouse in favorable coverts is nearly equal, thus indicating that no degeneration of the species is taking place.

5. Among grouse the possibilities of detrimental in-breeding seem exceedingly remote.

6. Only in case the birds are in the very best of condition will it pay to restock areas with grouse through the liberation of imported wild trapped birds.

7. Enemies, of which the skunk and the fox seem to be the most important, are probably responsible for breaking up at least one-third of all grouse nests in this state each year.

8. Enemies, of which the horned owl, goshawk, and fox seem to be the most important, are probably responsible for killing about 20 per cent of all the adult grouse in this state each year.

9. The number of nests broken up, and of adult grouse destroyed, but not the losses of young birds while still with the brood, can be reduced to a considerable extent through intensive predator control.

10. Sportsmen are probably not responsible for killing more than 15 per cent of the grouse in the average covert in any one year.

11. The rearing of grouse in captivity and on a large scale is apparently a practicable proposition.

12. Artificially reared grouse, while astonishingly tame in captivity, upon liberation rapidly acquire those wild characteristics which make them truly kings and queens among upland game birds.

Outstanding, interesting, and important achievements during the past year include:

1. The obtaining of 335 eggs from 29 hand-reared grouse.

2. The raising of 70 second-generation birds from these eggs, nearly all of which seemed to be the equal in every respect of their wild cousins.

3. The studying of 548 wild grouse nests, 59.4 per cent of which hatched and 40.6 per cent of which were destroyed.

4. The liberating of 29 wild grouse, 12 being females, of which five are known to have nested. Four of these raised broods averaging 4½ birds apiece, which is slightly above normal.

5. The rapid reversion to normal wildness of five tame, hand-reared grouse upon liberation.

6. The recording of a 33 per cent decrease in the destruction of grouse nests in an area where predator control had been practiced, as compared with a similar adjacent area where no control was attempted.

7. The actual observing on two separate occasions of a wild red fox in the act of breaking up a grouse nest.

8. The finding of grouse remains in five (16 per cent) of 31 fox droppings (both red and gray) from the Connecticut hills area, and in 24 (14 per cent) of 169 droppings entirely from red fox from the Adirondack region.

## Artificial Propagation.

No story in the annals of artificial propagation of game birds emphasizes more graphically the practical value of scientific research, carefully and intensively conducted, than does the record of the second year of experimental grouse producing.

Last year many a "doubting Thomas" attributed the satisfactory results to "just luck." But with the rearing of 253 grouse to September 1, 70 of which were second-generation birds, we are emboldened to suggest that the last great obstacle to the rearing of large numbers of physically fit ruffed grouse in captivity seem to have been removed. Thanks to the eternal vigilance and care of Dr. A. A. Allen, dean of grouse breeders, serving without pay, in charge of the Ithaca Experimental Station, and Mrs. Gardiner Bump, who returned to direct the work from May 15 to October 1 at the Catskill Experimental Station, the season's results proved successful beyond our most sanguine expectations.

It was astonishing how preconceived notions and fancied difficulties concerning the successful breeding of grouse and the securing of fertile eggs therefrom, vanished as the work progressed at the two stations. The results reveal that, under proper management, (1) hand-reared grouse will lay at least 17 to 27 eggs in captivity; (2) most of these eggs will be fertile; (3) the hatchability of these eggs will be high; (4) the resultant chicks when mature appear to be absolutely as good as chicks hatched from wild eggs; (5) little difficulty need be experienced in rearing the youngsters, or holding in wintering or in breeding pens a large breeding stock of hand-reared grouse.

The progress to date raises the question, "Will these relatively tame hand-reared grouse upon release revert to type?" To determine this, five hand-reared birds were liberated last December on a state game refuge. Out of the transporting bags walked the grouse and began to feed. Some were afraid of their strange surroundings; none was afraid of us. Each bird was conspicuously marked. Within a week field men assigned to observe these birds experienced difficulty in approaching closer than 60 feet to them. Over the winter two were caught by predators, one disappeared, and two survived—a most encouraging average when one considers that above 30 per cent of the wild adults resident on this area were killed by predators last year.

Doubtless, conditions vary to some extent in different localities, but this is a very important and encouraging study. It deserves careful examination. The fact that the gun takes such a relatively small toll (15 per cent) of grouse bears out the belief of every student-sportsman. No one can view the vast stretches of extremely inaccessible, rough, and in some instances almost impenetrable country constituting the grouse coverts of Pennsylvania and other states, and comprehend how they can be denuded of birds by shooting alone. That 20 per cent of adult grouse and 33 per cent of nests are destroyed annually by predators should be emphasized. In addition, doubtless, many immature young birds are sacrificed yearly to vermin of various kinds.

Perhaps the most important statement in the report is that relating to artificial propagation. That a way has now been discovered by which grouse may be successfully reared, opens up avenues for future stocking. It also offers a means to combat not only predators and vermin but to lessen the devastation due to the cycles of scarcity which occur with fair regularity in all areas inhabited by this bird. All conservationists and game breeders will eagerly anticipate the final report of this Commission, in order to determine the practicability and cost attending the artificial rearing of grouse. During the past hundred and twenty years numerous attempts have been made to raise grouse in captivity. Wilson (1829) and Schley (1877) mention efforts to raise the birds, from eggs hatched under a domestic hen; and in the *American Shooters' Manual* (1827) reference is made to attempts of the same kind. The eggs can be readily hatched, but the trouble has always been to rear the chicks. For this reason the report is especially valuable, for good birds have been reared to maturity from eggs supplied by birds in captivity.

The possibility of deterioration in subsequent generations of grouse in captivity is still to be determined but under proper conditions there seems no reason to anticipate trouble. The fact that predators play a large part in the destruction of nests, eggs, young and adult grouse, confirms the observations of all grouse hunters. Predators are particularly difficult to control on many grouse ranges on account of the wildness of the country.

Dr. Gardiner Bump, of the New York Conservation department, in her 1932 investigation regarding ruffed grouse conditions, reported that ground vermin destroyed eggs as follows: Of 548 grouse nests, 104 were destroyed by predators—foxes destroyed 34; skunks, 15; weasels, 13; raccoons, 5; dogs, 8; red squirrels, 5; woodchucks, 4; and snakes, 2. King has observed squirrels break open grouse eggs, and if they did not contain well-advanced embryos they were discarded. If, however, incubation was more advanced the contents were devoured. In passing, it might be stated that the groundhog, by providing gravel, is, to some extent, beneficial for grouse.

Cooper's hawks are not specifically mentioned in the report, but from my own experience I know that this bird destroys many adult game birds. Only a season or two ago I had the satisfaction of killing one of these hawks, which flushed from a newly killed grouse. This hawk is known locally in Pennsylvania as the chicken-hawk, blue-darter, or big stub-winged hawk. It is almost the size of a crow. It is often seen soaring in small circles, its flight an alternation of quick wing beats and sailing. The Cooper's hawk possesses great speed; adult birds are dark bluish-gray above, whitish-barred-reddish below; the under surfaces of the wings and tail are barred. This bird should be destroyed at every opportunity.

Colonel H. P. Sheldon, in his delightful chapter on "Grouse Shooting" in *Upland Game Bird Shooting in America,* says that the goshawk will seldom leave a covert until he has killed the last grouse in it. I have seen confirmatory evidence of this statement. Many sportsmen believe that the pheasant is more or less inimical to the grouse. I cannot bear out this statement from my experience, and Sheldon is of the same opinion. He says that repeated investigation has failed to prove the tendency, and, as most observers are aware, the two are frequently found in the same coverts. Great horned owls are destructive to all game birds.

It is well known that snowy owls, during severe weather, when there is a dearth of rabbits and grouse in Canada, frequently invade our northern states and do great damage to the grouse crop. Sharp-shinned hawks take all small birds, including young grouse. Jays and perhaps other hawks and owls are occasionally injurious. Crows notoriously are nest-robbers. Foxes are frequently found in most grouse coverts, and undoubtedly do great damage to the grouse, destroying incubating birds, eggs, young, and adults— the latter at all seasons, but perhaps especially during the winter months. Skunks, wildcats, lynx, opossum, weasels, minks, snakes (especially black snakes), perhaps occasionally raccoons, and certainly house cats and stray dogs—all are more or less destructive. Rats, such a scourge in some localities to quail and pheasant, probably do little damage to grouse. To this list King adds the chipmunk. The chipmunk regards the eggs as playthings and rolls them out of the nest, usually without breaking them. On one occasion King found a nest containing twelve eggs. Next morning they were gone. Suspecting a chipmunk, he searched and found all twelve, which he put back in the nest. Every one of them hatched.

That grouse undergo regular cycles of abundance and scarcity is well recognized. These approximate ten-year intervals, and, apart from the annual fluctuations, amount to about 90 per cent of the entire stock. King believes that, as a result of these cyclic decimations, we can have grouse-shooting only in so many years out of every ten, and that the question of determining in advance which years should be open for shooting can be answered with certainty by the census method. An experienced man can census from 1,000 to 1,500 acres per day.

Whether these cycles are the result of disease or a number of combined factors, such as floods, cold spells, and forest fires during the breeding season, excess of predators, or of other conditions, is not definitely known. Forbush states that internal parasites, external parasites (such as ticks or blood-sucking larvae), contagious intestinal diseases, pulmonary mycosis, or tuberculosis have all been named as contributory causes. H. H. Cahoon mentions a worm or parasite which has been seen on the head, and records that George H. Ryman, of Shohola Falls, Pennsylvania, brought two diseased birds to one of the grouse trials.

King, after exhaustive studies in Minnesota, states: "Whether we shoot this bird or not, their numbers will fluctuate according to a definite cycle." In 1930 and 1931, Dr. A. O. Gross, of Bowdoin College, reported that under ordinary circumstances parasites are of minor importance. When weakened by lack of food or severe weather, parasites may be of major importance in reducing the number of the birds. King states that there is reason to believe that grouse under four years of age are more subject to the cycle mortality than older birds. If it were proved that the decimations of the cycle mortality were due to an infection, the above statement might be explained upon the basis of an acquired immunity. To some extent these cycles seem to be more or less local, though usually the cycles involve birds which inhabit large areas. The fact that their distribution is continent-wide has not been proved. Indeed, there is some evidence to the contrary, but this is a point which requires further study.

There are cycles affecting many varieties of birds, mammals and fish. In the normal state, Nature usually takes care of those scarcities which are caused by cycles. But if there is a grouse scarcity caused by unseasonable weather, numerous predators, excessive shooting and, on top of this a disease cycle develops, the bird may be almost exterminated. In passing, attention may be called to the fact that there is a certain similarity in our grouse cycles to the cycles which occur in Red Grouse (*Lagopus Scoticus*) in Scotland and elsewhere. In Scotland the bane of young grouse is coccidiosis, and of the adult, strongylosis. This last-mentioned malady is largely concerned with the food supply. However, there are many radical differences between the cycles affecting Red Grouse and our American bird.

To summarize: The chief practical factors for the increase in the grouse population seem to depend upon rigid and continuous control of predators and the assurance of proper cover and food. The food supply can be helped by the planting of suitable fruit and berry-bearing bushes and vines, and perhaps the feeding of grain in winter and the early spring. It is hoped that artificial propagation may be an important factor in the future, but, to date, (1945) this has nót been accomplished on a scale sufficiently large to be of practical value.

*Grouse Shooting.* Much has been said in a previous chapter regarding grouse dogs. It may be worth while to repeat that the chief qualities to look for are intelligence and a good nose, and the more experience with the bird the better.

The really good grouse dogs have probably been trained by a grouse hunter, and are most likely to be found in a grouse country. A half-trained wild dog is far worse than none, as it will rout out every bird before the gun can get within range. As stated elsewhere, two experienced grouse hunters can kill a good many birds without a dog, and this is particularly true when scent is bad and birds are wild and do not lie. It is a matter of taste, but, to me, it is inferior sport without the dog.

With a dog which does not understand grouse and constantly flushes, the best thing is to mark the direction taken by the bird, bring the dog to heel, and attempt to walk up the game. Two men shooting together have a great advantage, but even one man, if he knows the habits of the birds, can often be successful without a dog, and certainly more so than if handicapped by some wild, half-trained animal.

The dog must know what is required of him. It takes a longer time to train a dog for grouse shooting than for any other game bird. All good dogs will point grouse, but relatively few have the ability to handle them properly. The perfect grouse dog knows where birds are likely to be, approaches as much as possible from the lee side, points the instant he catches scent and often from a distance. He is steady in the ordinary sense, but is willing carefully to follow a running bird when so ordered or when the bird moves out. He may have to follow the bird for a hundred yards. To watch a wise grouse dog, high-headed and stiff-legged, following a wily old bird is a sight worth going a long way to see. This is where the inexperienced hunter often makes a mistake, by cautioning his dog in the belief that he will cause a flush, whereas, in actual fact, the dog is really pointing every step of the way and making a fine job of it.

The grouse dog should be willing, travel at a good pace, be extremely biddable, work from signals or low orders, and constantly work to the gun. He should be a good, fast retriever. The intelligent, experienced dog will require few orders, and may work all day without having to be spoken to. Whistling and loud orders tend to make birds run, refuse to lie, and flush wild. The desirable qualities are likely to be found in an old rather than a young dog. Certain strains seem to be especially proficient in grouse hunting. It must be remembered that grouse, as compared to quail or woodcock, are difficult birds for a dog to handle. Because woodcock are often found in adjacent coverts, the grouse-dog should be able to handle these birds.

Grouse shooting generally requires harder walking and more of it than any other kind of upland shooting. The venue is always rough, generally hilly and sometimes mountainous. It is well worth while for the grouse hunter not to exceed his normal gait, and to try to maintain balance at all times. Indeed, balance is the secret of rough walking and of good shooting. There are coverts, often woodlots, which are so placed that it is possible to drive in a motor car from one to another; shooting in that case does not entail a great deal of walking. These are not usual, and, other things being equal, ability to cover ground enters largely into the sport and the number of shots secured.

Proper footwear and not too heavy clothes are important assets. Some men wear shooting-glasses to protect their eyes. Even the lightest gun will feel heavy after a long day's grouse shooting, so it is advisable to use one of not more than average weight. Foster found that the average distance at which grouse were shot in New England was 23 yards, and to this, most grouse hunters will agree. This estimate is from bird to gun, and not the distance at which the bird was found dead on the ground. In certain coverts where the leaves are off late in the season, fairly long-range shots are offered, but in general it is close-range work, and not over 25 or 35 yards. A close-shooting gun is, therefore, a definite handicap.

There is considerable difference of opinion among grouse hunters regarding the shot-carrying ability of these birds and the most effective size of shot to employ. For example, Spiller tells of a bird which came back over him and which was hit five times with an automatic. He relates another instance in which a grouse was half decapitated by a 303-rifle bullet, and, with its skull cavity entirely empty, flew for a considerable distance until it finally crashed into a tree bole. Frank Forester records an equally remarkable example of vitality. Half the brain and one eye of a bird were shot away. The bird flew a long distance, alighted in a tree, and ten minutes later, just as Forester had come up and was about to shoot a second time, fell dead.

That many grouse receive a fatal wound and are not gathered, is certain. Only recently I had the experience of seeing a bird flush rather wild, fly strongly, and top the crest of a hill a quarter of a mile away. I felt sure that I had missed this bird, but a wise old dog I had with me thought otherwise, and, after disappearing over the hill for ten minutes, returned with the dead bird. It was a wonderful bit of retrieving, and the dog had recognized a vital shot better than I had.

Many times, while following the lines of flight, in the hope of securing a second shot, a bird which was thought to have been missed, is picked up dead. My impression is that grouse are not so "soft" as many gunners believe and that they possess, in proportion to their size, almost as much vitality as quail. The body-stricken grouse will sometimes sail for a hundred yards and be dead by the time it is retrieved. Due to the thick cover in which grouse are usually found many hits are not recognized.

Provided that the gun gives a good pattern at the required range, No. 7½ shot is the most satisfactory size. With this, close-range shots can be handled, and it holds up better at longer distances. However, it is a matter of choice. Spiller recommends No. 9, and Foster also advocates fine shot, especially early in the season. The opinion of such experienced grouse shots should receive consideration. The success of fine shot, like No. 8's and No. 9's, is due largely to the thickness of the pattern, which makes the likelihood of head or neck wound probable. Furthermore, it has ample penetration at the short ranges at which it is customarily used. The feathers of a grouse offer little resistance to shot. It is not fair, however, to a splendid game bird to fire at it with fine shot at extreme range.

One of the reasons No. 9's are so often used is that woodcock and grouse are often hunted more or less together. Under this circumstance it is preferable to use only No. 9 rather than only No. 7½ sized shot. No one need feel handicapped by using No. 9 shot; it will kill grouse stone-dead up to ordinary range. It is at the longer distances or when the bird is hit a stray pellet that the larger shot is better. It is worth remembering that in grouse shooting, as, indeed, in any shooting in thick country, it is generally the first barrel that does the work. In the late season when the leaves are off, and the range may be somewhat greater, and if hunting grouse only, a heavier shot is to be preferred. The ideal gun for late in the season may be slightly more choked. Here the 12-gauge is notably superior to the small-gauge because of its larger shot charge and greater power. However, the really important point in filling the game bag is proper alignment.

In selecting a locality for grouse shooting, it is well to take into consideration the character of the coverts. Some places in which grouse may be found are almost impossible to shoot in. These places offer fine sanctuaries as far as the sportsman is concerned, but, as a matter of fact, they are often full of vermin. Ideal terrain is found in some of the New England areas which contain many deserted and overgrown farms. However, in shooting one often has to take the country that is available. Woodlots and young poplar groves are pleasant places in which to shoot. Blowdowns and windfalls are favorite places for grouse. Grouse often come down out of the hardwood ridges to feed in pockets after spells of cold weather.

In certain coverts, grouse have a tendency to keep near coniferous trees, and this is well to bear in mind when plotting a course through a terrain which contains only a few evergreens.

Grouse may be found deep in big timber, but such places do not usually carry as much food as those nearer the edges of the woods. Old apple orchards, grapevines, briar patches, partially grown-up cut-over areas, berry-bearing vines, fruit of all kinds, blowdowns and near beech trees are all likely spots in which to find the bird. Alder runs, especially if adjacent to springs or small swampy streams, are also favorite haunts of grouse.

Birds are sometimes found in the open, especially during fine weather and late in the afternoon; but this is the exception, and it is unusual for them to be far from cover. I have heard old gunners tell of a family of grouse fanning out in open swampland, as quail do in broomsage, but the modern grouse is too well educated for such methods. Schley records having seen a grouse associating for some days with a covey of quail, and attributes the curious behavior to the straying of the bird.

The choice day for hunting is one which is clear, nearly windless, and cool enough to make walking a pleasure. If it has rained recently the day is ideal. The scent is good and walking is far less noisy than when the leaves are dry. During a soft rain and in misty, damp weather, birds generally lie well. I have had good shooting in a light snowstorm, and the birds lay rather better than usual. Many Pennsylvania hunters believe that the best shooting follows an early, heavy, damp snowfall, which has largely or entirely melted off. There is a general belief that birds are hard to approach when leaves are falling or during the full of the moon, and that off-season drumming is more frequent during the latter period. Certain it is that on some days the birds are wilder and also more difficult for a dog to handle than on others in which conditions appear to be the same.

Early in the season grouse are perhaps not so wild as later and are less resourceful in tricks of self-preservation. Family groups are a little more likely to be encountered. In country in which grouse are not much hunted, two or more birds are apt to be found together even late in the season. In a hard-hunted area they often separate earlier in the season. On windy days scenting is bad, birds are wild, and they do not lie well. Just before a storm all birds like to fill their crops. I have had good shooting during drizzling rain, but in heavy storms all game birds, grouse included, seek dense cover and do not move around. Grouse, I think, feed more or less all day, but especially in the morning and late afternoon

Often during the middle of the day they will be found dusting or loafing in some sheltered sunny spot. Knowledge of what the birds are feeding upon is one of the secrets of successful grouse shooting. Examination of the crop contents is a point often overlooked.

The grouse is one of our finest game birds; the only criticism of it is that it does not lie particularly well to pointing dogs and is prone to flush wild. Lovers of this bird are perhaps glad of these traits, as the species is none too plentiful. Generally speaking, the grouse is a hard target. Unless one's nerves are conditioned by long experience, the roar of an exploding grouse is likely to result in the loss of valuable time, and especially so when the bird rises unexpectedly. Because of the character of the surroundings in which the bird is found, the hunter is often caught off balance and has to shoot, if at all, from a poor stance. Unexpected flushes are relatively frequent. On account of the thick cover the hunter is often lucky if he can get off even one barrel. The importance of balance and proper methods of woods-walking have been mentioned elsewhere. They are especially essential to the grouse hunter. A considerable proficiency in gun-pointing can easily be acquired on the skeet field or by the use of a hand trap, but without ability in woods-walking the grouse shooter will miss many easy shots. Some men never seem to learn; as with all shooting, success is a matter of long experience.

The bird is notorious for putting obstructions quickly between itself and the gun. Most grouse hunters will state flatly that the bird deliberately dodges behind trees, but this, I think, is matter for question. That it does get behind obstructions in a large proportion of cases is beyond doubt.

At all events, killing grouse with any degree of regularity is a hard proposition. Sometimes they present the easiest kind of shots, but these are the exceptions. Not a small proportion of the grouse which ultimately constitute the bag do so as a result of some glaring error in judgment on the part of the birds. Birds that come back over, or past, the gun, after having been flushed by a companion at a distance, or which are caught in some opening, or fly down a woods road, are examples of this lack of judgment.

Such chances for the gun come none too frequently and should be accepted thankfully. Sometimes grouse depend upon their invisibility and protective coloration and permit themselves to be passed, and later apparently lose nerve and flush in the rear, sometimes silently but more often going off like an exploding bomb.

Grouse generally look as if they were farther off than they are. No sportsman wishes to shoot at birds out of range, and thus wound a large proportion, but grouse shooting is very different from pheasant shooting in this respect, and it is usually safe to shoot in cover at any bird that can be seen. A grouse at 40 yards in the wood is an extremely long shot; it looks at least 50 or 60 yards distant. There is not much likelihood of shooting at birds which are out of range in the wood, except perhaps occasionally late in the season.

In the open it is a different proposition. When in cover the bird often will get behind a screen of leaves and twigs before the gun can be brought to bear upon it. In this case make a quick estimate and fire in the line of flight. It is surprising how frequently this shot can be brought off successfully. Shot penetrates through obstructions such as leaves, twigs, and treetops remarkably well. Sometimes a quick side step will help to give a clear view. In any event, after the shot, listen for the sound of the bird striking the ground. Even if this is not heard, search with the dog where the bird should have fallen. Often the thumping of its wings will locate the bird.

Sometimes the shooter feels sure that he has missed the bird and follows up its supposed line of flight. If such birds cannot be flushed a second time, it is often worth while to return to the place at which the shot was fired. A careful search will result not infrequently in finding the dead bird. As mentioned, the grouse possess considerable vitality. A body-shot bird will fly as long as its strength permits, and then often set its wings and sail. I have seen such birds fall over backward, dead, when they finally struck the ground. The air-wash and immobility of the dead birds account for the fact that these birds give off little scent and are often hard for a dog to locate. When grouse shooting there is no time to pick shots or count cartridges. Every chance should be accepted, no matter how difficult or impossible it may appear. He who hesitates has no chance to reconsider.

The same holds true for the use of the second barrel. If it is to be of any value, it must be used quickly. However, I do not believe that with the average grouse shot, more than a relatively small proportion of birds are killed with it. Occasionally there is a second bird or a laggard, particularly early in the season, but even then this is not especially common, and doubles are rare.

"Make sure of the easy shots and try all the chances which are within range" might well be a motto for the grouse hunter. Whether one or both barrels are used, load quickly, for· there may be unsuspected laggards. It is a good principle to follow quickly, as grouse may run after lighting. Some men make a practice of shooting at all grouse, even when plainly out of range, on the theory that this makes them lie better the next time they are flushed. I think that this is a doubtful practice and, if the bird is aimed at, is likely to result in wounding. Shoot at all birds within range by all means, but do not deliberately fire at grouse known to be 60 or 70 yards off. Grouse do usually permit close approach and tend to lie better to a dog after repeated flushing, but actual shooting is not necessary to bring out this trait. The difficulty often is to find them a second or third time. In grouse shooting it is vitally important to mark the line of flight. As stated, grouse are prone to fly uphill, and this is a much easier shot than if they plunge downward. In approaching the pointing dog it is well to bear this fact in mind and attempt to maneuver for the uphill shot. They rarely stop, but usually top the crest and then sail, sometimes veering, to the alighting point.

Drumming is often heard during the shooting season, and a careful stalk may result in a shot. Furthermore, drumming often indicates that a second grouse is in the vicinity. No matter how proficient a man may be with a shotgun, he will miss many grouse and fail to secure shots at others until he has learned to place himself properly. He must know grouse habits and get in the best location for a favorable shot. This seems to be a sixth sense with some men; others never learn. Shots are often easy from one place and difficult or impossible from a point 6 feet away. When two men are shooting together much depends upon teamwork and this is difficult to develop without long experience. A bold, fairly rapid approach to the pointing dog is best. Attempts at stealth are almost always detected and often cause a bird to run or to flush wild.

Occasionally the bird may not break cover promptly to the approaching gun. If the sportsman stops abruptly, the bird is apt to flush, so it is worth while to remember this habit and to stop at a spot from which a favorable shot can be obtained. Rarely can the grouse endure a second stop. This characteristic is also observed among grouse which are not being pointed by the dog but which intend to let the gun pass.

Whereas grouse are fast flyers and get under way quickly, they weigh sometimes around two pounds and in their initial rising flight do not have the blinding speed of quail under similar circumstances. When under way they probably average about 70 feet per second and on the down slant or with a tail wind, may far exceed this rate. Under favorable conditions and when well under way they are about as fast as any upland game bird. When shooting in thick covers it is a good general principle to kill the bird as quickly as possible. On all angle shots take a good lead. The conspicuous, rather long-barred tail induces most guns to shoot to the rear and below.

Unhurried speed is the desideratum. There are, of course, exceptions to this rule, among which is the wish not to spoil game for the table. Usually the farther the bird is permitted to get away, the faster is its speed and the harder it will be to kill, and the more likely it is that it will get out of sight behind an obstruction. One must size up the situation. The commonest shot over a point or when walked up is a rising one, and although the bird may not be traveling as fast as it seems, it can still be undershot easily. It will get out of range soon enough, or behind a convenient treetop even more quickly. It may go directly away or it may quarter, but its flight is generally of an impetuous sort without any tendency toward zigzagging.

Often the grouse will get up in front, rise sharply, and veer off to one side, offering an ideal target at the turn. It is worth remembering that when flushed on a hillside, grouse are apt to go up,

rather than straight away or down and that they usually head
for cover. Birds coming back and flushed from a distance are
going fast and straight, and are usually in range as soon as they
are seen. When possible take them well out—do not let them
get too near. The usual tendency is to wait too long. Not infrequently an incoming grouse is in very near when first seen. The
sportsman may either use the first barrel on the incoming shot,
and, if missed, may turn and use the second on the retreating
shot, or he may turn quickly, prepared to employ both barrels
deliberately on the outgoing bird. In the incoming shot the target
is blotted out by the muzzle, and the gun instantly fired without
checking the swing. In the outgoing shot the aim should be usually
slightly below the bird, in order to secure the proper lead.

The decision whether to take the bird as an incomer or to turn
and take it on an outgoing shot should be made instantly. If the
latter is decided upon, turn at once without the slightest delay.
The secret of success with these shots depends upon this speed
in decision. The expert will pivot at once and take the outgoing
bird deliberately and with certainty, while the tyro will turn
slowly and as a consequence be forced to employ a hurried snap
shot. The one has an easy shot, the other probably an exasperating
miss. Indeed, this ability to decide instantly, get started quickly
and to perform the preliminaries without delay, which thus afford
ample time for the important alignment of the barrels, is essential
in all covert shooting, and marks the experienced shot.

Grouse which are in a thick place almost invariably "get out
on the other side." When such birds are pointed, two men have a
great advantage. The same is true if one is hunting thick gullies
and small runs. One man can go in and the other remain on the
outside, or the dog may be worked in the middle and a man placed
on either side. An easily missed shot is a grouse, flushed from an
old stone wall or bank, which skims low over the ground. The
tendency is to shoot high and behind. The most difficult shot of
all is that of the bird which dives from a perch high in a tree. One
cannot well shoot too low on such an offering. Frequently these
perched birds dive from the side of the tree opposite from the
gun. It is often a mistake to get too near the tree trunk, as over-

hanging branches may obscure the vision, whereas a little farther off there may be a better chance to see the bird when it leaves its perch. Grouse seem to have an uncanny knack of knowing when they have been spotted in a tree, and take flight instantly. It is a pity the bird does not always do this and thereby save itself from the poor-spirited or greedy pot-hunter who lacks sufficient self-confidence to give it a sporting chance.

Perched grouse may fly in any direction, but usually it flies more or less away from the sportsman. There is also a tendency to fly in the direction in which the head is pointing and away from the bole of the tree. Thus, if the grouse is perched close to the bole on the north side of a tree, with its tail pointing to the east, the bird is apt to depart toward the west or northwest. When perched on a hillside he may plunge downward with incredible speed. Low-flying grouse are not apt to resort to trees. Grouse often take to the air while the sportsman is astraddle a wire fence, or his attention is taken by the difficulty of getting through some particularly thick spot from which it is utterly impossible to shoot. This habit has saved the life of many a grouse.

The corrected snap often has to be utilized, but at best it is overworked. However, it is frequently the corrected snap or nothing. The quick swing is a deadly method for many offerings. A man accustomed to shooting in cover soon comes to ignore or not even to see obstructions, as his mind and vision are concentrated on the bird. The disadvantage of this method is that a charge of shot may be placed in a tree trunk. However, when time permits, I believe it is the best method. A slower swing can be employed for the open shots.

Grouse shooting offers many chances for those who are masters of the interception method. Grouse shooting often has to be quick or not at all, and, whereas every opportunity should be accepted, I believe more grouse are missed because of hurry or tension than for any other reason. Balance, and perhaps timing (which, interpreted, means speed without hurry), is the secret of successful grouse shooting. The wise man profits by his mistakes, and there is no real way to learn to shoot grouse but to shoot them. An average of two grouse for five cartridges is excellent shooting, and anything better than this marks the expert, shooting at the top of his form. Sandys says that if half the birds shot at are bagged, it is good shooting. Schaldach believes one bird for three shells is excellent, and indeed it is. Anything approaching a long run is extremely rare and doubles are something to remember. It is a curious fact that such a fast-flying, heavy bird as a grouse can crash to earth and yet instantly be off running. The soft cushion of leaves on which they often fall probably helps them. Whatever the cause, they can do so, and the experienced sportsman will get his dog to the point of fall as quickly as possible. Such birds may run a considerable distance and are apt to hide under brush piles or in other places of concealment. It is an abomination to lose a cripple, but without a dog it can easily be done. The crippled grouse may run 25 or 50 yards or even more but they are not the ground coverers that are wounded pheasants in a like fashion.

Many grouse are obscured or out of sight at the time the shot strikes them, and as a result the gun does not see any flinch, alteration in flight, dropped leg or floating feathers, even if these indications are present. This results in a high proportion of unsuspectedly wounded birds. I am under the impression that most of the wounded birds die. As mentioned, it is not uncommon to find the bird dead which has been lined, and followed. Wounded grouse probably do not live long.

It is not uncommon to find pheasants and, occasionally, quail which have evidently been wounded some days before, but such is rarely the case with grouse. The latter usually run under some place of concealment and soon die. In one way or another there are many kills which are not recognized. Bailey states that one out of ten birds is killed without its being known to the hunter and in spite of the conviction that they were missed. On this basis he points out that many birds are wasted each year by inexperienced grouse shooters. All this emphasizes the advisability of making a thorough search, even if it is thought that the bird has been missed.

In some parts of the country grouse are shot with the aid of a dog, which is taught to tree the bird. Often a small mongrel is used. The dog flushes and follows the bird, and if it lights in a tree barks around the bole. The bird's attention is taken up by the dog and the gunner has only to spot the bird in the tree and kill it before it flies. This method was formerly common and is still not infrequently employed in parts of New England and perhaps elsewhere. Until the practice was declared illegal, grouse were frequently snared. A miniature, unobtrusive fence, made of twigs and débris, was built, and snares placed in openings. These little fences were often of considerable length. The snares were generally of fine copper wire or horse hair. Since the sale of grouse has been prohibited by law, snaring has been largely discontinued, although here and there it may be practiced occasionally. The marauder, with a pocketful of snares, generally carries a gun for appearance's sake. Snares should always be destroyed when found. Grouse are none too plentiful; they have many enemies, and the sportsman should be contented with a modest bag. Indeed, as far as all our native game birds are concerned the great bags of the past are gone forever. However, the smaller bags of today permit us to remember individual occurrences and shots more readily and thus store up pleasant memories. These are by no means the least delightful part of shooting.

CHAPTER IX          THE AMERICAN WOODCOCK
                        (*Philohela minor:* Gmelin)

> By the old holly-bush, where, up gushing
> The burn of the valley breaks forth,
> The woodcock, ere long, we'll be flushing,
> The Stranger that comes from the North,
> The sports of each season delight us,
> Not less of July than of May;
> Then why, when October invites us,
> Why not to the woodlawns away?
>                    —Henry Brandreth, *The Sportsman* (1833).

COMMON NAMES. Woodcock, cock (a term often used by sportsmen to denote both sexes), timberdoodle, bogsucker (parts of Canada), night partridge or pewee (Virginia), night peck (North Carolina), mudsnipe, blind snipe, woodhen, marsh plover, little woodcock, lesser woodcock, wall-eyed snipe, bigheaded snipe, red-breasted snipe, woodsnipe, big snipe, hill partridge, whistler, little whistler, whistling snipe, bush snipe, siphon snipe, briar snipe, possum snipe, twister, thick neck, cane snipe, owl snipe (Nova Scotia), mud bat, bar-capped snipe, red snipe, mountain partridge, swamp partridge, night flit, mud hen, bog bird, bog borer, hokumpake, shrips, Bushschnip (Pennsylvania Dutch), night becasse, Massachusetts woodcock, long bill, ground woodpeckers, Indian hens (south Missouri) and Labrador twisters (in the Northeast this name is applied to the small males constituting the last of the fall migration). The great multiplicity of names is no new thing, for even in 1827 it was remarked in the *Shooter's Manual* that the bird had a different name in each state.

The name woodcock is derived from the old English term of *wude-cocc* or *wudu-coc.* The bird was also sometimes called *wude-snite.* In some sections the pileated woodpecker is known as woodcock. There is only one species of woodcock in America, although occasionally stray European woodcock have been reported.

*Field Marks.* "The woodcock is larger than the robin. The long bill and the whistling sound made by the wings in starting from the ground will help identify the bird. It is rarely found in the open meadow or marsh where snipes congregate, but rather in swampy woods or upland gardens and cornfields" (Forbush).

It is infrequently seen on the ground; and flushes with a twisting, dodging flight. The ear of the woodcock is directly under its eye, not back of it as in most birds. Compared to many other birds, the brain is relatively large and is tilted upward, the base looking forward in the same relative position as that of a cap worn on the back, and not on the top, of the head. The bill, unusually long, is grooved, and the first three primaries are little more than quills.

By the curious position of the eye, the field of vision of the woodcock is greatly increased while they are probing deeply with their bills. As their chief food is found underground and obtained by a sense of touch, they have little need for their eyes at this time, save to keep watch for their enemies, which the position of their eyes enables them to do.

Woodcock vary markedly both as to size and weight: cocks weigh from about 5 to 6½ ounces and hens from 6 to 9 ounces. The males average 175.81 grams and the females 219.2 grams in weight (R. W. Tufts). Lewis reports having killed a bird which weighed 10 ounces and another which weighed 14 ounces. The latter may well have been a stray European woodcock, which is similar in general appearance to our *Philohela minor,* but nearly twice the size of our bird. The average weight of the European bird is about 11 to 11¾ ounces (Seigne). Indeed, Yarrel (quoted by Seigne) reports one bird weighing 27 ounces. Birds of 17, 18, and 19 ounces have been mentioned in *The Field* (London) during comparatively recent times. Only a few European woodcock have been killed in this country.

In southern Nova Scotia, during the end of the shooting season, woodcock grow extremely fat and birds of 7 or 8 ounces or over are not uncommon. Mendall and Aldous have shown that birds shot late in the season average more than in the early part, each sex gaining about 25 grams from early October to early November. In my experience, birds of 7 ounces or over are nearly always females and those under 5½ ounces are usually males. Mendall and Aldous, however, state that the results of the various methods of determining sex externally showed the bill measurements to be the most reliable. Birds with bills over 72 mm. were generally females, while those under 64 mm. were always males. Tufts records that of 121 males the average length was 63.46 mm., the shortest 59 mm., and the longest 69 mm., while the females averaged 71.89 mm., the longest 78 mm., and the shortest 66 mm. Knight believes that if the bill measures less than 2½ inches (62.5 mm.) the bird is a male, and that if the bill measures 2¾ inches from its tip to the end of the exposed portion of the culmen or upper ridge, the bird is a female. Males are thought to be usually a little darker than females. The sex can only be determined with certainty by dissection.

Newly hatched woodcock show the upper down as pale ocherous buff and are heavily marked with very rich warm sepia. The under parts are unmarked (Pettingill). Even at this age the bill is pronounced and the eye more or less characteristic. With these exceptions they resemble young bantam chicks except for their smaller size. The general appearance of the juvenile plumage is similar to that of the adult. For a summary of plumage descriptions for the adult woodcock, the reader is referred to those published by Pettingill in *The American Woodcock* and Forbush (1925).

*Voice*. Except during the breeding season the woodcock is a fairly silent bird. Pettingill states that the woodcock occasionally utters a few vocal notes upon being flushed, and at a few other times. Because the vocal and wing sounds are nearly of the same pitch, they are scarcely distinguishable. During the breeding season both sexes utter a loud cackling sound not unlike the quacks of a female mallard, but more subdued. There is also a clucking sound made by the hen to her brood. A series of squeals is sometimes uttered when the bird feigns injury in defense of its young. While on the ground and prior to the flight song the bird makes a harsh nasal sound which has been variously rendered as *"peenk, kwank peent.*" The *"peent"* somewhat resembles the call of a night-hawk (Forbush).

To quote further from Pettingill: "The flight-song is a striking combination of aerial maneuvers, mechanical and vocal sounds. Briefly it is a courtship display consisting of a slow spiral ascent and a more direct zig-zag return with an accompaniment of tremulous notes that are musical, varied, and refined." This is performed while the hen is on the ground near by. The flight lasts for about one minute. The average altitude attained is about 225 feet (Pettingill). These flights are repeated a number of times and are carried on over the singing field and may cover "a space of fully five acres." Between flights the male struts proudly before the hen and carries out various antics. A male may use two or more singing grounds. The *"peent"* can be heard for a moderately long distance and is generally uttered more or less regularly. During the courtship song the male is so preoccupied that he will permit a close approach. This is especially noticeable during the early stages of the courtship. There is evidence that suggests the male bird returns year after year to the same singing field.

*Courtship.* Courtships are carried out during the early morning and toward dusk, and have on rare occasions been observed in the fall. Occasionally the woodcock may be polygamous, but this is not generally the case.

*Nesting.* Nesting sites are always on the ground, sometimes in a wood or near its edge and occasionally in the open. Young, open, second growth is a common site. The nests are usually more or less concealed by herbage, branches, logs, and the like. A slight hollow is generally selected. The nest is scanty and composed of leaves and débris, which has been pushed aside and molded by the hen. Four eggs is the usual complement, although three is a not uncommon number, especially for late nests. Five is rare. There is probably daily laying, and incubation is probably by the female, but this is not certain and some observers believe the male participates in the function. The eggs average about 1.60 by 1.14 inches, are ash gray to light buff in color, with reddish brown or chocolate and stone-gray markings. The eggs are ovate but somewhat pointed and are arranged in the nest with the small end inward after the fashion of shore birds. Incubation is from nineteen to twenty-two days (Mendall and Aldous).

Woodcock sit close, and toward the end of incubation may permit themselves to be touched by the hand or even picked up. This is probably due to an accentuation of their well-known "freezing" habit rather than actual tameness. When disturbed on the nest the bird often feigns injury and attempts to lure the intruder away.

Egg laying by the woodcock is unusual in Pennsylvania before the first of April, but the date varies according to latitude. I have seen a nest containing three eggs in Monroe County, Pennsylvania, on April 15, at a time when there was light snow on the ground. Doubtless, early nests are occasionally destroyed by heavy snowfalls. Krider, who had an opportunity to study these birds when they were plentiful, stated that nests in Pennsylvania, before April 4, are rare.

The total nesting success is probably at least 75 per cent (Mendall and Aldous). Infertile eggs are infrequent. The young leave the nest in a few hours after hatching, never to return. For the first few days after hatching and during inclement weather they are brooded by the hen at night. It is probable that the male takes no part in the care of the young. I have never seen more than one adult with a brood. A curious bobbing action is often indulged in. This, unlike the tilting of the spotted sandpiper (*Actitis Linne*), appears to be the result of bending the legs. The hen and the chicks often walk away from the intruder, each and every one bobbing in this peculiar manner. It is probably a nervous reaction induced by apprehension, and is more common during the breeding season than in the fall.

Juvenile mortality does not exceed 10 per cent (Mendall and Aldous). All things taken into consideration, including shooting, storms, etc., it is probable that each pair of nesting woodcock add between two and three birds to the population annually.

The young squat and remain immovable in time of danger. Popular opinion holds that at such times the young may be carried by the mother, and moved from place to place. Various methods of transportation have been suggested. Neither Pettingill nor Mendall and Aldous have observed this habit, although the latter have flushed brooding females on more than four hundred occasions. It is probably of rare occurrence. These authorities suggest that occasionally the brooding bird may be flushed and accidentally carry away a chick between her thighs. Many reliable observers, including Audubon and Sandys, have reported seeing the young carried, but all are in doubt as to the exact method. It seems to be fairly well accepted that the European woodcock occasionally carry their young, but here also the method is not certain. All observers, however, agree that they are carried with the feet, legs, or thighs, and not with the bill. Seigne, one of the greatest living authorities on European woodcock, states positively that he has seen the young being transported by the parent on several occasions. Once the bird flew over his head within a distance of a few feet and the young bird was plainly visible between the thighs of its parent. Lowlander startled a woodcock that was flying past. The bird dropped a young woodcock which fell to the ground three or four feet away from him.

The development of young woodcock is rapid and at two or three weeks they can fly for some distance. In four or five weeks they can take care of themselves and by fall may be larger than their parents. It was formerly believed that woodcock raised two or sometimes three broods annually, but recent observers are of the opinion that only one brood is reared each year. If the first nest is destroyed, a second or even a third clutch will usually be laid. During the latter part of the summer both old and young birds lie very close.

*Range.* "In eastern North America, the woodcock breeds from northeast North Dakota, southern Manitoba, northern Michigan, southern Quebec and Nova Scotia, south to southern Kansas, southern Louisiana, and northern Florida; it winters from southern Missouri, the Ohio Valley, and New Jersey (rarely Massachusetts) south to Texas and southern Florida; it ranges casually to Saskatchewan, Keewatin, Colorado, Newfoundland, and Bermuda" (Forbush). Mendall and Aldous state that "formerly the woodcock nested as far west as eastern North Dakota, eastern South Dakota, eastern Nebraska, eastern Kansas, eastern Oklahoma, and possibly Colorado." However, there are no recent breeding records for any of these states.

*Migration.* These are made at night. According to both Jarvis and Davis, woodcock before their migratory flights are somewhat nomadic in their ways, changing their feeding grounds frequently, thus leading many to believe they are already on their southern journey. The migration is, compared to that of some birds, a rather slow journey, and its speed is to some extent governed by the weather. Much depends upon conditions. During the fall migration the birds are said to average about 25 to 35 miles per day. There is a common belief that the moon influences the time of migration and that movements of birds are more common during the full moon. This would seem to be logical, but scientific observers are by no means unanimous on this point. My own observations fail to show any relationship to the phase of the moon. These are based upon diary records for the last forty years and have been made in Pennsylvania, New Jersey, New York, Maine, Massachusetts, New Brunswick, and Nova Scotia. Northern woodcock, during their southern migration, probably travel 800 miles or more. It has been estimated that woodcock travel at the rate of about 200 miles per week. It would therefore require about one month or more for them to reach their destination, and as a full moon occurs every twenty-eight days, it would seem that they must be moving during all phases of the lunar changes. At all events, as Schaldach remarks, the theory that migration takes place chiefly during the full moon offers an excellent excuse for going shooting. Migrating woodcock arrive in southern Pennsylvania in the fall at about the same time as do the slate-colored Juncos (snowbirds). When wild geese are seen passing over in the autumn, woodcock may be expected. During the fall migrations, there appears to be no definite rule as to how long woodcock will remain in one area. Sometimes they stop in a favorable locality for a week or more; on the other hand, they may be gone tomorrow. The duration of stay in a certain covert is difficult to determine with certainty as one flight may be replaced by another and give the impression of a prolonged rest.

Weather has much to do with migration. Birds are apt to take advantage of favorable winds. When the flight is late in arriving, the birds seem to realize that they are overdue and the stay is usually short. Late migrations and those resulting from unseasonable weather tend to arrive in a body. Sudden cold spells are likely to hurry them, although it is not uncommon to find a bird or two lingering in some warm moist spot late in the season, long after the main migration has passed. During unusually dry weather, woodcock are apt to concentrate in damp areas and be difficult to find in their usual haunts, whereas in a wet season they spread out, often on higher ground. Certain coverts are selected and others which appear equally favorable are ignored. Migrations southward show considerable variations in dates, some years being much earlier than others.

In migrating, woodcock tend to follow waterways, but this is not as marked as with many other birds. Mountain ranges also influence the flight. There is a rather general belief among wood-cock shooters that the birds tend to follow a railway line during their migrations. This is questionable, and the explanation of such a theory may perhaps be found in the fact that railways frequently run through a good woodcock country and birds crossing, not following, the tracks strike the telegraph wires, and as a result are found dead on the right-of-way. Two or three such birds picked up on perhaps a mile of track lead to the belief that the birds have been following the rails.

Migrations are conducted at low altitudes—seldom at heights greater than 50 or 70 feet. This habit accounts for the frequency with which woodcock are killed by flying against overhead wires and other obstructions. Breastbone deformities have been observed frequently among woodcock. This is a not uncommon deformity among other birds, but it has been suggested that in the case of woodcock its rather unusual frequency may, in some cases, have resulted from striking obstructions. The birds travel singly, in pairs, or in loose flocks. During the early fall, while shooting is dependent upon local birds, the sexes are about equal. The main bulk of the early migrants are females. During the height of the migration both males and females are present and at the end chiefly males are found.

Woodcock come north early and there are records of nests having been found in the snow. The main flight, however, does not reach the northeastern part of its range until the last of March or early April, and in Pennsylvania, a little earlier. The fall migration reaches southern Pennsylvania and southern New Jersey during October, the main flight arriving from about October 21 to November 5 or even later. This varies somewhat according to the weather, however, and the earliness or lateness of the particular season. There are usually many birds left in southern Nova Scotia when the season closes, which is on November 1.

The three points of concentration for the eastern birds during the southern migration are southern Nova Scotia; Cape May, New Jersey; and Cape Charles, Virginia. Here the birds often bank up while awaiting favorable weather for their across-water flight. Strong north or northwestern winds and cold weather to the northward usually result in heavy southern flights along the coastal lane.

Banding has shown that many species of migratory birds exhibit the following characteristics: (1) Those individuals which occupy the northernmost part of their species' northern range occupy during winter the northernmost part of their species' southern range; (2) those occupying the southernmost part of their northern range move in numbers to the southernmost part of their winter range; (3) the individual robin which nests in your shade tree will be back to nest in the same immediate vicinity the next season. Banding has also shown that the same birds tend to use the same migrating lanes year after year. The fox-sparrow which accepts hospitality at your feeding station during its spring migration will, barring accidents, probably be back the next year. These are not hard-and-fast rules, and little is known along these lines regarding woodcock. There is, however, some reason for the belief that, if a group of migrating woodcock occupy a cover this fall, the same birds, if they survive, will return to the same cover with their progeny a year later.

Banding of woodcock has been attempted by L. J. Merovka,

federal game protector of Louisiana (1936-37); R. T. Norris, of the United States Fish and Wildlife Service; J. D. Beule; A. T. Studholme; C. Aldous, and H. Mendall, and others. During the winter of 1939-40, E. A. McIlhenny, of Aviary Island, banded 154 woodcock. Woodcock banding is a difficult procedure since adult birds are hard to catch.

Attempts have been made to secure the birds at night by means of a large net, something like a large, long-handled landing net, used in connection with a flashlight. Net traps have also been tried. None of these methods has been very successful and all have occasionally resulted in injury to the birds. Nor has the banding of the young been entirely satisfactory. Mendall and Aldous report forty-six returns from banding operations. This is too few from which to draw accurate conclusions. There is some evidence suggesting that the old birds migrate earlier in the fall than the young.

Knight quotes figures secured from the United States wildlife and conservation offices of various states which indicate that the probable distribution of the woodcock during December, January, and February is as follows: Louisiana 50 per cent, Arkansas 15 per cent, Texas 10 per cent, Mississippi 10 per cent, Florida 5 per cent, Alabama 5 per cent, other states 5 per cent.

*Food.* This consists chiefly of earthworms (68 to 86 per cent). The bill of the woodcock is long and straight, and contains many nerve endings which enable the bird to detect the presence of earthworms when he thrusts the bill into the ground. This sense of touch is centered in the tip, which is bulbous. The distal third of the upper mandible can be raised after the bill has been inserted into the ground, thus enabling the bird to secure worms without thrusting the open bill into the loam. According to Blanchan this peculiar ability to raise the anterior portion of the upper mandible was first observed by Mr. Gordon Trumbull. Woodcock also eat insects, and upon occasion even small seeds, such as bramble, mustard, knotwood, sedge, and golden foxtail. They often probe in ant hills. The chief feeding time is between dusk and sunup. Occasionally, especially during dark days or when food is scarce, woodcock feed more or less all day. When nights are very dark they are said to feed more at dawn and dusk and are more likely to feed during the daylight hours. However, weather does not greatly affect their feeding habits, certainly not so much as it does many other birds. Woodcock are large eaters. Job reports a captive bird devouring twice its weight of earthworms in twenty-four hours, and many other almost similar feats have been recorded. Their digestion is extremely rapid.

*Boring or Probing.* The latter would seem to be the more descriptive term, as worms are probably located chiefly by the sense of touch. Movements of the worm disturb the near-by earth and these are felt by the probing bill. The bill after its insertion into the mud acts somewhat as an antenna. It is quite possible that the woodcock also depend to some extent upon sound coming from the movement of the worm and sometimes locate them by hearing. They occasionally tap the ground with the end of the bill before beginning to probe, possibly for the purpose of making the worm move. Woodcock are fastidious regarding their bills and it is unusual to find them muddy. Grinnell describes the feeding act of a captive woodcock as follows:

He would push the point of his bill into the soil at an angle of about 80 degrees and by two or three deliberate thrusts bury it to the base. While doing this the left foot was slightly advanced and the body somewhat inclined forward. When the bill was wholly buried, he stood for a few seconds perfectly still as if listening. Perhaps he was doing so, but it seems more probable that he was waiting to see if he could perceive any movement in the earth near his bill. If none was felt he would withdraw his probe and thrust it in again a little farther on. If, however, he detected any movement, the beak was hastily withdrawn, rapidly plunged in again in a slightly different direction, and the unfortunate worm brought to the surface and devoured with evident satisfaction.

After feeding, the bill was cleaned by means of his feet, and sometimes the bill would be thrust a time or two into moss or he would wash it in a water dish. This bird ate over two hundred worms weighing no less than 8 ounces during twenty-four hours.

E. C. Kent describes the feeding of a tame woodcock as follows: "The cock walked over the loam with short quick steps, its head turned a little on one side, reminding me of the action of a robin hunting worms on a lawn. I am convinced that it was listening. Then it would slightly open its wings and drive the bill into the ground with a steady push." Sandys and Van Dyke, in describing the feeding of tame woodcock, say that sometimes when the bill was buried, forehead deep, there appeared to be a sucking motion and that minute bubbles would appear at the angle of the mouth. Indeed, in former times there was a well-established belief that both European and American woodcock obtained their food by suction.

> But man is a carnivorous production;
> He cannot live, like woodcock, upon suction.
> —Byron, *Don Juan.*

Several of the local names in this country also suggest the belief. More recent studies seem to have entirely disproved this theory.

*Early History.* The woodcock is a retiring and generally silent bird which occupies chiefly woodlands and swamps. Even today its presence is often unrecognized by persons living near its domain unless they are sportsmen or otherwise interested in bird life. The result is that in the early days of the settlement of the Atlantic coast there are relatively few references to woodcock. The bird is comparatively small and when killed provides little food. It is not particularly easy to trap or snare and its shooting in the day of flintlocks must have been a difficult feat. All these factors tended to protect the bird and make it unnoticed. That the bird was eaten by the Indians is shown by a statement of Father Paul Le Jeune (1634).

Lawson, in *The History of Carolina* (1714), mentions the excellent table qualities of the bird. Latham in 1785 was the first to describe the flight song. The woodcock was one of the first birds to have protective legislation enacted in its behalf: in 1791 a game law was passed which demanded a penalty of twenty shillings for the killing of heath hen, partridge, quail, or woodcock in the City of New York.

There is considerable evidence that the bird was abundant early in the nineteenth century. At that time, Forbush states, a good shot could average fifty birds per day within twenty-five miles of Boston. Frank Forester, who arrived in the United States in

1831, found many woodcock in various parts of New Jersey and elsewhere, but noticed a decrease in their numbers during his later years. Most of his shooting was done from Tom Ward's tavern in Warwick, and on the drowned lands of the Walkill, which at that time contained some of the best woodcock coverts to be found anywhere. Krider reported on the large number of woodcock, many of them nesting in the neighborhood of Philadelphia. On one occasion three men killed ninety-three cocks before midday. At another time, Krider and a friend killed sixty-three birds by 10 A.M. He also mentions ninety-six woodcock counted out by one man on a barroom floor in an hotel near Bethlehem, Pennsylvania. The birds were killed in one day. Frank Forester and a companion killed 125 birds in one day, and numerous similar records could be quoted.

Just when woodcock shooting became popular in this country is difficult accurately to determine. Although Lieutenant Colonel Peter Hawker shot English partridges with wonderful success with a flintlock and another great shot, John Holt, is reported to have killed twenty-three woodcock in twenty-five shots, it is doubtful if many sportsmen could accomplish very great success on our woodcock with this type of gun.

The percussion cap was invented in 1807 by John Forsyth, a Scotch minister. These were paper caps. The cap was improved but it was not until about 1818 that it began to come into use on sporting arms. Breech-loading guns were used in France about 1830, or earlier, but the muzzle-loader was common until many years later. Forester used one of the latter in all his early shooting.

It would appear, therefore, that woodcock shooting as a sport was not much practiced in this country prior to about 1820 or 1830, or indeed somewhat later. In the early days sportsmen were few and little shooting was done except in relatively accessible localities. The pernicious and almost universal practice of summer cock shooting, whereby half-grown birds were slaughtered in great numbers, did much to deplete the supply of local birds. Despite protest by Krider, Frank Forester, Dr. Elliot, Dr. Fisher and many others, this wretched destruction of immature birds continued until a relatively recent date. Since woodcock bred in a certain locality tend to return to the same general area to breed the next year, this shooting was particularly destructive to native birds, but flight birds from the North were not so severely affected. Indeed, to some extent this holds true today, because of the fewer number of gunners in the northern breeding areas as compared to the hard shooting the birds suffer in the Northeast and the Middle Atlantic states.

Prior to the prohibition of the sale of game, woodcock were a common sight in the markets of Philadelphia and as late as the eighties sold for about one or two dollars a pair. Most of the birds, however, went to the New York markets—an editorial in *Forest and Stream* in 1874 estimated the number at 1,800 weekly. Early writers were greatly concerned over the apparent disappearance of the woodcock during August. The truth is that many had been wiped out on their breeding grounds by summer shooting.

The remainder had left their nesting areas and sought seclusion in other types of terrain during their postnuptial molt. "Molting swamps" have been described by Edwin C. Kent and others, and are usually very dense cover. During the molting period, birds have been observed on dry hillsides. After the molt is completed the birds return to their natal site or former feeding localities.

*Habits.* The woodcock is everywhere a comparatively tame, gentle bird, and, even when hunted hard, tends to resort to "freezing" and dependence upon its protective coloration rather than running or flushing from a distance. Heavy winds seem to be the only thing that makes them wild, and even this does not affect them to the same degree as it does many other game birds. On bare ground, birds will sometimes run rather than squat or remain immovable.

Woodcock are crepuscular or nocturnal in habit, and feed chiefly from dusk to daylight. They seek a sunny warm spot in which to spend the day; sometimes this is on a hummock or log in a swampy area, or they may fly to a hillside.

During their southern migrations, woodcock are thought to exhibit a predilection for those coverts which face to the north. Sands logically suggests that this may be because that is the side of the hill at which the tired migrant first arrives. However, they so often use other exposures that this is no particular guide in locating them.

Sometimes the birds select a ground on top of a bleak mountain and at other times a valley. Cover and feed are the chief points governing the selection. Woodcock, however, are much more immune to cold than many observers seem to think. It is the freezing of their feeding grounds by low temperature which they cannot stand. As stated elsewhere, woodcock are heavy feeders and probably digest their food rapidly. Hence they require a constant supply. In the South, canebrakes are favorable grounds for feeding, as also are swamps and woodlands which possess a ground cover of fern.

I have killed five birds without moving as many yards and often had three or four down at once, but concentrations of this sort are unusual. Generally a small cover will contain only two or, maybe, three or four birds, and a similar distribution will be found in other coverts in the same locality. This rather straggling distribution is true of both native birds and migrants. The present scarcity of birds and their loose migrations may partially account for this scattered distribution. In my younger days I saw many concentrations, and this condition is also frequently referred to by other older writers and is occasionally seen today.

In captivity the birds soon become tame and may take worms offered from the hand. When frightened and cornered, the tail is raised and spread. Woodcock will wade in shallow water and on occasion can swim fairly well. While walking they sometimes bob, after the fashion of sandpipers. This movement appears to be an indication of unrest or fear. In walking through thick grass the bill is sometimes thrust ahead and moved sideways in order to separate the stems for the passage of the bird. The large eyes reflect a greenish light at night; this fact was formerly taken advantage of to "light" and kill the birds, at night, in some areas in the South.

Even during the courtship period fights are few and the bird is generally peaceful. Krider saw two woodcock engage in a combat which lasted for several moments. They tugged with their long bills and flapped each other with their wings.

Woodcock roost on the ground, probably sleeping during most of the day. Anatomists state that because of the structure of the foot the bird cannot grasp a perch. Pettingill has collected a few instances in which woodcock have been seen in trees despite the fact that it does not possess a perching foot. They have been observed on logs elevated some distance above the ground, but even this is a rare occurrence.

Rich has on two occasions seen a woodcock light in a tree and knows of six other instances. He is of the opinion that this tree-alighting is less rare during the nesting period. I have often seen them crouched on a low fallen log or tussock which projected over a shallow pool of water, and have seen dogs point them in these situations. With few exceptions the bird remains on the ground except when in flight.

*Hardiness.* The woodcock can withstand considerable cold provided the ground does not freeze and shut off their supply of food. As far as is known, they suffer from few diseases and are not subject to epidemics of infectious origin. Contrary to some opinions, Pettingill is of the belief that the first winter plumage is acquired by an almost complete post-juvenile molt. There is no prenuptial molt. This authority also states that the time of the postnuptial molt depends to some extent upon the general localiy. Northern specimens of molting birds show them to have been collected from August 1 to as late as October 18.

*Flight.* Woodcock rarely, if ever, fly during the bright daylight hours unless disturbed. The flight of immature birds is weak and labored. They rise to the top of the alders or other low cover, fly for a short distance, and drop rather suddenly into the covert—very different from the flight of the full-plumaged, vigorous, late October woodcock. Woodcock rise in many different ways, depending somewhat upon the cover and various other factors. Perhaps the most characteristic flush is a sudden twisting rise, often veering from side to side to avoid obstructions and then darting off on a moderately straight line over the top of the cover for a distance varying from 50 to 150 yards or more. Occasionally the bird may make long flights and apparently leave the locality. When flushing, woodcock generally fly toward an opening in the cover. This is worth remembering when walking to the pointing dog. A frequent rise is an almost perpendicular one. This is probably due to the desire to find an open space, i.e., in this case above the cover. Although woodcock can dart away through a thicket, they prefer to have ample room through which to fly and thus avoid obstructions. This characteristic suggests that in some lights the birds' eyesight is none too keen and possibly explains the frequency of the perpendicular rise.

The length of the flight is influenced to some extent by the height of the initial rise. Thus, in tall coverts, the flight is likely to be longer than in low ones. At the end of the flight, the bird drops suddenly and dips into the cover, fluttering and twisting occasionally to avoid obstructions. The downward flight is checked by fanning back-strokes of the wings. This dipping into cover is so abrupt that it may deceive the inexperienced shot into the belief that he has killed the bird.

The woodcock's action in alighting is extremely graceful. The legs and feet drop down gently to touch the earth, and the bird crouches on the ground or may run a short distance. Sometimes the bird suddenly turns in its flight as if losing its balance, and darts or slide-slips to the ground with half-closed wings, squatting where it pitches. I have frequently observed the bird dart to the ground after it had been flushed by my companion. Sometimes, under those circumstances, it will light in the open a few yards from the edge of a covert and often within a short distance of the observer. It squats instantly but will be off on rapid flight upon the slightest movement of the observer. This habit of alighting near a man further strengthens the belief that, in certain lights, the bird does not see particularly well.

During the woodcock's initial, perpendicular rise the body is held upright. On other occasions they go off at a lesser angle. Occasionally a woodcock flies low, especially if flushed at the edge of a covert from which it crosses open ground. These low-flying birds get under way fast, and if in the woods, dart here and there until they find a straight path, when they are off like a bullet. Woodcock flushed either from bare ground or from low, thin cover get under way especially rapidly. This characteristic is also noticeable among quail. Flushed woodcock may go in any direction and occasionally come back in the face of the gun. Generally, when flushed at the edge of a covert, they fly up and inward. There is no rule for direction, except that when crouched they usually fly in the direction in which the head is pointed. The speed of flight varies during its initial stages. The low-flying bird is usually fast, while a big hen bird flushing out of low alders may float away like a toy balloon. Much, probably, also depends upon how badly scared the bird is and whether it has been shot at previously.

Usually, when flushed, the flight is accompanied by a peculiar, querulous, musical, and characteristic whistle—a sound no other bird makes. However, they can rise silently. It is probable that, like the whirr of the grouse, this whistle is the result of the extremely rapid wing motion that comes from being startled, and is made in an effort to escape quickly. With birds flying overhead, which have been flushed at a distance, the whistle is not heard nearly so often nor is it pronounced when zigzagging. I have frequently had birds pitch down near me without giving any whistle. Nor do birds rising spontaneously from cover in the early morning or those flying to or from their feeding ground produce the whistle—at least as far as my somewhat limited observation of this type of flying goes. However, Davis says that he has heard the whistle on these occasions. Often the hen will slip away from the nest silently. The whistle is produced by the first three primaries, which differ from the others, being little more than quills. These stiff, partially bare primaries are used by artists and are sometimes spoken of as the "printer's feathers." Molting birds generally make only the faintest whistle. Jarvis states that he has held a woodcock by the legs and heard the whistle as the bird fluttered to escape. To make sure that the noise was made by the wings, the neck and bill were grasped, and still the whistle persisted; but when the wings ceased beating the whistle ceased. Davis carried out a similar test in which the results were exactly the same as those secured by Jarvis. Sometimes the flushing bird utters a vocal sound which is quite similar in tone to that of the whistle of the wings.

The woodcock gets under way moderately quickly, but is often hampered during its initial rise by branches or vines, which it attempts to avoid. Sometimes it is momentarily hung up in these, a phenomenon I have never seen happen to any other bird. Its general flight is of moderate speed, but because of its erratic banking and swerving due to the cover in which the bird is found, it usually produces an impression of being faster than it actually is, although its dart-away cannot be termed slow. Indeed, sometimes it can produce considerable speed. It is its dodging flight and the thick cover which cause the bird to be missed. During flight the long bill is usually pointed slightly downward and forward and the feet and legs are drawn up among the body feathers. It has been suggested that the quick spring from the ground is sometimes assisted by the long bill, the latter being used as a lever. When crouched ahead of the pointing dog the tip of the bill often rests on the ground.

*Enemies.* The same enemies which destroy grouse also destroy woodcock. On account of its crepuscular habits, owls (even some of the smaller species) probably kill a rather high proportion. The sharp-shinned hawk is a rather small bird, yet it takes a large share of adult woodcock, as well as immature birds. Some years ago, in Maine, I saw a sharp-shinned hawk dive down and catch a woodcock which had been killed by my companion. I am glad to say that the second barrel ended the hawk's career. Due to the woodcock's protective coloring, its quiet, retiring habits during daylight hours, and the thick cover in which it lives, the bird is less harried by hawks than other species, such as the quail.

Fur-bearers undoubtedly take their share, especially during the breeding season when nests and eggs are destroyed. Even red squirrels have been known to destroy woodcock eggs. The incubating birds' habit of sitting close make them, if discovered, an easy prey to predators. The scent of the brooding woodcock is difficult to detect and this fact undoubtedly saves many incubating females and nests. In the less settled localities, wild cats and lynx probably destroy a certain number. Seigne states that, in Ireland, foxes destroy many European woodcock, and it is probable that they likewise are injurious to our own birds here. Domestic cats are well known to be serious offenders. A farmer in Nova Scotia informed me that one of his cats commonly brought woodcock to his house during both the spring and the fall and occasionally at other times. Forbush states that one cat destroyed eighteen woodcock in one season, and there are at least thirteen other similar records.

Pettingill draws attention to the fact that the woodcock is an unsuccessful species, incapable of readjusting its highly specialized form and habits to combat the many changes which have been brought about by the white man. Because of the low altitude at which it flies, both during migrations and at other times, man-made obstructions such as overhead wires, fences, and motor cars, etc., are particularly fatal to the woodcock and undoubtedly account for the death of many thousands annually. Lights attract the birds and a certain number are destroyed at lighthouses. Most woodcock gunners of experience have seen birds become momentarily entangled in vines and twigs during their initial rise and, as mentioned previously, it is possible that at least in certain lights their sight may not be extremely acute. It has been suggested that they may be comparatively nearsighted and that this may account for their frequent death against obstructions.

Forest fires, which are so frequent in Maine, Canada, northeastern Pennsylvania, and, indeed, throughout the birds' breeding range during the period of nesting and when the young are incapable of prolonged flight, undoubtedly are a factor against the successful raising of broods. The close sitting of the brooding hen, as well as their other habits, probably result in the destruction of a considerable number of adult birds during these fires.

Nest-trampling by cattle has been recorded, although, with the exception of the breeding season, the presence of cattle improves woodcock coverts. Occasionally the birds are destroyed in muskrat traps. Deforestation and drainage are constant factors working against the woodcock.

*Weather.* Prolonged, severe cold spells and heavy snowstorms during the nesting period destroy nests and probably some adult birds also. Such a cold spell occurred in April, 1939, in New Brunswick. Many woodcock were killed; no less than a dozen were found in St. John alone. Unseasonably cold weather in the fall from which the birds fail to escape, at times probably causes many deaths. Severe storms, accompanied by extremely low temperatures, occurring in the woodcock's winter range are known to destroy countless thousands.

Such a storm occurred in 1899 in South Carolina. Wayne says:

The cold wave was the severest recorded for 200 years. On Monday, February 13, the thermometer registered 14 degrees above zero, with the ground covered with snow from four to five inches deep on a level, while drifts were two feet deep. On Tuesday, at 6:55 A.M., the thermometer registered 6 degrees above zero. Woodcock arrived in countless thousands. Prior to their arrival I had seen but two birds the entire winter. They were everywhere and were completely bewildered. Tens of thousands were killed by would-be-sportsmen, and thousands were frozen to death. The great majority were weak and emaciated and were unable to withstand the cold. One man killed 200 pairs in a few hours. The majority not killed died of cold and starvation.

During these freezes, woodcock frequently resort to open pastures in an effort to secure food and there fall easy victims to their various enemies. A somewhat similar freeze occurred in the Gulf States area in the winter of 1939-40, and the destruction of great numbers of woodcock was reported by McIlhenny and others. Generally, the woodcock withstand weather conditions satisfactorily, but unusual and unseasonable cold spells occasionally result in an enormous mortality. Most birds can withstand even unusually low temperatures for a time, provided they have an adequate food supply. If this is not available, they fall easy victims. Prolonged droughts during the rearing season are also unfavorable for the young birds.

*Fire Lighting.* Lighting of woodcock was formerly practiced to a considerable extent in certain localities in Louisiana and other sections of the South. Since the enactment of laws prohibiting the sale of game this form of poaching has been largely stamped out.

Fire hunting was probably introduced by the French. It was carried out (preferably on a misty night) as follows: The shooting was done with a shotgun and light loads. A broad-brimmed hat was worn and a Negro carried an old-fashioned warming pan in which pine knots were burning. The shooter kept as much as possible in the shade, and the glare was cut off by his wide-brimmed hat. Cocks were seen on the ground and permitted close approach; they were killed on the ground or as they flew off. The woodcock's eyes reflect light and many were merely killed on the ground with a stick. In the early days it was not an unusual thing to kill one hundred birds in a night.

Formerly, when cocks were plentiful in England, large numbers were taken in nets which were suspended in favorable places. As far as I know our birds have escaped this form of persecution.

The above conditions militate against the woodcock—the chief adverse factor, however, is the gun. Long seasons, summer shooting, the sale of the birds, and the increase in the number of gunners due to the fine sporting qualities of the woodcock quickly had their effect, and their original abundance was greatly decreased. This soon became apparent and the best type of sportsmen, aided by conservationists, were instrumental in having legislation enacted which largely abolished many of these evils. However, this was a slow process, and much harm already had been done and the woodcock population largely depleted.

With the smaller head of birds, their normal slow rate of increase, the effects of unseasonable storms and unfavorable hatching seasons, became much more serious. Despite the benefit of the present short season and bag restrictions, these favorable factors have been more or less counterbalanced by the steadily increasing number of gunners. In the final analysis the woodcock is an easy bird to kill. It lies well and if missed on the first shot can generally be flushed a second time.

Dusking and skylining were practiced until comparatively recent times. This consisted in the shooter taking a stand outside of a cover either at dawn or dusk and shooting the birds as they left or returned to their resting sites. Large numbers were often killed in a short time. I have seen a dozen or more men lined up outside a covert at Cape May during the early morning. Knight states that as late as 1930 there was a large annual illegal kill and that a few years later there was an estimated legal kill of woodcock of 396,128.

On account of its migration and the large area occupied by this bird an accurate estimate of its numbers is extremely difficult to arrive at and a few local or isolated reports are of little value. Tufts is of the opinion that the woodcock is increasing in numbers and gives the following figures from his own shooting records:

Average Number of Birds Flushed Per Hour of Actual Hunting Time Assisted by a Good Dog:

1929, 3; 1930, 2.30; 1931, 3.04; 1932, 2.60;       *average* 2.73
1933; 3.59; 1934, 4.71; 1935, 4.59;                       *average* 4.37

He further states that, from discussing this phase of the matter with others who hunt in various parts of New Brunswick and Nova Scotia, the impression is general that the bird is increasing in numbers. However, he questions whether woodcock can stand greatly increased hunting. Mr. Tufts is an experienced observer whose opinion should carry real weight.

Pettingill attempted to determine whether or not woodcock were increasing or decreasing under the then present (1932, 1933, and 1934) conditions. To his questionnaire, which was directed to state and provincial game departments, he received twenty replies, ten of which indicated an increase, two a decrease, and three implied that the species was holding its own. Five did not answer directly. As far as this goes, it is a satisfactory report and speaks well for the efficiency of the present laws governing shooting. Despite the results of this survey, Pettingill stated (1936): "It is believed that unless certain radical conservation measures are enacted at once, it will be only a matter of years before the species is lost to us."

Mendall and Aldous (1943) have compiled a table of the "Annual Kill of Woodcock During the Period 1935-1939 Inclusive (as reported by states and provinces)." The average annual kill varied from 51,737 in Michigan to 300 in Prince Edward Island and totaled something over a quarter of a million birds. Pennsylvania alone in 1941 had a kill of 31,328, and in 1942 a kill of 27,729.

It would be beneficial if the Federal authorities in charge of migratory birds would secure from all states and provinces, from which they are available, the annual bag records, following somewhat the method adopted by Mendall and Aldous. A study of the gross annual kill from year to year, while it would be subject to certain fluctuations due to changes in laws and other conditions, should be of value in showing general trends causing increase and decrease. Furthermore, such data could easily be broken down to show local variations. The benefit of such a plan is so obvious that something like this is doubtless done at present, but if so, figures have not been published. Charts showing annual figures in five-year periods could be published with advantage in one of the shooting journals. Sportsmen do not object to restrictive laws, provided they are shown to be necessary.

Naturally, the woodcock population fluctuates more or less from year to year, and, like salmon, they have their good and bad seasons. Woodcock cannot be bred in captivity or artificially propagated. What is needed is a set of figures going back twenty-five or thirty years. As far as I know such studies are not available or on a sufficient scale to be conclusive.

The woodcock is a bird difficult to protect. Its susceptibility to unseasonable weather, the fact that it raises only one small brood each year, its mortality from forest fires, its habit of flying into obstruction, and its popularity as a game bird—all mitigate against its future. Indeed, there seems to be some tendency toward five- or ten-year cycles. Although in 1944 there was a Federal open season of only two weeks, the migrating bird may pass from one zone to another and therefore be in territory in which it may be legally killed for as long as six weeks.

Shooting seasons and bag limits have been reduced to the minimum. Staggered seasons, such as were attempted for small game in Pennsylvania a few years ago, have not proved entirely satisfactory. Experience with other game birds has shown that closed seasons for a year or two have not worked out nearly so well as was expected. Furthermore, as far as woodcock are concerned, its migratory habits would require a countrywide closed season, which might be difficult to obtain and even more difficult to enforce.

There has been a closed season on quail in Ohio for many years. This was instituted under the guise of protecting the quail as a song bird. This has not been satisfactory and there would be more quail in that state today if the bird had been left under the management of the sportsmen and their organizations. As a matter of fact, practically all efficient game legislation which has been accomplished during the last half century has been fostered by the sportsmen of the country and their organizations. Sportsmen's journals, such as *Field and Stream, American Field,* and, formerly, that fine old paper, *Forest and Stream,* and others, have uniformly endorsed sane conservation measures. A high gun license would certainly reduce the annual woodcock kill; however, it is more than doubtful whether such an unpopular law could be passed, even were it desirable.

The arrangement of synchronized seasons for woodcock and other game birds would be beneficial and practical. For example, Pennsylvania has an open woodcock season in October, during which a certain number of grouse and other game birds are killed illegally. Then the grouse season opens in November and the woodcock in turn suffer from illegal killing. How much game is illegally killed in this way is difficult to determine.

Grouse, pheasants, and quail are usually in good condition toward the end of October. By delaying the woodcock season until October 20 or 25 some early migrants might get passed, but these would help the breeding stock. Such a plan would be especially practicable in the northern states and Canada, where grouse and woodcock constitute the chief game birds and is in force in some places. As far as Pennsylvania and some of the Middle Atlantic states are concerned, there are probably more guns out in November than during the present woodcock season, and if that season were put back it would result in cocks being killed which otherwise would have been spared because they were out of season. However, I believe a combined season would work well and be beneficial to all species. It would also go far to stop out-of-season shooting. If the stock of woodcock warranted it, the ideal would be a one-month season coinciding with that of other small game. In this connection it should be remembered that as far as migrants are concerned they can only be shot while they are here and their stay is not long. Also native woodcock would be leaving before the season was over. Furthermore such a plan would eliminate much of the present illegal shooting.

In the British Isles a good deal has been done by special planting and cutting to improve woodcock coverts. Connet states that attempts to introduce woodcock into areas outside their normal range have failed constantly, as have other efforts to bring the European woodcock to this country and our own bird to European coverts. The same author also calls attention to the fact that several "big days" are less destructive to the woodcock population than many "small ones," and that success in increasing the stock of woodcock has been attained in England, but that there the coverts were left undisturbed except for several nonconsecutive days of shooting.

To summarize: under the most favorable circumstances the woodcock raises only a small brood. Predators are less destructive than to many other game birds. Nesting losses average about 30 per cent, approximately one-third of which is due to predators. Juvenile mortality is about 10 per cent (Mendall and Aldous). Occasional severe storms, both on their breeding grounds and in their winter range, wipe out enormous numbers. There is a large and regular toll of birds killed by flying against obstructions. It would appear that under present laws the woodcock is about holding its own.

*Shooting.* Woodcock are usually easy birds for a dog to handle. Their habit of "freezing" to immobility in the presence of danger makes premature flushes infrequent. Few game birds will permit closer approach than the woodcock. Indeed, it is not uncommon to see a woodcock almost under the nose of a pointing dog. Often birds are seen ahead of the pointing dog, a squatted oval brownish mottled mass, the large, dark shining eye being conspicuous. At other times they may strut with trailing wings and spread tail like a miniature turkey cock in front of the dog. The latter behavior is more common when the bird is under some shelter, such as a bush or overhanging branches. Strutting in front of a dog is thought by many observers to be a sign of fear or apprehension. No matter how thick the cover, woodcock like to have a moderately clear opening above them through which they may escape. This perhaps explains their frequent strutting when pointed under an overhead obstruction. Curiously enough, birds which are seen on the ground ahead of a pointing dog are rather frequently missed. I have known men who for this reason hated to have such a bird pointed out to them. When a bird is seen on the ground it is usually best to walk to it at once and flush boldly. It is something like a fence to a fox hunter—the longer one looks the more difficult it appears. Size up the situation, note the direction in which the bird's head is pointing and get the game in the air without delay. For some it is perhaps best not to look for the bird on the ground.

Due to the fact that the birds are less numerous, the shooting season shorter, the bag limit restricted, and perhaps because their sale is eliminated, good woodcock dogs are scarcer than in former times. As woodcock are generally found in thick cover the dog must keep close to the sportsman and constantly work to the gun. In some types of cover the dog should go out fairly well, but the rule that he should be within sight or sound of his bell is a good one for most occasions. This does not mean that the ideal dog is slow or pottering; on the contrary, he should be busy, industrious, active and keen, and investigate all good holding ground. The dog which will not go into heavy cover or seeks the easy way will never be good on woodcock. The woodcock dog should work at as fast a pace as surroundings permit. The idea that the woodcock dog is an old, superannuated, worn-out animal is quite incorrect.

Some dogs do not like woodcock. Such dogs are I think more common today than they were years ago. Some will refuse to retrieve the birds; other extreme cases carry their dislike to the point where they refuse even to point or to have anything to do with woodcock. Many dogs do not exhibit the same intensity and style when pointing woodcock as they do on other game birds. With certain dogs, the characteristics of the point will denote the variety of game which has been found. Many fine dogs are extremely intense when pointing grouse and merely do a good workmanlike job on cock. Some dogs also dislike snipe. The same characteristic is sometimes observed in England in regard to the European woodcock.

Prevention is better than cure, and the way to prevent this dislike from developing is to introduce the dog to woodcock while he is still young. If, at this time, he is made to know that woodcock are desirable game, and is encouraged in their pursuit, the dislike will not often develop. It is a good plan to work the youngster with an older dog which is accustomed to the bird. If, after a fair trial and an attempt to work upon the dog's competitive spirit and jealousy, he still refuses to point woodcock or to have anything to do with them, he had usually best be discarded, although he may be excellent on other varieties of game birds. He will probably never be a really good woodcock dog.

Most dogs, if they do not take readily to woodcock hunting, can be educated to do so. Many, however, will refuse to retrieve the bird. If so, hold the dog on his point and let another dog do the retrieving for a few birds. Let the dog smell the retrieved birds and if he makes any effort to mouth the bird, toss it a few yards away and have him retrieve it. If he does not retrieve promptly, send the other dog to do the job.

Vail suggests the following which has the advantage of not requiring a second dog. Hold the dog steady on his point and let the handler retrieve the bird. Let the dog smell the bird. Repeat this two or three times. As soon as the dog makes any attempt to mouth the bird, throw it away a short distance and require him to retrieve. If he does so, then kill another bird over his point and he will usually retrieve. This method is often successful with dogs which refuse to retrieve these birds, and it is also a good routine procedure upon introducing a dog to woodcock shooting.

Still another plan is to sew up a dead woodcock in a piece of rabbit or fox fur. If he is well broken to retrieve, he will usually bring this in. If so, cut a hole in the fur, bring out the bird's head and neck, and require him to retrieve. Thus, gradually cut away more fur at each retrieve, until none is left. Do not hurry or tire the dog. Carry lessons over at least two days.

I have seen a number of dogs that would not handle woodcock, but none of them had ever seen a cock until they were broken and over three years of age, hence more or less fixed in their ways. Sometimes, however, young dogs evince this dislike. Some strains are more likely to exhibit this dislike than others. Once overcome, many ultimately make good, useful woodcock dogs, but are not often so keen and enthusiastic as they might be. However, this is not always the case. Some become keen enough as far as hunting is concerned, but although they will retrieve the birds, evidently do not like to do so. Once firmly established, the dislike is difficult to eradicate. At one time I had an old dog (a good retriever of other game) that would point woodcock, but would refuse to retrieve them or even point dead. He would ignore the dead or even crippled bird entirely. By working with him, exciting his jealousy by having another dog retrieve the bird, and wrapping a woodcock in a piece of an old foxskin, as described above, he finally got so he would bring them in well, but he never evinced any pleasure or pride in the act as he did with other birds, and until his retirement was as likely as not to drop the bird at my feet instead of delivering it to hand. While carrying the bird he would curl up his lips as if the taste or smell was abhorrent to him.

Dogs which do not like to hunt woodcock are the exception. Many oldtime trainers preferred to break their charges on woodcock rather than on any other bird. When birds are sufficiently plentiful they afford excellent opportunities for the young dog. In addition to working in a restricted range, the woodcock dog should be extremely biddable, steady on point, and possess a good nose. If the dog will work to signals, so much the better. He should be a good retriever, and, since grouse are often found in the same general terrain, should be able to handle these birds. A dog which is predominantly white, rather than dark, is much easier to see and to keep track of in thick cover. On account of the thick cover, setters are usually better than pointers. However, as stated elsewhere, it is largely a matter of individual superiority and personal preference.

The use of a bell is often advantageous. Some men think that both grouse and cock hold better to the belled dog. This I doubt. However the bell does not seem to disturb the bird to any extent and aids in keeping track of the dog's whereabouts. If two dogs are used, bells of different tones may be employed in order to distinguish them one from the other. Some handlers tie the bell to the collar with a piece of weak string in order that the dog can break loose if the bell becomes entangled. This is apt to result in the loss of a good many bells. I prefer to keep the dog collar loose, so that he can pull his head out of it if he really gets hung up. It is a rare occurrence for a dog to get hung up so tightly that he has to pull his head out of the collar. I believe it is preferable to employ only one dog for each gun. Owing to the restricted range at which the woodcock dog works, one active, industrious dog can cover all the ground thoroughly. When two men are shooting, they are apt to be separated, and if each has a dog which will work to him, and if the dogs are well broken and will back promptly, two dogs are then ideal. Intelligent dogs soon learn where birds are likely to harbor and hunt such areas without orders.

Some men prefer a well-broken spaniel for cock shooting, for spaniels are a little smaller and lower than setters or pointers and

can get into thick cover well. It is from its use on European woodcock that the cocker spaniel derived its name. Good sport can be
had with a well-broken spaniel, especially in those localities in
which the cover is unusually thick, but I believe that pointing dogs
generally give better and more interesting shooting.

With the fewer birds which we have today, woodcock shooting
is an uncertain sport. To be sure, many localities contain a certain
number of native birds which can be more or less depended upon.
The bulk of the shooting, however, is often derived from the migrants. As previously mentioned, the date of the arrival of migrating
birds is uncertain and varies considerably. Cold weather to the
northward, perhaps clear nights and certainly favorable winds tend
to make the birds move southward. By watching the weather reports and the thermometer readings to the northward a good deal
can be learned about expected flights.

Furthermore, no man can say how long birds will remain in any
given locality. This applies both to local birds and migrants, but
with special force to the latter. Today, they may be here in numbers and tomorrow the coverts may be barren or hold only a bird
or two. Fine, clear, warm weather tends to make the migration
slow, but there is no absolute rule about this. During wet seasons
the birds tend to scatter, while, after prolonged dry spells, they are
often more or less concentrated in damp areas. Thus, after long
spells of dry weather, woodcock are not apt to be found in open
coverts or sparse wood, but instead in wet bottoms or deep, impenetrable thickets where the soil never entirely loses its moisture.
Conversely, in extremely wet weather the more elevated grounds
are sought. Very late in the season and after most of the birds have
left a few stray woodcock may often remain around a favored
swamp or wet spring in a sheltered area. Woodcock like, and,
indeed, require, moist ground for boring, but unlike their cousin
the Wilson snipe, they do not like actually to get wet or to wade in
the water more than is necessary. However, if it is required of them,
they can swim fairly well.

A normal season usually offers the best shooting. Their habit of
resting during the daytime and moving about for food during the
twilight hours should be remembered. It is probable that a certain

amount of sporadic feeding occurs during the daytime, especially on dark days. Birds which are migrating during the night must also utilize daylight hours to some extent. Unless particularly severe, the weather makes no great difference in the feeding habits. Sometimes the birds rest during the day on or near their feeding grounds, or they may fly to some warm, often southern slope of thick cover, and there sleep and loaf in the sunshine. Flight birds particularly exhibit a tendency to use hillsides, especially those covered with small alders, birch or poplars, whereas local birds are more apt to be found near their natal sites, or in the bottom lands. However, there is nothing certain about the location of flight birds and they may also be found in the latter localities.

There is no sure way of distinguishing a migrant from a local bird. As stated, migrants are perhaps more likely to be found in hillside cover and are a little more apt to be bunched up and to produce concentrations. Hens migrate first, hence if there is a marked predominance of females present, it is probable that they are migrants. A predominance of males may merely indicate that the earlier migrating hens have left and the cocks may be local birds. Some gunners think the migrants are wilder and that they fly faster. This is doubtful; nor is there any reliable distinguishing mark in the appearance of the birds. Sometimes late in the season, however, a number of small fast-flying males are encountered—the so-called Labrador twisters—which often seem to be wilder and faster than the ordinary run of woodcock. These usually constitute the tail end of the fall migration, and give some color to the belief that migrants are harder to kill than local birds. Warm hillsides are more apt to be utilized by the woodcock toward the end of the season and in cold weather. A moderately warm, pleasant day after a mild rain is usually favorable for shooting. A strong wind is not desirable. Woodcock will use one cover year after year and may be absent from others which look just as good to the sportsman.

Sometimes in the course of years the cover will become grown up and the birds will desert it. When the grass becomes at all dense, it is unfavorable for boring. Knight calls attention to the woodcock's preference for Canadian blue grass. As already mentioned, the presence of cattle usually improves a covert. Hoof-prints remain damp and offer favorable sites for boring and the cattle droppings probably increase the number of worms. I have seen woodcock boring directly through dried cow droppings, but generally their probing is in soft earth or mud. Woodcock seem to have no fear of cattle and I have flushed them almost from under their feet. They are particularly partial to the almost black, soft muddy type of soil found under alders. The presence of cattle also acts beneficially in keeping cover from getting too thick and thereby cutting off sunlight. Cattle trails through alder swamps and in rocky cover are favorite sites for woodcock. I know of at least three coverts which were at one time used regularly by these birds and are now deserted because the cattle have been removed and, as a consequence, a thick ground cover has developed.

Probably the distribution of earthworms is one of the chief attractions to woodcock in selecting a cover. Slightly moist or even muddy, loose, sandy loam is one of the most favorable types of soil. In such a soil, when moist and covered with lowland or black alders, earthworms are usually abundant, and hence such places are a favorite feeding ground. As many as twenty-six earthworms to the cubic foot have been found in such soil. These alder runs and thickets are common in the Northeast and in many parts of Pennsylvania, as well as in many other localities. In Nova Scotia, Maine, and Pennsylvania, and in fact wherever present, they are likely to contain woodcock.

More or less stony areas, consisting of sycamore scrub and low willows, provided the ground is moist and partially covered by low green grass, attract woodcock. In some localities the bottom land alders and other cover, while containing woodcock, are so thick as to make shooting, except along the edges, almost impossible. Recently burnt-over land is attractive to the bird. The hillside coverts generally provide pleasant shooting. Bennett calls attention to the fact that woodcock are often found in the neighborhood of crabapple trees and I have found them in such places. The ground under young aspen and small or medium-sized birch trees is often favored; but when the trees get large they lose their attractiveness for the bird. Sometimes some special small area seems to offer particular charm to woodcock and if a bird is killed from it another will take its place in a short time.

Knight, in his excellent monograph, shows a picture of such a spot, not more than a few yards in extent, from which twenty woodcock were killed in three seasons. Sometimes singing fields and breeding sites can be located in the spring and such areas are almost sure to contain local birds when the season opens. In sour acid soil, such as is often found under tamaracks, black spruce, and other conifers, worms are scarce and woodcock are rarely found. Soil which is permeated with iron rarely contains many worms. The same is true of sandy, gravelly ground. Woodcock rarely use areas in which there is much moss. The woodcock does not frequent salt meadows, nor, according to Chandler, are the birds abundant in coal regions.

Areas partially grown up after timbering or fires are often used by woodcock. Second-growth hardwoods or mixed growths often hold birds. Hardwood of any size, provided the earth is moist and there is considerable undergrowth, may hold birds. Brushland is often utilized, especially early in the season. On mountainsides, briar patches or crabapple-hawthorn thickets are sometimes selected. Wild oats, when not too thick, and partially covered with low undergrowth, are often used. Woodcock are found under white birches and it is believed the soil under these usually contains large numbers of earthworms. Young upland birches are especially favored by the birds. Overgrown apple and pear orchards also are often utilized. Birds may be found in sparse bracken and light growths of ferns and under sumac trees. In New England, bayberry bushes intermixed with red cedars are frequently chosen. The edges of thickets are common resting places.

Generally speaking, cock prefer a light overhead cover. Quail and other game birds frequently resort to such thick cover that they have to make a preliminary run to clear it in order to flush. Not so with the woodcock, which likes to have space to ascend in. Naturally the cover will vary with the locality. In southern Nova Scotia, probably 75 or 80 per cent of birds are found in alder patches. Around Ellsworth, Maine, briary hillsides are favorites.

In Sullivan County, New York, the cover around small springs on the hillsides is much used. Small ravines, often conspicuous by reason of little patches of green grass in the neighborhood of a spring, are favored by woodcock. Green briar thickets, often underneath hardwoods and in blowdowns, are choice sites in southern New Jersey and Maryland. In Pennsylvania alders, briary undergrowth are selected.

Woodcock are said occasionally to frequent cornfields, especially in the Middle West, but I have never found more than a stray bird or two in such situations. Woodcock are so selective that in a strange country it is of great advantage to secure the services of a local man in order to find out the location of the best coverts. Woodcock shooters, however generous in other respects, are often secretive in regard to woodcock coverts. At dusk and dawn in favorable locations birds are frequently seen flying to and from their feeding grounds and an attempt to "line" the birds by the direction of their flight is sometimes worth while. Such opportunities are doubtless infrequent, but on one occasion, while motoring from Digby to Yarmouth, Nova Scotia, I remember seeing a heavy flight crossing the road. We stopped the car and watched as well as the failing light permitted. Fifty birds must have flown across the road in a few minutes. We returned the next morning and found the spot in which they had been feeding, but most of the birds had departed—probably to a resting ground.

To summarize: a stray migrant may drop almost anywhere. In selecting a cover the birds seem to desire two things, i.e., food and a resting site. Sometimes these are combined in one area, at others they are separate. The feeding grounds must contain accessible earthworms. Such sites, if recently used, show evidence of occupation, but aside from this (and the fact that cocks have been formerly known to use them) the average sportsman has little to go upon in determining what are and what are not good feeding grounds, except for the general appearance, which may be deceiving. Woodcock like to rest during the day in a dry place. This may be merely a hummock or a low log surrounded by water and situated in a swamp, but it is a dry spot. On other occasions and apparently for no determinable reason, they will leave their feeding grounds in the morning and fly to some favored resting site. These resting sites may be totally different in character from the feeding grounds. I have seen them even on high mountain sides covered with oaks and maples. They are not always near what is generally classed as good woodcock cover. Resting sites may show droppings, but borings are infrequent. Woodcock are, however, fairly constant in their choice of both feeding grounds and resting sites. Without local knowledge, therefore, much time is likely to be lost.

Borings and chalk marks, or, as they are sometimes called, "splashings" and "whitewash," are a sure indication that woodcock are either present or have been recently. The rather neat borings are apt to be in cattle tracks, old paths, or anywhere the soil is loose or damp; but they are not often seen in thick grass. They may be single, straggling, or in clusters. The latter is the most common and look as if a small-calibered pencil had been thrust into the ground. They generally enter at an angle of about 80 degrees, and are 1 to 3 inches deep. Near the borings and in other areas the so-called chalk marks are present. These are the whitish semi-liquid droppings of the bird. As the woodcock is a large eater there are usually many chalk marks scattered about. The boot toe or a stick test can help to determine their freshness. Sometimes footprints of the birds may be seen.

*Shooting.* A light, perfectly fitting gun which gives an optimum pattern at 20 or 25 yards is ideal for woodcock shooting. The gun for upland shooting which gives optimum patterns at 25 and 35 yards is entirely satisfactory for woodcock shooting, provided small charges are employed, and these are all that is necessary. For a 12-gauge gun, 2¾ or even 3 drams or its equivalent and 1 ounce of No. 9 shot is an excellent load. It is equally satisfactory for grouse in case these are encountered. Seven-eighths of an ounce of shot is enough for the 20-gauge. Woodcock shooting is usually close-range work and fine shot is preferable. Some woodcock shooters use 10's or even smaller shot. No. 9 shot penetrates obstructions well and spoils few birds.

For extremely short range, the edge of the pattern may be utilized. This employing of the edge of the pattern has been mentioned a number of times. It is a useful procedure and the knack is not particularly difficult to acquire. The easiest way to perform it is to lead a bit high and about 8 inches or a foot ahead of the proper allowance. This will put the bird in the edge of the pattern at about 15 yards, provided the barrel is an improved cylinder. In all covert shooting it is better to kill the bird quickly than to wait until it gets farther off. Delay often results in the bird getting behind an obstruction. Furthermore, it is gaining headway all the time. Also, quick shooting gives a better chance for the use of the second barrel in case there is a miss with the first. Quick shooting does not necessarily mean snap shooting, but dwelling on the aim with the idea of letting the target get farther off is an almost sure way to miss. If one must wait—and no one wishes to blow a bird to pieces—it is better to delay going into action for a fraction of a second. The most effective method, however, is to shoot as soon as the opportunity is offered. Using the edges of the pattern would be difficult or almost impossible at ordinary range, but it is not so hard to accomplish at the short distance at which it is required. Regardless of whether the delayed shot or edge of the pattern method is attempted, most men who shoot woodcock ultimately become eligible for what Knight calls the W.D.A.—Woodcock Demolishers Association.

When woodcock rise almost perpendicularly they are not going very fast. Take them on the rise or at the latest when they have reached the top of the cover. There is apt to be a slight pause at the top of the flight. This is an excellent time to shoot, especially when the rise has been a short one and time has not permitted a shot during the initial upward flight. When the perpendicular rise is a long one, as is likely to occur in timber or tall saplings, birds should usually be shot at while they are ascending. They are most often shot over points, and there is no excuse for not being ready. Quick shooting is necessary at times but try to make sure with the first barrel, for even at best there may be no time for the second. It is the judicious use of the first barrel which fills the game pocket in all covert shooting. I have shot for a week in Nova Scotia and not been able to use the second barrel a dozen times.

Probably the improved snap will be required more frequently on woodcock than on any other game bird. Even in this type of shooting it is generally overworked. The quick swing is far more accurate and preferable whenever it is possible. Fairly open shots are easy; it is generally the obstructions and twisting rise that cause the misses. Shooting is much easier after the leaves are off.

What has been said, in the chapter on grouse, regarding the importance of selecting a favorable point from which to shoot holds true in woodcock shooting to an almost equal extent. It is well worth while when walking up to the pointing dog to look over the ground. Select the best footing and a site from which the most open shot is likely to be obtained. A few feet may make the difference between a clear shot and one which is almost impossible. It is generally best to walk in behind the dog, as this is likely to result in a going-away or quartering shot. Woodcock are uncertain, however, and may go in any direction, even returning into the face of the gunner. Only one thing is certain, and that is, that at the edge of covert and when approached from the outside they are almost sure to fly inward. However, if the sportsman is inside the cover and the bird on the edge it may attempt to cross an open space to go to another near-by covert. In common with most game birds, a sudden pause while approaching the pointing dog often results in the bird taking to the air. If the sudden stop is to be tried it is obviously wise to select a location from which an open shot can be obtained. Sometimes the trick will work when the bird is in a thick cover. A sudden stop at the edge may result in a flush and a fairly easy shot, whereas if the gun had entered the thicket the shot might have been impossible. At all events, it is sometimes worth trying. When seen crouched ahead of the pointing dog, the bird is apt to fly in the direction in which its head is pointing.

Although, as mentioned elsewhere, probably more woodcock are wounded and lost than the average shooter suspects, the bird is not much of a shot carrier and a few pellets will generally bring it to the ground. Nor is it a difficult bird to retrieve, as it rarely makes much serious effort to run when wounded. A good retriever is, however, a great asset, as birds frequently fall in dense cover and even dead birds are difficult to find because of the underbrush and their protective coloring, which blends with fallen leaves. It is probable that a number of birds are killed which do not immediately fall to the shot nor show evidence of being hit, but fly off some distance and die in a relatively short time. Furthermore, the thick cover often makes it impossible to see a floating feather or an alteration in flight or to follow the bird with the eye for any considerable distance. The short range results in deep penetration of the shot, and with the small size usually used there are many stray pellets at the edge of the pattern, any one of which driven into the body cavity will probably result fatally. Knight thinks that 10 per cent of woodcock are lost in this way, and that perhaps 25,000 or 30,000 birds are thus wasted annually.

On account of its large head it is not very rare for a killed woodcock to lodge by the neck in the fork of a limb. Birds which are wounded and able to remain upright are often harder for the sportsman to see than those which are cleanly killed. As stated previously, during its flight and fall the bird has had an "air wash" and if killed cleanly may not give off much scent, so no matter how good a retriever the dog may be it is well for the sportsman himself to "mark the fall." Since wounded woodcock do not run much, make the dog hunt dead thoroughly at the point where the bird has been marked. As shots often have to be taken through treetops, and the like, a thorough search should be made for all such birds, unless they are known to have been missed. With a good retriever relatively few woodcock are lost, as compared with other game birds. Sometimes a bird which is missed will nevertheless drop voluntarily to the ground at the shot. When going to the point at which a bird is supposed to have fallen, it is well to be prepared for such an eventuality.

Woodcock do not usually fly very far, and if their line of flight is marked they can generally be flushed a second time within a hundred yards or so. Birds which are flushed in high cover have a tendency to fly farther than those in which the initial rise is relatively low. Unlike grouse, the more frequently woodcock are flushed the wilder they become and the farther they fly. When not shot at or missed it is pretty certain that the bird can be put up again—at least once, but probably twice and possibly three times. The bird will usually leave the locality after the third time, if not before. Indeed, two chances are about all one is likely to get. In the South the shooting is less attractive than in the North.

Five or six woodcock for ten cartridges and six or seven for each ten birds shot at is excellent shooting. Probably 50 per cent of the birds shot at would be about the average. Because of the varied cover in which woodcock are found, estimates are especially difficult. In some covers, after the leaves are fairly well off, moderately long runs are not particularly infrequent, but when the cover is really heavy, and if one accepts all chances offered, anything over half the birds shot at may well mark the expert. The best thing to do is to take enough cartridges, accept every chance, and not bother to count shells.

Captain Paul A. Curtis said a man seldom performs indifferently on cock. Generally he either shoots about up to the top of his form, or else he is too poor to be good company. People generally like what they do well and it is a fact that for many sportsmen woodcock shooting represents their ideal sport. Many men who will hardly inconvenience themselves to shoot other birds will go to any trouble to obtain good woodcock shooting. There is something about the woodcock which is especially attractive—perhaps its beauty or the mystery which surrounds its habits—at all events the saying "Once a woodcock shooter always a woodcock shooter" holds true with many lovers of the dog and gun.

Woodcock shooting is practiced at a time of year when the weather is likely to be delightful and the coverts are of unrivaled beauty. Barring heavy wind and other conditions which result in poor scenting, the type of day selected for shooting does not make much difference in one's ultimate success or failure. Dark days often result in poor background, but otherwise birds, if present, can be found nearly as well as in clear weather. I have had excellent shooting during a mild early snowstorm and during misty or softly rainy weather. Indeed, during these latter conditions birds seem to lie particularly well and scent has often been good. During clear warm weather cocks are often more sluggish and lack the speed and dash they exhibit on a frosty morning or during a heavy wind. Moderately slow and careful hunting is the most effective. Woodcock generally lie close when in thick cover and this is where they are usually found. No matter how good the dog, it must be given time to investigate likely areas, otherwise birds will be passed by. This is particularly true where one bird has been found or borings or chalk marks have been observed. It is also the case of coverts known to have held birds in former times. Woodcock do not move around much during the daytime. Therefore scent is apt to be more localized than in the case of more active birds.

Much has been written about the woodcock. Recently two especially valuable monographs have appeared, namely, *The American Woodcock,* by O. S. Pettingill, Jr., and *The Ecology and Management of the American Woodcock,* by H. L. Mendall and Clarence M. Aldous. Both of these excellent studies have been extensively drawn upon for material in this chapter. They should be read in full by all those interested in the natural history of the woodcock.

(*Colinus virginianus virginianus:* Linnaeus)

---

*The corn-land loving quayle, the loveliest of our bits.*
                                    —Drayton, *Poly-Olbion.*

NOMENCLATURE. The term "quail" has caused much discussion. The European quail is migratory, polygamous, and dark fleshed. In size and appearance our American is not entirely dissimilar—a fact which probably led to the early settlers of our country to misname the American bird, just as was done in the case of many others, notably the American robin, which is in reality a thrush.

Mayer says that "in the North and East he is called Quail; in the South and West he is Partridge; while everywhere he is known as Bob White." His advice to call him "Bob White," as he calls himself is excellent. However, during the sixty years since Mayer's writing the term "quail" has become more generally used than formerly. There are many varieties of quail in this country. The term "bobwhite" is distinctive and therefore the better name. However, names are largely a matter of established usage and, despite what scientists and others may advise, most of us will continue to employ the term to which we have become accustomed.

Sandys and Van Dyke say that Pennsylvania sportsmen have sometimes referred to a "willow-legged" quail, meaning a bird with a greenish-tinted leg. It is also common to hear a "swamp" quail and "woods" quail which are generally large, well-fed birds that occupy a swampy or woody territory. These latter terms are local names for a single species.

*Field Marks.* "The bobwhite is much smaller than a ruffed grouse and slightly larger than a woodcock, but distinguished from it in flight by its small head, extremely short bill, and different wing motions." (Forbush states that the length of quail varies from 9.5 to 10.75 inches; spread 14 to 16 inches and weight 6 to 9 ounces. Warren states the woodcock's length is 10 to 12 inches, spread 15 to 18 inches and weight 4 to 9 ounces. Baird places the woodcock's length at about 11 inches and its spread at 17 to 19 inches. To me, during flight, the woodcock looks the larger bird.) "In rising it whirrs loudly and flies at no great height with speed and fast-beating wings, then sails with wings sharply curved downward. It does not flutter and sail alternately, like the smaller meadow lark, which is sometimes called 'marsh' quail, and which in flight shows white outer tail feathers. The black and white markings on the head of the male bobwhite are conspicuous at some distance; similarly placed buff markings on the female are not so noticeable" (Forbush).

A rare red phase has been described. The late C. E. Buckle reported several of these beautiful quail present in a covey of otherwise normally colored birds on H. Ames' plantation, near Grand Junction, Tennessee. I have been informed that these red quail are now being raised in captivity on the Ames plantation. If so, it would seem probable that a pure breeding red race might readily be established in much the same manner as was the melanistic pheasant. A. R. Starr states that the Cuban quail is strikingly red—so deep in color that no one fails to notice it.

In 1937, I saw a bobwhite that was distinctly of the red phase. This bird was killed a few miles south of Windgap, Pennsylvania, by R. C. Martin, now of Elizabethtown, Pennsylvania. He told me that the bird was so noticeable he singled it out of the covey, and that there were two other similarly colored birds. It was a large quail, whose red, while not so brilliant as that in the specimen from H. Ames' plantation, now in the possession of The Academy of Natural Sciences of Philadelphia, was, nevertheless, very distinct and noticeable.

*Weights.* Starr places the average weight of well-fed adult bobwhites at 7 to 7¼ ounces. H. L. Stoddard (Thomasville-Tallahassee region) gives the average weight as being from 5.71 to 6.25 ounces; but in South Carolina the same authority quotes average weights as varying from 6.11 to 6.54 ounces, the heaviest being 7½ ounces.

In North Carolina, Mayer shot fifty birds averaging 7 ounces. Lewis records twenty New Jersey birds averaging 8 ounces; and Schley states that he has frequently killed bags in Maryland that averaged a similar weight. No larger or finer bobwhites than the Pennsylvania birds are found anywhere. The largest bird I ever weighed was killed in Montgomery County, Pennsylvania. It weighed 8¼ ounces. Northern birds are usually larger than the southern variety. There is not much difference between the weight of hens and cocks.

*Sex Ratio.* Many observers have noted a predominance of males. So, when a choice is offered, it is better to shoot the cocks and spare what Sandys aptly calls the "seed" hens.

*Longevity.* Bobwhites have been known to live eight or ten years in captivity, but sufficient data are not available from which to hazard a surmise as to the average length of their life in the wild state.

*Range.* The bobwhite may be found from Southern Ontario and the northern eastern states, southward to Mexico, and westward to Wyoming, South Dakota, Mississippi, Michigan, Texas, the Gulf states, Colorado, and New Mexico. A smaller, darker bird inhabits Florida, and various altered or sub-species are found in Arizona, Texas, Mexico, and elsewhere. The bobwhite is now infrequent or absent in much of its original northern range. Lapsley states that for quail we have nearly one hundred million acres of potential habitat in America. On an average, about three acres are required for each quail, although this varies greatly according to the character of the land.

Following the settlement of this country small primitive farms sprang up, creating conditions favorable for the bobwhite. The birds consequently increased in number. More recently, with newer methods of farming and cleaner fields, a less favorable environment has developed. This, added to the increase in shooting, and other conditions, has resulted in fewer birds than heretofore or their total extinction in many areas where they were formerly plentiful. This is particularly so in many of the middle and northern states, but is less noticeable in the South. In some parts of the South, due largely to the care given to the bird by sportsmen, quail have increased.

*Courtship.* This frequently takes place before the coveys break up in the spring. Even after the birds have paired off, covey reformation sometimes occurs if unduly severe weather develops.

During the courtship, fights frequently occur between males, and, in rare instances, between females. These conflicts do not often result fatally, although Stoddard has observed males that have been killed. Once mated, evidence seems to prove that polygamy is extremely rare. The time at which the covey breaks up in the spring depends upon the weather.

The first calls of the bobwhite are an indication of pairing—in Pennsylvania this is usually in April. Stoddard says that there is some indication that old birds remain mated in the covey throughout the winter and are the first to leave the covey in the spring.

*Nesting.* The nesting period is a long one in Pennsylvania, running from early May until September, or even later. Destruction of early nests probably accounts for many of the late ones. Laying starts in most cases between mid-May and the end of June. The nesting site may be in a grass field or in partially overgrown areas. Roadside nests are frequent; they are rarely found in woods and are always on the ground, in a small depression. Nests are usually under some cover, such as a hummock of grass, brush, etc., and invariably are well concealed. They are composed of dead grass, leaves, pine needles, and other near-by available material. The majority have well-formed arched roofs which help to conceal the nest from egg robbers. Sometimes a tunnel gives entrance to the nest.

*Laying.* There is a daily or slightly less than daily laying of eggs. Bobwhites have been known to lay in chicken nests, and vice versa; guinea-hen nests have also been utilized. Eight to eighteen eggs, with an average of about fourteen or fifteen, comprise the usual number laid for one setting. Larger numbers of eggs in one nest usually are the result of two hens occupying the same nest. In confinement, hens have been known to produce enormous numbers of eggs, but in these cases the eggs are removed from the nest daily.

The eggs are short, ovate, pointed at the small end, and vary quite widely in size, averaging about 1.12 to 1.22 by 0.92 to 0.96 inches. They are pure white and tend to become shiny toward the end of incubation, when the shell becomes more brittle. Incubation is most often performed by the hen, but the cock's taking over of this function is not rare.

Stoddard calls attention to a curious behavior on the part of bobwhite, but one that probably has a great deal to do with the security of the nesting. It is the absolute avoidance of the nest and its immediate vicinity by the mate of the incubating bird. If disturbed from the nest, the incubating bird usually feigns injury, in an effort to lead off the intruder.

*Hatching.* Eggs are hatched in about twenty-three days and are pipped at about the twenty-first day. Before hatching, each chick with extreme neatness breaks a hole through the shell with the little spur which is situated near the end of the upper mandible. Its function fulfilled, this spur or egg tooth drops off two or three days later. When the chick emerges, the empty shells remain in the nest. About 86 per cent of the eggs hatch (Stoddard).

However, many nests are failures. Stoddard states that of 602 nests that contained eggs, 37 per cent were known to have been destroyed by natural enemies, and about an additional 20 per cent were abandoned for one reason or another. He also thinks that 60 to 80 per cent of the nesting attempts over the southeastern quail territory may normally be expected to be unsuccessful.

All eggs in the same nest hatch at about the same time. The young leave the nest almost immediately and the incubating bird is joined by its partner. Thereafter the family remain together, except for occasional straying, until the following spring. Occasionally young birds stray and join other broods; this accounts for the presence of bobwhites of different ages and sizes in the same covey. This habit of joining other coveys sometimes occurs in the winter; also if two coveys are reduced in number by shooting or other causes, they may join forces. This may lead the sportsman to believe he has found a moderate-sized unshot covey, when in fact what he sees may be the result of the joining together of two badly depleted bevies.

The young are brooded at night, during bad weather, during extreme heat or cold, and at many other times. Either or both parents perform the act. The young are active almost from the time they leave the shell and, when the alarm note is given by the adult, will hide and "freeze."

*The Chicks.* The chicks are covered with chestnut down below, and on the sides of head with grayish buff. There are two light streaks on the back and a black streak behind the eye. At two weeks of age, they can flush weakly and juvenile plumage is beginning to appear. At two months of age young bobwhites can fly fairly strongly for a good distance and are just beginning to assume adult plumage. Weak-flying young birds in the fall are often called "cheepers" or "squeakers." By fifteen weeks of age the birds are practically mature.

Old birds can usually be distinguished from those under a year and a half by the rounded end of the first and second primaries; in younger birds these feathers are more pointed than in the adult. Young birds have soft bills, and clean (not hard or scaly) legs. I have seen young half-grown birds in the North on the first of November. This is unusual; much depends upon a late or early spring as well as other conditions. Doubtless nest destruction often results in late second or third nestings, and accounts for many of the immature birds early in the shooting season.

Bobwhites are excellent parents. It was formerly believed that two broods were raised each season, a theory now known to be incorrect. The best-informed authorities agree that only one brood is reared. If the nest is destroyed, the hen is likely to lay a second time, and perhaps even a third attempt may be made.

It was formerly believed that bobwhites migrated. Since the time of Audubon, frequent descriptions of migrations and of autumn running seasons have appeared. As a result of his exhaustive study of southern bobwhites, Stoddard can find no evidence of such a trait, nor have references to this habit been common in recent times. Indeed, all the evidence, including banding, tends to show that the bird is sedentary, remaining in one locality. Under the proper environment these birds are peculiarly local, and will live their entire lives within a mile or less of where they have been hatched. Stoddard, A. R. Starr, and others make positive statements to this effect—indeed, Stoddard says that "they will often not wander more than one-fourth of a mile." This habit of staying on a restricted area is well known to sportsmen and dog trainers. Even those birds imported from Mexico have a decided tendency to stay put. This habit makes stocking and the putting down of artificially raised birds a successful venture.

*Food.* The diet of the bobwhite varies according to the locality and season. Grubs, ants, grasshoppers, and insects of various kinds, many of them injurious, constitute a large part of the food at seasons when these are available. Weed seeds and small grain are freely eaten. Lespedeza, common in the South, is an excellent food that grows well in nearly all soils except those which are strongly alkaline. It provides a seed crop in which there is a sufficient proportion of hard seed to carry the bird through the longest winters, and it furnishes green pickings which quail utilize in the spring (Goode). Beggarweed and peas, both wild and cultivated, are also favorites. Bobwhites are especially fond of buckwheat, and also relish the corn droppings that are present in the field after harvesting. In favorable years, long-leafed pine mast makes up a large part of the diet in many parts of the South. Berries, acorns, and the seeds of maple, beech, wild fruits, and grasses are also part of the diet of the bobwhite.

A plentiful food supply and cover affording easily reached protection from hawks are the desiderata of the bobwhite. It is important that the food supply be adequate at all times. In some areas, food is plentiful during some months and scarce during others.

Bobwhites require gravel; they may suffer from its loss when snow covers the ground for long periods of time. Bobwhites are essentially ground-feeding birds. This, apart from crusts of snow, is one of the reasons why prolonged heavy snow by largely cutting off their food supply, is apt to result disastrously. It is also an indication for sheltered winter feeding stations.

*Feeding.* Although feeding habits are influenced by the season, local conditions, and weather, the birds if undisturbed are generally extremely regular, and in this respect are not unlike domestic poultry. It is thought by many countrypeople that if chickens are out feeding in doubtful weather, the day will clear; but if, during a drizzle, the hens stay under shelter, the weather will be bad. Quail hunters often act on these signs.

When quail forage forth or move from place to place they spread out and a big covey may occupy an area of 60 feet or more. Sometimes three or four stray off a considerable distance from the main body. In pleasant weather, quail feeding starts early. In hot weather, they feed early and late and spend most of the warmer hours in relative inactivity, often near water. Because during this resting period they do not move around much, they are hard for a dog to find, unless he happens to stumble over them. For this reason the middle of the day is generally the worst time in which to hunt.

The birds do not like to get wet, and if vegetation is very moist, they will select an open, dry feeding ground, or may delay feeding for a time. Toward midday they seek some comfortable place in which to rest and dust. Dusting beds, roosting sites, and droppings are sure indications that a range is being used. In cold weather, some sunny sheltered site, often with a southern exposure, is chosen. After some three or four hours of loafing the birds forage forth and feed until roosting time.

Before a storm all birds fill their crops, and at such times bobwhites may feed more or less all day long. During bad weather they are apt to keep in sheltered spots as much as possible. Surface water is not essential to quail and is of real value only in maintaining an adequate food supply. Bobwhite can subsist upon the dew and moisture obtained from food. The presence of water or its absence, upon good quail lands, is immaterial (Stoddard). However, when surface water is present it is generally utilized. Lapsley points out that feeding habits may be altered if vermin are present, the land plowed recently, and, what is important to the sportsman, that on dark days they feed more in the open than during clear weather.

*Roosting.* There is a widespread belief that bobwhites fly to their roosting sites, thereby leaving no trail of scent available for foxes or other enemies. As daylight was beginning to fail, on a number of occasions, I have seen birds that I thought were flying to their roosts. This is obviously a difficult thing to prove with certainty, and it is quite likely that they may sometimes walk and at other times fly.

Roosting sites may be in almost any partially overgrown area—scattered briar patches are favorite places. All the roosting rings which I have seen have had one thing in common, i.e., a free area above, through which the birds may flush without danger of entanglement from overhanging branches.

The birds roost in a circle with their heads out, probably in an effort to guard against surprise attacks. Observation of birds in confinement shows that it takes some little time for them to settle down for the night, and that they press closer together in cold weather than in warm. Young birds raised in confinement, which have never seen an adult, assume this formation. In cold weather they huddle so close together that their tails are forced upward.

When coveys are unusually large they may divide, and two rings will be found moderately close together. Even when coveys are reduced to two or three birds, the same tendency to form a ring with the heads outward is still adhered to. Rings are conspicuous, due to the circle of excrement, which is white-topped. Roosts are almost invariably on the ground, although Sandys and Van Dyke state that under certain conditions the birds may spend the night in grapevines or trees.

*Flight.* The young can fly at an early age, but they require about four months to acquire full vigor. Adults leave the ground as if shot out of a gun and appear to be going at full speed almost at once. This is especially noticeable in birds flushed from bare ground or from sparse cover. They usually head for the nearest cover within their covey range. There is no hesitation and rarely any turn. If the gun gets between them and the cover, in an effort to drive them to open country, they will fly in his face. They evidently know where they intend to go before they leave the ground, and no amount of heading is of any avail.

A practical point to remember is that when flying into timber under which there is little or no undergrowth they are apt to go in low—10 feet or less—but if there is a high growth of ground cover they are sure to be high enough to clear it comfortably, often with a lot of space to spare. When flushed on a hillside, they usually fly to the brow and then drop, often curving after they disappear.

The average covey flight is perhaps about 200 yards, but it varies with the terrain, for they may fly a quarter of a mile or more. Singles and flights in thick cover do not average quite so far as this. If flushed at the foot of a hill or on the hillside a covey generally goes up and over the crest of the rise. These flights are often long ones.

Birds found early in the day are said to average shorter flights than they do in the afternoon. Much depends upon the cover. In the rain, flights are shorter than in clear weather. Birds that have been hunted hard are apt to fly farther than those which are less wild. Also, early in the season, flights are shorter than in the late season.

There is a good deal of difference of opinion as to whether bob-whites are wilder than they were formerly. The general opinion is that they are, that they stay nearer cover, fly farther, use woods more, and the coveys have less of a tendency to "fan out" in broom sage or other open places. This is less noticeable in the early part of the season. Late-season birds are capable of several prolonged flights, but in the pre-season, dog-training period young birds tire noticeably, and second and third flights are shorter and weaker. If wet, the flight, even of strong adult birds, is reduced in speed and duration.

The flight is generally fairly low, straight, and bold, although a slight curve may be present. Even in the woods there is comparatively little dodging and twisting as compared to that done by a woodcock. Quail are expert fliers and even in thick cover they rarely collide with obstructions. Sometimes singles go off barely above the grass top, but more often there is a gradual rise. This is especially the case with coveys. This tendency to rise continues until beyond gunshot; it is more real than apparent.

Quail generally fly over rather than around or under obstructions. Wing action is extremely rapid, and the flight ends in a long slanting sail. Sometimes this is misjudged and the wing beats are resumed. Often toward the end of the flight coveys will veer to one side or the other. This is more common toward the end of the season than at the beginning, and when there has been much shooting. Singles are not so prone to adopt this trick, although occasionally they do. They do, however, frequently cut back.

The bobwhites are fast fliers, but their speed is often over-estimated because of the whirr of their wings and their small size. Probably 30 to 35 miles per hour would be a fair estimate of their speed. In similar surroundings and flying at the same speed, large birds always appear slower than small ones. At a distance the tendency is to underestimate the speed of an airplane or even a large bird, such as a goose or swan. For the same reason, there is a tendency to overestimate distance and speed in the case of small birds, such as quail, and in the latter the whirr of wings adds to the deception. A Cooper's hawk is of course a very fast bird, but these pirates can overhaul a bobwhite in almost no time.

On alighting, the bird may freeze instantly, but more often it runs or moves about a little. Coveys are a little more apt to move than single birds. Much depends upon the type of cover in which they have come down. Usually the birds can be found for a reasonable length of time near where they have been marked down. Occasionally entire coveys will take to their legs, but this is unusual. On flushing, the bobwhite makes a loud whirr with its rapidly beating, short, curved wings. After the bird gets under full headway this whirr ceases. The birds can flush silently, for, like the grouse, this characteristic whirr is the result of their attempt to get under way rapidly, and when the bird is not frightened, the sound is not always heard. A covey that has been in the air for some time and is passing close by does not produce the noise, nor is it evident when the rising is undisturbed and the birds flying from one feeding ground to another or going to roost.

The bobwhite is a ground bird; however, it is not uncommon for them to perch on fence rails or low elevations. The male frequently selects such a site from which to issue his bobwhite call. Occasionally, during the shooting season when the covey is flushed, some, or, less frequently, all of the birds will resort to trees, in which case they are often quite difficult to see. While not so hard to shoot as a grouse under similar circumstances, when they leave their perch they are difficult enough to take the conceit out of most good shots. Birds are said to resort to perching more in hilly or mountainous country, or when the ground is covered with snow. Certain coveys seem to have a predilection for this habit. The act of perching upon trees is probably not a natural habit, but one acquired in an effort to avoid danger.

Bobwhites have a habit of standing upright and rapidly flapping their wings, as if exercising their wing muscles. The noise thus produced can be heard for some distance. This action is indulged in rather frequently and is often practiced when two coveys meet. It has given rise to the erroneous belief that the birds were fighting. During flight the feet are drawn up among the body feathers, and not stretched out under the tail. Sandys and Van Dyke report that they have seen birds end a flight by dashing into a snowdrift like grouse and ptarmigan. As mentioned elsewhere, these birds occasionally tower upon receiving a wound.

*Covey Habits.* The bobwhite is essentially a social bird. The finding of a single bird during the shooting season indicates that the covey has been scattered, often by a hawk or perhaps by another sportsman. The remainder of the covey is probably in the neighborhood.

After a covey is scattered, its members reassemble as soon as they believe the danger to be past. Probably one of the old birds will sound the call, which is gradually answered by the scattered birds which thereupon reunite.

At the covey rise, all the birds usually go off in the same general direction. The covey usually rises as one bird, but not infrequently there may be one or two laggards. These are prone to follow in the general direction taken by their mates. Stoddard states that banding has shown that in late summer and fall, coveys may be composed of one to three pairs of adults and their surviving young, frequently with the addition of one or more cocks or pairs that have failed to raise broods. Occasionally young stragglers that have strayed from their parents join the group. When flushed, such compound coveys may split, one part going one way and the other going in yet another direction.

As mentioned before, the covey range is extremely restricted. It is well known that a covey is likely to occupy a certain locality, year after year, without apparent increase. Banding has shown that while the covey remains on its favorite range individual members wander off, especially during the nesting period, and may be replaced by birds from other bevies. This practice has a tendency to prevent inbreeding.

The average covey contains about twelve to fourteen birds. Much larger coveys, of from twenty-five to thirty birds, have been observed. These large coveys are generally the result of unions between two or more bevies. If at the beginning of the shooting season, however, the coveys are uniformly large, it is the sign of a good hatching season, while if the coveys are small, the reverse is true. All evidence points to the fact that the old theory which indicated it was necessary to shoot up and scatter the covey to prevent inbreeding and deterioration is absolutely fallacious. Birds may do and for generations have done, splendidly in neighborhoods in which there has been no shooting and little or no disturbance of their natural habits.

*Voice.* Almost everyone who has lived in the country is familiar with the whistled "bob-white, bob-bob-white," "buckwheat," or "more wet, no more wet," as it may be sometimes interpreted, which is so common in the spring. To others the whistle seems to say "Peas most ripe! most ripe!" or "Sow more wheat! more wheat!" The bobwhite whistle is uttered only by the cockbird. According to Stoddard the caller is almost invariably an unmated bird that is in search of a hen. Stoddard found that one unmated cock issued no less than 1,295 full voiced "bobwhites" in a single day and as there is a predominance of males the frequency with which the call is heard is explainable. Stoddard describes fifteen calls, among them the "lost," "alarm," "scatter," and other calls. Quail often whistle in the morning before, or shortly after, leaving their roost. The birds in a covey often twitter ahead of the pointing dog. Due to the success of raising the bobwhites in confinement, much has been learned regarding their habits and mode of life. When properly treated, the birds become as tame as chickens. I myself have seen a dozen birds run to and feed from the hand when the door of the coop was opened.

*Predators.* Bobwhites occupy an extensive range, and as a result are subject to numerous natural enemies, which vary in the amount of injury which they do to the quail crop in different localities.

In the South, cotton rats and certain southern snakes destroy an enormous number of birds, whereas, in the North, a totally different group of natural enemies are at work. Of the winged enemies, the Cooper's hawk, or blue darter, is the most injurious. This bird has well earned its title of "quail hawk," as the bobwhite appears to be its favorite prey. The sharp-shinned hawk, while smaller, is also uniformly destructive—in fact, most of the *Accipiter* and falcons, with the exception of the sparrow hawk, are destructive. Numerous other hawks and owls also prey upon quail in varying degrees in different localities. The argument that winged predators are beneficial in that they destroy sick and weak birds is greatly overworked. Wild and domestic cats, stray dogs, foxes, skunks, minks, weasels, and various other fur-bearers all destroy quail and may or may not be important factors, according to their prevalence.

Black snakes are everywhere destructive to eggs and young birds, and in the South many other egg and young eating varieties of reptiles are present. Stoddard states that in a single year two thousand snakes were killed upon one plantation. Where game is scarce, predators may be scarce, but in those localities in which intensive game preservation is practiced, predators are likely to be found in abundance unless means to control their numbers are instituted. The more game, the more predators, is axiomatic. Game attracts all sorts of predators, often from a long distance. Severe depredations to game stock from predators may occur without the casual observer being aware of the presence of vermin. Hawks are generally noticeable, but most of the fur bearers work chiefly at night and their presence may be unsuspected. A few traps set in favorable places often yield surprising results.

Despite the fact that farmers are generally favorable toward bobwhites, the clean farming which is becoming prevalent in the middle and eastern states reduces both cover and feed and is an important factor in the reduction in the bobwhite population. Occasional severe winters also destroy many northern birds. During snowy weather bobwhites huddle together under some cover and often become covered with snow. If a hard crust forms on top, the birds become imprisoned and die. Heavy snow also covers feed and grit and the combination results in heavy mortality. During severe weather quail have frequently been observed to come to a barnyard and feed with chickens. There is much truth in the old saying that "a well-fed quail never dies of cold," and, indeed, this applies with more or less aptitude to all game birds.

Floods during the nesting season destroy a certain number of nests and young. Fires also are sometimes very destructive. Probably the chief reason for the reduction of the quail population is the system of "free shooting," resulting as it does in the overshooting of many areas, for gunners, like the predators, tend to swarm into areas in which game is plentiful. The motor car has done much to make previously remote sections accessible. Daily bag limits have generally been reduced to the minimum, seasons have been greatly shortened, and season limits, which necessarily are largely dependent upon the "honor system" for enforcement, are small. Despite all these favorable factors for increase, the bobwhite has in many localities become a scarce bird.

The best bobwhite shooting today is in the South, where the winters are mild. An even more important factor in the South is that a great number of preserves have sprung up, upon which public shooting is prohibited, and where the scientific management of quail has been introduced, with the result that the birds have increased in numbers in many areas. Stoddard has performed a splendid service in his advice to many plantation owners. The Southerner has learned that the quail crop is a valuable one, marketable for worthwhile returns. A different situation exists farther north, where land is generally more valuable, and the farming is more intense, and other factors—many of which mitigate against the future of this fine game bird—are present.

Much can be done by improving cover, increasing the natural food, eliminating predators, and preventing overshooting. Bobwhites can now be raised in captivity and may be purchased from many game farms. They are not difficult to rear. Smith's *American Game Preserve Shooting; The Quail Breeding Manual,* from the Game Conservation Society, and the valuable monograph by H. L. Stoddard, *The Bobwhite Quail,* give detailed information regarding bobwhite breeding and stocking. Formerly many birds were imported from Mexico. Even these foreigners showed little tendency to wander, and bred with the local birds.

When there is a natural stock, it is, for many reasons, generally preferable to rely upon improvement of local conditions rather than stocking. But where birds are badly depleted, exterminated, or quick returns are desired, stocking offers a means of replenishment. Care must be taken to secure healthy stock, and it is a waste of time and money to put them down unless favorable conditions exist. Probably the best time for stocking is shortly before the mating season. Birds planted during or just before the shooting season are not altogether satisfactory. Nature produces about 4 to 7 per cent more cocks than hens, and in stocking about twelve hens to thirteen cocks is the proper ratio.

Crates containing the birds should be placed near and facing a covert. The door is then raised and replaced by a piece of cardboard, to which a long string is attached. A few handfuls of feed are scattered in front of the crate. The crate is now left until the birds settle down and the cardboard is then removed from a distance by pulling the string. Leave the open crate alone—do not go near it to see if birds have left. Remove the crate the next day, and scatter feed. Continue feeding as long as the birds return for food.

Given suitable environment, bobwhite is usually a hardy, healthy bird. Stoddard's monograph contains an excellent review of diseases and parasites to which quail are subject.

*Shooting.* In quail shooting the quality of the dog is far more essential than that of the gun. The requirements of a quail dog vary widely. In the South, where one shoots from horseback or even from a buckboard or motor car, often over a flat terrain where perhaps covey rather than single-bird shooting is specialized in, the dog should be fast and wide. A brace or more of dogs are put down and fresh dogs are used in the afternoon. Sometimes the so-called covey dog is not very good on singles, and if these are to be shot the big-going dog may temporarily be taken up and a dog of more restricted range utilized. This also gives the fast dog a rest. Under favorable conditions a dog that is good on singles should find two-thirds to three-fourths of the birds, but terrain, cover, scenting conditions, and other factors enter largely into the problem. Covey dogs are specialists on quail.

Southern shooting is the typical quail shooting. The weather is apt to be delightful, and what walking has to be done is often relatively easy. Unless the birds get into "bay heads" or swamps, the shooting is often fairly open. Only one kind of game bird is likely to be encountered and the entire setting is one of charm and attractiveness. To the Scotchman the term "fish" means a clean adult salmon and nothing else, so in the South, "birds" indicate quail. Turkeys are turkeys; woodcock are woodcock, but birds mean quail.

Southern shooting brings to mind a long avenue of great live oaks draped with Spanish moss, a white plantation house, soft-spoken, hospitable people, smiling darkies, the leisurely start in the morning, the fast-moving dogs, one of which suddenly freezes near the edge of a pea patch, the approach and back of his mate, the drive home as the light is beginning to fail, the Negro cottages, the smell of burning fat wood, large, shallow open fireplaces, and a hundred other delightful pictures typical of the Southland. There will probably be a deer hunt. There are few more pleasant places than some old, disused woods-road surrounded by sparsely placed long-leafed pines and occasional small patches of broom sage, with the sun just sufficiently warm to make it acceptable. Perhaps your hostess will honor you by her presence on the deer stand. At all events, it is entirely delightful and it does not matter much whether or not you get a shot.

The southern is a type of quail shooting different from that practiced in the North, where the country is closer, the sportsman is afoot, and probably other varieties of game besides quail may be encountered. Here a dog of the type described in a previous chapter is required. The bag is apt to be mixed and the dog should be able to handle all "four varieties." Over-ranging is a nuisance when afoot and is unfair to the dog. Apart from finding the covey, the northern dog is almost uniformly required to handle singles; to do this, he should come in and work close. Such a dog should have a good nose, be steady, biddable, work to the gun, handle at all times, and be a good retriever. There is no game bird which provides more enjoyable dog work.

The gun previously described for upland shooting is satisfactory. For the man who shoots nothing but quail, the stock may possess slightly more drop than in the case of a gun used for all sorts of upland shooting. However, even for the low-flying quail it is preferable to err on the side of a too straight stock rather than one in which there is too much drop. Seventy-five or 80 per cent of bobwhites are killed at ranges of 25 yards or under. Buckingham says that 90 per cent of first bird-kills, gun to retrieve, average a shade over 16 paces, and second-barrel kills average 8 or 9 yards farther. This authority also states that for every dead quail grassed at a true 40 yards, five thousand are sacked at 25 yards or closer. Bobwhites generally lie close, and there is rarely any excuse for accepting long shots which result in a high proportion of wounded birds.

Breeches and some form of comfortable walking-riding boot combination are best when horses are employed. The soft-legged boot of the Botte Sauvage type is preferable. A fleece-lined holster is also preferable, as plain leather, if tight, is prone to rub off blueing.

A dry spring generally produces plenty of birds; on the contrary, heavy rains during the hatching season often result in a poor crop.

When hunting quail from horseback, before starting, determine whether your mount will stand or whether he has to be tied each time the rider dismounts to shoot. If the latter is the case, be sure to tie him securely, for a lost horse may mean a long walk. In the South, a darkey usually accompanies the guns, and, in addition to carrying various extras, will act as horseholder and often as marker. From horseback, the dogs are more easily seen, are less likely to get lost, one can get to points quicker, can signal better to the dogs, travel faster, cover more ground, and mark birds better than if one is afoot. Northern dogs generally require a little time to learn to handle from horseback. When hunting from horseback always unload before mounting.

A carryall or "possible sack" is useful. This is a long bag closed at both ends, with a longitudinal slit in the middle. It is a home-made affair of thin canvas or other strong material—in some I have seen the ends have been enlarged. It holds extra shells, a raincoat, lunch. It rides at the back of the saddle. Incidentally, it is also useful when duck shooting.

Two guns are enough; more are dangerous and make for poor shooting. When two men attempt to shoot a single, and three or more, a covey, good shooting by all is apt to suffer. Make haste slowly. Give the dog a chance and do not crowd him. Too many dogs are often a detriment. Two are usually enough, and one is often preferable for singles. This is particularly true when using headstrong, jealous, or not particularly well-trained animals. One dog is more easily controlled than too many.

Generally, early-in-the-season shooting is easier. Later, the birds are stronger, and, especially if they have been shot much, fly farther, exhibit a greater tendency to seek heavy cover, and become more educated. Occasionally educated coveys will run as soon as a dog or a man enters the field. Late in the season there is a noticeable tendency for coveys to stay near covers. The so-called education of quail has been mentioned elsewhere, and, whereas I believe this condition exists, some of the apparent education may be the result of less cover than formerly. Quail have always been wise birds.

*Weather.* Pleasant weather is generally the best for quail shooting. On warm, windless days birds will often lie like stones. During bleak, windy weather scent is apt to be poor and birds flush wild. They often run and rise wild during rain. Extreme dryness is bad for scent. Generally, not much is gained by an extremely early start, and it is better to let the birds get well under way in their morning feeding. However, in fine weather the start should be earlier than if it is cold and wet. As a matter of fact, during the latter, birds are always harder to find, and in really bad weather it is wise to stay at home. As far as quail are concerned, there is no advantage in getting afield while the cover is soaking wet from dew or a previous night's rain. Coveys will be passed by and dogs and men both be tired by afternoon when the best of the shooting should be had. A long luncheon hour helps both sportsman and dogs. During pleasant weather hunt late in the afternoon, for this is often the best part of the day. However, I personally like to get home betimes. There will always be another day.

As mentioned a number of times, quail are extremely local, and where a covey is found one day it is apt to be present near by on another. When shooting over strange country, therefore, the assistance of a local guide often helps in locating birds. During prolonged wet spells look for birds on the higher ground uplands, sparse woods, and dry bramble patches, etc. During dry spells, bottom lands and overgrown stream, ditch or slough edges are likely spots.

Knowledge of local and seasonable feed, water, and dusting sites is of assistance. Coveys are generally found toward the edges of fallow fields, in light covers, and along the edges of woods, especially those in which the undergrowth is not particularly thick. Corn, buckwheat, and other fields in which harvest droppings from small grains are present offer favorable feeding areas. Heavy weed fields are often utilized because of the weed seeds and the cover afforded.

Bobwhite are frequently found in the neighborhood of abandoned farms where they are attracted by the weed seeds, and early in the season by the small fruits that are likely to be present. Old and little used railway rights-of-way are favored because of the weed seeds that are usually present. In some cases fallen grain from passing freight cars adds to the attractiveness of this site. The finding of fresh droppings, scratchings, loose feathers, dusting beds, and roosting rings are indications of the presence of birds, as are, of course, quail calls. If there is snow on the ground, hunt the swamps, briar patches, brush piles, second-growth woods, rank weed stands, around thickets, and southerly hillsides. The finding of fresh cartridge cases, the sound of shots, and single birds indicate recent shooting. Singles may, however, have been caused by a hawk scattering the covey.

There is one almost unbreakable rule, and this is that when a covey is flushed it will invariably fly directly to cover, usually to the densest and most impenetrable one available. No amount of interception or heading will prevent this. Here the covey may light as a body, but it is apt to spread out more or less. At the alighting point singles may be found or a few scattered birds may flush together. In some instances the entire covey will stay together and rise as one bird. If this occurs, and they can be followed a second time, they are generally found more or less scattered. Covey flights are apt to be longer than those made by single birds and singles are prone to lie closer.

In former days, when it was believed that quail could withhold their scent, Frank Forester and others advised delay in following a covey. This may occasionally have some advantage. More often delay is disadvantageous, and birds may run, or scattered birds may reunite and another covey rise result. It is better to mark them closely and follow them promptly.

Many of the older writers stressed the importance of killing the old hen on the first covey rise, believing that this made it easier subsequently to secure the singles. Early in the autumn the old hen is usually the first bird to break cover. Later this is not the case, and she is often among the last to take wing. With our present later opening seasons, the old hen is more difficult to recognize, and what advantage there may be in killing her is minimized.

In flushing bobwhite, try and arrange for an outgoing or quartering shot. Quail are almost sure to head for cover. The worst shot of all is to have the covey come back, as the birds will do if the gun gets between them and cover. Other things being equal, it is best to flush by walking up from the rear of the pointing dog. Try to select good footing, and in cover, a clear path. Coveys are usually flushed relatively easily; singles, especially when in thick ground cover, often require some kicking out, certainly more than do many other game birds. While not as certain to cause quail to flush as grouse, the sudden stop will often make them break cover. If it does not do so, a loud deep expiration, imitating the whirr made by a departing bird, may do the trick.

While bobwhites generally go straight away or quarter, they are gradually rising, but not often to any great height. Sometimes they are found in thickets of second growth, saplings, or, especially in the South, in tall second-growth pine trees. Here the birds often rocket upward to the top of the trees, and should be killed either during their ascent, or, at the latest, at the top of their flight. In general it is easier to kill all game birds as soon as the opportunity arises. The farther they go, the harder the shot usually becomes. There are exceptions to this rule, but it is generally true. This does not mean hurried shooting, but it does mean elimination of delay. The quail, which goes off low in cover, is a hard shot. When singles lie close they often permit the sportsman to walk past them and flush in the rear. This is especially the case in cover. If birds are scarce and one wants a bag, do not be in too great a hurry to leave a scattered covey. It pays to hunt close. Be on the alert at all times. No matter how good the dog, the sportsman himself often stumbles on a few singles.

Among scattered birds never pass a brush pile or other thick cover without investigation. As much as possible, work the dog so he will have the benefit of the wind, and give him time. In hot weather especially, arrange the hunt so the dog can get water.

Nash Buckingham, well-known author, field-trial judge, and authority on quail, gives the following advice regarding quail shooting in his recently published and delightful book *Mark Right!*: "Pick out one certain bird. One man should do all the dog handling, unless each shooter owns a dog and happens to find his dog on point. Don't hurry. Practice repression. Remember to center your bird at the proper distance. The novice should observe, absorb, ask advice and, above all, try to put adequate suggestions into practice." In this chapter the author of that incomparable story, *De Shootinest Gent'man,* gives much valuable advice which should be read *in toto* by all interested in quail shooting. The same authority also advises to take every opportunity to shoot with experienced quail hunters. More can be gained by a few days afield with an experienced "bird" hunter than any amount of book learning. All this is excellent advice.

Most misses are the result of too hurried shooting and lack of calmness. The rise is usually short and over a point. Although the flight is rapid, there is plenty of time. One has only to refrain from shooting and watch the flush or observe someone else shoot to be convinced that there is no need for hurry. Note the ample time given by the birds during the pre-season dog-training period.

The whirr, initial speed, suddenness of the flush and small size of the bird all tend to make the inexperienced shot feel that he has not much time. These factors are augmented at a covey rise. Except in cover there is rarely any necessity for great speed, and usually plenty of time for a deliberate aim.

Ripley advises finding the flushed bird over the barrels. It is interesting to know that nearly one hundred years ago the famous sportsman Lieutenant Colonel Peter Hawker gave the same advice in nearly the same words in regard to shooting English partridges. This is good advice and emphasizes what has been said in a previous chapter regarding the importance of going into action quickly and the elimination of delay. The time intervening between the flush of the bird and that moment when the man assumes balance and starts to bring his gun to his shoulder should be cut to the minimum in all sorts of shooting and is especially necessary in cover. The novice, upon hearing the bird flush, is prone to turn his head, locate the bird, then change his stance (often not turning his feet and body sufficiently), raise his gun, and fire hurriedly, each of these acts being more or less a separate unit, whereas the entire procedure should be one synchronized movement. The term "finding the bird over the barrels" is very descriptive of what should be done in order to save vitally important time for the alignment. Of course, much depends upon a so-called "quick eye," i.e., the ability to locate the bird with the least possible loss of time.

In cover, the quick swing or the corrected snap are usually the most productive methods. Here again it may be worth repeating that all snap shots are emergency measures and should be resorted to only when more accurate alignment is impossible. They are generally overworked, and this is especially the case of the true snap shot. Most men would do better if they could entirely eliminate the latter from their repertoire.

For their size quail possess considerable vitality and will carry off quite a lot of shot. Undoubtedly many wounded birds fly a considerable distance and are not gathered. There may be no flinch, alteration in flight, dropping of a leg, or floating feathers. I have often seen quail fly 150 yards, only to fall and then be picked up dead. If one does not know that the bird has been wounded it is apt to be lost. Often a bird will flinch at the shot, alter its course, or slow up. Birds acting in this way are generally gathered. The small-gauge guns so frequently employed for quail shooting undoubtedly somewhat increase the number of cripples, as does the use of No. 10 shot. For a 12-gauge gun, bored as previously described, 2¾ drams or its equivalent and 1 ounce of No. 9 shot early in the season and No. 8 shot later, make an ideal load. Three drams and 1 ounce is the next best substitute. Tens are cripplers and 7½ or larger tend to thin the pattern and spoil birds for the table. Large-sized shot has been advocated by a few because it has a tendency to pass completely through a bird, and hence eliminates the discomfort of biting on a pellet. However, this is not always the case, and relatively large shot may readily strike a bone and remain in the bird. Some men believe that soft shot has greater stopping powers than hard. More soft shot is used in the South than elsewhere. I believe chilled shot to be the best.

Quail shots may be very easy or very hard. Early in the season and in little shot preserves they are often easy, but late in the season and in cover they are much more difficult. The open shots should be killed with a fair degree of regularity. The flush is generally over a point and at close range. In cover the birds are faster than a woodcock, but the flight is more direct. Under these circumstances, Holland thinks them harder to shoot than a grouse. However, so much depends upon conditions that comparison is difficult. Both birds may be hard enough to test the best of shots.

The sudden flush and loud whirr of wings save many birds. The experienced quail shot should average fairly well, but taken by and large and accepting all fair chances, successful quail shooting is not nearly so easy as it appears on paper. Perhaps a fair estimate would be that the average shot will bag four or five birds for every ten cartridges, the good shot five or six, and the expert perhaps seven. Starr thinks that 40 per cent is a fair average. Mayer says that if 60 per cent of birds fired at are secured it is excellent shooting and that 33.3 per cent for the novice is satisfactory. Schley says that 60 per cent is good shooting. Curtis states that if you can average one bird for two and a half shells you are shooting well, one bird for two shells is very good, and one bird for one and a half shells marks the expert.

We all are prone to remember our good days and, to a lesser extent, our bad ones; but we are likely to forget our many average performances. In any case, the counting of cartridges spoils sport and tends toward the refusal of hard shots and the picking of easy ones. Almost any experienced shot can run quite a string by the latter method if birds are plentiful. Furthermore, the counting of shots is likely to impair the confidence necessary for top-form performance. One of the tests of a good quail shot is the number of doubles that he can make from covey rises. The secret of successful double shooting, apart from the selection of birds, is to concentrate on the first shot and then instantly select a second bird. Be quick but do not hurry. If the first bird is missed, shoot the second barrel at it. Do not switch. If only two birds rise and both are in range, shoot at the farthest first.

It is usually necessary to depend upon the dog to retrieve cripples. Get him quickly to the place where the bird was seen to fall, and make him hunt close. Once he gets the scent, however, he can generally tell better than the sportsman where the bird has gone. Dogs which are taught to break shot to retrieve, lose fewer cripples than those which are steady. Never leave a wounded bird without a really conscientious effort to find it.

If two or more men are shooting together a definite plan as to how the shots are to be taken should be arranged beforehand. With two shooting, they usually walk up from the rear, one on each side of the pointing dog, and when the covey rises each shoots at the birds on his side. If the covey goes to the left, the man on the right shoots the rear birds, and vice versa, if the birds head to his side.

To shoot successfully it is necessary to choose a bird. Select one on the side, rear, or front of the covey, depending upon which way it goes. Never under any circumstances select a bird in the center of the covey, and, worst of all, never shoot blindly into the center on the general principle that the birds are so thick that one or two are sure to be killed. The latter idea is false and usually results in a miss. The birds are generally more scattered than they seem to be.

"Browning" a covey also wounds many birds. It is a bad principle, unsportsmanlike, and is never resorted to by the experienced shot. In shooting single birds, it is generally best to alternate, or if two dogs are working, one man may follow each dog. In quail shooting it is vitally important to watch where the covey goes, and before shooting some arrangement should be made as to who is to do the marking. The man selected for this purpose should have good eyesight and knowledge of quail, he should ignore the dead or falling birds and keep his eyes fixed upon the vanishing covey. Small coveys, especially late in the season, should be spared, and certainly there should be no effort to shoot singles from it. No covey, no matter how large, should be too heavily shot. At least five birds should be left; seven or eight is better. Too persistent hunting leaves desolation in its wake. Goode says that observation and experience have shown that an average kill of half the quail population in a given area is the maximum that may safely be taken each year. This is a good rule to adopt. If the choice arises, shoot the cocks and leave the "seed" hens. As a general rule, to which there are a few exceptions, the dog should not be permitted to flush, whether singles or covey—this should be done by the sportsman.

Quail can easily be netted, trapped, or snared, but all such methods are illegal, unless a special permit has been secured. These practices are not now nearly so prevalent as formerly, when the sale of quail was legal. Lewis records an instance in which nine hundred quail were caught in nets near Havre de Grace, Maryland, in a single season. Audubon also describes netting these birds. In 1851, a steamboat, on a single trip, brought 1,680 quail to the New Orleans market. In the eighties quail sold in Philadelphia for $2.50 and $3.00 per dozen. The author of the *American Shooter's Manual*, published in Philadelphia in 1827, says "The Partridge is considered excellent eating, and generally sells in our market for from six to twelve cents apiece; the facility of taking them by snares and traps and the high price they sell for brings great numbers to the markets of our large towns and cities." Wilson

(1829) states that from August to March numbers were brought to the markets and sold for from twelve to eighteen cents apiece. They were often brought alive and sportsmen would sometimes buy them and keep them until spring, when they would be liberated. Near Keokuk, Iowa, four hundred quail were netted in one afternoon. In 1852, three men near Lynchburg, Virginia, killed one hundred birds, each, in one day. While this may not be a record, it is the greatest slaughter by gun and dog of which I have knowledge. Shooting quail on the ground is a foul, murderous practice and may result in wiping out almost an entire covey with one shot, but it is not so infrequent as the average sportsman might believe. Apart from being a vile deed perpetrated upon the best and most universally loved game bird in America, it is ruinous to the training of the dog.

Whereas the future of the quail in the North is uncertain, in the South it seems assured. The delightful winter climate in most of the southern quail states, the attractiveness of the sport, the bird's splendid sporting qualities for both dog and gun, the ability to raise the quail in large numbers under artificial conditions, its willingness to stay put and not roam—all these factors have led to the formation of many private and club preserves where the birds are carefully protected. The legislation of the southern states has in general adopted liberal laws regarding shooting. This is a wise procedure, as the owners of preserves are for the most part, fine, law-abiding sportsmen and rarely require restrictive laws. Also they are the ones who are especially desirous of increasing the quail population. Short seasons and unduly small bag limits would be ruinous to these preserves. The owners or lessees of such preserves are usually the best friends the bird has. Furthermore, suitable quail land carrying a good head of birds is a marketable commodity, and in the South the so-called "free shooting" is much less prevalent than it is in the North.

*Kill your rail handsomely in the field, missing not more than one in twenty, present him properly and with due appreciation on the table, and eat him with the gratitude that he deserves.*
                    —R. B. Roosevelt, *Florida and the Game Water Birds.*

R AIL are not upland game. Because so many upland gunners enjoy an occasional day of rail shooting, the following abbreviated chapter has been inserted. Most of the qualities that have earned for quail, grouse, and woodcock the title of game birds are lacking in the rail. The upland gun is accustomed to working hard for his birds, and the absence of the constant interest and companionship of a fine dog is sure to be felt. On the other hand, rail shooting possesses some definite compensations. It comes at a season when there is little else to shoot unless a long journey is undertaken. It is suitable for those men who are not quite up to the more strenuous sport of following a dog. It is excellent practice at a time of year when practice is needed. The gun probably gets more actual shooting in three or four hours on the rail marsh than he would in four or five days with the more sporting birds. Rail shooting is often preceded by a pleasant drive. The river itself, while not so interesting as a trout stream, and lacking the impressive grandeur of many salmon rivers, is, nevertheless, not without its charm. The marsh, with its varied greens and browns and occasional marsh flowers, such as the buttercup, together with the surrounding autumn foliage, is a thing of real beauty.

Most sportsmen are interested in wild life of all kinds, and perhaps especially in birds. Apart from game birds, the marsh teems with them. Red-winged blackbirds are present in hoards, and constantly flying from place to place. The drab reed birds, the males of which are hardly recognizable as the bobolink of the

319

spring, are always numerous. As in all areas in which bird life is plentiful, many hawks are found. The graceful marsh harrier is almost sure to be seen. Perhaps the handsome Osprey may be observed hovering stationary over the river, or the splash of his dive may attract attention. If he has been successful, he will emerge from the river, shake off the water, turn the fish head foremost in his talons, and fly off to some dead tree where his prey will be devoured. The mouselike marsh wrens are certain to be seen slipping unobtrusively through the reeds. Gulls are plentiful on the river, and herons and numerous other interesting birds, many of them infrequently seen by the inland sportsman, are often found. A few years ago I saw a small flock of the rare sicklebill curlew. It is the season of migration, so visitors as well as local birds are apt to be in evidence.

The domelike muskrat houses are present on many marshes, and occasionally their occupants may be seen swimming low in the water, towing stems of grass, or the v in the water may attract attention to them. I have twice detected minks slipping along the shore, and once, during an early morning tide, interrupted a raccoon at his fishing. Fish and reptiles are often present, and it is this abundance of wild life that affords half the pleasure of rail shooting.

To the shooting man rail usually means the sora. However, under the title of rail shooting a number of varieties of game birds are often encountered. Among the most frequently met are the sora, Virginia rail, king rail, clapper rail, and, occasionally, the yellow rail and the black rail. Wilson snipe, coots and ducks, especially the blue- and the green-winged teal, black ducks, mallards, wood ducks, pintails, baldpates, and others are often present on the rail marsh.

RAILS. The *Rallidae*, or rail family, is a large one and includes the coots and the gallinules. Most of the rails are small or medium-sized birds, possessing rather elongated, narrow bodies, which enable them to slip between the reed stems. Their legs are moderately long, heavy, and muscular. Their feet are large, permitting them to run easily over semi-submerged vegetation. They are not webbed. The hind toe is long. Toes are without lobes. The wings are short and rounded. Except when on migrations, their flights are weak and generally short. When flushed, the legs hang down loosely, but when in full flight tend to trail out behind. The migrations of some of the rails are surprisingly long when the feeble character of their flight is considered. Some travel from New England to South America.

All the rails are expert divers and swimmers; all are pedestrians of the first order and prefer to run rather than to fly when disturbed. Some inhabit salt, others fresh or brackish marshes, or reedy, grassy places. Most of their life is spent running about in the thick cover of the marsh herbage. They travel quickly and easily over semi-submerged vegetation or soft mud, and hop or swim lightly across puddles. All the rails are somewhat nocturnal. They nest on the ground or among the reeds, and usually lay large clutches. The young leave the nest as soon as hatched.

The rails have many enemies, including reptiles, fish, birds, and animals. Floods and unseasonable weather doubtless destroy many nests and eggs. Vast numbers are shot by sportsmen. Were it not for the large families which most of the rails rear, they would now be scarce birds. Many of the rails are extremely vocal. Most of them are not strictly gregarious, but are usually found associated through a community of interests. They are catholic in their tastes, their food embracing insects, small fish, worms, reptiles, even small snakes, and many seeds from marsh grasses and reeds. Rail are often numerous in localities where their presence is unsuspected by their human neighbors. The yellow, like the black rail, is too small and scarce to furnish sport, and on account of its rarity should not be shot except for scientific purposes.

THE YELLOW RAIL (*Coturnicops noveboracensis*). *Field Marks:* "6 to 7.5 inches in length; yellowish color; the wing in flight shows much white" (Forbush).

It is a relatively rare bird and its chief habitat is eastern North America; it is known to nest in New England. Rich believes the yellow rail more common in New England than the Virginia rail. This is certainly not the case in New Jersey. Forbush states that he has seen the bird alive only once, but adds that a considerable number are taken in Massachusetts. It is, perhaps, less susceptible to cold than the sora, but its habits are otherwise generally similar to the latter species.

Like all rails it flies only as a last resort, but with somewhat more speed than most of the other rails. The only two that I have seen were killed by my pusher with his pole. Wayne states that his dog caught nine yellow rail and flushed but one. Rich reports that of six specimens he obtained, five were captured by a dog.

The nest is placed on the ground in a marsh and is composed of dried grass. Eggs are usually six or eight in number, buffy in color, and marked with blotches and spots of pale brown. They measure about 1.10 by 0.8 inches.

BLACK RAIL *(Creciscus jamaicensis). Field Marks:* "The little black rail measures about 5 inches and is the smallest of the rails. It is very dark; must not be confounded with the young of the other rails, which also are small and dark" (Forbush). In the fall it can be identified by its size.

Its range is eastern North America. It is a rare species, but less rare in the southern part of its range. The black rail is known to breed in New England, and probably also nests elsewhere. When running through the reeds it suggests a field mouse.

Nests are composed of dried grasses and are placed on the ground in a marsh. The eggs are six to ten in number. They are white, speckled with small reddish brown dots which are more plentiful at the large end. Eggs measure about 1.05 by 0.80 inches.

The voice is a high-pitched *"chi-cro-croo"* (Sanford). Rather than fly, the black rail will sometimes submit to capture, hiding its head in the marsh vegetation and cocking up its tail.

VIRGINIA RAIL *(Rallus virginianus).* Nomenclature: Red rail, little red rail, long-billed rail, fresh-water rail, fresh-water marsh hen.

*Field Marks:* "8.5 to 10.5 inches in length; bill 1.5 inches; size of a bobwhite; long, reddish bill and rich brown breast distinguish this bird from the sora" (Forbush).

*Range:* "North America. It is by no means a local bird, as might be implied by its name. It probably breeds from Canada to North Carolina; winters chiefly in the South" (Forbush).

*Voice:* "Kep, kik, kip"; song, a grunting *"wak-wak-wak"* and "*cut-cûtta*" (Brewster). These somewhat piglike grunts are often heard in the early morning and late afternoon. Females, when disturbed or apprehensive emit a "*ki-ki-ki*" or "*kiu*" like a flicker (Eaton). Brewster says, "When heard at a distance of only a few yards it has a vibrating, almost unearthly quality and seems to issue from the ground directly beneath one's feet." The Virginia rail inhabits chiefly fresh or brackish marshes.

Forbush describes a nest among driftwood and grasses under an alder bush at the edge of a run. The nest is composed of grasses, and is sometimes placed on a tussock, and is usually well concealed. The site of the nest is generally in a remote part of the swamp. Nuttall says, "The female is so much attached to her eggs after sitting as sometimes to allow of being taken up in the hand rather than desert the premises." Rich believes that the Virginia rail may occasionally raise two broods in a season. Clutches number six to a dozen eggs and are pale buffy white, spotted with brown and obscure lilac. Eggs measure about 1.26 by .096 inches. Incubation commences as soon as the first egg is laid, and as a consequence hatching time varies. Incubation requires about fifteen days. The young leave the nest as soon as the last egg is hatched.

The food of this rail is extremely varied. Cahn reports that a captive Virginia rail consumed various insects, small fish, small crustaceans, worms, and frogs. On one occasion this bird devoured a snake 12 inches in length, taking two hours for the operation. After he finished the meal it was noted that this was the only time during its captivity that the bird seemed satisfied with the amount of food supplied. Seeds of various marsh herbage probably constitute a large part of the diet. However, the diet of the Virginia rail probably contains more animal matter than that of the sora. According to Samuels, it feeds chiefly during twilight and early dawn, and remains concealed in the grass during the greater part of the day.

During some years the Virginia rail is fairly common and may constitute 5 per cent or even more of the bag. Usually not more than one or two are killed by a single gun on a tide, and often none is seen. The Virginia rail are more plentiful toward the end of the shooting season than at the opening. It is a timid, shy, retiring bird, often living in large, inaccessible swamps, boggy meadows, and marshy river borders. When approached, it is apt to retreat by running to heavy cover, and is, therefore, often not observed. It does not resort to flight unless forced to do so. The Virginia rail is probably more plentiful than generally believed. In size, manner of flushing, and character of flight it resembles the more common sora, but is easily distinguished from the latter by its reddish-brown color and longer bill. In the spring, the Virginia rail arrives in Pennsylvania and New Jersey about May 1. Some remain and breed, others continue farther north. They depart for the south about October 10-15, the date varying somewhat according to the weather conditions. Like most rails, a heavy frost sends the bulk of the Virginia rails southward.

KING RAIL *(Rallus elegans)*. Nomenclature: Big red rail, red-breasted rail, fresh-water marsh hen.

*Field Marks:* "Much larger than the Virginia rail (17 to 19 inches; closely resembles it, but sides of head less gray; size of clapper rail, but much brighter in color; olive brown above rather than gray, and breast cinnamon rather than buff, as in the clapper" (Forbush). Looks like a large edition of the Virginia rail.

*Range:* Eastern North America. Breed from Ontario and New England to Texas, Florida, and Cuba. Winters in the southern part of its breeding range.

It nests on the ground, but these are raised 6 to 18 inches by means of withered weeds and grasses (Bachman). Wayne has found numerous nests in rushes and buttonwood bushes 8 to 18 inches above water. The nest is sometimes on a tussock of marsh grasses. It is a rude platform made of dead grass and weeds. Eggs are seven to twelve in number, buffy white or creamy, and heavily marked with rufus or light purple. Eggs measure about 1.68 by 1.2 inches.

*Voice:* A loud *"bup, bup, bup,"* repeated rapidly a number of times. Many of the rails emit a sort of treetoad rattle. In the case of the king rail this has a rather pronounced metallic, ringing quality.

The king rail may be looked upon as the fresh-water prototype of the clapper rail. It is most likely to be met with moderately late in the fall and is rarely encountered on the rail marsh at the opening of the shooting season. Except during the breeding season it is nearly always observed singly. The king rail is a handsome, somewhat scarce bird and the rail shooter is not apt to kill more than one during two or three seasons. Often he does not even see one for an even longer period. As far as the sportsman is concerned, the habits of the king rail are similar to those of its smaller relatives. It is not especially wild; flies slowly with dangling legs, and is easily brought down with fine shot such as is usually used for sora.

CLAPPER RAIL *(Rallus crepitans crepitans)*. This bird is often called the marsh hen.

*Field Marks:* "Resembles the Virginia rail and the king rail in form, but is much larger and grayer or paler than our common rails. In salt-water marshes mainly. . . . The clapper rail can be distinguished from the king rail by its generally grayish instead of brownish or blackish upper parts and by its paler underplumage" (Forbush).

*Range:* "The salt marshes of the Atlantic coast from New England to the Gulf of Mexico" (Forbush).

It breeds in salt marshes in the northern part of its range. It not infrequently is found in brackish marshes and not often in fresh water. Nest is on the ground or a pile of rushes. It is usually placed on a less watery site than that of the sora. Seven to twelve eggs are laid. These are buffy white, sparsely marked with reddish or purplish. Formerly eggs were collected for food. Wilson states that as many as 1,200 clapper-rail eggs have been gathered by one man in a single day.

*Voice:* "Grak, grak, grak," at first loud and rapid, ending on a lower and slower note (Chapman). At all times a noisy bird, it is especially so during its breeding season. The clapper rail may be regarded as an accidental visitor to the average fresh or even brackish rail marsh. It is an extremely difficult bird to flush except during high tide. At times of low and moderate heights of water it dodges about among the reeds and refuses to take wing. The clapper rail may sometimes be caught by an active dog. At times it presents a curious appearance with its head tilted downward and its tail pointing skyward. The birds often live in colonies, but are not strictly gregarious. The food of the clapper rail consists largely of animal matter, but, like most rails, it devours seeds at periods when these are available, and may sometimes be observed climbing the reed stalks to secure the grain at the top of the plants. It is a poor bird for the table. Clapper rail are shot from a boat pushed over the marsh at high tide in much the same manner as are sora. Number 8 shot is suitable.

Sora *(Porzana carolina).* Nomenclature: Sora, rail, Carolina rail, rail-bird, chicken bill, meadow chicken, common rail, crake, soree, water hen, "Ortolan."

*Field Marks:* "Nearly as large as a bobwhite (8 to 9 inches), but slimmer; short (0.75 inch) yellow bill distinguishes it from the long-billed Virginia rail" (Forbush). They appear darker, and in some lights the males look almost black. The males may be distinguished from the females by their ashy-blue breasts and black throats. The young males lack much of the dark and bluish markings.

*Range:* "North America. Breeds from British Columbia, southern Mackenzie, central Keewatin and Gulf of St. Lawrence, south to southern California, Utah, Colorado, Kansas, Illinois, and New Jersey; winters from northern California, Illinois, and South Carolina through the West Indies and Central America to Venezuela and Peru; accidental in Bermuda, Greenland, and England" (Forbush). The sora is the most widely distributed of our rails.

*Nesting:* Soras mate each season. Relatively few sportsmen have seen the nest. The nest is often in a watery part of the marsh and is placed upon the ground, often on top of an elevated tussock in an open meadow. Often the nest is in a dense growth of cattail flags *(Typha latifloliara).* It is usually well hidden. Sometimes a point under thick vines is selected, others are in briar patches. It is usually just above high-water mark and is composed of marsh grass. It is a moderately bulky, basket-like affair, and sometimes partially arched over. The eggs number eight to eighteen. These are glossy buffy or white, sparsely speckled, and spotted with rich brown or purplish markings. Often so many eggs are laid that it seems remarkable that such a small bird can cover all of them. They are frequently arranged in layers in the bottom of the nest and their position is probably shifted by the sitting bird in order that all may get sufficient heat. Eggs average about 1.24 by 0.9 inches and are ovoidal in shape.

Incubation is carried out by both birds. It begins as soon as the first egg is laid so that hatching is not simultaneous. Incubation lasts about two weeks. The old birds sit close and will continue on the nest even if it is partially submerged by floods. The young leave the nest as soon as the last egg is hatched.

Incubation commences early in May in New Jersey and Pennsylvania. The young are covered with glossy down and present a general dark or blackish appearance. They possess a red protuberance at the base of the upper bill and a tuft of yellowish feathers on the throat. The young can swim, dive, and hide, and soon follow the mother through the marsh. If the eggs are destroyed, sora probably lay a second time, but if the young are destroyed a second clutch is unlikely. The sora may breed in the midst of civilization.

*Food:* Various kinds of animal matter, including worms, insects, small fish, crustaceans, and perhaps small mollusks. Gibbs questions that reptiles are eaten. Sora are voracious eaters and soon become fat when the supply of autumn seeds from the marsh grasses becomes available. They are particularly fond of wild rice (*Zizania aquatica*) or wild oats. Food is gathered from the ground by quick pecks, but, like most of the rails, the sora often deftly climbs the reeds and grasses to reach the seeds and grain which hang in tassels at the top of the stems. They are assisted in climbing by their hind toes.

*Voice:* This is characteristic. Like most of the rail family, the sora is quite vocal and possesses a variety of calls. The most common is a *"kuk"* or *"peep."* Chapman describes a clear whistled *"ker-wee,"* now and again interrupted by a high-voiced clear rolling whinny of about twelve to fifteen notes, which, like the call of alarm, is taken up and repeated by different birds all over the marsh. Often when a rail marsh is approached it is silent, but if a stone be thrown into some thick clump of cover, or an oar sharply rattled, numerous rail can be heard responding from various directions. Brewster describes a call which resembles the scatter call of quail. The call of the rail is somewhat difficult to locate, and the bird seems to possess a certain ventriloquistic ability. Rails can often be heard calling at evening. They flush silently.

*Migration:* Sora arrive in the Mid-Atlantic states about the middle of April; some continue northward, others mate and remain until the first hard frost in the fall, when the main body, which has by this time been greatly augmented by migrants from the north, depart for a milder climate. After leaving New England and other northern breeding grounds, the birds congregate in large numbers in the marshes of the Delaware River, Chesapeake Bay, and other favorable localities. Migrations arrive in waves, one often overlapping another. Thus heavy concentrations are built up at favorable points. Just how long individual birds or groups remain in suitable areas is unknown, and probably varies with conditions. According to Audubon, the migration is made in compact flocks of five to one hundred individuals. Some of these groups shorten their migration by cutting across bays and headlands; others follow the shore. It is at about this time that the wild grains upon which they feed become ripe. It is during this period of aggradation that the birds become fat and afford sport to the rail shooters. The date for leaving New Jersey and adjacent areas varies somewhat according to the weather, but the first hard frost usually sends the bulk of the birds southward. On one day the marshes may be filled with rail and the next practically empty. The majority have usually left by the middle of October or even earlier. Sora are apparently extremely susceptible to cold weather and are good weather prophets. This habit of almost simultaneous departure of the bulk of the birds on the advent of the first cold weather in the autumn gave rise to the belief, still held by some old marsh-men, that rail turned into bullfrogs during the winter months, and buried themselves in the mud. This theory was strengthened by the fact that the frogs ceased to croak and disappeared for the winter at about the same time as the rail left. It is not, however, uncommon to find a few stray birds lingering after the reeds are almost flattened, about the last of October or even the first week of November. Lewis states that the fall of 1846 was remarkably mild, and, as a result, many rail delayed their departure until November 25.

Migrations are carried out during the dark hours. Large numbers often arrive in a single night. There is no rule about this, but a marsh may contain only a few birds one evening and hold large numbers the next morning. That rail bank up in suitable marshes is certain. Migrations are performed at a low altitude, as proved by the large number of sora killed by flying against telegraph wires and other man-made obstructions. There is some evidence that, under favorable conditions, the speed of the migrants may be greater than would be expected from such weak-flying birds. There is little question that the birds take advantage of favorable winds, as definite increase in numbers in the New Jersey marshes is generally observed after suitable winds have been blowing during the period of migration. Sora are known to cross wide stretches of water. Some of them go to Cuba, and others as far as Venezuela and Peru. One migration lane is evidently along the Atlantic seaboard, and others undoubtedly exist farther inland. I have occasionally flushed a rail from a grass field far inland, when working dogs in the fall. I have never seen a dog point a rail, and my dogs paid no attention to them. There is a tendency for the migrating birds to follow waterways. Little is known as to whether families migrate together, or whether old birds come first, or what the sex ratio is during different stages of the migration. During the shooting season old and young birds of both sexes are present.

*Habits:* Sora are retiring birds and their presence is generally not suspected except by sportsmen, naturalists, and those whose business takes them on the marsh. Even then, many birds may be present and but few seen during stages of low water. To flush many birds, a boat must be run over the marsh, and this cannot be done except at high tide. The rails spend most of their time running about the marsh and retreat by running upon approach. As a consequence, relatively few are observed unless they are actually pursued. Rail when walking take long steps and when running may span 12 inches or more. Rail sometimes leave the marsh and utilize nearby grass and weed fields; but do not remain long in these areas. When running and walking sora present a sprightly, odd, and somewhat mouselike appearance. They look much slimmer when frightened. At close range it can be seen that the bill is often pointing downward, the head being carried low and the stubby tail elevated. At other times the head and tail are both elevated, the bird exhibiting a neat, rather jaunty appearance. The tail is frequently flirted about in a nervous manner. If undisturbed, they pick with quick strokes of their bills at food on the ground, and often climb the marsh grasses to obtain the seeds.

Rail, in common with certain varieties of ducks and other birds, evidently possess considerable curiosity, and if quiet is exercised, will often run to the edge of the cover to investigate a strange sound. Rail are probably active to some extent at night and can often be heard calling at twilight, early morning, and occasionally during the darker hours. This is especially true during moonlight, but their calling is not confined to these periods. During high tide there is a tendency for the birds to work toward the landward edge of the marsh, where more cover still remains above water. Although they can swim lightly, but rather slowly, they definitely prefer to be on their legs, and, even at high water, will run over semi-submerged mud and vegetation, moving from one bit of cover to another, and resorting to flight only when they are forced to do so. Hence the necessity for the pusher to send his boat along at a good pace, as the slow boat permits many birds to run into thick cover, from which they are often difficult or impossible to flush. Many are also passed by a slow boat, as the birds have time to run out of the course of the sportsman. During the period of high water, single birds are often seen resting on some elevated spot from which they can be easily flushed.

Many New Jersey rail marshes have an old bank on the landward side. These are usually covered with small or medium-sized trees, bushes, vines, and grasses, which form an almost impenetrable cover. The experienced sportsman or pusher shoots the deeper part of the marsh first and works inland as the tide rises. At flood water, with a good tide, there is no better place to find rail than along these banks. The pusher should parallel the bank, preferably, in the direction which will result in shots being secured to the left side. Many birds will be found in such localities and nearly all will go to the bank. Birds can often be seen running, splashing, or semi-flying to the cover out of gunshot ahead of the boat, but the majority fly, offering excellent targets. Under these circumstances they usually fly low, intending to light upon the lower part of the bank, from which site they instantly run into the cover and are of course lost.

Rail seem definitely to sense an ebbing tide and can be put in the air more easily while the water is rising. As soon as the tide begins to fall birds are harder to flush. However, the height of the water is the chief factor and good shooting can usually be had, even on the ebb, as long as the water remains at a good height. I have seen periods during big storm tides when good shooting could be had all day, as even so-called low water was then higher than a normal flood tide.

Rail are not strictly gregarious and are not found in flocks except during their migrations. However, where one bird is found in the marsh, others are likely to be near by. This is probably the result of favorable covers and the presence of an abundance of food. As a result, pockets of birds are usually found, some areas containing many more than others. Collections of marsh buttercups are favorite sites for rail to collect in. The edges of marsh creeks, which are usually bordered by thick, high reeds, are good cover. As the tide rises, rail seek such places and the latter sites are often utilized. Except during really high water, many more rail are present than are flushed.

*Flight:* Except during migrations, or for the purpose of moving from one adjacent marsh to another, rail do not often resort to flying unless forced to do so. Such spontaneous flights are usually at night. One may watch a marsh which is full of rail and rarely see a bird fly voluntarily. This is not because they are idle, for they are usually moving about, but is due to the fact that they prefer to use their legs rather than their wings, and remain in cover. Perhaps because of this trait, or as a result of it, their flight is weak and heavy, most birds flushing ahead of the boat, flying a short distance, and dropping back rather suddenly into the marsh. This habit may deceive even the experienced rail shooter into the belief that the bird has been wounded or perhaps killed. The average flight is seldom more than 150 yards, and often not a third of that distance. Rail are occasionally missed because they drop suddenly back into the marsh just as the trigger is being pulled. The flushed birds frequently head for heavy cover, such as a dense clump of reeds, and the distance to such cover governs, to an extent, the length of the flight. Sometimes, especially in thick cover, they merely flop up and drop again almost instantly. The flight is slow, steady, and rarely exceeds 20 or 25 m.p.h., and is perhaps even less. Rail usually take advantage of a strong wind and their speed is increased and somewhat longer flights are usual. As has been mentioned, the flight is usually short, but there is hardly an experienced rail shooter who has not seen them occasionally cross wide streams, such as the Delaware River, when hard pressed by boats. During such flights, it can be noticed that, after going a distance, the birds pick up speed and appear to fly more energetically. The dangling legs are more or less tucked up under the tail feathers and the generally labored character of flight, so common while in the marsh, is less pronounced or absent.

The average rise is at a distance of about 12 to 15 yards ahead of the boat. Much depends upon the cover. When this is thick, birds tend to lie close—sometimes so close that the cover has to be beaten by the pushing pole before they can be flushed. During high water, and especially when the cover is sparse, the birds are wilder than in low water. When shooting, most of the rail rise ahead of the boat and fly straight away or quarter. Some turn back and not a few spring at the side. Many of the latter also turn back. Occasionally a bird permits the boat to pass and flushes in the rear. Usually such birds head back and are often seen only by the pusher. The flight is usually straight and low. There is rarely any twisting or dodging, though late in the season, when the birds are strong and the marsh vegetation largely flattened down, I have seen them zigzag like a snipe. Usually, the greater the altitude of the flight, the longer it will be. During heavy wind, rail sometimes rise with it, more often against it or go with it diagonally. Unless they rise with the breeze they are apt to turn and dart off down-wind. On alighting, they may drop suddenly into the marsh, often appearing to have been hit; or if especially they are at a fair height, they may turn and drop with uplifted wings into cover. In entering the reeds they often do so from above and not from the side. Wing beats are not especially rapid and no definitely audible whirr is produced. Particularly in thick cover, rail can often be heard running through the dry reeds as a preliminary to flight. However, this is not like the preliminary run of a pheasant and employed to get up speed, but appears more to be a means of getting out of the way, or of finding an opening for flight. They often cause a splashing in the water as they take off. Occasionally an educated bird is encountered, which routinely flushes wild and makes long flights. These birds are not common and may perhaps have been previously shot at and escaped.

As previously mentioned, sora give the impression of being somewhat nervous birds. Many of the older writers record instances of rail falling to the shot without having been hit. Some of these birds are said to have been dead upon being picked up; others have recovered or have been "playing possum." Krider reports having been informed by a pusher whom he believed reliable, that the latter had seen a rail fall dead at the simple report of a cap, the gun having missed fire. The late Morton Reeves, of Mauricetown, New Jersey, who was a famous pusher in days gone by, told me that he had seen similar instances on two occasions. However, unless the birds were carefully picked and subjected to a rigid examination, it would be impossible to exclude the presence of a single pellet, perhaps in the brain or some other vital point. Furthermore, a bird may occasionally be hit by a wad which might leave no mark. I have talked to many pushers and sportsmen and can find no reliable instance of a rail falling without being hit. However, it is only fair to remember that birds are not usually examined with this thought in mind. A rail is shot at, picked up, and dropped on a heap of dead birds in the bottom of the boat. The head and neck may not be picked, and even if it is noticed that there is no shot mark on the body, it is apt to be assumed that the bird has been killed by a wound in the head.

Sandys and many others refer to a sort of fit or spasm to which they believe rails may sometimes be subject. This may not have any relation to the report of a gun and is prone to develop if the bird imagines itself to be hopelessly cornered. In this condition, the bird topples over and may be picked up in the hand. It may subsequently recover. Sandys states he has seen a rail suddenly stiffen when the only apparent disturbance was the sound of a boot rustling in the herbage. He says others have spoken of having attempted to pick up a skulking bird which, to their astonishment, stretched out and seemingly expired as the hand was extended toward it. Statements such as these may well be accepted cautiously, unless accompanied by adequate proof.

*Enemies.* Little is known of the enemies and diseases of rail, or indeed of other factors influencing their abundance or scarcity; but it is well known that they have their good and bad years, and this periodicity is often quite marked. Sometimes their scarcity can perhaps be explained by local conditions, but this is not always the case. Nesting as they do on the ground and often not far above high-water mark, probably many nests and eggs are destroyed by unseasonable floods and high water. How often, under such conditions, second clutches are laid is unknown. If the eggs are destroyed, most species of birds lay a second time. Second clutches, however, usually tend to be smaller than first and the young are generally handicapped in other ways. If the young brood is destroyed, second layings are probably infrequent. The rather wide nesting distribution helps them, as floods are often local.

Leaving the nest soon after hatching, the young are small and, following the mother through the grasses and reeds, they are exposed to many enemies. Marshes are well known to be favorable hunting rounds of vermin of various kinds. Doubtless, despite their activity and ability to hide, dive, and swim, many young rail, and occasionally adults, fall victims to predators, such as minks, weasels, raccoons and probably foxes and skunks. According to Blackman, rats are said to have exterminated the rare Laysan rail from one of the islands of the Pacific. However, the Laysan rail was flightless and conditions in its habitat were different from those of our rails. Bullfrogs are known to eat young rail. Fish, such as pickerel, eels, catfish, bass, and perhaps gars, probably account for some deaths, and doubtless also finish off many cripples and devour lost birds.

Rail are also vulnerable to snapping turtles and snakes. Wayne has seen a moccasin eating the eggs of a king rail. Herons and cranes destroy young rails. Hawks occasionally take an adult or an immature rail, and the same may be said of owls, for rail are more or less active at night. However, I have observed hundreds of hawks while rail shooting, and have seen them catch reed birds and red-winged blackbirds; but have never seen one take a rail, and doubt if they do so very often. However, a rail sitting out on a tuft of grass at high water is probably a sight which the hungry sharp-shinned or Cooper's hawk could not resist. Crows, so common on many marshes, probably destroy eggs and young. Literally thousands of rail are killed annually by gunners. Even with the present Federal limit, the kill must be enormous. Rail are probably the easiest of all game birds to shoot. They are not in any sense shot carriers, a single pellet or two of fine shot being sufficient to bring them down. They are relatively tame birds and easily approached. Even if the sportsman lacks experience, this can usually be supplied by the pusher and the actual shooting can be accomplished with considerable success by the novice. As previously stated, the rise is usually at short range, the flight is slow and straight; there are usually no obstructions in the way of cover, and the birds are therefore easily killed. Many gunners are at work and, under favorable conditions, it is nothing unusual for nearly every sportsman to secure his limit. Probably the average rail marsh which is fairly accessible will yield five hundred to one thousand birds per season or more.

Two factors especially tend to save the rail from extermination: (1) their large broods and (2) the fact that only a relatively few marshes are shot. There are many thousands of acres of marshland inhabited by rail which are either inaccessible or unsuited for shooting. Most of the non-tidal marshes fall in the latter category, as it is impossible to push a boat over them. All the marshes that for one reason or another are not shot over are valuable sanctuaries. Under existing circumstances rail seem to be holding their own. There is always a certain amount of illegal shooting—generally a disregard for the limit. Game wardens sometimes take a boat and push the marsh during the flood tide, and examine licenses and check on the number of rail in the boats. More often, the wardens wait at the landing places. In an effort to escape detection, greedy gunners sometimes tie their excess birds in a bunch and anchor them somewhere in the marsh or to the bank, and recover them later. A few birds are sometimes concealed in cartridge boxes or in the clothing before landing. I have heard of instances of pushers and gunners coming ashore with their shirts, and even trousers, filled with birds. Any of these latter methods could be detected if a strict search were instituted, but this is rarely done. Sometimes homeward-bound motor cars are stopped and searched. I think that, as far as New Jersey is concerned, there is not a great deal of illegal shooting—certainly not as much as when the 15-bird limit was in force. Both Federal and local wardens do their work well and are generally conscientious men. Federal wardens obviously have many advantages. The present limit of 25 birds is a good one; the former limit of 15 was too small and encouraged infringements.

Lewis (1851) and Roosevelt (1884) state that rail were formerly taken along the James River in Virginia, and perhaps in other areas by fire hunting, in much the same manner as were woodcock in Louisiana, the birds in this case being knocked down with a paddle. Lewis reports that the enormous number of 960 have been killed by three Negroes during the short space of three hours. I have not heard of fire hunting being practiced in recent times.

Rail are difficult birds to trap and the only illegal methods from which they suffer to any extent is shooting. In New Jersey the season opens September 1. At this time most of the birds are thin. The chief aim of shooting is sport and not food; however, shooting should be reserved for those periods during which game is in prime condition. Thousands of rail are in the New Jersey marshes by September 1, and many hundreds or thousands are killed before they are in good condition. In my opinion the opening of the season should be delayed until September 10 or 15, when the birds are in better condition. As a matter of fact, early shooting is often not pleasant, due to hot weather and the presence of mosquitoes. Such a change in the game laws would probably result in a somewhat smaller annual kill, which itself would act as a safeguard for the future and improve the shooting during the open season.

*Shooting.* The equipment for rail shooting varies somewhat from that necessary for upland shooting. A light, double-barreled, open-bored, well-fitting gun is desirable. As quick loading is often required, it should be an ejector. The gun used for upland shooting is satisfactory. If the sportsman likes to shoot a small bore, the rail marsh is an ideal place for its use. Rail are easily killed and the range is short, so light loads are all that are necessary. For a 12-bore, 2¾ drams and ⅞ of an ounce of No. 11 shot is ideal. The next best is the 3-1–11 load. A waterproof metal cartridge box, holding one hundred shells, is useful, as boats may be wet or shooting may have to be done in the rain. A few loose cartridges are usually carried in the right-hand pocket of the shooting jacket, where they are quickly and easily available. Some men prefer a cartridge holder of the type used by clay-pigeon shooters, which is strapped to the waist and holds about twenty shells. The Panta-belt which will be described in the chapter on "Equipment" is convenient. As the weather may be warm, a light shooting coat is desirable.

A motor car is apt to be used for getting to the marsh. If so, there is no reason not to take everything that may be necessary. Extras can be left in the car if it is found that they are not needed. Boat bottoms are often wet and slippery, and a pair of overshoes may be useful. Weather is often hard to forecast and, apart from this, on the Atlantic seaboard most of our really big storm tides are the result of heavy, easterly winds. These are usually accompanied by rain. Rain itself in no way prevents good shooting, so, unless one is willing to forego what is often the best shooting of the season, some provision must be made for keeping dry. The best rig I know consists of a pair of rubber hip boots, waterproof trousers, cut off a little below the knee and worn over boots and a waterproof blouse. The Navy used to make these waterproofs. They are about the correct weight—loose, strong, and, above all, waterproof under all conditions. By taking off the regular shooting coat and substituting the waterproof blouse one could shoot about as well as in an ordinary shooting jacket. At all events, some provision for rainy weather should be made.

Take along a greasy rag for the gun. In wet weather, a coat of grease on the gun will save a lot of trouble. Put some grease on a greasy rag in the cartridge box and forget about it until it is needed. Small as the chance, there is always the possibility of a fall overboard or capsized boat. A few dry clothes are an insurance against a wet drive home. Especially, early in the season, mosquitoes may be troublesome and are sometimes a plague, particularly near the landing place or when there is no breeze on the marsh. A pair of loose shooting gloves and a small bottle of mosquito repellent are worth including in the outfit. The regular shooting hat is satisfactory. Glasses are a nuisance in the rain; but there is not much that can be done to keep them dry except to wear a wide-brimmed hat, and to keep handy a dry handkerchief. They are a comfort in high reeds. In hot weather, and if the drive home be a long one, some arrangement for keeping the birds cool may be necessary. One of the tin-lined baskets containing a compartment for ice, which are made for fishermen, answers the purpose. A basket of this kind is also useful to take on the marsh on a warm day, as the condition of birds is not improved by lying on the bottom of the boat in the hot sun, even though they may not actually spoil.

A great part of the success or failure of rail shooters depends upon the pushers. A poor shot will probably get more birds with a good pusher than an expert with a man who does not know how to handle a boat. The pusher should be strong, reliable, sober, willing, a good marker, know the marsh, and, most important of all, possess the skill to push a rail boat safely, smoothly, and at a good pace. Most of them are good men, but there is a great difference in their ability to push and mark. With the best intentions, some are constantly jerking the boat; run at great speed for a few minutes, and then reduce the pace to almost nothing; are frequently colliding with submerged obstructions or otherwise not doing their work well. Personally, I like a man to be quiet in the boat. Some are great talkers. However, noise in the boat does not greatly influence the number of shots obtained. Some pushers regularly come in with the limit and these men are much sought after and, as a consequence, often have to be engaged some time ahead. A good pusher is punctual and generally has a tight, clean boat and proper outfit. Although the price asked by most pushers is high, the work is hard and a good man is well worth the money. A poor pusher is expensive at any price.

The rail boat should be smooth running, steady, light, easy to handle, water-tight and draw as little water as possible. The best boats are flat bottomed. Round-bottomed boats are apt to be unsteady. Some pushers rig a bag net toward the stern, in which to place dead birds. Others use a covered basket. At all events, some provision for keeping birds dry and out of the sun should be made. Some boats are rigged with a small low canvas cover over the bow, in order to keep seeds and débris out of the cartridge boxes. The pushing pole, sometimes called a "gaff," is moderately light, smooth, about 12 to 15 feet in length, and approximately 4 inches in diameter. It is equipped at one end with a foot or claw which prevents it from penetrating the soft bottom. Each pusher has his favorite pole. A pair of short oars or a paddle should be taken. A shallow net on a light 5-foot handle is useful for picking up dead birds. Wire is better than twine for the netting. Some pushers carry three or four white blocks of wood, which they throw out to mark the point of fall in case two or three birds are down at once. These are useful. A jug of water for the pusher completes the outfit.

The rail marsh contains many high reeds, and birds, and gunners are often numerous. The latter are not infrequently excited or careless. There is no other form of shooting which involves so much risk of being shot. The average pusher has been shot at least once, some a number of times. This is usually nothing more than a peppering with fine shot, but fine shot may destroy an eye, and even the remote chance of being hit is enough to spoil sport. It is a good plan to tell a new pusher to keep well away from all other boats. If he does not do so, have no hesitation to warn him again. All pushers like to see their men get the limit and it is human nature to edge in on another boat that has run into a pocket of birds. It is a poor business to work too close and perhaps interfere with another man's shooting, quite apart from the ethics involved. Furthermore, a few rail are not worth the risk of being shot. The rail marsh is essentially the place of all others where an ounce of prevention is well worth the proverbial pound of cure. Avoid crowded marshes, keep an eye on the whereabouts of near-by boats. They often slip up unnoticed through thick reed. Treat others as you would like to be treated and do not endanger them or shoot even in their general direction.

The sportsman should take with him on the marsh only those articles he really needs. There is little enough room in the boat and excess equipment gets in the way. Everything should be stored away, generally in the bow of the boat, and nothing left loose which may be swept overboard by overhanging reeds or branches, or get underfoot. Loose articles may also readily cause a fall.

Apart from the ability of the pusher and, to a lesser extent, the skill of the sportsman, success in rail shooting depends very largely upon the height of the water on the marsh. Owing to the birds' habit of skulking, rail shooting can usually only be practiced upon tidal marshes. The higher the tide the better, as the boat can be more easily pushed over the marsh, and birds then have less cover and are obliged to fly more frequently when come upon. At low water, a man may flounder about for hours and not even see a rail. Afternoon tides are generally thought to be better than those in the morning, and big tides generally occur during the full of the moon. Perhaps the chief factor in influencing the height of the tide is the direction of the wind. On the New Jersey coast long-continued, strong winds from the eastward, northeast, and southeast bank back the water and bring about extra high tides on the marshes. These storms are generally accompanied by rain and when the birds are in, it is during them that the cream of the shooting can be secured. Birds flush well during rain, fly fast in the wind, and it is possible to push easily over many high meadows which previously have been little shot. During these heavy storms is the time of all times to get to the rail marsh. Often few boats are out. Westerly winds make low tides. With normal tides it is possible to push over the marsh during the last two hours of the flood and the first one and a half or two hours of the ebb. The time to start is usually best known by the pushers. Pushing is hard work and too early starting may readily result in a willing pusher tiring himself out before the high water arrives. The rail shooter should provide himself with a local tide-table. However, high winds often play havoc with the schedule, some holding back the water from the marsh and others banking it up. Where telephone communication is available, it is often safer to rely on it, rather than to place entire dependence on the tide-table. Furthermore, winds on the coast may be different from those inland, and as a result plans have to be altered.

The man shooting rail for the first time will find himself handi-capped in two ways: first by the movements of the boat and second by the fact that he cannot move his feet while shooting. In order to maintain balance and help the pusher he should select a point in the forward part of the skiff. Ask the pusher if he is in the right place properly to balance the boat. Sometimes there is a seat just back of him. If so, the shooter can assist himself in maintaining his balance by keeping the calf of his right leg braced against it. Old-time gunners sometimes wore a pad or bandage over the leg to prevent bruising from this cause, although this precaution is not usually necessary. In some boats there is a cleat, under which it may be possible to slip the toe of the left boot. When this is present it helps considerably in maintaining balance and prevents the tendency to sway backward if the pusher gives a strong shove for-ward or a sudden start. The stance should be easy and comfortable, but with the feet about 4 inches farther apart than if shooting from level ground. The wider spread gives better purchase against sudden starts and stoppages of the boat, which are sure to occur occasionally. The latter often are caused by collision with under-water obstructions. It also helps to maintain the balance required to overcome the normal movements of the boat. The rail shooter has to stand in more or less the same position for three or four hours. This is more tiring than the novice might think. Do not stand too stiffly, and move around a bit or sit down when the opportunity occurs. The gun is held more or less at the ready, but it is a good plan to change grips and its position, to prevent the arms and hands from becoming tired.

In order properly to face shots at the side, when shooting from land, the shooter unconsciously changes the position of the feet. In the rail boat any such movement is likely to tilt the boat and result in a miss (usually undershooting), if not a fall or worse, and the shooter must depend upon a pivot without changing the position of the feet. Very few men can safely change the position of their feet under these circumstances; the novice should certainly never attempt it. As a result, side shots, especially those to the right, must usually be taken quickly or not at all. With birds far around on the right, it is usually better not to attempt to shoot. Usually the bird can be marked down and often flushed a second time if it is thought worth while to follow it. It is best to follow them at once. Delay gives the bird time to run and conceal itself, and as a consequence it is harder to force into the air. No matter how quickly they are followed, some birds seem simply to evaporate and are never seen again. Birds sometimes flush very near the boat. Pushers make a practice of beating near-by heavy cover with their pushing poles, and this sometimes routs a close-sitting bird.

In covert shooting, it is often advisable to use the edge of the pattern for birds that are too close. The reason for this is that the target will often get out of sight behind cover before it gets off to a proper distance. In rail shooting, this is not the case, as the shooting is usually in the open and it is best not to shoot too fast with the first barrel. Let the close-flushing, outgoing birds get off the proper distance. Otherwise, despite the small loads generally used, many birds will be badly shot up. No one wants to waste game and a smashed bird is a wasted one and useless for the table. The edge of the pattern is sometimes useful for near-by rail at the side which may have to be taken quickly or not at all.

When two birds flush simultaneously, it is generally good policy to take the hardest shot first, which generally means the one farthest away, or to the right. Rail shooting is generally close-range work and the flight is slow compared to that of most game birds. As a result, less lead is required. Because this is so plainly obvious, there is a tendency to be afraid of taking too much lead, and quite as many birds are missed by shooting behind or below as escape because of too great lead. This is especially the case with the low reed-skimming targets, in which the aim should also be a little high.

Rail shooting is generally easy after the gun has become accustomed to the motion of the boat. However, as mentioned, a good many shots have to be taken quickly. During heavy winds the rail's flight is speeded up and there are many more difficult and sporting shots offered than on windless days. The gun should at all times keep a sharp lookout for rising birds. The pusher usually stands upon the stern of the boat, and as a consequence has a better view than the gun, who is standing on the bottom of the boat and is about a foot or so lower. The pusher will call "Mark Right" or "Left," as the case may be, if he thinks his man does not see the rail rise, and should check and steady his boat at this time.

It is said any novice can kill a rail, but it takes a good man to find it. Marking of dead and live birds is the duty of the pusher, and good men become remarkably proficient. They usually mark dead birds by noting that they have fallen near some special stalk of grass or marsh flower, which to the novice is so inconspicuous that its location would be lost if the eye was taken off the place for one instant. Even if three or four birds are down at once, a good pusher will pick them up quickly and unerringly. It is sometimes of assistance for the shooter also to mark the fall of dead birds, but his real business is to load at once and be on the alert for another bird which may flush while the first is being gathered.

While everyone hates to lose a cripple, and every effort should be made to secure it, in the case of rail very prolonged search generally ends in failure. The wing-tipped rail will sometimes run a short distance, and this is often enough to effect its escape, but what makes it even harder to find is the rail's habit of diving and holding on to underwater grain stems, with only the bill above water. In this position, their submersion, more or less protective coloration, and immobility makes them extremely difficult to find. Furthermore, rail can run under water (Maynard). Some pushers believe the cripple often deliberately drowns itself by holding to underwater roots. This is extremely doubtful, although badly wounded birds may dive and become so entangled amid grass stems that they cannot regain the surface. At all events, crippled rail are hard to find, and if a bird is seen to be only wounded, the second barrel should be used without hesitation. Indeed, an instant's delay often means a lost bird. The flight is frequently so low that there is no time to use the second barrel on the falling bird while it is in the air. If this is the case, shoot instantly at the point of fall, regardless of whether or not the bird is visible. Often when a bird cannot be found promptly the pusher will run his boat sideways over the point of fall, and in the resulting slick the bird can be easily seen.

For various reasons, some men prefer to sit down while rail shooting. The seated shooter is much lower than the standing man and, as a result of his restricted range of vision, he is at a distinct disadvantage, especially in high reeds or with low-flying birds. Unless one is physically handicapped, the standing position is decidedly the better. If the shooter elects to shoot from a seat, a fairly high one is preferable. About the best is a piano or stenographer's stool which has been equipped with supports and braced firmly to the bottom of the boat. The seated shooter is less exposed to falls; it is less tiring than standing and he has greater command of side shots, since he can turn much farther around.

The average good shot should boat about fifteen or seventeen rail for every twenty-five cartridges expended. There will probably be about two additional birds which have been knocked down but not retrieved. The expert will probably secure approximately twenty for the same number of cartridges. Curtis believes a good shot should boat about one rail for every two cartridges. Long runs are not at all uncommon, and one hears of twenty-five or even occasionally of fifty birds being killed consecutively. If the gun cares to pick his shots, very few should be missed. Heavy winds speed the birds up and reduce the ratio of kills per shell. During heavy winds, rail often rise wildly and speed away with astonishing rapidity for a bird generally so sluggish in its flight. Twisting and dodging, or a sudden turn to take advantage of the gale, are also not uncommon. It is harder to shoot well in some marshes than in others and a pusher who handles his boat unsteadily may readily cause many misses.

Pushers vary in their marking ability. Some lose few birds and, as a result of accurate marking, can pick them up promptly. Loss of time militates against a good bag, as, during normal tides, the best of the shooting is necessarily limited to a short period and has to be done during the few hours of high water. Marshes vary greatly; some are always hard to find dead birds in, and others are the reverse. Naturally, the higher the water the more vegetation which is covered, and the easier it is to locate dead birds. In a heavy marsh it is often best to pass up a shot or two rather than have four or five rail down at once and thereby overtax the marking ability of the pusher. If the shooter elects to take all such shots, he should himself mark the last bird killed and not take his eyes off the point of fall until the bird is boated. Under ordinary circumstances there are about two birds knocked down and lost for every twenty boated.

Rail are sometimes shot by wading the edges of tidal marshes. At high water many of the birds have worked inland to obtain cover along the margins of the marsh. Dogs are used to flush the birds and retrieve them. Krider records that an acquaintance of his shot successfully in this manner, his two dogs swimming around him in the water. This method is still practiced in parts of New England. Spaniels are generally employed. In some types of cover, Rich says, it is almost like woodcock shooting. Bags are usually smaller than when pushing, but, with the present small limit, this is not so important. I have no personal knowledge of this method of shooting and believe it is rarely attempted on the Delaware River at present. It is not hard to imagine that under good conditions this might be a very attractive method of shooting.

In former times rail were undoubtedly more plentiful than at present. Lewis records thirty-five of the record bags secured below Philadelphia and recorded by Major Price of the National Hotel in Chester, Pennsylvania, during the season of 1846. These varied from 81 to 154, twenty being one hundred birds or over, all killed on a single tide. Lewis further states that on September 8 of the same year J. M. Eyre, of Chester, Pennsylvania, killed 195, which is possibly a record slaughter. A Mr. Hubbell is said to have boated 175. During the season of 1849, rail were very abundant, and over one thousand were brought into Chester alone during a single day. These records are especially remarkable when it is remembered that they were made with muzzle-loading guns. Rail shooters in those days had developed various special loading tools, shot and powder containers particularly devised for rail shooting, with the idea of permitting rapid loading. Sometimes, if a powder container was left open, a spark falling in it would result in an explosion. Holland says that our own forefathers sometimes wore high silk hats while rail shooting, perhaps for the same reason that red is frequently worn by deer hunters today. However, many old prints depicting fishing and shooting show sportsmen wearing high hats. Matches were frequent and considerable rivalry existed, which sometimes led to various shady methods, such as staking out a bunch of dead birds on the marsh, to be picked up during the shooting period, or concealing a large number of birds in the boat before starting. During the eighties rail sold in the Philadelphia markets for from $1.50 to $2.50 per dozen. Rail are still plentiful. Before the Federal limit was in force, I killed fifty rail during the first hour and fifteen minutes of a big tide, and came ashore long before high water. My boat did not go out of sight of the landing at any time. I feel sure I could have killed fifty, and probably a hundred more birds had I so desired. During a storm tide in 1943, I killed a limit in twenty minutes and my pusher subsequently took out two other shooters, each of whom got his limit. The pusher later told me he could have handled two more gunners on the same tide, had they been available. However, these birds were shot with breechloaders, whereas seventy-five or one hundred years ago much valuable time was lost in loading the older type of weapon.

## CHAPTER XII

SCENT, WOUNDED BIRDS, AND
                                                          TOWERING

---

*Here lies one, who never drew*
*Blood himself, yet many slew,*
*Gave the gun its aim, and figure*
*Made in field, yet ne'er pulled trigger.*

*Armed men have gladly made*
*Him their guide, and him obeyed.*
*At his signified desire*
*Would advance, present, and Fire.* ...

*Stout he was, and large of limb,*
*Scores have fled at sight of him.*
*And to all this fame he rose;*
*Only following his Nose.*

*Neptune was he call'd, not He*
*Who controls the boist'rous sea,*
*But of happier command,*
*Neptune of the furrow'd land;*
*And your wonder vain to shorten*
*Pointer to Sir John Throckmorton.*

—W. Cowper, *Poems.*

---

SCENT. Little is known about the scent of game birds. Most of our knowledge is derived from the behavior of bird dogs in the field. As a result of the pursuit of game birds with keen-scenting dogs over long periods of time and under varying conditions, certain facts stand out which can be accepted. The most experienced dog handlers, however, often differ widely in their opinions upon many points relating to scent.

Whether the scent originates from the oil bag or elsewhere is at least uncertain. The entire bird appears to be permeated, as can easily be proved by smelling a freshly killed grouse or wood-cock. Some men believe the scent originates from the feathers or underlying skin and still others attribute it to the feet or vent. Anyone who has drawn a game bird in preparation for the table or has smelt a badly smashed bird whose entrails are perhaps partially protruding, is aware of the fact that the intestines possess a definite odor. The droppings also are probably not without scent. Different varieties undoubtedly possess different smells. Some dogs will refuse to point or have anything to do with woodcock or snipe, refusing to take them in their mouths, but will delight to retrieve or hunt other species.

It is not uncommon for certain individual dogs to point different species in a different manner, which also indicates a difference in smell. Often the owner can tell which species is being pointed by the attitude and behavior of the pointing, or even roading, dog. Even a man can easily differentiate between the rank smell of a crow or purple grackle and the rather gamey odor of a recently killed game bird. These are elementary statements to the man familiar with bird dogs.

Stoddard states that a large number of bobwhites struggling in a trap, when the air is damp and stagnant, emit an odor so powerful as to be offensive to even the dull human nose. If the birds have been motionless for a time, very little odor is noticeable. Spiller relates an instance of a man who got down on his hands and knees and crawled to his pointing dog. Just as he came level with the dog he was able to smell the woodcock, which presently flushed.

Many fundamental problems regarding scent are unsolved or only in a state of theory. There is little positive scientific knowledge based upon controlled or laboratory investigation on many phases of the subject. How a hound, on coming on an old trail, can almost immediately determine the direction taken by the quarry, or why on some days dogs seem to have great difficulty in handling birds, yet on others, which appear in every way similar, are able to handle them very well—these are among the familiar examples, and problems which remain to be solved. Most dogs will ignore a penful of pheasants, but readily point a stray bird, five or ten feet outside the wire screen. However, this is probably dependent upon intelligence rather than a matter of scent. Recently liberated pen-raised birds probably smell differently than wild birds. Occasionally, particularly in the case of quail, dogs are not so keen on them. Possibly fear may increase or alter scent and be the explanation for this. It might be expected that fear would be more pronounced in wild than in tame birds.

Various theories can be advanced, but none has been proved. Scent is composed of minute, ultra-microscopic particles emanating from the bird and involuntarily disseminated by them to the adjacent atmosphere, herbage, or earth. The fineness of these particles is extreme. If the air conveying an odor is filtered through a tube packed with cottonwool, the odor is still discernible by the olfactory sense. This test filters out all microörganisms more than 1/100,000 inch. Undoubtedly, movement of the birds tends to liberate these particles and make the scent stronger.

It is possible that individual birds of the same species may vary in their scent, just as people do. It seems not improbable that their food, mental state—such as fright, health, dampness of feathers, bodily temperatures—may all have a bearing upon the amount and possibly the character of the scent given off. Some men claim that their dogs can distinguish between cock and hen pheasants. Richardson states that a fox that is heated as a result of being run by a pack of hounds gives off more scent than in its normal state. Great exhaustion of the quarry diminishes the scent. A number of birds, such as a covey of quail, undoubtedly emit a stronger odor than a single bird, and can, as would be expected, be winded by a dog at a greater distance.

If a bird has a body wound and is not bleeding, it may give off little scent. If it is bleeding, it is a different matter, as probably the blood itself can be smelled by the dog—blood scent, as it is called. Blood scent probably accounts for the fact that an otherwise absolutely staunch dog will frequently point and then jump in, catch and retrieve a wounded bird.

A bird which has a wing broken near the body and which, as a consequence, drags on the ground or flaps against grass stems as it attempts to escape, gives off plenty of scent and is easily followed by a dog. A very different condition exists with the merely wing-tipped bird, whose feathers are apt to be held close to the body and whose wing does not drag. Such a cripple is much more difficult for a dog to trail.

It is probable that, while dogs can generally distinguish different varieties of game birds by their scent, this is not always the case, perhaps because of weakness of scent. Dogs are taught to ignore the scent of non-game birds, and generally they do so. Possibly game birds give off more scent than many other birds, but untrained dogs, precocious puppies, and even occasionally experienced dogs will sometimes point larks or sparrows, the so-called "stink" birds of the dog trainers, and these do not always seem to be sight points. Experienced dogs will also often point turtles and snakes.

Scent has been aptly likened to a faint column or cloud of smoke, invisible to the eye, but detectable by the sense of smell. This cloud diffuses around the bird and is carried in various directions by air currents. Some of it lodges on herbage or may be directly deposited there by actual touch, as is the foot or settled scent. It has not been definitely decided whether the sense of smell depends primarily on a chemical or a physical process. Odoriferous particles come in contact with the free ends of the peculiar rod-like cells found in the olfactory mucous membrane. The free olfactory surface is covered with a thin layer of fluid and all odoriferous matters must be dissolved in this fluid in order to reach the rodlike cells. This is somewhat analogous to taste and is an almost instantaneous process. Youatt states that the dog possesses an unusually large olfactory nerve.

The fact that the mucous membrane must be wet and the particles of scent dissolved explains why moist air generally results in better scenting conditions. It is well known that woods odors or the scent of flowers are most distinctly perceived in the morning after a shower, when the atmosphere is damp. Probably the atmosphere in which the average man lives tends to impair his sense of smell, as it does that of house dogs. Outdoor men generally are much keener than indoor men in this respect.

I had this fact demonstrated a few years ago, while poling to camp after a late evening's salmon fishing on a Canadian river. I remember the incident well because we had killed a phenomenal lot of fish, one of which was a very leviathan. When we were about a mile from camp the bow Indian said, "I smell camp" and his brother in the stern said, "Me, too." Only after we had progressed about half a mile could I faintly detect the pleasant, slightly pungent odor of wood smoke. Here conditions were favorable—the still, damp air of late evening.

Studies have shown that the effluvia of animals and birds is of a higher specific gravity than air, and hence tends to sink to the ground. In general, scent is extremely persistent, a drop or two of musk may be detected in a closed room for years. The durability or persistence of scent accounts for the cold trailing so commonly observed in hounds. Dogs live in a world of scent and depend upon their sense of smell far more than the casual observer has any idea of. Dogs detect their masters and each other chiefly by smell. If one remembers the analogy to the smoke column and carries it farther, thinking of the effluvia as very fine, invisible soot, the advantage of dampness for its absorption on the olfactory mucous membrane, instantaneous as it is, many of the secrets and vagaries of scenting become less difficult to understand.

It is generally thought that the game bird, while setting on her nest, gives off little scent. This belief is at least questionable. It certainly does not imply a voluntary withholding of scent. The bird has been immovable for some time; this has permitted the cloud of effluvia which originally surrounded it to disseminate. Because of lack of movement, little fresh scent has been thrown off. This, plus the fact that the nest is generally more or less surrounded and covered by rank, lush vegetation, such as is present in the spring or summer, perhaps explains why even good dogs have difficulty in locating birds, under these circumstances.

A bird which pitches down fresh from an air wash and which remains immovable and, from fright, keeps the feathers tightly pressed to the body, gives off little scent. It is relatively infrequent for a quail to "freeze" instantly upon alighting. Usually it moves enough to give forth scent. Nevertheless, this occasional instant freezing is almost certainly the basis for the now generally discarded theory that quail can voluntarily withhold their scent. Frank Forester was one of the observers who believed quail could withhold their scent, and, as a result, he advocated leaving the scattered covey of quail until the birds had time to move around and develop fresh columns of scent. The practice was sometimes right, although the theory was wrong. When a bird freezes, the immovability is not the result of a deliberate effort to withhold scent, but an effort to escape detection by keeping still. The slight trail of scent which followed the bird in the air during its flight is soon dissipated, and, to a certain extent at least, the longer the bird remains immovable the more difficult it is to scent. This is particularly true if there is some air stirring. But, after the bird relaxes, loosens its feathers, or moves about, more scent is liberated.

The freezing habit, so common in game birds, especially woodcock and quail, is therefore protective in two ways: their immobility makes them difficult to see, and it tends to lessen scent. However, this is more theoretic than practical, and is more than counterbalanced because it permits close approach by the sportsman, and when man or dog gets very near the immovable bird it often loses its nerve and in its effort to run or fly discloses itself or because of extreme proximity the scent is detected. Wide experience has shown that Forester's plan of waiting is generally an unnecessary waste of time, for if much delay is practiced the birds may run. Field-trial handlers—a group which should know—almost invariably hustle their charges to marked-down birds.

A bird killed dead in the air offers a somewhat similar example. Even the best dogs will often pass close to such a bird without detecting it. The air wash and immobility of the stone-dead bird limit the amount of scent that is present. This is especially noticeable when the bird has been killed high in the air. If the stricken bird struggles its movements often disclose its whereabouts, and it may be located by either sight or sound. Eliminating the latter methods, however, wing-beats or other movements liberate scent and the bird that has thrashed about but is absolutely dead by the time the dog arrives in its vicinity is much more easily located by the latter.

The analogy to a column of smoke, drifting off low to the ground before a light breeze, explains why the clever dog always tries to work against the wind. When a bird shakes itself or fluffs its feathers it emits a heavy cloud of "smoke." This drifts off in the moving air, or, if there is no wind, gradually spreads out in all directions. It is only conjecture, but probably the scent particles, being heavier than air, slowly sink. Rotting vegetation and different degrees of temperatures probably influence scent.

One hears a great deal about foot scent and body scent, often as if these were two totally different varieties of odors. Certain animals possess scent glands in or near their feet or hoofs, but birds do not. Foot scent and body scent are in all probability the same, the only difference being in the localities of the minute particles which produce the sense of scent. However this is not proven. In foot scent the effluvia is on the ground or grass, whereas in body scent it is in the cloud of particles floating in the air. Naturally, the former remains "put" longer and the sensible, experienced dog lowers his head in order to get nearer the origin of the scent when body scent is absent. If the thickness of the effluvia is the same, it is the first whiff which is the strongest, like the first smell of a flower. Most sportsmen have seen a dog point with a dead bird in its mouth. Doubtless many such performances are sight points; but not all of them, as it is this sudden whiff of fresh scent which probably explains the performance.

Smoking has a tendency to inhibit temporarily the sense of smell —a point for the man to remember who transports his dogs in a smoke-filled motor car. Unusual dryness and high wind are conditions always unfavorable for good scenting. Water appears to be bad for scent, although it seems probable that it may lie for a time upon the surface of a still pond or puddle. Running water of course carries foot scent off immediately. Extreme dampness with a preponderance of puddles is probably not favorable to scenting. Water and extreme dampness appear especially to affect foot scents. During heavy rains scenting conditions are not good, but during light drizzles, mist, or fog, dogs sometimes scent well. Dogs can handle snipe and woodcock on partially flooded ground. A hound belonging to Lieutenant Colonel Richardson successfully followed a murderer over flooded land. Ordinarily, snow does not materially interfere with scent, and dogs often perform very well in light falls, quite apart from the fact that sight points are more frequent at such times. As mentioned elsewhere, I have seen a dog point a grouse that had plunged into, and was completely buried in, a snowbank, and have also witnessed points of quail and pheasants which have become covered by falling snow. Fox hunters believe that freshly plowed land is detrimental to trailing. Manured land and tarred roads interfere with scenting conditions. Ground temperatures and even almost imperceptible air currents also play a part in influencing scenting conditions. Fatigue, poor health, frozen ground, and other factors are often detrimental to good scenting. Occasionally a bird may pitch back of a large rock or over the crest of a hill. This may break the air current and produce a pocket in which scent is very faint or absent. Foot or settled scent is generally poor on absolutely smooth, bare, hard ground, and does not continue long on such a surface. Dusty foliage is detrimental to good scenting. Certain herbage is said to be so potent as totally to swamp the scent of birds. However, a dog may be drenched with skunk odor and continue to work, and apparently without marked detriment to its scenting powers. It is common for some dogs to roll in foul-smelling filth without its appearing to interfere with their ability to find birds. It is probable that the dog to a marked degree possesses the faculty of distinguishing and analyzing a mixture of odors and fixing attention on only one. Passy and Binet, as a result of a series of experiments with scented papers, concluded that dogs react to bodily odors but not to perfumes. This is what would be expected. However, Kalischer succeeded in demonstrating that dogs could distinguish between the odors of nitrobenzene, benzaldehyde, and other chemicals. As previously mentioned, rank, green vegetation is unfavorable for scenting. During late summer and early dog-training period dogs are often unjustly condemned because of this fact. Scenting conditions are rarely at their best until cool weather, and after there has been a killing frost. I have seen this proved time and again.

Since the olfactory mucous membrane must be moist, anything which dries this membrane interferes with the dog's scenting ability. If, on the other hand, there is an excess or alteration of the character of the normal secretion, due to irritation or disease, this also acts deleteriously. The latter may result from various local, and sometimes general, conditions. Everyone knows how a slight cold in the head interferes with the ability to detect odors (*anosmia*). Probably temporary, minor, local conditions are present more often than most of us think, and put a dog off in his scenting. Some dogs have a better nose naturally than others. The shape has nothing to do with this. It is what is inside the nose that makes the difference. Experience in using the nose is also an extremely important factor. Occasionally, distemper or other general illnesses may either temporarily or permanently affect a dog's nose. Men are occasionally born with a total lack of the sense of smell, and it is possible that this holds true for dogs.

It can readily be seen that the whole subject is a very complex one, and dependent upon many factors. So do not blame your dog too much for an occasional lapse—it may readily not have been his fault. The wonder is that dogs perform as well as they do.

RUNNERS AND WOUNDED BIRDS.

> *I am right sorry for your heaviness.*
> —Geoffrey Chaucer, in "The Squieres Tale."

The opinion has frequently been expressed that no one should go afield until he or she has learned safety and acquired a certain degree of proficiency in shooting. Preliminary practice with a hand trap or other forms of clay-pigeon shooting will prevent many embarrassing and irritating misses. Game birds are too scarce to use for this form of practice. No one should be content to merely knock a bird down; birds should be cleanly killed. Everyone cripples birds occasionally, but the good shot does this much less frequently than the novice.

One of the most frequent causes for wounding game is shooting when the bird is beyond the killing range. All sportsmen should know the killing range of their guns—not merely how far a stray pellet may chance to knock a bird down, but the distance at which the pattern will insure killing. With the average 12-gauge field gun and ordinary loads, 40 yards is the extreme maximum range for the first barrel, and is too far for an outgoing pheasant and for a grouse if No. 9 shot is being used. Obviously, what is extreme range for an open-board field gun may be well within killing distance for a closely choked weapon shooting 1¼ ounces of fairly large shot. Small gauges are more likely merely to wound than large. They shoot less shot and their killing patterns are therefore smaller and often thinner than the large-gauge guns. With them birds must be centered more accurately. Nobody can center all the birds shot at, and those birds not centered are often wounded. Too fine shot is also prone to cripple. Fine shot is an excellent killing agent up to certain ranges, but beyond this it results in many wounded birds. The shooter should bear in mind the maximum killing range of the size shot he is using. A pheasant may be killed stone dead with No. 9 shot at 20 or even 25 yards, but at 40 yards is almost sure to be merely wounded.

An example of this is found in live-pigeon shooting. Live-pigeon shooters have given much study to the most effective size of shot. Sevens are generally accepted as the standard size and 28 yards is probably about the average rise. Bogardus shot many matches against time. All these were at short rises and in them he used No. 9 or No. 10 shot. In other words, he found that, at short range, fine shot was the most effective; but in his 28-yard rise shooting he employed larger shot. Small-gauge advocates are apt to use smaller shot than those shooting 12-gauge guns, in order to thicken their patterns. This is a good thing, provided they remember that small shot does not hold up so well at extreme ranges. With the exception of rail shooting, I do not think that anything smaller than No. 9's should ever be used in the field.

The novice is pleased when he makes an extra long shot, but the experienced man knows that it is a lucky chance and that at that distance many more birds are wounded than are brought down. To adopt the attitude that an extra long shot may kill—or, if not, may wound and thereby help subsequently in securing the bird —and, if a miss, is only a wasted cartridge, is a distinctly unsportsmanlike one to assume. Wounding is a waste of game, apart from the miserable fate which awaits many crippled birds. True, some wounded birds are gathered. Others, however, fall victims to vermin; still others ultimately die from the starvation which results indirectly from their wounds, often days or even weeks later. Who has not had his dog pick up some wretched cripple, reduced to skin and bone, with perhaps a wing or a leg hanging by a few shreds, a bill shot away, or with gangrened wounds? Even if the bird ultimately recovers, sterility may result, if it has been pricked by the shot in the region of the ovary.

These facts are unpleasant to contemplate, but they are, nevertheless, true. There is no use in being maudlin or sentimental, and birds do not suffer so much as more highly organized animals, but consideration for the suffering of game which is shot should be and generally is a definite part of the code of every good sportsman. Most errors in this respect are caused by thoughtlessness, but they are, nevertheless, inexcusable. Furthermore, ungathered wounded birds encourage the presence of vermin. Shooting is the finest sport in the world, but this is its black side. Every conscientious and decent sportsman will do everything in his power to reduce to the minimum the number of escaping cripples. In the case of clean kills, birds probably suffer little.

In man, undoubtedly, much of the suffering due to injury is the result of apprehension. An extremely minor surgical operation without anaesthesia entails much more suffering than the unexpected gash of the finger due to the slip of a penknife. Also so-called highly strung men undoubtedly suffer more than those of phlegmatic temperament. I have been shot in the legs at about 35 yards range, with No. 8 shot, and the sensation was that of being struck hard with a lath. We have the word of Dr. Livingstone that he noticed no pain while being mauled by a lion, and many more or less similar experiences could be cited. The caponizing of cockerels does not appear to cause much pain, and the birds are often about, feeding a short time after the operation. I think, therefore, we may take comfort in the fact that the actual shooting of game birds does not normally entail great suffering; certainly less than often results from death by hawks or vermin. It is the later effects, resulting from crippling, which are undoubtedly the worst. From some fifty odd years of experience I am convinced that even with the utmost care, far more birds are wounded than the average sportsman has any conception of.

I remember on one occasion, when shooting back of Elsworth,

Maine, three of us found a flight of woodcock rather late in the afternoon. The birds were on a briary hillside. We killed nineteen and, because it was getting dusk, quit before having worked out all the cover. Our dogs were good retrievers and cock are easy birds to retrieve. We were not aware of losing any dead or cripples and woodcock are not much in the way of shot carriers. With the intention of working the rest of the cover, we went back to the same hillside the next morning. The flight had gone, but our dogs picked up no less than six dead or wounded birds.

This instance is exceptional, but every experienced shot knows how frequently cripples are found. This is particularly true of large, strong, thick-feathered birds, like pheasants, which not only require a hard blow to kill, but which, on account of their size, are often thought to be nearer than they actually are. Apart from the humanitarian side, no one wants to cripple, and all, of course, do their best to shoot straight.

Many of us, however, do shoot at birds which are out of range. Everyone should learn to judge distance. If the sportsman has played baseball he knows the distance in feet between the pitcher's box and the plate. A tennis player knows the length of the court. These are aids in judging distance when shooting. Another good plan is to learn the length of the stride—50 paces usually equal about 40 yards, but of course this varies with the individual. It helps immensely occasionally to practice estimating distances when walking. It is surprising how accurately distances can soon be judged. In the woods the tendency is to overestimate distance, and over water or with clear sky background, one is likely to underestimate. An exception to the latter statement is found in overhead birds, and particularly if there is a perspective, such as tall trees. A 70- or 75-foot tree is a high one, and an overhead bird 25 feet above it, although only actually about 33 or 34 yards high, appears a very long shot indeed. In the city, pigeons flying across a street between tall buildings always appear farther away than they are. Also small, moving objects near at hand appear to be traveling faster and to be farther away than larger objects. The airplane, perhaps flying at a rate of 200 or 300 miles per hour, when seen at a distance, does not seem to be traveling extremely fast. Quail, especially, are often thought to be at a greater distance and to be flying faster than they are. The whirr of wings also adds to the idea of speed.

Long shots inevitably cause a high percentage of wounded birds. If the sportsman owned a preserve containing a hundred birds which he expected to kill during the season, he would certainly not thank a guest who wounded many birds, and thus reduced his season's total bag by a number of escaping cripples. Yet this is exactly what out-of-range shooting means to the state's supply of game. All military surgeons know that wounds are cumulative in their action. Thus, two wounds, other things being equal, are more than twice as dangerous as one. In the case of birds, shot wounds probably equal the number squared. Thus, two pellets are nearly four times as likely to knock down a bird as one, and three are nearly nine times as fatal.

Not only does range, size of shot, penetration and degree of choke influence the killing effect of shot, but also the angle of flight of the bird. In crossing shots, the head, neck and vital organs are exposed. With incoming birds the head, neck and wings are unprotected and clean kills or misses are apt to result. With overhead birds or high incomers the same is true, and in addition the heart and lungs may be readily reached. The vital organs are fairly well protected by the bony structures when the game is going away from the gun. A bird on the ground is much harder to kill stone dead than in any other position. Apart from the fact that it is often partially protected by irregularities of the ground, stones, etc., it represents a relatively small target and its tough wing feathers usually must be penetrated before the shot can reach a vital organ. If time permits, do not shoot too quickly at a cripple on the ground, and aim at the feet of quail and woodcock and at the legs of larger birds. Birds on the ground are not infrequently missed as a result of carelessness or hurry. Always use the second barrel on a wounded bird which may escape no matter at what distance or how tempting other shots may be.

Some of the important points in securing crippled game are: watch all birds shot at, until out of sight. When shot from a covey a wounded bird often lags behind or flies off by itself. The tendency for the dog handler is to watch the dog. When two men are together, the duty of marking can sometimes be delegated to one if he is not at the moment shooting. If there is a man along who is not shooting he can sometimes do all the marking. The marker should have good eyesight and be experienced. There is a natural tendency for each man to watch only the bird he himself has shot at, and this he should usually do. If there is reason to believe the bird is hit, mark the site of its alighting by breaking a branch, or by noting some landmark. Do not mark with your gun. The bird may flush or you may have trouble finding the gun later.

Crippled woodcock do not as a rule run far or make any serious effort to hide. Quail often run or hide under a brush pile or log or in dense cover. A wing-tipped grouse usually hits the ground, running, and may go a considerable distance or may hide under some thick cover. Pheasants are the worst runners of all, and may go a quarter of a mile or more, and at a surprising speed. They usually run fast and in a fairly straight line and often end by hiding in some thick cover. It is a common belief among gunners that crippled pheasants will deliberately secrete themselves in ground-hog and other holes, but I have never seen this proved. On only two occasions have I been present when it seemed probable, and, in these instances, the bird may have escaped elsewhere. That a bird closely pursued by a dog might run down a hole in an effort to escape seems likely, but under other circumstances is less probable. A dog accustomed to retrieving will hunt close in the area in which he is directed. If the dog gets to the point of fall quickly it should find all dead birds and get the scent of most runners. It is probably largely a matter of experience, but some dogs mark the site of fall much better than others.

No sportsman can depend entirely upon his eye for marking. The dog should be allowed to do practically all the retrieving of both dead and crippled birds. With the reliable, experienced retriever it is better to let him do the searching. If the gun walks around too much he is likely to destroy the scent, and he may even inadvertently bend down a large tussock of grass over the bird and make it difficult for the dog to locate. Only when the dog is evidently at fault or fails is it advisable for the owner to take an active part. However, he should put the dog on the line at once if a cripple is seen escaping. Sometimes if the point of fall is approached from another side, from which the wind is more favorable, the dog will get the scent. For all retrieving, and especially for hunting cripples, use a dog—any dog is better than none. In general, wounded birds are difficult to find. If the bird can run and the cover is moderately thick, the man without a dog has little chance of securing it. Even a small terrier will rout around under cover and discover many cripples which would otherwise have been lost. Usually game birds make no outcry upon receiving a wound, although I have heard an outgoing cock pheasant give a squawk upon being solidly centered by a load of sixes. It has been suggested that the usual voicelessness of birds under these conditions is sometimes of benefit to them, as otherwise the wounded might attract attention to their whereabouts and hence fall more ready victims to predators. Under the stimulus of fright, game birds sometimes cry out, but even this is rather unusual. However, I have heard quail and grouse become vocal upon being attacked by a hawk.

If accurately marked, most wounded birds can be gathered, provided a good dog is available. If the point at which they go down cannot be seen because of cover, their line of flight should be followed. Most of them will be found dead or offer an easy shot when flushed. Occasionally wounded birds veer from their original lines of flight after they have disappeared behind an obstruction and these, as well as those in which the hit is not recognized by the shooter, are not often found. Runners also add to the lost. Whether or not the bird will run depends largely upon the character of its wound, the cover, and the species. Wounded birds should be searched for at once. Delay permits scent to become dissipated, gives time for birds to run from the point of fall and thus causes an increase in the proportion of lost birds.

As a final word on this unpleasant subject, never leave a bird which may have been wounded until after a really conscientious search has been made, and you are sure that it cannot be gathered.

TOWERING BIRDS.

> *Now darting upward, now down again*
> *With a twist and a turn that was strange to see.*
> —William Gilmore Simms, in "The Grape-Vine Swing."

The true towering bird is a strange and curious sight, especially for those who witness it for the first time. The bird has generally been shot at from some distance, but may have been hit at close range by the edge of the pattern. Usually the bird has been going almost directly away from the gun and rising, but it may occur as a result of a passing shot. On receiving the wound, the bird often checks momentarily in its flight, flies slower and slower, and then rather suddenly rises, straight up or almost perpendicularly, and falls, without a movement, stone dead.

The stricken bird rises to a considerable height. It may travel some distance before the sudden rise starts. Once the sudden rise (tower) begins, the bird does not go much farther away, but, owing to the height which it may have attained, may be blown by the wind. However, in the absence of wind it falls straight and rapidly, as a stone-dead bird will. It is usually found on its back with outspread wings, but this is not always the case. This is the typical behavior of the true towerer, and once seen it is unmistakable. Sometimes the birds fly more erratically, but the latter behavior is more characteristic of the false, or what Schley terms the "mock" towerer. Sometimes the false towering bird rises in diminishing circles, or may fall as a result of colliding with an obstruction, such as a tree trunk or branch.

The false towerer is not apt to attain so great an altitude as the true towerer, and often falls somewhat slowly, and in any position. The wings also may be in any position. Its fall is not so plummet-like as that of the true towerer. The false towerer may be merely stunned, and may fly when the attempt is made to gather it.

Many theories have been advanced to explain towering. Until comparatively recently the differentiation between true and false towering was not understood. Both were classed under one heading. It is known that certain brain centers control certain definite sets of muscles, and that an injury to a brain center may cause response by certain definite muscular movements. As a result of this knowledge and the fact that some of these birds (the false towerers) were found to have been wounded in the head, it was formerly believed that all towering birds had received a head wound, and that it was a brain injury which caused their peculiar actions.

However, in recent years, a series of autopsies have been performed upon birds which have towered in the true sense of the word—notably those studies of the late W. B. Tegetmier, of the staff of *The Field* (London). These dissections have shown conclusively that true towering birds were shot in the lungs, usually by a single pellet of shot. This conclusion has been confirmed by X-ray photographs.

Sir Edmond Spriggs reported an interesting series of investigations in *The Field* (London) of April 1, 1939. His article is accompanied by a number of excellent X-ray photographs. As a result of these studies, it is now generally accepted that a genuine towering bird has ben hit by an odd pellet of shot in the lung or lung cavity, and that the flow of blood has smothered the bird. The bird often flinches or exhibits other evidence of being hit, and flies less rapidly. As the lung cavity fills with blood, attempts to breathe become more and more difficult, and the bird opens its beak widely and throws back its head farther and farther, in an effort to secure air, and this action causes it to rise (the tower) and finally to fall over backward and drop to the ground.

I have examined two true towerers. Both were quail; both received a single pellet in the front part of the body. There was no wound elsewhere. Both showed the lungs and pleural cavities more or less full of blood. I have frequently seen head-shot birds fly in a peculiar manner, often striking obstructions, and, until the appearance of Tegetmier's study, assumed that all towering birds were so wounded. An internal hemorrhage, not involving the lung, may result in a flight of greater or less length, and be followed by a more or less sudden fall, the bird generally being dead when picked up. But these birds' behavior lacks the characteristic sudden rise of the true towerer, and there is no reason to call them towerers, which term might well be reserved for the lung-wounded birds, whose actions are always quite similar and characteristic.

Towering birds are infrequent. The examination of a single bird is not always conclusive or accurate. The above-quoted observations are the only studies of a series of instances of towering birds of which I am aware, and because they cover a number of cases and have been carried out carefully by competent observers they should, I believe, be accepted—certainly until further studies have been made which disprove them.

Towering is apparently somewhat more frequent among English game birds than in this country, and for that reason we have less opportunity for examination of them than our English cousins. It is possible that wounds other than those in the lungs may occasionally result in somewhat similar behavior on the part of the victim. The false towering bird has often been hit in the head or sometimes merely grazed. This bird may fall instantly, or, if the wound is of less serious character, may fly in an erratic manner for various distances, and even in some instances may go upward. A practical point to remember is that if the bird falls slowly, it may flush again when an attempt is made to gather it. A bird sustaining a wound in the bill or spine may fly erratically. Birds wounded in the eye not infrequently fly in curves or circles, often colliding with obstructions. True towering is fairly rare in American game birds. The bobwhite quail and ruffed grouse are the only varieties which I have seen exhibit this behavior. This itself is somewhat curious and is not explained by either of the theories which have been advanced in explanation of towering. I have probably seen about 2,500 grouse and quail killed, and among these I can remember eight or nine that seemed to be true towerers. On the other hand, I have probably seen close to 15,000 or 18,000 other game birds killed, including wild fowl, and do not remember a single towerer among the lot. However, the number of towering birds which have come under personal observation is small, and too few from which to draw conclusions. Foster and Rich mention instances in which grouse have towered, and Schley and others refer to towering quail. Abroad a somewhat similar situation exists, in that most of the towering birds are partridges, the common or gray partridge *(Perdix cinerea),* or the red-legged or French partridge *(Caccabis rufa).* At all events, true towering is rather rare and it may perhaps occur in species other than those mentioned.

---

*He who esteems trifles for themselves is a trifler—he who esteems*
*them for the conclusions to be drawn from them, or the advantage*
*to which they can be put, is a philosopher.*
                                        —Edward Bulwer-Lytton, *Pelham.*

ONE's equipment should be selected for both comfort and
utility. Comfort is a definite factor in good shooting.
Equipment of the best quality is the most satisfactory
and, in the long run, the cheapest. It is preferable to buy less,
but of the best quality. As a matter of fact, it is a great mistake
to overburden one's self with numerous pieces of equipment many
of which are not required.

The necessary equipment will naturally vary with the seasons,
the weather, and the locality. Some men may be much more
sensitive to cold than others, therefore what may be suitable in
this respect for one will be ineffective or unsatisfactory for another.
Both local and personal needs should guide the sportsman. A
little care in the selection of an outfit makes all the difference
between an uncomfortable and a pleasant outing—this is particularly true in regard to footwear.

As far as clothing is concerned, the upland sportsman must please
himself, but, if he is to do much walking, it should be light in
weight. It is better to start off a little cool than to perspire all day
in extra warm clothing. Nothing will sap one's energy so much
as to be too warm. As long as the hands, feet, and neck are comfortable, it is possible to travel in comfort all day, even in cold
weather, with comparatively light clothing. On a frosty morning,
the invariable tendency is to wear too much.

Most upland shooting requires tramping through heavy cover
and briars, and the legs must be protected from thorns. Furthermore, watertight or nearly watertight boots are desirable. As much

immunity as possible from briars and wet feet is essential if any comfort or enjoyment is to be had.

While appearance is of secondary importance, there is no reason for the sportsman to look like a ragamuffin. Coats and breeches quickly get oily and dirty, but they are relatively inexpensive, and, for the man who shoots much, two sets may be had, and one occasionally sent to the cleaner's. No one wants to look like the proverbial fashionplate, but there is no reason for wearing filthy, uncomfortable clothing; yet this is what many men do who otherwise are particular in their appearance. Men will spend large sums for a gun or motor car, yet cling to some foul old jacket that even a tramp would throw away.

*Coat.* The chief function of the coat is to act as a windbreak, to carry necessary articles in the pockets, and perhaps to turn a little rain. It should be equipped with "pivot" sleeves or a pleat in the back, so that it will not bunch at the shoulders during the act of mounting the gun. Generally, ready-made shooting coats have entirely too many pockets, most of them badly placed. Two large patch pockets for cartridges, one handkerchief pocket on the left (for the right-handed man), game pockets, and a small inside pocket for matches, are all that is desirable. The cartridge pockets should be lined with thin, flexible, soft leather.

Game pockets should be large and deep or what the English call a hare pocket. The kind having an outside opening, in the back, is secure, but the slit opening catches on every wire fence, hence openings inside the coat are preferable. Detachable pockets lined with thin rubber which permit washing are excellent, but they should be well secured to the coat. Their disadvantage is that they do not permit much ventilation and in warm weather do not keep game well. There is no reason that they should not be made without rubber lining and therefore be washable. Two buttons for suspension are not sufficient. Slash pockets, opening in front, are excellent.

The material of the coat should be thin, strong, and not stiff. Waterproofed material is good, provided it permits ventilation; otherwise it is an abomination. The coat should be loose enough to be comfortable and to permit the wearing of a light sweater underneath. Many coats are entirely too loose. The ill-fitting, hard, stiff, sheetiron-like coats that are often sold are the worst possible articles to shoot in, because they nearly always bunch at the shoulders.

The so-called skeleton coats are useful for warm weather, but even these, if the right shoulder-piece is hard, often bunch at this point. The skeleton coat has some disadvantage in thick cover and has a tendency to catch on branches, barbed wire, etc. The collar of the shooting coat should be so cut that it can be turned up and buttoned across the neck if desired. The patch pockets in which cartridges are usually carried should be practically waterproof and covered with a wide, deep flap. An excellent plan is to have a zipper placed under the flap and if desired it can be left open when quick loading is desired. Zippers are also useful to close the game pockets. The front of the coat and other pockets are best equipped with buttons.

*Breeches.* Whether trousers or breeches are selected is a matter of taste. If the former, they should be short and reach barely to the ankle or slightly below the boot top. Trousers are cheap, washable, and excellent to walk in. They are best worn outside the boots, in order to prevent weed seeds and the like from working into the boots.

If breeches are selected, they should be looser at the knee than ordinary riding breeches and have no unnecessary bagginess at the hips. A fair criterion of breeches is that they can be pulled on easily over the stockinged foot without unfastening the buttons usually placed below the knee. Indeed, the buttons had best be dispensed with altogether and the usual slit entirely eliminated. Laces or buttons are unnecessary and often constricting. The cuff should extend about two inches below the boot top. If not too tight, the elastic type of cuff is excellent, but it must be renewed each season.

In order that the trousers or breeches may be briarproof, they should be reinforced on the front and sides. This can be accomplished by doubling the material or by facing with leather—the latter method I have found very satisfactory. In his excellent book, *New England Grouse Shooting*, the late W. H. Foster, who gave considerable thought to the question of outfits, recommended that kangaroo skin be utilized. He says it is flexible, light, and durable. Two watch pockets (one of which can be used for a compass), two large front pockets, and two hip pockets are advisable. A zipper is a very safe way of closing the pockets. In one of the pockets, money, car-key, and other valuables may be carried; and in the other, matches. Zippers may with advantage replace all buttons on the breeches or trousers.

The chaps devised by the late Captain Curtis are sometimes useful, especially if one expects to spend only a short time afield and does not wish to take the trouble to change. They can be worn comfortably over knickerbockers or trousers. Chaps are made of waterproofed duck and should be loose enough to pull on easily over boots. They are to all intents and purposes loose, short, overall legs, and are attached to a belt. They can be purchased at most of the large sporting-goods houses. However, a pair of extra size Duxback trousers answers the same purpose and costs about half as much.

The material for breeches or trousers should be strong, only moderately thick, tightly woven, and not noisy. Cartridges are most easily carried if distributed in the various pockets, so the distribution, size, and strength of the latter are important.

Most shooting clothes are made of a dead grass, or some similar, color. A bit of bright color or white on the coat, or else a red hat, may occasionally be worth while as a protection, for the same reason that deer hunters favor this color. As long as it is fairly clean, white is very conspicuous. White coats are excellent; they are worn a good deal in the South. Conspicuousness is also of practical value in order to enable your dog or companion easily to locate your whereabouts. As far as the former is concerned many scientists believe that dogs are color blind but even if this is the case, white is probably more easily seen in the woods than a dark color.

*Boots.* These should be fitted to wear over one pair of thick stockings, or two pairs of moderately thin hose. Army observers have found that the foot broadens nearly a quarter of an inch after a day's marching.

Since the sportsman has to traverse wet places and often wade small streams, the footgear should be as nearly waterproof as possible. High rubber boots are too hot; but in some localities, such as the woodcock swamps of Maryland, they may be almost a necessity. A rubber shoe with light leather or canvas upper makes a good compromise, and is fairly waterproof if the uppers are kept well greased. Neatsfoot oil is excellent for leather boots, but a hard grease or vaseline, applied in a warm room, is even better. A little beeswax added to the grease will make it more permanent.

The boot should be laced, and not buttoned or fitted with catches. Some men prefer more heel and support for the foot than that given by this type of boot. An inlaid sole or a light steel or aluminum arch supporter helps in this matter. The outside sole should be well roughened, for autumn leaves are slippery. The crepe-bottomed sole is satisfactory. If leather soles are used, a few well-placed hobnails help, but they add to the weight and are noisy on rocks. Corrugated composition soles over the leather are better than leather alone.

Boots which come about halfway up the calf are satisfactory for most localities. Very high boots have a tendency to bind the leg, and their extra height is generally unnecessary. If a high, laced boot is to be worn, pull the laces moderately tight to about an inch above the ankle, then tie a knot and lace the leg loosely. The boot must be comfortable and not too heavy. Too big a boot is almost as bad as one which is too small. Army observers have found that by lightening each boot one pound as much energy is saved as if eight pounds were taken off the soldier's back. Provided proper support for the foot and ankle can be secured, and the sole is not too thin, the boot cannot be too light. Heavy boots are tiring, especially for those not accustomed to their use. Their only possible advantage is that they may wear a little longer. No one can have a good day afield with poor, ill-fitting or unsuitable boots.

*Stockings.* Much of the comfort of the foot depends upon the stockings, which are best made moderately broad across the toes, and which should fit the foot—many are too narrow across the front part of the foot. When intended to be worn with breeches, they should come almost to the knee, be of the best wool, and be fairly thick. Many men find it most comfortable to wear silk

socks underneath the wool. Ordinary garters can be worn with the latter and a fairly loose circular garter used for the wool stocking, the top of which is turned down over the garter. It is worth while to get a pair of broad-toed, wooden forms for the woolen stockings, otherwise they will soon get too tight for the foot.
• A little boric-acid powder in the stocking and boot is an excellent preventive against blisters, and, liberally applied, helps even if chafing has occurred. If chafing has developed, a liberal application of soap to the inner side of the sock is of some help.

*Underclothing.* A light, soft, flannel shirt with a loose, moderately low collar makes a good shooting shirt. The lightest wool underwear is all that is ordinarily required. If this is not warm enough, however, a light sweater can be worn over the shirt. It is comfortable to have when one rests at lunch, but it is generally too warm for walking. It is a mistake to switch to heavy clothing for shooting, and it is best to be governed by what one is accustomed to wear.

*Raincoats.* Raincoats and waterproofs are a nuisance. In the clothing described above one may be fairly dry in a light drizzle, but in a heavy rain it is better to abandon upland shooting for the time being.

*Gloves.* Many men shoot without gloves, but I think it is a good plan to make a practice of wearing a moderately thin soft, loose, glove on the left hand. This is a protection against scratches, as this is the hand which is used chiefly to fend off branches and briars. In cold weather a warmer glove may be necessary, and its trigger finger can be cut off. However, I do not like bulky gloves, and the loss of tactile sense tends toward accidents. Tight gloves are always cold.

*Headgear.* The best headgear I know is the sporting helmet or grouse helmet made by A. J. White of London. This is of brown felt, with a moderately narrow brim extended somewhat in the front and back, a moderate crown, and a cork insert under the sweatband. It is a bit odd-looking to American eyes, but it gives good protection from glare and rain. It is of about the correct weight, and, most important of all, is not easily knocked off by branches and undergrowth. However, any felt hat with a moderate brim will answer the purpose. I do not like caps, but this is a personal matter. Some people find them satisfactory. A white hat is conspicuous, and therefore has advantages from the standpoint of safety, or a broad red band may be sewn on the crown.

*Belts.* The Pannabelt, manufactured by Alex. Martin, 20 Exchange Square, Glasgow, Scotland, offers a convenient means of carrying extra cartridges. It consists of two flat, pocket-like bags, mounted on a broad belt. It will accommodate twenty-five 12-gauge shells quite easily. It comes in leather or canvas, and is equipped with flaps which may be fastened down. It is best worn under the shooting coat. It is also a good receptacle for shells while rail or clay-pigeon shooting.

*Glasses.* When shooting in cover some men always wear a pair of large glasses for protection. These may be of colorless glass or they may be slightly tinted. If the latter, light amber is perhaps the best. Amber-tinted glasses protect one's eyes from sun glare and do not cut off much light. Indeed, it is claimed that light amber adds contrast, especially on dark days or toward evening. Personally, I prefer colorless glasses. The Bausch and Lomb Company have recently perfected an excellent glass for this purpose. Some sort of tinted glasses are almost a necessity for shooting on the snow.

If the sportsman normally wears distance glasses, he should get a larger pair for shooting. It should be remembered that in shooting the head is dropped forward on the gun stock, and the upper part of the glass utilized. If he has to wear reading glasses for near work, a small circular insert in the lower part of the shooting glass is far more convenient than the ordinary bifocal arrangement, which is a nuisance in woods walking. If glasses of any sort are to be worn spectacles are best and the frame and ear supports should be carefully fitted and comfortable.

*The Shooting Bag.* A good plan is to have a shooting bag, which contains a change of clothing, a large towel, extra cartridges, tobacco, matches, a small flask, and extra motor-car key, and a small first-aid kit. The latter is like a pistol—it may be carried for years and not used, but when wanted, it is wanted badly. The change of clothing is somewhat similar. What Knight calls the "get wet bag" is very convenient to have in case of an unexpected wetting. In any event it is comfortable to take off shooting boots and put on dry stockings and shoes for the drive home. My first-aid kit contains a one-ounce bottle of 5 per cent tincture of iodine, as an antiseptic; one ounce of boric-acid powder (this can be added to water and used in any strength as a wet dressing for cuts or eye irrigation); one 1-inch gauze bandage; one 2-inch gauze bandage; one small roll of 1-inch adhesive (this should be fresh each year); one 1-ounce package of raw cotton; a hemostat; a small pair of sharp, pointed scissors; a small pair of dressing forceps; one medicine dropper; salt tablets; and, when shooting in some sections of the South, a snake-bite kit may well be added. This first-aid kit is kept in a sealed tobacco tin and is always in the shooting bag. Put one there and forget about it until it is needed. It is insurance in case of accident to either dog or man.

Some men suffer severely from leg-cramps. These may be due to a number of conditions, but the following, cures or helps some cases: 1. Wear everything loose from the waist down. No belt or circular garters. Use suspenders for the trousers and stockings. 2. Gradually increase the amount of exercise and do not overdo it. 3. Drink plenty of water during, and following, the exercise. 4. Take two or three salt tablets during exercises, and two or three more at hourly intervals following the walk. Salt tablets can be purchased at any drugstore and do not require a prescription.

The shooting bag is kept packed at all times and it is necessary to add only lunch, water, and cartridges. See that it is ready the night before; otherwise it is only a matter of time before some needed article, even the shooting license, will be forgotten.

What to take for lunch is also a personal matter. Some men want a heavy, and others a light meal. Excellent lunch kits, that are generally sold for the motorist, can be secured. Certainly some hot tea, coffee, or soup makes a pleasant addition to the usual sandwiches. If it is intended to return to the car for lunch, there is no reason to stint one's self. I have never seen a thermos bottle which could be comfortably carried in the pocket—all are too bulky. If not coming back to the car, many content themselves with a few sandwiches, and half of these generally go to the dog, despite resolutions to the contrary. At best, a heavy lunch is a poor walking companion. Men vary, but a good many do not shoot so well after a heavy meal. On the other hand, a rest and a little food often help a man to shoot better. Much depends, however, upon one's habits and the time breakfast was eaten.

It is often well to take some drinking water, best carried in a large thermos, in the car. Occasionally the terrain is dry, and in such a place water must be carried for the dogs. Dogs need plenty, and cannot work without it. I think it is generally better for the dog not to be fed until the return home in the late afternoon or evening, and therefore dog food is not carried on one-day trips. The dogs should have a light breakfast before starting—a half to three-quarter pound of meat and a cracker is about correct.

Keep an old bath towel in the car to dry off the dog before starting home. A dog comb and blunt-pointed scissors, to remove the worst of the burrs, are also useful. The above, plus the dog whistle, license, and gun, will fit most requirements.

Since most shooting is done from a motor car, there is no reason to stint one's self with what can be taken in the car. Most of the extras, however, will go in the shooting bag, which is a compact and convenient way to carry them and prevents mixing up articles with those belonging to a companion. Here they are not in the way or apt to be forgotten or lost. The bag is, of course, left in the car while shooting.

SAFETY.

*Warnings and portents, and evils ominous.*
—William Shakespeare, *Julius Caesar*, Act II, Scene 2.

*I am escaped with the skin of my teeth.*
—Job, 19:20.

Accidents afield are caused by carelessness. Sometimes the carelessness is the result of youth or inexperience, but by no means is this always the case. Prolonged use of the gun usually results in greater care, but in some individuals familiarity seems to breed an indifference. Some men are so naturally careless that no amount of education will eradicate it. Others are so excitable that they always are unsafe. Furthermore, liquor and gunpowder do not mix.

Men who do not, or will not, handle firearms carefully should not be permitted to own them. However, since this is not generally practicable, they should be and can be shunned as shooting companions. If a companion is careless, he should be warned on the very first offense, however minor. No feeling of friendship or fear of offending should prevent his at once being taken severely to task. Nothing will bring back your life, or your former health after you receive a charge of shot in your body. Even though no accident occurs, a careless companion will surely spoil a day's shooting. It is difficult to get much pleasure or even shoot well if one has to be constantly watching the direction in which a companion's barrels are pointing. If spoken to in the right way, most men will take the warning in good part.

Accidents may occur in so many different ways that it is impossible to enumerate them all. However, a study of the common causes and types of accident should help in their prevention. Through the courtesy of Mr. Seth Gordon, Executive Director of the Pennsylvania Game Commission, it is possible to supply the following data:

It will be noted that these data include accidents with both rifles and shotguns. It has seemed preferable to present them as supplied by the Pennsylvania Game Commission and not to attempt a further breakdown. From a study of these statements a few facts stand out rather prominently. Nearly 25 per cent of self-inflicted accidents are fatal, as against about 6 per cent of the accidents inflicted by others. There is about ten times more danger of being shot by others than there is of receiving a self-inflicted wound. More than half of all accidents (58.7 per cent) fall under the rather broad heading of "Did not see victim in line of fire." "Hunter slipped and fell with safety off" accounts for 23.1 per cent of all fatal accidents. The summary of accidents during a ten-year period generally bears out these conclusions.

I have seen two near-accidents happen because of cold hands. In one case the hands were bare and numb with cold; in the second instance, heavy gloves were being worn. In both cases the loss of tactile sense was the direct cause of the hunter inadvertently pulling the trigger. Both instances occurred among a group of men.

## 1942 HUNTING SEASON ACCIDENTS
### Compiled by Pennsylvania Game Commission

| | Fatal | | Non-fatal | | Total | |
|---|---|---|---|---|---|---|
| *Total Accidents* | No. | Per Cent | No. | Per Cent | No. | Per Cent |
| Self-inflicted ........ | 8 | 30.8 | 23 | 7.0 | 31 | 8.8 |
| Inflicted by others .... | 18 | 69.2 | 304 | 93.0 | 322 | 91.2 |
| *Kind of Game Hunted* | | | | | | |
| Large game ......... | 5 | 19.2 | 23 | 7.0 | 28 | 8.0 |
| Small game ......... | 21 | 80.8 | 304 | 93.0 | 325 | 92.0 |
| *Causes of Accidents* | | | | | | |
| Gun placed in dangerous position .......... | 4 | 15.4 | 25 | 7.6 | 29 | 8.2 |
| Ricochet or stray bullet | 0 | 0 | 57 | 17.4 | 57 | 16.2 |
| Did not see victim in line of fire ........ | 11 | 42.3 | 192 | 58.7 | 203 | 57.5 |
| Hunter slipped and fell (with safety off) ... | 6 | 23.1 | 26 | 7.9 | 32 | 9.1 |
| Shot in mistake for game | 4 | 15.4 | 8 | 2.7 | 12 | 3.4 |
| Loading or unloading guns ............. | 0 | 0 | 9 | 2.7 | 9 | 2.5 |
| Firearms exploded (unsafe firearms) ..... | 1 | 3.8 | 10 | 3.0 | 11 | 3.1 |

*Summary of All Classes of 1942 Shooting Injuries*

Fatal: 26 (7.4 per cent); Non-fatal: 327 (92.6 per cent); Total: 353. One fatal accident for every 24,952 licenses; one non-fatal accident for every 1,984 licenses. Reports indicate that 648,759 hunting licenses were issued in 1942.

### 1942 HUNTING ACCIDENTS COMPARED WITH PREVIOUS TEN-YEAR PERIOD

| | 1932 | 1933 | 1934 | 1935 | 1936 | 1937 | 1938 | 1939 | 1940 | 1941 |
|---|---|---|---|---|---|---|---|---|---|---|
| Fatal .......... | 54 | 31 | 28 | 55 | 23 | 45 | 50 | 44 | 43 | 26 |
| Non-fatal ....... | 275 | 252 | 254 | 252 | 159 | 336 | 438 | 346 | 419 | 370 |

| | Totals | 10-Yr. Average |
|---|---|---|
| Fatal ............. | 399* | 39.9 |
| Non-fatal .......... | 3101† | 310.1 |

\* Of this total 30.8% were self-inflicted and 69.2% inflicted by others.

† Of this total 6.7% were self-inflicted and 92.9% inflicted by others.

In both cases, the gun was loaded and the safety off, whereas it should have been empty and the breech open.

Another cause for an accidental discharge is for a twig to catch in the trigger while the shooter is pushing through heavy cover.

It is impossible to enumerate all the rules for safety, but some of the most important are:

1. Never permit a loaded or unloaded gun to point at or in the direction of any living thing which you do not intend to kill. The careful man will develop a muzzle consciousness that will make him instantly aware if his barrels momentarily are brought to bear even near a companion. *Presuppose that every gun is loaded* and treat them all with respect. This is the most important rule of all and failure to observe it is at the bottom of more accidents than all other causes put together.

2. Never take a loaded gun into a house or tent or habitation of any kind.

3. Never take a loaded gun into a motor car. Make a point of opening the gun in the presence of the other occupants of the car, so that they can also see that it is empty. This is not only insurance for yourself, but also common courtesy.

4. Never rest a loaded or unloaded gun against a tree, wall, motor car, etc. It may fall or be knocked down by a dog, and, if it does not explode, a dented barrel is the least that may be expected. Lay the gun down, preferably with the breech open. If it is damp, lay your hat under the lock. Always unload the gun when you have finished shooting.

5. Unload the gun when crossing obstacles, difficult fences, walls, streams, or ditches, or when descending slippery embankments, etc.

6. Unload the gun before you hand it to a companion while crossing an obstruction, and do so in such a way that he can see that the gun is empty. Never hand a gun, muzzle first. Keep the muzzle pointing directly upward.

7. Never, *never* drag a gun toward you by the barrels. Accidents from failure to observe this precaution are numerous and usually fatal.

8. Have trigger pulls and safety mechanism checked once a year.

9. Do not neglect to look through the barrels before loading and look to see that the safety has returned to "safe" after loading. On starting out, make sure that no improper cartridges are in the pockets. If guns of different gauges are owned a stray 20-gauge shell may readily have been left in a pocket, and if a 12-gauge gun is used the next time, it may easily be dropped into the chamber of the

12-gauge. If the combination of a 12-gauge and 20-gauge or a 16-gauge and 28-gauge gun are kept, make a rule to use different colored cartridges in each. This is not only a convenience, but a safety measure.

10. Do not shoot Damascus or other barrels which are not guaranteed for the loads to be used, nor employ shells too long for the chamber.

11. Open the breech of your gun if you are standing talking to someone. This may be a mere courtesy, but no one can enjoy a chat if he has to keep one eye constantly on the direction in which a companion's barrels are pointing.

12. Do not fiddle with the safety. Develop the habit of pushing the safety forward, as a part of the act of mounting the gun to the shoulder. Keep it at "safe" at all other times.

13. Keep your fingers on the trigger guard, not on the trigger, until you are ready to shoot.

14. Keep the barrels pointing forward and upward if you stumble or slip, as everyone does sometimes.

15. Open the breech after a stumble and make sure that no mud or snow has gotten into the barrels. Do the same if you have fired a defective cartridge, for there may be a wad stuck in the barrel. This habit saved me from a burst barrel on one occasion. On another occasion, I found both barrels filled with mud after a stumble, although I had felt sure I had kept the muzzle well up. Always look through the barrels before loading.

16. Never shoot low where you cannot see, and remember that shot may ricochet on a stone, ice, frozen ground, tree trunk, or even a branch. I once saw a bird shot on the ground in thick cover, and an unseen dog, which was pointing it, was killed. Always identify the target, and if in doubt, refrain from shooting. No bird is worth a risky shot.

17. If a bird flushes and turns back low, the tendency is to concentrate on the target and swing too far, thus endangering a companion who may be walking parallel with you. Low birds going toward a hedge are always dangerous. Hedges often border lanes and paths on which children may be playing or adults walking. Fur-

thermore, it is unlawful to shoot near a highway in many states.

18. Keep track of your shooting companion's whereabouts at all times, especially in cover. This is also self-protection. Some red or white on the hat or coat helps in this respect. When approaching game, keep level. Do not lag or get ahead. Keep barrels pointing high.

19. Carry the gun on the shoulder with the triggers up. This not only keeps the barrels pointing high, but is a position from which mounting the gun can be done more quickly than with the triggers down. Another safe way is to keep the gun under the arm, with the muzzle pointing to the ground. It may be worth while to remember, if you carry an empty gun carelessly, that while you may be aware of its safety, your companion may have grave doubts and be extremely uncomfortable. This may be reminiscent of the man who said: "I see you are using No. 6 shot." "How do you know?" asked his companion. "I can see down your barrels," was the answer. The story is ancient and impossible, but has been used for generations as a gentle hint to the careless.

20. Carrying the gun in the crook of the elbow is a dangerous position, especially if a companion is on the left side.

21. Do not hesitate to warn a dangerous or a careless companion. It is safer to leave him. At close range a shotgun produces a dreadful wound, and even from a distance may cause the loss of an eye.

22. At all times err on the side of safety. A thousand birds will not make up for a companion shot. Do not be greedy.

23. Develop habits of safety, so that they become automatic. It is especially important that the boy or novice should be so instructed from the first time he handles a gun. Even apart from actual danger, habits of safety are ordinary courtesies. No companion can be comfortable or enjoy a day's shooting if he has to be constantly watching his shooting partner. Having occasionally to look into a gun muzzle, even at a distance, will spoil anyone's pleasure.

24. Do not get excited.

25. Exercise care regarding the dog. He is busy doing his work and cannot get out of the way or warn a dangerous companion.

In 1856 William Bishop, a gunmaker and sporting character living in London, published a pamphlet entitled *Caution as to the use of Firearms*. In this he pointed out forcibly the dangers entailed by the careless use of these weapons and urged the adoption of a set of simple rules. This jovial and eccentric gunmaker was a recognized authority and his warnings carried weight. Bishop's article is one of the earliest published on this subject.

### A Sportsman's Advice

If a Sportsman true you'd be,
Listen carefully to me;

Never, never let your gun
Pointed be at anyone;
That it may unloaded be
Matters not the least to me.

When a hedge or fence you cross,
Though of time it cause a loss,
From your gun the cartridge take,
For the greater safety's sake.

If 'twixt you and neighbouring gun
Birds may fly or beasts may run,
Let this maxim e'er be thine:
"Follow not across the line."

Stops and beaters oft unseen
Lurk behind some leafy screen;
Calm and steady always be,
"Never shoot where you can't see."

Keep your place and silent be
Game can hear and game can see;
Don't be greedy, better spared
Is a pheasant than one shared.

You may kill or you may miss,
But at all times think of this:
All the pheasant ever bred,
Won't repay for one man dead!

*—Shooting Times and American Field.*

DIARY.

*The life of every man is a diary in which he means to write one story, and writes another, and his humblest hour is when he compares the volume as it is with what he vowed to make it.*

—James M. Barrie, *The Little Minister.*

I would suggest that every sportsman keep a shooting diary, or some sort of log, in which to record his days' sport. Even if only the names of guides, weather conditions, localities, dogs used and their behavior, dates and game secured are entered, it will be useful. Accuracy is essential, otherwise the diary is valueless. Short observations of the behavior of game, scenting conditions, and even descriptions, are delightful, but the diary should not develop into a chore. If one cares to, and has the ability, add short word pictures— even mere fragments. In future days, these will recall pleasant outings which otherwise might have been forgotten. Especially valuable to the shooter of migratory birds are recorded dates, by which really valuable data can be built up. Photographs make a delightful addition to the diary. They should be dated and marked with a legend; otherwise, as time goes on, details are certain to be forgotten.

ETIQUETTE.

*For a man by nothing is so well bewrayed,*
*As by his manners.*

—Edmund Spenser, *The Faerie Queen,* Book vi.

A good deal has been written on the etiquette and amenities of shooting, but it can all be covered by the words, decency, ordinary courtesy, and good manners. Most sportsmen are good fellows, and if they err, do so from ignorance, thoughtlessness, or excitement. The ideal companion is on time; is safe at all times; walks an agreed course and keeps in touch; gives occasional signals while in cover; calls "Mark!" promptly when birds are coming your way; shows consideration for game; at all times keeping his eyes open and his mind on the business at hand; and generally lives up to the Golden Rule.

Some of the types to avoid—and they are infrequent but may occasionally be found in various degrees and phases—are: the greedy, jealous, nervous, reckless, or selfish shots; the bragger (about either his dog or his shooting); the "long-shot fiend"; the unsolicited coach; the claimer of all shared birds; the poacher, who shoots birds which plainly belong to you (the keen novice will often do this—and is not included in this category—and everyone occasionally does inadvertently claim birds which do not belong to him but the hardened sinner requires different treatment); the vocal critic of your dog or shooting; the loud-shouting and noisy man; the man who kicks or otherwise mistreats his dog, or gives orders to yours; the "know-it-all"; the excuse-maker; the big flask man; the postmortem addict; and the chronic complainer. At most, if you are wise none of these should spoil more than one day's shooting. Almost as bad, but by no means so frequent, is the overcourteous individual, who does not accept his shots in order to give you shooting.

Apropos of the poacher, and the difficulty with some of these thick-skinned gentlemen, the following incident occurred some years ago: Two men, whom we may call A and B, were woodcock shooting in New Brunswick. A was shooting over his own dog and B was dependent upon a guide's. One morning, B's guide did not turn up and A asked B to shoot with him. It soon developed that B was a confirmed poacher and claimer, and after he had claimed at least two extremely doubtful birds, which A handed over, A began to realize the sort of companion he was shooting with, and worked out a scheme which he thought might shame B out of his evil ways.

In a few minutes, A killed a cock far to his right, which B could not possibly have shot at. A's dog retrieved all birds to him. A politely handed the bird to B, with the remark that B had made a long shot. B did not hesitate, but pocketed the bird, remarking that he was using a very hard shooting gun.

As they trudged along, A cogitated how to deal with the situation. His first plan had failed signally, and B already had at least three of A's birds. For the rest of the day A pocketed every bird, regardless of who had killed it. In relating the incident he said that at the end of the day he calculated he had about squared up the account. A's guide told me that at the end of the day B was breaking shot and running for his birds like a retriever.

B left the small hotel in which they were staying the next day, but his version of the day's shooting, as related in New York, is not printable. However, it appeared that *B*'s reputation was well known.

I have twice witnessed attempts to steal game. Once I shot at a grouse in thick cover. In an effort to determine the result of the shot I stooped down and was able to see the bird fall near a companion. He looked cautiously around, did not see me, and quickly pocketed the bird. A few minutes later, there was a single shot and a shout, "I got him!" I walked over and asked for my bird, explaining that I had seen him pick it up. At the end of the day the man had only one bird which he had killed late in the afternoon. On another occasion, when I was fourteen or fifteen years of age, I was shooting with an older man who had the reputation of being somewhat of a scamp. I killed a grass plover stone dead, and marked the fall accurately. We both hunted for the bird a long time without apparent result. Finally my companion suggested giving up, but I was loath to do so, and continued my vain search for nearly half an hour. In my unsuspecting innocence, and despite knowledge of my companion's reputation, it was not until years later, when something recalled the occurrence, that the fact that he must have pocketed the bird dawned upon me.

*Oil Finish.* The woodwork of many cheap shotguns is finished with varnish. This scratches badly and an oil finish is much more handsome. If one desires to change a varnished stock to an oil finish, a fairly good amateur job can be done, but much depends upon the quality of the wood. It may be converted as follows:

Remove the varnish with a varnish remover, which can be purchased at any paint shop. Then scrape off with a dull knife blade, a piece of glass, or sandpaper. Get all the old varnish off. Thoroughly wet the woodwork with gasoline and wrap it in a moistened cloth for from twelve to twenty-four hours. This will raise the fiber of the wood. Rub smooth with the finest steel wool. Repeat the moistening and the smoothing until absolutely all the raised fiber disappears. Then repeat twice more; it is absolutely essential to secure a really smooth surface. After the final wetting and rubdown, no suspicion of raised fiber should be detectable anywhere with a hand magnifying glass.

When thoroughly dry, apply the best quality linseed oil. Use this liberally and rub it in with the palm of the hand. The more one rubs it in, the better. Dry off with a soft cloth, and repeat the application of oil and rubbing daily for a number of days. After the first application of the oil, apply sparsely, and only by placing a little oil on the palm of the hand, and rub this well in. At the completion of each treatment do not neglect thoroughly to rub off all excess oil. The more oil that is rubbed in, the darker the wood will become; therefore naturally dark woods do not require quite so much oil.

*The receipts of cookery are swelled to a volume; but a good stomach excels them all.*

—William Penn, *Some Fruits of Solitude.*

SELECTION. Unless raised on a licensed game farm, it is illegal to sell any game bird that has been killed in the United States. Such birds are usually marked with a metal tag. They are generally young, and in good condition. Pen-raised pheasants are good but pen-raised quail are inferior.

It does not improve the flavor of game to be crammed, while warm, into an ill-ventilated pocket of a shooting coat. When possible, all game birds should be cooled first. They also keep better if this is done, but it is generally impracticable.

Generally speaking, young birds are better than old. This is particularly true of pheasants. The old cock pheasant is apt to be tough, no matter how it is prepared. In young birds, the skin of the feet and legs is apt to be smooth and not roughened or scaly. The feet, distal wing, bones, and leg joints can easily be bent or broken, and the lower bill is weak and may not support the weight of the bird. In very young birds, pinfeathers may be present. The quills in old birds are hard and white. In quail and grouse, the outer wing feathers are more pointed in young than in old birds. The spur of the young cock pheasant is a dull knob, hardly half an inch in length. A long, heavy, sharp spur is a sure indication of age. In normal seasons, about two-thirds to three-fourths of birds killed in the field are young birds.

Birds in good condition, i.e., fat, feel heavy for their size. Personally, I do not like game which is high. In freshly killed birds, the surface of the eye is full and round, but after twenty-four to forty-eight hours it becomes dull, sunken, and flattened.

The first sign of gaminess is a tainted odor from the mouth when the bill is opened, and around the vent; the latter area soon becomes discolored. Badly shot birds and those which have been permitted to become wet and draggled do not keep well.

Some authorities advise drawing the bird at once. If this is done and the cavity wiped dry with a dry cloth, it will keep longer, but the meat tends to dry. Unless it is intended to keep the bird for an unusual length of time, I believe it is preferable not to draw until ready to use. If there is any likelihood that grouse have been feeding on skunk cabbage seeds, as they occasionally do, they should be drawn immediately after killing.

*Hanging.* Game birds are best eaten either immediately after killing or when they have been hung for a time. If not used within ten hours at the latest, they are apt to be tough, stringy, and lacking in flavor. Their excellence when eaten shortly after killing was proved to me years ago, at the Currituck Sound Shooting Club, at Knotts Island, North Carolina. The membership of this club is composed of men who know good food and how it should be prepared. Some of them were members of the famous Fish House, all of whom are amateur cooks, and some of whom are among the best amateur chefs to be found anywhere.

It was the practice at the Currituck Club, on returning from shooting, to select a duck from the day's bag and have this cooked for dinner the same evening. The birds were splendidly cooked, but even discounting this fact and an out-of-doors appetite, these ducks were, with the exception of some late-in-the-season-killed Chesapeake Bay canvasbacks, the best I have ever eaten—tender, fine-flavored, and especially full of juice. The latter was noticeable as soon as a fork was put in the breast, and I have never seen a duck yield more juice even when put in a press. Since then I have often eaten birds the same day as killed, and they are always good.

This, however, does not apply to pheasants: they should always be hung for some time. If not cooked the same day as killed, game birds are best hung for from four to fourteen days. However, quail are excellent after three or four days' hanging. Birds will keep for at least two weeks if the temperature is uniformly cold and dry, but one or two warm spells may spoil them. If there is danger of their spoiling they may be put in the refrigerator. Do not place directly on the ice.

Even if the birds do not spoil after two weeks, the meat tends to become dry and loses flavor. This is particularly noticeable of birds which have been in cold storage. They should be hung where neither sun, rain, nor snow can reach them. Cats, rats, and even dogs may be destructive. A screened porch with a northern exposure is an excellent place in which to hang game. It is best to hang them in pairs. For choice, do not hang against the wall but from hooks in the ceiling so that the air can circulate freely. Early in the season, when flies may be present, it is sometimes a good plan to put each pair in a paper bag, but this prevents ventilation and is not advisable, except when flies are prevalent.

Some years ago there was a somewhat lengthy discussion in one of the sporting journals as to whether it was preferable to hang birds by the head or the legs. As I remember, no conclusion was arrived at. I prefer to hang game by the legs, unless the bird has been previously drawn.

Use the badly shot birds first. If there are a number of birds killed on different days, a tag marking the date is worth while. When game is given as a present, it should always be tagged with the date killed. In the September 1944 number of the *Field and Stream*, Archibald Rutledge has an amusing article entitled "Game I've Given Away." In this he calls attention to the advisability of knowing that the recipient likes game before presenting it. This is sound advice. In this article the author says that the liking for game is often an acquired trait. However this may be, it is wasteful to present it to the unappreciative.

Pheasants keep better than grouse, quail, or woodcock, and, generally, ten days or two weeks is none too long for them to hang. The old test of hanging a pheasant by the tail and not using it until the carcass drops, results in a pretty high bird. Do not have birds plucked until you are ready to prepare them for the table. With small birds, such as rail, or, in the old days, reed birds, which do not require much hanging, this does not matter. It is perhaps hardly necessary to state that birds should never be skinned.

Plucking should be done carefully, in order not to break the skin.

If the skin is broken, apart from spoiling the appearance of the bird, the meat tends to become dry and loses body juices, and cooking is not so uniform as it should be. After plucking, tie a string tightly around the base of the neck and then cut off the head. This tends to keep in the body juice.

Some people like to eat the brains of snipe and woodcock, and therefore it is wise to leave the head on. If this is done, skin the head and neck, remove the eyes, and tuck the bill under the skin of the shoulder. This was formerly always done when woodcock, snipe, or plover were served in restaurants; the practice also established the identity of the bird.

Wings may be cut off at the second joint. Many inexperienced cooks have a pernicious habit of washing the entire bird, including the body cavity, before cooking. No water should touch the bird after it is drawn. If there is much blood in the body cavity after drawing, this may be wiped out with a damp cloth, but on no account should the bird be immersed in water. This is a sure way to lose much of the flavor. Some chefs parboil birds of doubtful tenderness. Parboiling is certain to destroy the flavor of a good bird and to spoil a mediocre one. If birds are cold, put them in a pan breast down near the fire, to warm for twenty or thirty minutes before placing in the oven.

It is attention to detail that marks the difference between a good and a bad cook. Unless the household contains a gun-lover, the average American family is not often able to enjoy game, and, as a consequence, relatively few cooks know much about preparing it. All are too apt to treat game birds as if they were chickens. All sorts of fats are often used, whereas only good butter or bacon should be employed. Most of our game birds possess a delicate flavor, which is easily destroyed. Peppers, spices, and all condiments should be the best, and preferably fresh.

*Pheasant.* This is a moderately good bird, but at best does not compare with many of our native game birds. It is especially important to select a young one—a hen is the best. Do not attempt to roast an old bird any more than you would roast an old stewing chicken. Truss as a chicken. Use no filling. Give it about thirty to forty minutes' brisk roasting. The tendency of this meat is to be dry. It should be cooked through, but every minute after this amount of cooking increases the dryness. The secret of a juicy pheasant is not to overcook, and to baste frequently with good butter. The latter can hardly be done too often. Some chefs tie a piece of fat bacon over the breast before cooking, but this does not eliminate the necessity for frequent basting. Prepare separately a gravy of stock and giblets, brown and add a dash of lemon juice. Serve with bread sauce. (Bread sauce is appropriate with any white-meated game bird.) Braised celery, French fried potatoes, potato chips, or wild rice are good accompaniments to pheasant. Burgundy or a full-bodied claret is an appropriate wine. If you are young, and a lady is dining with you, offer a sidecar, forget about the red wine, and order a well-iced bottle of "Widow." Most women like champagne; few young ones appreciate Burgundy. As a matter of fact, and contrary to the general belief, a moderately dry champagne is a good accompaniment. If one gets tired of the ordinary roast, try peeling and seeding a couple of handfuls of grapes and placing them in the body cavity before cooking.

*Roast Pheasant in Red Wine.* Use an uncovered pan and roast in a hot oven (400°F.) for twenty minutes; then reduce heat (250°F.). When nearly done, season with salt and pepper and pour over the bird two or three claret glasses full of claret. Continue roasting until done. Strain and serve the remainder of pan drippings as a gravy.

Pheasants and quail are sometimes larded. Larding improves thin, dry birds. For the larger bird allow one lardon for each side of the breast and one for each leg (upper joint). For quail, use one lardon on each side of the breast. Bacon is best. Use a strip about a sixth of an inch wide. Insert with a larding needle and leave a short end projecting. Insert lardons at right angles to the breastbone and in the direction of the grain of the meat. Another way to prevent dryness is to pour over the bird half a cupful of hot melted butter, permitting some to enter the body cavity, and cover the pan and roast for the necessary time. The hot pan drippings may be poured over the bird just before serving.

*Broiled Pheasant.* Select a young hen, split it down the back, and broil as one does a young chicken. A charcoal fire is best. Serve with butter sauce and a squeeze of lemon. This is a good luncheon or breakfast dish.

*Broiled Breast of Pheasant.* Pluck and cut off each side of the breast in one slice. Broil on a quick fire, serve with butter and lemon sauce. This also makes an excellent breakfast or luncheon dish. The carcass may be utilized for stock, or, appropriately seasoned with a little red wine such as Madeira or sherry you will have a good soup. Heel taps from bottles of wine are entirely satisfactory and should be kept for this purpose.

*Braised Pheasant.* This is not a bad way to utilize a pheasant whose tenderness is questionable. Place the bird in a closed casserole, add a good stock, small carrots, small onions, small potatoes, small turnips, tomatoes, diced ham, salt, and a *bouquet garni* of herbs. Cook thoroughly. Let this braise in the oven with the heat above the lid of the casserole. Turn the bird if necessary. Add a glass of Madeira during the final stage. The bird should be brown and served in a casserole dish with its own juice. If available, chestnuts may be added to this dish. Parboil or half roast the nuts, and peel. Add them to the stock, to boil slowly for ten minutes before serving. The above is a recipe given by Major Hugh Pollard in *Shooting by Moor, Field and Shore,* edited by Eric Parker.

From South Dakota, that land of pheasant plenty, where pheasants are plucked by machinery, canned for future use, and even utilized for sausage meat (dress and bone one pheasant, dice half a pound of lean pork, grind both meats and mix together, add seasoning to taste), J. L. Russell recommends *Fried Pheasant in Sour Cream:* Cut a young pheasant into four pieces; roll the pieces in flour and fry in an open pan on top of the stove. Use sour cream in place of the usual frying fats.

Holland, in the February 1944 issue of *Field and Stream,* recommends cooking pheasant in a Dutch oven, with some of your favorite vegetables.

E. F. Warner recommends *Roast Salmi of Pheasant,* which is prepared as follows: Cut cold, roast pheasant in even pieces; set aside. Then break up what is left of the bird into small pieces. Make a brown sauce of butter and flour. Thin this with beef-broth soup stock and one tablespoonful of Madeira or sherry. Bring to a boil, add the broken pieces, and again bring to a boil. Strain and pour into another pot. Add the cut pieces of pheasant and let simmer until the meat is thoroughly warm. Place the meat on a platter and pour gravy over it. Serve with croutons.

*Boiled Pheasant.* An old bird may be used. Truss and boil as a chicken. Serve with a good white sauce, to which is added a generous dash of white wine and some truffles.

*Pheasant Sandwich.* An old bird can be utilized. Roast as usual. Cut off the white meat, removing all the skin and sinews. (Use only the best of the meat. Many chefs think anything will do for a sandwich, whereas only the choicest meat should ever be employed. On a plate it is possible to see what is served and to discard any undesirable portions. This is not the case with a sandwich, hence only the best and most carefully selected meat should be used.) Run the meat through a fine grinder, season to taste (freshly ground pepper from fresh peppercorns is far better than the ordinary pepper, and Nepal is generally preferable to paprika or red pepper). Add sufficient thick cream and a good stock until the meat is of the proper consistency. Use good bread, cut thin, with the crusts removed, liberally covered with sweet butter. Place each sandwich in a separate waxed-paper envelope. Keep the sandwich cool. This makes an excellent sandwich for a day's shooting, and if it can be washed down with a glass of one of the heavier clarets, it is a good lunch. The remainder of the bird can be utilized for stock or soup.

Chicken meat may be used instead of pheasant's, and various combinations of seasoning or meats may be utilized. One or two teaspoonfuls of the liquid from a bottle of Major Gray's Chutney may be substituted for the cream, or a piece of ham may be ground up and mixed with the pheasant meat. Virginia ham is best. Or a slice of raw tomato with a crisp lettuce leaf and some mayonnaise dressing, to which has been added a dash of English mustard, may be put in a sandwich. A piece or two of crisp bacon may be added. The sliced meat from any good game bird, provided it is tender and free from sinews, is suitable. The secret of a good sandwich is to use only the best materials, cut the bread thin, spread the sweet butter with a liberal hand, fill as full as possible with the meat, have it freshly made, place at once in an oiled paper container, or wrap in a clean napkin, the outer surface of which has been dampened, keep in a cool place, and, if possible, in a covered receptacle. The meat is usually best if a little more highly seasoned than if it is to be used on a plate. Whole, cold roast game birds are excellent and should be wrapped in a napkin, the outer folds of which are dampened and placed in oiled paper. Lunch may be topped off with a sweet sandwich. Orange marmalade with nut bread is good. Many persons like fruit; an apple is never so good as when eaten out of doors. Although it is a matter of personal taste, I think that about the most satisfactory liquid to go with a shooting lunch is hot tea. Coffee deteriorates more in a thermos than does tea. Some like a glass of claret; but wine is cold comfort on a crisp fall day. Others prefer a small split of Bass' Ale. I think something hot is preferable; a soup is excellent.

*Ruffed Grouse.* With the possible exception of a fat grass plover —which bird is now, I fear, gone forever—or a late-in-the-season shot, celery-fed Chesapeake Bay canvasback, ruffed grouse are perhaps the finest game birds in America for the table.

*Roast Grouse.* Just the proper length of hanging is important. Prepare as suggested for pheasant. Roast briskly for about thirty to thirty-five minutes. The bird should be thoroughly done, but avoid overcooking. Baste frequently with good butter, which has been placed in the roasting dish. Never use other fats. Use no filling. Place in a hot dish, pour a little of the pan drippings over the bird, and serve with bread sauce. No jelly—the entire idea is to preserve the flavor of the grouse. An excellent menu to accompany this fine bird is as follows: Lynnhavens (Lynnhavens are apt not to be prime before December. They are a large oyster, with a rough shell and a slightly yellowish tinge to the surface of their meat, which should be full and firm. They often contain oyster crabs. Many large, white, fattened oysters are passed off as Lynnhavens, but they are nothing like the real Lynnhaven in flavor. Lacking Lynnhavens, a good salt oyster or caviar may be substituted)—clear, green turtle soup; a dish of terrapin; roast grouse; wild rice; celery salad; Camembert or Roquefort cheese; café noir. A fine Burgundy is the appropriate wine, and see that the "Boy" is very slightly above room temperature and unshaken. Do not waste this on the unappreciatives. Roast grouse is excellent cold and makes a fine luncheon dish. As every big game hunter knows, grouse can be cooked in a reflector oven, out of doors.

Grouse may also be split and broiled. They are good in any way, but roasting is the best.

*Woodcock.* Tastes differ regarding the excellence of this bird— many people are enthusiastic about it. Much depends upon the preparation and proper hanging. Woodcock killed in the South are not generally so well flavored as the northern birds. The bird is best roasted. Woodcock spoil easily and in the old days of summer shooting many were spoiled in the jacket pockets before they reached home. Some prefer not to draw these birds, leaving the "trail" *in situ,* but do remove the crop and gizzard. The trail comes out easily after cooking. I prefer to remove the insides. If the head is to be left, remove the eyes and skin the head and neck. Roast on a round of thick toast to catch the drippings, and serve on this. Baste frequently with butter. A woodcock is a small bird, and one easily overcooked. It should be well browned on the outside. An old-fashioned meat-jack does this to perfection. The meat next to the breast bone should be distinctly red, but no tinge of real bluishness should remain. From about fifteen to eighteen minutes, depending on the fire, is usually about the right length of time to cook woodcock. I have seen woodcock toward the end of the season in Nova Scotia which were covered with a thick layer of fat, but usually they possess only a moderate amount. If the birds are thin, they may be roasted with a slice of bacon pinned over the breast, but I prefer to omit this. A little drawn butter, plus a squeeze of lemon juice, may be added for a sauce. Claret is an appropriate accompaniment to woodcock.

Major Pollard recommends the following recipe for European woodcock. I have tried it with our birds and it is an excellent dish.

*Woodcock Flambé.* Roast the bird for ten minutes. Joint and carve off the meat and pile it in a hot silver dish. Crush the carcass and strain all the gravy into a saucepan. Thicken this to a sauce with salt, pepper, butter, and a little mild paprika or Nepal; stir in cream to thicken. Now serve your cock, pour over this a glass of warm brandy, light it and let it burn off, and then pour on your sauce. Our birds, being about half the size of European woodcock, require less cooking. Mr. Schaldach recommends woodcock split and broiled on a grill over hardwood coals. Do not overcook. Season with salt and pepper. Colonel H. P. Sheldon recommends for broiled woodcock, a sauce made of butter, sour cream, currant jelly, mustard and a little Burgundy. These ingredients are melted together and the birds dipped into the sauce frequently while broiling.

Woodcock may be cooked in a chafing dish. Mr. Davis recommends the following: Remove breast meat and legs and cook in chafing dish until done. Previously prepare a sauce consisting of thin brown gravy, to which has been added a glass of sherry or Madeira, salt, pepper, and a dash of Nepal and the juice of half an orange. Mix well, heat and pour over meat. Serve hot, not merely warm.

*Bobwhite Quail.* There are many ways of cooking this excellent bird. Like all white-meated fowl, they should be cooked through and should avoid any suspicion of being underdone. However, any cooking beyond this point promotes dryness and destroys flavor. They are usually overcooked.

*Roast Quail.* This is properly the most popular method of preparing this bird for the table. Pluck, draw, and truss with white string. Dredge very lightly with melted butter and flour. Roast in a moderately quick oven for from fifteen to eighteen minutes. Baste frequently with butter. Serve with bread sauce. A red wine is appropriate. A strip of bacon may be pinned over the breast before roasting—this improves the flavor and prevents drying, but do not, on this account, omit the basting. Some cooks place an oyster or two in the body cavity before roasting. This is served intact. Quail may also be stuffed with sausage meat, which should be not too highly seasoned—a few truffles added to it is an improvement.

Cold roast quail is excellent and makes a good addition to a shooting lunch. At the Oakland Quail Club in South Carolina the members have a pleasant custom of having guides prepare a hot lunch, the *pièce de résistance* of which is a freshly killed quail, split down the back, and cooked with butter in a frying pan. The frying of any game is generally an abomination, but these quail are really excellent.

Broiled quail are apt to be dry and tasteless. Braised quail *en casserole* are excellent and often a pleasant change from the frequent roast. The dish is prepared in the same way as described for pheasants. In New Orleans I have eaten a casserole of quail prepared with shrimp, rice, and a few tomatoes, to which a generous supply of claret had been added. The concoction was highly seasoned and far better than it sounds.

Another Louisiana recipe mentioned by Dr. F. A. Martin and J. L. MacHugh, and quoted by W. A. Hanger, is as follows: *"Perdrix à la créole sur du pain grillé.* (1) Fry six quail in olive oil. (2) Cut fine one cup of onions and six pods of garlic. (3) Let smother until onions and garlic are cooked. (4) Add two cups of hot water and season to taste with salt and red pepper. Cook until done. (5) Put one bird to each piece of toast and a small quantity of gravy. Eight doves may be substituted for the quail."

Frank Forester recommends a pie composed of alternate layers of hen quail and beefsteak, to be eaten either hot or cold.

*Sauté Quail à la Mouquin.* Dress, clean, and trim half a dozen quail. Have ready one-half cup of butter, two scallops finely chopped, two or three finely chopped cloves, garlic, one teaspoonful finely chopped chives, half a bay leaf, two cloves, a few fresh peppercorns, one pint Rhine wine, Sauterne or other white wine, one pint good cream, butter, salt, freshly ground white pepper, dash of Nepal. Cook and stir the butter, scallops, garlic, bay leaf, peppercorn and cloves continuously for eight minutes. Sauté the birds in the sauce until brown. Add the white wine and simmer half an hour. Remove the birds, strain the sauce into a casserole, and slowly add the thick cream. Add the remaining seasoning. Bring to a boil and serve in a casserole. This is a good dish, but much of the flavor of the quail is lost.

Roasting is generally the best way in which to preserve the flavor of game birds, but toward the end of the season the eternal roast is likely to become tiresome. Any good French cookbook will supply innumerable sauces and methods of preparing game. Although these are devised for European birds, generally they can be adapted to ours, and the pheasant is common to many countries. Split, grilled, deviled or spatch-cooked birds are pleasant for a change, especially if prepared over a wood fire. Red currant jelly, grape jelly, or various combinations of tomatoes and young onions can be utilized.

*Salmi of Woodcock or Quail.* This is not a bad dish for a change, although much of the flavor of the birds is lost. Separate the raw meat from the bones and fry in butter for only a few minutes. The meat should not be cooked through. Place the carcass in a duck press or mortar, mash, and stew carcass with herbs and a wineglassful of claret or Madeira. Season with freshly ground peppers and mace. Remove the carcasses. To this stock add a few small onions and a little tomato sauce. Simmer the meat in the stock for from twenty to thirty minutes. Place the meat on a shallow dish, pour the sauce over it and serve hot.

*Rail.* Tastes differ regarding the excellence of this bird for the table. The flavor is characteristically its own. The sora is the best. Rail do not keep very well, and do not require long hanging. This is especially true of birds killed during warm weather, of those that are badly shot, draggled, wet, or have been exposed to a hot sun in the bottom of a boat. For these reasons it is customary to pluck the birds at once. The term pluck is somewhat of a misnomer, inasmuch as the expert does not pick off any but the large feathers; the others he rubs off with the ball of the thumb and the palm of the hand. He starts at the tail and works upward. A good man can remove the feathers in three to five minutes. The birds should be plucked clean, and this can be accomplished more easily if they are dry. Wings and feet are cut off. As some people like to eat the brain, the neck and head are skinned and the eyes removed. The bird is drawn, leaving the liver in place. Wipe out the body cavity with a dry cloth. Do not use water or wash the bird. They can then be placed on a plate in the refrigerator. They are best eaten the same day as killed or on about the third or fourth day. Fat birds are decidedly the best. The best are usually those shot during the latter part of September or in October. A small, thin rail is tasteless and hardly worth cooking.

*Roast Rail.* Place a few teaspoonfuls of butter in a covered pan and roast in a hot oven. Birds should be slightly brown upon the outside, but the meat should be distinctly red not pink. Baste two or three times with pan drippings. Guard a tendency to overcook, because this not only ruins the flavor, but melts away most of the fat. Rail continue to cook after being removed from the fire. Place on toast from which the crusts have been removed. Pour over them the pan drippings and serve hot, not merely warm.

Rail are often cooked in a chafing dish. The same principles are involved as if they were roasted. Toast is often omitted. The advantage of the chafing dish is that the birds can be served piping hot. Two or three birds are usually allowed for each person.

If a sufficient number of birds are available, the livers may be sautéed in a little butter and make an excellent breakfast dish. A few rails are good for breakfast, but the hungry man will require something additional, such as a kipper or some broiled fish. Even large, fat birds provide relatively little meat. One hungry writer referred to them as table bric-a-brac. Rail also makes a pleasant luncheon dish. When served at dinner, they may be utilized as the main course or, better, served with the salad. A plain salad with French dressing is best. Never serve rail with vegetables having a pronounced taste. French fried potatoes which have been well iced before cooking, potato chips, or a scraped bantam-corn pudding are good accompaniments. A red wine is suitable, and Burgundy probably the best for dinner.

*Bread Sauce.* This is an excellent accompaniment for any white-meated game bird and is made as follows: two cups of good cream; one-third cup of fine, stale, white bread crumbs; one small or medium-sized onion; six or eight cloves; one-half teaspoonful of salt; a dash of Nepal pepper; three to four teaspoonfuls of good butter; one-half cup of coarse, stale, white bread crumbs. Scald the cream for one-half hour in a double boiler, with the fine bread crumbs, onion, and cloves. Remove the onion and cloves, add the seasoning and the butter. Stir well, sprinkle with the coarse bread crumbs. This should be well softened before serving. Another alternative is to brown the coarse bread crumbs in a little butter and sprinkle on top. I prefer the former recipe.

# BIBLIOGRAPHY

Alken, E. *The National Sports of Great Britain.* New York: D. Appleton & Co., 1903.
American Kennel Club. *The Complete Dog Book.* New York: Blue Ribbon Books, 1938. New, rev. ed.
*The American Shooters Manual.* Philadelphia: Carey, Lea and Carey, 1827.
"Ashmont." *See* Perry, J. F.
Askins, Charles. *Game Bird Shooting.* New York: Macmillan Co., 1931.
——. *How to Hunt.* New York: Field and Stream.
——. *Modern Shot Guns and Loads.* Marshallton, Del.: Small Arms Technical Pub. Co., 1929.
——. *Wing Shooting.* Denver, Col.: Outdoor Life, 1928.
Audubon, J. J. *Birds of North America.* London: pub. by author, 1827-1838.
—— (plates) and Bachman, J. (text). *The Viviparous Quadrupeds of North America.* New York: V. G. Audubon, 1842-54.

Bach, R. H. Quoted by Cartwright, B. W.; *see* below.
Backman, T. M. *Natural History,* Sept. 1945.
Bailey, R. *Field and Stream,* Sept. 1944.
Bailey, W. W., and Nestler, R. B. *See* McAtee, W. L., ed., *The Ring-Necked Pheasant.*
Baird, S. F. *Birds of North America.* New York: D. Appleton & Co., 1860.
Beard, D. *Guns and Gunning.* Chicopee Falls, Mass.: J. Stevens Arms & Tool Co., 1908.
Beebe, William. *Pheasants: Their Lives and Homes.* Garden City, N. Y.: Doubleday, Page & Co., 1926.
Bennett, L. J. *American Field,* February 27, 1943. *See* also, McAtee, W. L., ed., *The Ring-Necked Pheasant.*
Bent, Arthur C. *Life Histories of North American Birds.* Washington: U. S. National Museum, Bulletin 135, "Rails," 1926.
Betten, H. L. *Upland Game Shooting.* Philadelphia: Penn Pub. Co., 1940.
Bigelow, H. *Flying Feathers.* Richmond, Va.: Garret & Massie, 1937.
Blaine, D. P. *Encyclopaedia of Rural Sports.* London: Longmans, Green, Reader, and Dyer, 1870.
Blanchan, N. *Birds That Hunt and Are Hunted.* New York: Doubleday, Page & Co., 1905.

Bogardus, Adam H. *Field, Cover and Trap Shooting.* New York: pub. by author, 1878.

Brooke, Sir Victor. *Shooting.* London: Longmans, Green and Co., 1896. The Badminton Library.

Brown, W. F. *How to Train Hunting Dogs.* New York: A. S. Barnes & Co., 1942.

Buckingham, Nash. *Mark Right!* New York: Derrydale Press, 1936.

———. *Tattered Coat.* New York: Derrydale Press, 1939.

———. *Field and Stream,* Aug. 1945.

Buckle, C. E. *American Field,* April 23, 1937.

Burges, A. *The American Kennel and Sporting Field.* New York: J. B. Ford & Co., 1876.

Burrard, Gerald. *The Modern Shotgun.* New York: C. Scribner's Sons, 1931. 3 vols.

Buytendijk, F. J. J. "L'odorat du chien" (Scent of the Dog), *Arch. neerlandaise de physiol. de l'homme et des animaux,* V (1920-21), 434.

Byng, A. H. and Stephens, S. M., eds. *Autobiography of an English Gamekeeper.* New York: Macmillan & Co., 1892.

Cahn, A. R. *The Auk* (1915), p. 91.

Cahoon, H. H. "Whirring Wings," *American Field,* CXL (1943), No. 49; CXLI (1944), No. 6.

Cartwright, B. W. *Field and Stream,* Aug. 1945.

Chalmers, Patrick R. *The Shooting-Man's England.* Philadelphia: J. B. Lippincott Co., 1936.

Chapman, F. M. *Birds of Eastern North America.* New York: D. Appleton & Co., 1906.

———. *Autobiography of a Bird-Lover.* New York: Appleton-Century Co., 1933.

Churchill, R. *How to Shoot.* London: G. Blès, 1925.

Collinge, Walter E. *Journal of the Land Agents Society,* June 1917.

Colquhoun, J. *The Moor and the Loch.* Edinburgh: W. Blackwood & Sons, 1878. 2 vols.

Comeau, N. A. *Life and Sport on the North Shore.* Quebec: Daily Telegraph Print House, 1909.

Connett, E. V. *Wing Shooting and Angling.* New York: C. Scribner's Sons, 1922.

———, ed. *Upland Game Bird Shooting in America.* New York: Derrydale Press, 1930.

Cooper, C. A. ("Sibylline"). *See* Leffingwell, W. B., ed., *Shooting on Upland, Marsh and Stream.*

Coxe, W. H. *Smokeless Shotgun Powders.* Burnside: DuPont Co.

Creytz, A. von. *Der Hund in Dienste,* der Schutz- und Polizaitruppe. Berlin: Schoetz, 1913. P. 65.

Criddle, S. *The Field* (London), Jan. 27, 1945.

Crowe, C. E. "Hookworms," *American Field,* June 25, 1932; Dec. 3, 1938.
———. "Heartworms and Microfilaria," *American Field,* CXL (1943), No. 49.
Curtis, Paul A. *American Game Shooting.* New York: E. P. Dutton & Co., 1927.
———. *Guns and Gunning.* Philadelphia: Penn Pub. Co., 1934.
———. *Sporting Firearms of Today.* New York: E. P. Dutton & Co., 1922.

Davis, E. W. *Woodcock Shooting.* Printed for private distribution, 1908.
Day, James W. *Sporting Adventure.* New York: G. P. Putnam's Sons, 1937.
Delke, P. D. *See* McAtee, W. L.
Dinks, Mayhew and Hutchinson. *The Dog.* New York: Stringer and Townsend, 1857. Ed. Frank Forester.
Dugmore, A. R. *Wild Life and the Camera.* Philadelphia: J. B. Lippincott Co., 1892.

Elliot, D. G. *Game Birds of North America.* New York: F. P. Harper, 1897.
Eveshed, A. F. C. Quoted by Collinge, W.; *see* above.

Forbush, Edward H. *History of Game Birds, Wild-Fowl and Shore Birds of Massachusetts.* Boston: Mass. State Board of Agriculture, 1912.
———. *A Natural History of the Birds of Central and Eastern North America.* Boston: Houghton Mifflin Company.
Forester, Frank. *See* Herbert, H. W.
Foster, J. C., Jr. American Setter Family Tree, *American Field,* July 10, 1943.
Foster, W. H. *New England Grouse Shooting.* New York: C. Scribner's Sons, 1942.

Game Conservation Society. *Game Birds.* New York: The Society, 110 Grand St.
———. *More Game Birds by Controlling Their Natural Enemies.* New York: The Society.
Gibbs, M. "The Sora," *Oologist,* Vol. XVI (1899).
Goode, R. J. *American Field,* April 29, 1944.
Graham, J. A. *The Sporting Dog.* New York: Macmillan Co., 1904.
Greener, W. W. *The Gun and Its Development.* London: Cassell & Co., 1910.
———. *Modern Breech-Loaders.* London: Cassell & Co. 2nd ed.
Griffith. Quoted by Day, J. W.; *see* above.
Grinnel, J. *Scientific Monthly,* May 27, 1927.
Grinnell, George B. *American Game Bird Shooting.* New York: Forest and Stream Pub. Co., 1910.
———. *See* Mayer, A. M., ed., *Sport with Gun and Rod.*

Hall, M. C. *Parasites and Parasitic Diseases of Dogs.* Washington, D. C.: U. S. Dept. of Agriculture, 1925.

Hallock, C. *The Sportsman's Gazetteer.* New York: Forest and Stream Pub. Co., 1877.

Hammond, S. T. ("Shadow"). *Hitting vs. Missing.* New York: Forest and Stream Pub. Co., 1898.

——. *Practical Dog Training.* New York: Forest and Stream Pub. Co., 1886.

*Handbook on Shotgun Shooting.* New York: Comm. on Promotional Activities, Sporting Arms and Ammunition Manufacturers Institute, 1939.

Hanger, W. A. *See* Connett, ed., *Upland Game Bird Shooting in America.*

Hardy, H. F. H. *English Sport,* London: Country Life, 1932.

Hawker, Peter. *Instructions to Young Sportsmen.* London: Longman, Brown, Green, Longman, & Roberts, 1849. 11th ed.

Hearn, A. *Shooting and Gunfitting.* London: H. Jenkins.

Herbert, H. W. (Frank Forester) *American Game.* New York: C. Scribner, 1854.

——. *Complete Manual for Young Sportsmen.* New York: Excelsior Pub. House, 1873.

——. *Frank Forester's Field Sports.* New York: W. A. Townsend & Co., 1860. 2 vols.

——. *Life and Writings of Frank Forester.* New York: Orange Judd Co., 1882. 2 vols.

——. *Sporting Scenes and Characters.* Philadelphia: T. B. Peterson & Bros., 1881.

Hightower, J. *Field and Stream,* May 1944.

Hochwalt, A. F. *The Pointer and Setter in America,* Cincinnati: Sportsmen's Review Pub. Co., 1911.

Holland, R. P. "Ring-Necked Roosters," *Field and Stream,* XLVIII (1944), No. 10.

——. *Shotgunning in the Uplands.* New York: A. S. Barnes & Co., 1944.

——. *Shotgunning in the Lowlands.* New York: A. S. Barnes & Co., 1945.

Jarvis, W. ("Mont Clare"). *See* Leffingwell, W. B., ed., *Shooting on Upland, Marsh & Stream.*

Jensen, A. V. and Anderson, O. P.; *see* Knapp, J. S. below.

"Joe, Jr.—Gladstone Match." *American Field,* Dec. 27, 1879; reprinted May 29, 1943. *See* also Hochwalt, A. F. above, chap. iii.

Johnson, H. M. "A Note on the Supposed Olfactory Hunting-Response of the Dog," *Journal of Animal Behavior,* IV (1914), 76-78.

Johnson, Melvin M. and Haven, Charles T. *Ammunition.* New York: Morrow & Co., 1943.

Jones, O. *The Sport of Shooting.* London: E. Arnold & Co., 1928.

Kalischer. Quoted by Buytendijk; *see* above.

Keith, Edward C. *A Sportsman's Creed.* New York: C. Scribner's Sons, 1938.

Kent, Edwin C. *The Isle of Long Ago*, New York: C. Scribner's Sons, 1933.

King, R. T. *How to Encourage Wildlife*. Syracuse, N. Y.: State College of Forestry, 1940.

———. *Roosevelt Wild Life Bulletin*, April 1943.

———. "Ruffed Grouse Management," *Roosevelt Wild Life Bulletin*, Vol. VIII (1943), No. 3. N. Y. State College of Forestry (Syracuse).

———. Quoted by H. Premarck; *see* below.

Knapp, J. S. "Cornell Studies of Gun-Shyness," *American Field*, April 1, 1944.

Knight, J. A. *The Woodcock*. New York: A. A. Knopf, 1944.

Krider, John. *Krider's Sporting Anecdotes*. Philadelphia: A. Hart, 1853.


Lancaster, C. *The Art of Shooting*. London: McCorquodale & Co., 1898.

Lapsley, A. B. *See* Connett, E. V., ed., *Upland Game Bird Shooting in America*.

LeCompte, E. L. "Peculiar Behavior of Bob-Whites," *American Field*, CXL (1943), No. 31.

Leffingwell, William B. *The Art of Wing Shooting*. Chicago: Rand, McNally & Co., 1895.

———, ed. *Shooting on Upland, Marsh and Stream*. Chicago: Rand, McNally & Co., 1890.

LeJeune, Paul. Quoted by O. S. Pettingill, p. 271.

Lemmon, R. S. *About Your Dog*. New York: F. A. Stokes Co., 1928.

Lentz, W. J. "Nutrition and Diet," *North American Veterinarian*. Vol. XIX (1938), No. 4.

Leonard, J. L. *The Care and Handling of Dogs*. Garden City, N. Y.: Garden City Pub. Co., 1928.

Leopold, A. Quoted by B. W. Cartwright; *see* above.

Lewis, E. J. *The American Sportsman*. Philadelphia: Lippincott, Gambo & Co., 1855.

———. *Hints to Sportsmen*. Philadelphia: Lea & Blanchard, 1851.

Lloyd, Freeman. *Spaniels and Their Training*. New York.

Longsdorf, H. E. *American Field*, Mar. 25, 1944.

"Lowlander." *The Field* (London), Feb. 24, 1945.

Lytle, H. *Breaking a Bird Dog*. New York: D. Appleton & Co., 1924.

———. *Forest and Stream*, Nov. 1944.

———. "The Sportsman Dog," *Field and Stream*, XLIX (1944), No. 7.

———. *How to Train Your Bird Dog*. Dayton, Ohio: A. F. Hochwalt Co.


Marksman. *The Dead Shot*. London: Longman, Green, Longman, & Roberts, 1861.

Mayer, A. M., ed. *Sport with Gun and Rod*. New York: Century Co., 1883.

Maynard, C. J. *Birds of Eastern North America*. Newtonville, Mass.: C. J. Maynard Co., 1896.

McAtee, W. L., ed. *The Ring-Necked Pheasant and Its Management in North America.* Washington, D. C.: American Wildlife Institute, 1945.

McIlhenny, E. A. "Effects of Excessive Cold on Birds in Southern Louisiana," *The Auk,* LVII (1940), 408-10.

McLellan, Isaac. *Poems of the Rod and Gun.* New York: Henry Thorpe, 1886.

Mendall, H. L. and Aldous, C. M. *The Ecology and Management of the American Woodcock.* Orono, Maine: Maine Coöperative Wild Life Research Unit, 1943.

Moffit, E. B. and Vail, Elias. *Elias Vail Trains Gun Dogs.* New York: Orange Judd Pub. Co., 1937.

Money, A. W. *Pigeon Shooting.* New York: Shooting and Fishing Pub. Co., 1896.


*Naturalist's Library.* Edinburgh: W. H. Lizar's. Ed. W. Jardine. Vol. III.

"Nessmuk." *Woodcraft.* New York: Forest and Stream Pub. Co., 1900.

Nichols, B. *Field and Stream,* May 1944; Oct. 1944; Mar. 1945; July 1945.

———. *The Field* (London), Nov. 4, 1944.

Nuttall. Quoted by Samuels, E. A.; *see* below.


Parker, Eric. *An Alphabet of Shooting.* London: Field Press, 1932.

———. *Elements of Shooting.* London: Field Press.

———, ed. *Shooting by Moor, Field and Shore.* Philadelphia: J. B. Lippincott Co., 1929. Lonsdale Library, Vol. III.

Passy and Binet. Quoted by Buytendijk; *see* above.

Payne-Gallwey, Ralph. *Letters to Young Shooters.* London: Longmans, Green & Co., 1893. *See* Walsingham, T. DeG.

Pearce, J. *See* McAtee, W. L., ed., *The Ring-Necked Pheasant.*

Pearson, A. M. "Quail Fond of New Lespedeza," *American Field,* CXL (1943), No. 29.

Peek, H., ed. *The Poetry of Sport.* Boston: Little, Brown & Co., 1896.

Perry, Joseph F. ("Ashmont") *Kennel Secrets.* Boston: Little, Brown & Co., 1924.

Petrides, G. A. "How to Tell Their Age," *Field and Stream,* XLIX (1944), No. 7.

Pettingill, O. S., Jr. *The American Woodcock,* Memoirs of the Boston Society of Natural History, Vol. IX (1936), No. 2.

*Pheasant Breeding Manual.* New York: More Game Birds in America, 110 Grand St., 1936.

Phillips, J. C. *A Sportsman's Scrapbook.* Boston: Houghton Mifflin Co., 1928.

Pollard, H. B. C. *Game Birds and Game Bird Shooting.* London: Eyre and Spottiswoode, 1936.

———. *See* Parker, E., ed., *Shooting by Moor, Field and Shore.*

Premack, H. "Ruffed Grouse Research," *American Field,* Dec. 13, 1943.

Purdey, T. D. S. and Purdey, J. A. *The Shot Gun.* New York: C. Scribner's Sons, 1937.

*Quail Breeding Manual.* New York: More Game Birds in America, 110 Grand St., 1939. Rev. ed.

Rice, R. L. *Frontiers,* Feb. 1946.
Rich, W. H. *Feathered Game of the Northeast.* New York: T. Y. Crowell & Co., 1907.
Richardson, E. H. *Forty Years with Dogs.* London: Hutchinson, 1928.
Ripley, O. *Bird Dog Training Made Easy.* Columbus, Ohio: Hunter, Trader-Trapper Co., 1929.
———. *Sport in Field and Forest.* New York: D. Appleton & Co., 1926.
Robinson, M. A. *Field and Stream,* July 1945.
Roosevelt, R. B. *Florida and Game Water Birds.* New York: Orange Judd Co., 1884.
Ruskin, D. B. *American Field,* June 17, 1944.
Russell, J. A. *American Cookery,* Nov. 1941.
Russell, R. L. *The Whole Art of Setter Training.* London: Field Press.


Samuels, E. A. *Our Northern and Eastern Birds.* New York: E. Worthington, 1883.
———. *With Rod and Gun.* Boston: Samuels and Kimball, 1897.
Sandford, L. C. *et al. The Water-Fowl Family.* New York: Macmillan Co., 1903.
Sands, L. *The Bird, The Gun and The Dog.* New York: Carlyle House, 1939.
Sandys, Edwyn W. *Sporting Sketches.* New York: Macmillan Co., 1905.
——— and Van Dyke, T. S. *Upland Game Birds.* New York: Macmillan Co., 1902.
Schaldach, W. J. *Coverts and Casts.* New York: A. S. Barnes & Co., 1943.
Schley, F. *American Partridge and Pheasant shooting.* Frederick, Md.: Baughman Bros., 1877.
Sedgwick, N. M. *The Young Shot.* London: A. & C. Black, 1940.
Seigne, J. W. Quoted by J. W. Day; *see* above.
——— and Keith, E. C. *Woodcock and Snipe.* New York: C. Scribner's Sons, 1936.
"Seneca." *Hints and Points for Sportsmen.* New York: Forest and Stream Pub. Co., 1891.
Sharp, H. *The Gun: Afield and Afloat.* London: Chapman & Hall, 1904.
Sheldon, H. P. *See* Connett, E. V., ed., *Upland Game Bird Shooting in America.*
Smith, Laurence B. ("Lon"). *American Game Preserve Shooting.* New York: Windward House, 1933.
———. *Shotgun Psychology.* New York: C. Scribner's Sons, 1938.
Somers, J. *Proc. & Trans. Nova Scotia Inst. of Natural History,* VI (1886), 81.
Spiller, B. L. *Grouse Feathers.* New York: Derrydale Press, 1935.
———. *Firelight.* New York: Derrydale Press, 1937.

*Sportsman and His Dog.* London: J. and D. A. Darling, 1801. Ed. by the author of *Scottish Sports and Pastimes.*

Sprake, Leslie. *The Art of Shooting.* London: Seeley, Service & Co., Ltd., 1930. Lonsdale Library.

———. *Pheasant Shooting.* London: P. Allan, 1936.

———. *See* Parker, E. ed., *Shooting by Moor, Field and Shore.*

Spriggs, E. *The Field* (London), April 1, 1939; April 29, 1944.

Starr, A. R. *See* Leffingwell, W. R., ed., *Shooting on Upland, Marsh and Stream.*

Stoddard, H. L. *The Bobwhite Quail.* New York: C. Scribner's Sons, 1942.

"Stonehenge." *See* Walsh, John H.

Tauskey, R. W. *et al. Complete Dog Book. See* American Kennel Club.

Tegetmier, W. B. Quoted by E. Parker, *Elements of Shooting.*

"Thormanby." *Kings of the Rod, Rifle and Gun.* London: Hutchinson and Co., 1901. 2 vols.

Tufts, R. W. *Fish and Game News Bulletin* (Frederickton, N. B.), Sept. 1936.

"Ubique." *Rod, Gun and Saddle.* New York: W. A. Townsend & Adams, 1869.

Vail, Elias. *See* Moffit, E. B., above.

Vale, R. B. *Wings, Fur and Shot.* Harrisburg, Pa.: Stackpole Sons, 1936.

Walsh, John H. ("Stonehenge"). *Hints to Sportsmen.* London: G. Routledge & Son.

Walsingham, T. DeG. and Payne-Gallwey, R. W. F. *Shooting.* London: Longmans, Green & Co., 1892. 4th ed. Badminton Library.

Warren, B. H. *Birds of Pennsylvania.* Harrisburg, Pa.: Pub. by authority of the Commonwealth, 1890.

Waters, B. ("Kingrail") *Training and Handling of the Dog.* Boston: Little, Brown & Co., 1889.

Watson, J. *The Dog Book.* New York: Doubleday, Page & Co., 1906. 2 vols.

Wayne, Arthur T. *Birds of South Carolina.* Charleston, S. C.: Charleston Museum, 1910.

Wilson, A. *American Ornithology.* New York: Collins & Co.; Philadelphia: H. Hall, 1829. 3 Vols.

Western Cartridge Co. *Upland Game Restoration.* East Alton, Ill.: The Company, 1940.

Youatt, W. *The Dog.* New York: Leavitt and Allen, 1857.

Young, T. *Dogs for Democracy.* New York: Ackerman, 1944.

# INDEX

Accidents; *see* Safety
Ammunition, 133-38
  balled shot, 137-38
  tracer cartridge, 136

Balled shot, 137-38
Black Rail, 322
Blinking, 63-65
Bobwhite Quail, 292-318
  courtship, 295
  covey habits, 303-04
  dog, 307-08, 308-09
  eggs, 295
  enemies, 304-05
  feeding habits, 298-99
  field marks, 292-93
  flight, 300-03, 312
  food, 298
  former abundance, 317
  future, 306
  illegal methods, 317
  locales, 311
  nesting failures, 295-97
  nomenclature, 292
  perching, 302-03
  population, 306, 309, 317, 318
  predators, 304-05
  range, 294
  red phase, 293
  roosting, 299-300
  sex ratio, 294, 307
  shooting, 307-10, 313-17
    gun and ammunition, 309
    missing, cause of, 313-14
    percentage, 315
    Southern, 307, 308, 309, 318
    type of shots, 312-13
    weather, 310
  stocking, 306-07
  voice, 301
  weight, 293-94
  young, 296-97
Bolting, 67
Boots, 368-69
Brittany spaniel, 24-25
Bursts, 131-33

Canadian Grouse, 218
Canker of ear, 96
Cant, 163
Chaps, 368
Clapper Rail, 325
Cleaning gun, 129-31
Clothes; *see* Equipment
Coccidiosis, 94-95
Cocker, 23

Cookery, *see* Game for Table
Corrected snap shot, 148, 249
Cover, thick, 172
Cripples, retrieving, 316, 359
Crossing shots, 152-53, 359

Dead game, care of, 176, 384
Dents, gun, 131
Diary, 380
Distemper, 84-86
Dog, 13-105
  age, 34-35
  backing, 46, 48
  bathing and grooming, 74
  biddableness, 38
  blood lines, 35-36
  blood specimen, 105
  blinking, 63-65
  Bobwhite quail, 307-08, 308-09
  bolting, 67
  brace, a, 38
  breaking
    car, 52-53
    house, 53
    yard, 53
  breeds, 15
  Brittany spaniel, 24-25
  buying a trained, 31
  canker of ear, 96
  car-sickness, 53, 98
  care of, 68-105
  class and style, 47-48
  coccidiosis, 94-95
  cocker, 23
  color and marking, 26-27, 52
  conditioning, 28
  conformation, 52
  courage, 52
  crossbreds, 23
  desirable qualities, 26-28
  desire to hunt, 38
  distemper, 84-86
  droppers, 23
  dropping to shot, 46
  English setter, 20
  euthanasia, 100-03
  evaluation, 32
  false pointing, 47
  fear of storms, 36-37
  feet, sore, 99
  field and bench, 18
  fleas, 96
  flushing, 46
  food, 68-74
  fright disease, 95-96
  Gordon setter, 20

405

*Dog—(Continued)*
grouse, 46, 55, 239-40
gunshyness, 63, 65-67
handling, 58-63, 169
health, 36-37
intelligence, 36
intestinal parasites, 86-96
Irish setter, 20
kennels, 77-79
Llewellin setter, 20
lost, 63
medicine and surgery, 81-83
medicine, giving, 103
nose, 42
pedigree; *see* Dog, blood lines
Penna. Field Trial Club standard, 55
pheasant, 206
pointers, 16-17, 22
puppy, 25-26
range, 38
registration, 35
reporting, 46
retrieving, 48-52
running fits, 95
scenting ability, 347-55
selection, 31
setters, 20
sex, 32
spaniels, 23
springer, 23
steadiness, 43
surgery, 81-83
tail, sore, 98
temperature, taking, 105
trainer, selection of, 28
urine specimen, 105
woodcock, 22, 277, 278-79
worms
heart (filariasis), 95
hook, 88-92
round, 94
whip, 94
Drumming, 226

English setter, 20
Equipment, 365-73
boots, 368
chaps, 368
coat, 366
glasses, 371
gloves, 370
grouse shooting, 240
headgear, 370
lunch, 372
Pannabelt, 371
rail, 336
raincoat, 370
shooting bag, 371
stockings, 369
trousers or breeches, 367
underclothes, 370
Etiquette, 178-79, 380-82
Euthanasia, 100-03

False pointing, 47
Fitting gun, 114
Fleas, 96
Flinch, 163-64
Flushing bars, 199
Fright disease, 95-96

Game birds, scent of, 347-55
Game for Table, 384-96
bread sauce, 396
grouse, roast, 391
hanging, 385-86
pheasant
boiled, 390
braised, 389
broiled, 388
breast, 389
roast, 387
in red wine, 388
Salmi, 389
sandwich, 390
quail, 393-95
roast, 393
Salmi, 394
sauté, 394
rail, 395-96
chafing dish, 395
roast, 395
selection, 384
woodcock, 392-93
chafing dish, 393
flambé, 392
roast, 392
Salmi, 394-95
Good manners; *see* Etiquette
Gordon setter, 20
Grip of gun, 143
Grouse, 216-51
Canadian, 218
courtship, 218
crazy season, 228
cycles, 237
dog, 46, 55, 239-40
drumming, 226
early history, 222
enemies, 232, 236
field marks, 216
food and economic status, 220-22
flight, 230
gun and ammunition, 241-42
habits, 222
illegal methods, 251
locales, 242
log, in hollow, 232
molts, 217
nest, 219
nomenclature, 216
N. Y. Conservation Dept. report, 232, 236
perching, 249
predators, 232, 233, 236
propagation, artificial, 233
range, 218
roosting, 223

*Grouse—(Continued)*
  shot-carrying ability, 241
  shooting, 239-51
    equipment, 240
    percentage, 249
    type of shots, 244
    weather, 243
  snow, in, 223-25
  tame and wild, 225
  treeing, 231
  tunnels, 224
  vitality, 241
  voice, 217
  weight, 217
  wounded, 241, 250
  young, 220
Gun, 106-38
  accidents; *see* Safety
  ammunition, 133-38
  balance, 122
  barrels, 111
  bursts, 131
  case, 127
  choke, 112, 359
  cleaning, 129
  dents, 131
  fitting, 114-22
  gauge, 106
  locks, 123
  master eye, 120
  oil finish, 382
  one-armed man, 118
  pair, 125
  pumps and automatics, 127
  quality, 125
  recoil, 164-66
  stock, 114
  storage, 131
  tests of fit, 119
  tests for new, 128
  trigger, 123-25
  weight, 107
Gunshyness, 63, 65-67

Handling, 58-63, 169
Heartworms, (filariasis) , 95
Hookworms, 88-92

Intercepted shot, 149
Irish setter, 20

Kennels, 77-79
King Rail, 324

Leg cramps, 372
Loading, 145
Lost dog, 63
Llewellin setter, 20

Marking the fall, 360
Marsh hen; *see* Clapper Rail
Master eye, 120
Melanistic Pheasant, 186
Methods afield, 167-79
Misses, 149, 158
Mounting gun, 144

Overhead shots, 209

Pattern, 135, 286, 315
Penna. Field Trial Club standard, 55
Pheasant, 180-215
  courtship, 184
  destruction by mowing, 198
  dog, 206-07
  drives, 213
  favorable terrain, 204
  field marks, 180
  flight, 208
  food and economic status, 186
  history, 180-81
  illegal methods, 214
  insecticides, 200
  Melanistic or Black, 186
  molts, 185
  nest, 184
  nomenclature, 180
  predators, 194-98
  preserve, 200-03
  rearing, 191
  roosting, 183
  shooting, 203
    percentage, 213
    public grounds, 202
    Western, 213
  stocking, 188
  tracking in snow, 212
  vitality, 208
  voice, 183
  wounded, 211
Pigs pointing, 15
Pointers, 16-17, 22
Powder headache, 164
Preserve, the, 200-03
Predators and control, 194-98, 233-34, 236-37
Propagation, grouse, 233-36
Public shooting grounds, 202

Quail; *see* Bobwhite Quail

Rail (*Rallidae*) , 319-46
  black, 322
  Clapper, 325
  equipment, 336
  factors saving, 335
  fire lighting, 336
  fits, spasms, 333
  former abundance of, 345
  flight, 331
  gun and ammunition, 336
  habits, 329
  illegal shooting of, 336
  King, 324
  marking, 343
  Marsh, the, 319
  migrations, 328
  natural history, 326
  predators, 334-35
  pusher, the, 338, 344
  safety measures, 339
  shooting, 336

*Rail—(Continued)*
  over dogs, 345
  percentage, 344
  type of shots, 341
Sora, 326
tides, 340
Virginia, 322
wading for, 345
wounded, 343
Yellow, 321
Range of shot, 135
Recipes; *see* under Game for Table
Recoil, 164-66
Releasing safety, 146
Retrieving, 48-52
  cripples, 359
Roundworms, 94
Running fits, 95

Safety
  cause of accidents, 374
  frequency of accidents, 375
  rules, 376
Scent, 347-55
Second barrel, 157
Setter
  English, 20
  Gordon, 20
  Irish, 20
  Llewellin, 20
Shared birds, 177
Shooting hints, 139-166
  assembling gun, 140
  cant, 163
  causes for missing, 149, 158
  corrected snap shot, 148, 249
  crossing shots, 152-53, 359
  grip of gun, 143
  intercepted shot, 149
  lead, 151
  loading, 145
  mounting, 144
  powder headache, 164
  practice, 155
  raising head, 163
  recoil, 164
  releasing safety, 146
  safety, 140
  second barrel, 157, 315
  stance, 141
  swinging shot, 149
  time, 155
  trigger pulling, 147
  true snap shot, 148
Shot
  balled, 137-38
  range, 135
  size, 136
Signs of birds, 169
Snap shot, 148
Soil conservation, 194
Sora Rail, 326
Springer, 23

Stance, 141
Stock, oil finish, 382
Stocking
  pheasants, 188
  quail, 306
Storage of gun, 131
Swinging shot, 149

Teamwork, 174, 316
Tests for new gun, 128
Time, shooting, 155
Towering, 362
Tracer cartridge, 136

Virginia Rail, 322-23

Whipworms, 94
Whistle signals, 61
Woodcock
  banding, 260
  boring, 262
  captivity, in, 266
  chalk marks, 286
  courtship, 255, 266
  covers, 282
  dog, 277, 278
  early history, 263
  field marks, 253
  fire lighting, 272
  flight, 267, 289
    song, 254
  food, 261
  former abundancy, 263
  future, 273
  gun and ammunition, 286
  habits, 265
  hardiness, 267
  migration, 258
  nest, 254
  nomenclature, 252
  perching, 266
  predators, 270
  protection, 275
  range, 257
  roosting, 266
  sex determination, 254
  shooting, 286
    equipment, 286
    percentage, 290
    type of shots, 287
    uncertain, 281
  vitality, 288
  voice, 254
  weather destruction, 271
  weights, 253
  winter distribution, 261
  wounded, 288
  young, 254, 256
Woods walking, 173
Wounded bird, 211, 241, 250, 288, 314-15, 343, 355-60

Yellow Rail, 321